EARLY RADIO

For Nick and Xavier, fans of sound machines

EARLY RADIO

An Anthology of European Texts and Translations

Edited by
Emilie Morin

With Translations by Emilie Morin, Marielle
Sutherland and Nicoletta Asciuto

EDINBURGH
University Press

Edinburgh University Press is one of the leading university presses in the UK. We publish academic books and journals in our selected subject areas across the humanities and social sciences, combining cutting-edge scholarship with high editorial and production values to produce academic works of lasting importance. For more information visit our website: edinburghuniversitypress.com

LEVERHULME
TRUST _________

This work was funded by a Leverhulme Trust Research Fellowship

Edinburgh University Press Ltd
13 Infirmary Street,
Edinburgh, EH1 1LT

First published in hardback by Edinburgh University Press 2023

Typeset in 10/12.5 Adobe Sabon by
IDSUK (DataConnection) Ltd, and
printed and bound by CPI Group (UK) Ltd
Croydon, CR0 4YY

A CIP record for this book is available from the British Library

ISBN 978 1 4744 8514 2 (hardback)
ISBN 978 1 4744 8515 9 (paperback)
ISBN 978 1 4744 8516 6 (webready PDF)
ISBN 978 1 4744 8517 3 (epub)

CONTENTS

ACKNOWLEDGEMENTS

I am grateful for the funding that supported my research. An award from the University of York's Research Priming Fund (2017–2018) enabled me to conduct the initial scoping work in archives and libraries. A British Academy Small Grant (2019–2020) supported the commissioning of translations and practical translation work. A Leverhulme Trust Research Fellowship (2021–2022) enabled me to complete the anthology. Nicoletta Asciuto and Marielle Sutherland were the most wonderful collaborators I could have wished for, and I am grateful for the energy and flair they brought to the translation work. Marielle Sutherland advised on stylistically awkward pieces at the end, enabling the completion of difficult translations. Thanks are also due to Kate Murphy, for sharing ideas and notes with such generosity, and for suggestions on the near-final product; Sana R. Chaudhry and Evan Lower, for peerless research assistance; my colleagues in the Department of English and Related Literature at York, especially Kevin Killeen, who read all my funding applications, Trev Broughton, who advised on the Italian texts, Helen Smith, who made much of working life immeasurably better, and Helen Barrett, Claire Chambers, Matt Campbell, Cathy Moore, the late Philip Morris and Vicky Nesfield, for precious support. Thanks to the Department and the F. R. Leavis Fund for covering the cost of indexing. Thanks to the two external readers at Edinburgh University Press, for helping me give this anthology its final shape, and for their deep engagement; Birgit Van Puymbroeck, Rebecca Roach, Loïc Bertrand and Emily Bloom, for helpful suggestions; the Electronic Soundscapes network –

David Clayton, Esme Cleall, Marta Donati, Rachel Garratt, Graeme Gooday, Jean-Baptiste Masson, James Mooney and Beryl Pong; Marina MacKay and Richard Hand; the many others who encouraged me along the way, too numerous to name here, but appreciated all the same. Thanks to the archivists and librarians who supported this work, especially Matthew Chipping at the BBC Written Archives; Corinne Gibello and Luc Bellier at the Bibliothèque Nationale de France; Jörg-Uwe Fischer, Susanne Hennings, Jan Plate and Andreas Rühl at the Deutsches Rundfunkarchiv; the staff of the Institut National de l'Audiovisuel, the Bibliothèque Littéraire Jacques Doucet, the British Library, Boston Spa, particularly Tamsyn Chadwick and Bev Wise; Isabelle Cluzand and Aurélie Zbos at Radio France; Elaine Hickes, Carmen Rhodes and York's inter-library loan team. For help with copyright searches, thanks to Ralph Montagu at the *Radio Times*, Emilie Hache at the Répertoire BALZAC, Sarah Baxter at the Society of Authors, Caroline Jessen and Dörthe Perlenfein at the Deutsches Literaturarchiv Marbach, Sean Vis at the BBC Written Archives, Len Markham, Mark Nixon, the Fondazione Arnoldo e Alberto Mondadori, John Dack and Christine North, Roland Spahr at S. Fischer Verlag, Frank Göbler, Marc Jacquin, Sabina Becker, Stéphane Bonnefoi, Caroline Bianco, Maggie Smith at the Saltaire Collection, Jennifer Purcell, Victor Martin-Schmets, Nora Mercurio and Elena Cascio at Suhrkamp, Zoltan Földvári at Földvári Books, and Katherine Reagan at Cornell University's Rare and Manuscript Collections. It was a pleasure to work with Jackie Jones, Ersev Ersoy and Susannah Butler at Edinburgh University Press, and with the eagle-eyed Jenna Dowds. All my gratitude, as ever, to Nicholas Melia and Xavier, the great joys of my life, and to the Morins and the Melias.

Grateful acknowledgement is made to the following individuals for permission to reproduce or translate materials in copyright and previously published elsewhere: Susan Watts, for permission to reproduce Sheila Borrett's 'Scene – and Unseen!'; Foulques de Jouvenel, for permission to translate 'Colette nous parle de la TSF'; Danielle Mérian, for permission to translate France Darget's 'Comment jouez-vous devant le micro?'; D. J. MacCarthy, for permission to reproduce Desmond MacCarthy's 'The Art of Broadcasting Talks'; Jacques Fraenkel, for permission to translate Robert Desnos's 'La clé des songes au Poste-Parisien'; Stephan Döblin, for permission to translate excerpts from Alfred Döblin's 'Literatur und Rundfunk'; Valerio Castelli and Maria Castelli Luti, for permission to translate Enzo Ferrieri's 'La radio come forza creativa'; Bertrand Vinot, for permission to translate excerpts from Gabriel Germinet's *Théâtre radiophonique: Mode nouveau d'expression artistique* and 'L'Art radio-phonique au service du désarmement moral'; Julia Crampton, Adrian Moyne and the Board of the Tyrone Guthrie Centre, Annaghmakerrig, for permission to reproduce Tyrone Guthrie's Introduction to *Squirrel's Cage and Two Other Microphone Plays*; Annie Teulière, for permission to translate Augustin Habaru's

'Il faut découvrir la radio'; Friederike Kasack, for permission to translate Hermann Kasack's 'Mikroreportage'; Annette Mallin-Ryder, for permission to translate excerpts from Annette Kolb's *Beschwerdebuch*; Jacqueline Schaeffer, for permission to translate Pierre Schaeffer's 'Problème central de la radiodiffusion'; Paul Sieveking, for permission to reproduce excerpts from Lance Sieveking's *The Stuff of Radio*; Sophie and Clémentine Olchanski, for permission to translate Alex Virot's 'Réflexions sur le radio-reportage.' Articles from the *Radio Times* and the *Listener* are reproduced by kind permission of Immediate Media; these are B.E.N.'s 'Feature Programmes,' Barbara Burnham's 'Adaptations,' R.E. Jeffrey's 'Wireless Drama,' Ella Fitzgerald's 'Wireless and Women,' Grace Wyndham Goldie's 'Listening to Comedy' and 'Let Us Be Thrilled,' and the following: Mabel Constanduros's 'My First Broadcast,' also reproduced by permission of Bob Constanduros; Laurence Gilliam's 'Actualities' and 'Features,' also reproduced by permission of Bill Gilliam and John Gilliam; Rose Macaulay's 'The Arm-Chair Millenium,' also reproduced by permission of the Society of Authors as the literary representative of the Estate of Rose Macaulay; Olive Shapley's 'Night Romance of the Roads,' also reproduced by permission of Christina Hart, Dan Salt and Nicholas Salt; Charles Siepmann's 'Talks,' also reproduced by permission of Kate Siepmann and Sarah McNamara.

Every effort has been made to trace the copyright holders, but if any have been inadvertently overlooked, the publisher will be pleased to make the necessary arrangements at the first opportunity.

NOTE ON THE SELECTION, TRANSLATION AND PRESENTATION OF TEXTS

Radio was frequently and abundantly discussed throughout the 1920s and 1930s. The texts in this anthology were selected on the basis of their interest, clarity and representativeness, and because their authors had a practical involvement with radio – of speaking at the microphone, of writing for radio, of writing about radio. Priority was given to lesser-known authors and to texts not already available in English translation. Work by widely translated authors, such as Rudolf Arnheim, Bertolt Brecht or Siegfried Kracauer, and texts already available elsewhere have not been included in the selections. Except for Walter Benjamin's 'Auf die Minute,' the texts featuring here have not previously appeared in full in English translation (although English-language scholarship on early European radio features some translated fragments – notably, from Walter Ruttmann's 'Neue Gestaltung von Tonfilm und Funk. Programm einer photographischen Hörkunst' – as well as variant translations of other short excerpts from other texts included here). The German texts selected predate 1933: Weimar-era materials have been widely cited in scholarly sources but do not tend to be available in translation, and it was more important to bring into the public domain translations from this vibrant time in radio's history than Nazi-era texts, not least because such texts, including essays denouncing the Nazi uses of radio, have been translated for other anthologies.

The selections offered here were drawn from a vast range of publications, including the annual handbooks of national broadcasting companies; large-circulation radio magazines such as *Der Deutsche Rundfunk, Die Sendung,*

Funk, *TSF Programme*, *La Parole Libre TSF*, *Le Petit Radio* and *Radio-Magazine*; the magazines of broadcasting organisations such as the *Radio Times*, the *Listener*, *Radiocorriere* and *Die Werag*; modernist literary magazines speaking to urban Europeanised readerships such as *Vox*, *Il Convegno*, *Lumière et Radio*, *Der Querschnitt* and *Die Weltbühne*; popular radio magazines primarily aimed at women, such as *Radio Pictorial*; large-circulation newspapers that published ambitious radio journalism, such as *Comœdia*, *L'Intransigeant* and *Der Wiener Tag*; magazines focused on other arts, such as *La Revue Musicale* and *Film-Kurier*; literary periodicals aligned with the nationalist right, such as *L'Illustration* and *Le Journal de France*, smaller publications aligned with the communist and socialist left, such as *Arbeiter-Sender*, *Radio-Liberté* and *Le Populaire*, and conference proceedings and essays published elsewhere.[1] Some texts included here have been previously anthologised in their languages of origin, in publications that emphasise their significance.[2]

[1] On these publications, see Claude Bellanger, Jacques Godechot, Pierre Guirral and Fernand Terrou, *Histoire générale de la presse française, tome 3: de 1871 à 1940* (Paris: Presses Universitaires de France, 1972); Pierre Milza, *Le fascisme italien et la presse française: 1920–1940* (Bruxelles: Complexe, 1987); Thomas Bauer, *Deutsche Programmpresse 1923 bis 1941: Entstehung, Entwicklung und Kontinuität der Rundfunkzeitschriften* (Munich: Saur, 1993); Marc Martin, *Médias et journalistes de la République* (Paris: Odile Jacob, 1997); Carola Tischler, ed., *Inventar der Quellen zum deutschsprachigen Rundfunk in der Sowjetunion (1929–1945): Bestände in deutschen und ausländischen Archiven und Bibliotheken* (Potsdam: Verlag für Berlin-Brandenburg, 1997); Debra Rae Cohen, 'Intermediality and the Problem of the *Listener*,' *Modernism/modernity* 19, no. 3 (2012): 569–92; Tony Currie, *The Radio Times Story* (Tiverton: Kelly, 2001); Andrea Sangiovanni, *Le parole e le figure: Storia dei media in Italia dall' età liberale alla seconda guerra mondiale* (Rome: Donzelli, 2012); Peter Brooker, Sascha Bru, Andrew Thacker and Christian Weikop, eds, *The Oxford Critical and Cultural History of Modernist Magazines, vol. III: Europe 1880–1940, Parts I and II* (Oxford: Oxford University Press, 2013).

[2] Shaw's 'The Drama and the Microphone' features in *The Drama Observed, vol. IV: 1911–1950*, ed. Bernard F. Dukore (University Park: Pennsylvania State University Press, 1993), 1408. Kuh's 'Angst vor dem Radio'; Kasack's 'Mikroreportage'; Weill's 'Zum Thema "Musikalisches Hörspiel"'; Kyser's 'Wie schafft man Hörspiele und Hörspielliteratur?'; Jessner's 'Rundfunk und Theater'; Gunold's 'Wege zum akustischen Drama'; Tucholsky's 'Freier Funk! Freier Film!' and 'Rundfunkzensur'; Schickele's 'Paneuropa der Sender'; Toller's 'Internationaler Rundfunk' feature in *Radio-Kultur in der Weimarer Republik*, ed. Irmela Schneider (Tübingen: Gunter Narr, 1984). Kisch's 'Weh' dem, der sieht!' and 'Der Funkreporter vom Roten Platz: "Am Moskauer Mikrophon kann man nicht lügen!"'; Hardt's 'Das Echo der Hörerwünsche'; Kolb's 'Radiofreuden und Radioleiden'; Alfons Paquet's 'Rundfunk und Staat' feature in *Literatur und Rundfunk 1923–1933*, ed. Gerhard Hay (Hildesheim: Gerstenberg, 1975). Benjamin's 'Auf die Minute' features in Walter Benjamin, *Gesammelte Schriften IV, vol. 2*, ed. Tillman Rexroth (Frankfurt: Suhrkamp, 1972), 761–3. Dermée's radio journalism features in Céline Arnauld and Paul Dermée, *Œuvres complètes*,

The texts are accompanied by biographical sketches and footnotes directing readers to relevant scholarly sources. For these sketches, I drew additional information from online archives and repositories of newspapers and periodicals including the BBC Programme Index (formerly Genome), Proquest Newspapers, the British Newspaper Archive, The Listener Historical Archive, 1929–1991, Gallica, Retronews, Delpher, BelgicaPress (KBR), Radiocorriere TV, Digiteca, arthistoricum.net, ANNO, ARD-Hörspieldatenbank, Deutsches Rundfunkarchiv Datenbank, Hemeroteca Digital, letempsarchives.ch and HathiTrust Digital Library. Much of the work was conducted during Covid-19 lockdowns, when libraries and archives were closed and some physical sources were inaccessible; during this time, unofficial repositories of periodicals such as archive.org, introni.it, Doctsf and worldradiohistory.com yielded valuable information.

Copyright considerations shaped construction throughout: indeed fair use or fair dealing, which makes the writing of monographs possible, does not apply to anthologies or to translations. Securing permission to reproduce or translate work by well-known authors is relatively straightforward, because the copyright holders' names and contact details feature on databases such as WATCH or can be obtained from archives. For little-known authors, however, there are no pre-established records, and finding information can be immensely difficult. Much time was spent from 2017 to 2021 conducting copyright research that often seemed like the stuff of detective fiction, collating and cross-referencing information from obituaries, genealogy sites, acknowledgements in PhD theses, telephone books, online forums, LinkedIn and Facebook. Many copyright holders responded warmly and supportively, but many possibilities also had to be discarded owing to silence, refusals, copyright uncertainties or the absence of workable leads.

The task of translation was never easy. Some texts relied on a flamboyant style; many featured idiosyncrasies difficult to render in English. Wherever style was awkward in the original, we tried to preserve some awkwardness in the translation, without automatically resorting to the 'flattening' that tends to occur in the transfer to English. When it came to radio vocabularies, however, it was impossible to avoid this flattening effect. Where French and Italian texts speak of radio through a language of relatedness and intimacy, as *radiophonie*

---

ed. Victor Martin-Schmets, 7 vols (Paris: Classiques Garnier, 2013–2019). Desnos's 'La clé des songes au Poste-Parisien' features in Desnos, *Œuvres*, ed. Marie-Claire Dumas (Paris: Gallimard, 1999), 846–48. Ferrieri's 'La radio come forza creativa' and 'Inchiesta sulla Radio' feature in *La radio! La radio? La radio!*, ed. Emilio Pozzi (Milan: Greco e Greco, 2002). Ruttmann's 'Neue Gestaltung von Tonfilm und Funk. Programm einer photographischen Hörkunst' features in *Walter Ruttmanns Tonmontagen als Ars Acustica*, ed. Jeanpaul Goergen (Siegen: Massenmedien und Kommunikation, 1994), 25–6.

and *radiofonia*, English texts speak of radio broadcasting. Where French, Italian and German sources invoke a public of *sans-filistes*, *galénistes*, *galenisti*, *dilettante di radio*, *radio-amatori*, *Radio-Interessenten*, *Radio-Amateure* or *Funk-Teilnehmer*, English sources speak of radio listeners; and where French and German texts invoke the *metteur en ondes*, *Regisseur* or *Hörspielregisseur*, English texts speak of radio producer. The vast range of terms invented and deployed for radio drama in French and German has no real equivalent in English either.

Some adjustments were made to facilitate reading: section breaks marked by asterisks in the originals have been replaced by indented paragraphs in the translations whenever they were excessively numerous. Tenses have occasionally been modified. Words emphasised by means of inverted commas in some Italian and French originals have been italicised in the translations. Hyphenation patterns were not consistent in the radio vocabulary of the period; in English-language texts hyphenation has been kept as it was in the originals, and in the translations hyphenation is consistent with English usage during the period. 'We', frequently used in the French originals instead of 'I', has been turned into 'I' or more idiomatic turns of phrase in many cases. Man is the sole referent for humanity in most of the texts included, including in texts authored by women; this feature has been preserved in the translations in most cases (anything else would be historically inaccurate and would fail to convey the barriers faced by women) but tweaks have been made to reflect the spirit of the originals when necessary. Some of the originals featured typographical errors; any error that could be a typesetting error has been silently corrected in the translations, but when the error is more likely to have been the author's it has been kept and has been identified as such. Respecting historical word usage was a priority that informed all other translation choices.

INTRODUCTION

EMILIE MORIN

It has proved difficult to reimagine the beginnings of public broadcasting. Radio was a medium that unleashed fierce passions, and accounts of the early years can be uncharitable: 'In the beginning of radio was boredom,' wrote Hans Flesch, in an essay associating the 1920s with an unrelenting dullness.[1] The issue, for Flesch, was that the radio listener – 'grateful for every sound, every word he heard, regardless of what and how he heard it, so long as he only had reception' – expected little beyond the capacity to witness a technological miracle.[2] Others shared this sense that the wonders of sound transmission were not sufficient in themselves, and believed that a great deal of work was needed if radio was to live up to its true potential. Bertolt Brecht, notably, described radio as an instrument of thoughtless imitation; 'an acoustic department store' ruled by 'cacophony and dissonance,' which made it at best possible to 'learn to breed chickens in English' to fragments from a Wagner opera.[3] Likewise,

---

[1] The translations throughout this introduction are by the author unless otherwise indicated. Hans Flesch, 'Rundfunk Heute,' *Der Querschnitt* 10, no. 4 (1930): 245–7.

[2] Hans Flesch, 'Kulturelle Aufgaben des Rundfunks' (1926), in *Aus meinem Archiv: Probleme des Rundfunks*, ed. Hans Bredow (Heidelberg: Vowinckel, 1950), 95; trans. M. Brook, cited in Axel Volmar, 'In Storms of Steel: The Soundscape of World War I and its Impact on Auditory Media Culture during the Weimar Period,' in *Sounds of Modern History: Auditory Cultures in 19th- and 20th-Century Europe*, ed. Daniel Morat (New York: Berghahn, 2014), 243.

[3] Bertolt Brecht, 'The Radio as a Communications Apparatus' (1932), in *Brecht on Film and Radio*, trans. and ed. Marc Silberman (London: Methuen, 2001), 41–2.

when Edward Gordon Craig recounted his experience of listening to radio for the first time in 1922 or 1923, he did not have one good word to say, but complained that he had 'never heard any fine speaking coming out of the machine,' and wondered 'whether very good readers, the very best thinkers and artists, ever read into the radio machine.'[4] These anecdotal observations fit with common assumptions about the dawn of broadcasting technologies, and resonate with later accounts, in historical surveys as well as memoirs, presenting the first decade of public radio as a prehistory largely unrelated to its golden age. When Lionel Fielden, notably, recalled the early work done at the BBC's Savoy Hill studios, he wrote: 'we had one aim and one aim only – to find Voices to fill the Hours. [. . .] The first objective was to avoid silence. And this was not, at first, as easy as it sounds.'[5]

Much in the visual iconography of radio, too, invites us to perceive the beginnings as a time of little artistic worth, a time when little happened: the photos reproduced in radio magazines and technical publications from the interwar period show a predilection for aerial masts towering over fields and plains, microphones in empty studios, deserted control rooms, transmitter panels and walls covered in new machinery. When technicians are in the frame, they are rarely in action; when actors are photographed, they are often in costume, seemingly craving a theatre stage; when listeners are portrayed with their set at home, their facial expressions are enigmatic and the emphasis is placed on the machine, with its arrangement of cables, headsets, switches and dials. Yet for each account, each photograph describing this time as strangely devoid of life and movement, there are others showing how seemingly immoveable technological and creative limits were played with, subverted or overturned. To many of those who worked in radio broadcasting, wrote for and about radio, and to their millions of listeners and readers, radio provided a window onto other worlds, real and imaginary. Much in the literature and journalism of the 1920s and 1930s bears testimony to the wonder, joy and enthusiasm that greeted the opportunities unleashed by radio; cities, countries, languages and cultures came into close proximity at the turn of a dial, with philosophical and political implications that were thrilling for some, troubling for others. The purpose of this anthology is to show that this other history, too, can be told. Throughout the interwar period, radio unleashed an immense creativity, and a type of experimentalism that often arose from a combination of deep optimism, flair, humble persistence and haphazard working conditions.

This anthology features texts articulating many of the questions, hopes, ambitions and doubts that surrounded radio's place in society, culture and the

---

[4] Edward Gordon Craig, 'Can Wireless Aid the Art of Drama?,' *Radio Times*, 27 September 1929, 666.

[5] Lionel Fielden, *The Natural Bent* (London: Deutsch, 1960), 105.

arts during the best part of the 1920s and through to the late 1930s. These materials, drawn from the abundant volume of journalism and essayistic writing that bolstered the rise of public broadcasting in Europe, record the development of an art of commentary around radio broadcasting that emerged across nations and cultures, and was shaped by debates around radio's cultural applications and implications as a new art form and a technology requiring different listening practices. In these texts we can also discern ways of imagining radio that have endured over time, and resonate with discussions around sound art and radio drama that began much later. The authors featured include many writers and artists – some established, other less so – who were conversant with literary and cinematic modernism, though often idiosyncratically, and crafted or discussed new approaches to writing, speaking and acting that capitalised on radio's lack of a visual dimension, embracing its capacity to create striking narrative and auditory works with modest means. Throughout, the focus remains on Europe, and on ways of thinking about radio tied to the perspectives and practices of state-controlled broadcasting systems, and to their shared ideals of education and public service. Journalism and essays representative of British, French, German and Italian radio cultures constitute the core of the selections; authors from other countries including Czechoslovakia, Belgium, Ireland and Austria are also included. British, French, German and Italian radio cultures led the way for spoken word radio during this period – the first three owing to solid broadcasting organisations, large numbers of wireless set owners and wavelength allocations that worked to their advantage, and the fourth owing to the quality of its programming and cultural offerings.[6] These countries set the tone in other ways too, defining how radio was thought about and discussed, and nurturing theoretical thinking through a lively, high-quality radio press informed by transnational influences and dialogues, which actively solicited input from writers and artists eager to reflect on radio's imaginative and expressive capacities. A prevalent way of conceptualising radio's myriad possibilities was to discuss its related functions, as 'a means of transmission and dissemination' and 'a means of expression,' to borrow Rudolf Arnheim's terminology, or as a creative force and a medium of education and dissemination, to use the categories defined by Enzo Ferrieri in a landmark essay included in this anthology.[7]

The radio journalism of the interwar period – which encompasses specialised radio magazines, regular columns in daily and weekly newspapers, and a

---

[6] See Rebecca P. Scales, *Radio and the Politics of Sound in Interwar France, 1921–1939* (Cambridge: Cambridge University Press, 2016), 139; Pierre Miquel, *Histoire de la radio et de la télévision* (Paris: Editions Richelieu, 1973).

[7] Rudolf Arnheim, *Radio*, trans. Margaret Ludwig and Herbert Read (London: Faber and Faber, 1936), 14.

looser corpus of essayistic writings published in literary and arts periodicals – remains the most reliable barometer of the artistic discoveries made in broadcasting throughout this foundational time. Indeed, the scripts of radio talks and radio plays were not always preserved; many original documents have been lost; print runs of periodicals are often incomplete; correspondence is at best fragmentary, when it does exist. Before 1928, recordings were inexistent,[8] and they remained scarce thereafter for many reasons – because recording was impossible or overly difficult, because materials were not deemed worthy of preservation,[9] or because recordings were accidentally lost or damaged beyond repair. Some of the recordings that have survived – notably, of Olive Shapley's social documentaries, Walter Ruttmann's work on sound montage, Robert Desnos's and Paul Deharme's experiments with dream narratives – show that this was an immensely exciting time, marked by great artistic accomplishments.[10]

Already in the 1930s, there were concerns about the difficulty of preserving radio creations and about their fragility. The importance of collecting and archiving recordings was recognised early on; a resolution adopted at the 1937 International Congress of Radiophonic Art in Paris, guided by the radio dramatist Suzanne Malard in particular, advocated for new sound archives, including an international archive of radio recordings.[11] But the gap between aspiration and practice remained great, such was the challenge posed by the abundance of broadcast materials and their perceived lack of significance against programming ebbs and flows. Hilda Matheson offered a vivid account of this problem, comparing broadcasting to 'an immense key-board stretching out of sight at both ends,' extending from 'the whisper of the infinitely small and intimate

---

[8] Recording at the BBC was only deployed during the 1930s, for materials deemed particularly significant. This was also the case in France: the Institut National de l'Audiovisuel does not hold recordings of French radio broadcasts from before 1933. In Weimar Germany, recording began earlier, and the Deutsches Rundfunkarchiv's first recordings date from 1928; prior to that, everything was broadcast live and broadcasts could not be recorded for technical reasons. That said, German journalists started using gramophone and wax disc recording for news gathering in mid-1929. See Paddy Scannell and Peter Cardiff, *A Social History of British Broadcasting vol. 1: 1922–1939: Serving the Nation* (Oxford: Blackwell, 1991), 145–46; Carolyn Birdsall, 'Sonic Artefacts. Reality Codes of Urbanity in Early German Radio Documentary,' in *Soundscapes of the Urban Past: Staged Sound as Mediated Cultural Heritage*, ed. Karin Bijsterveld (Bielefeld: Transcript, 2013), 146–7.

[9] This was the case for Weimar-era *Frauenfunk* programmes; see Kate Lacey, *Feminine Frequencies: Gender, German Radio, and the Public Sphere, 1923–1945* (Ann Arbor: University of Michigan Press, 1996), 8.

[10] Preserved as part of the British Library Sounds collection, by the Deutsches Rundfunkarchiv and by the Institut National de l'Audiovisuel respectively.

[11] *Compte-rendu des travaux du Premier Congrès International d'Art Radiophonique* (Paris: Bureau International d'Art Radiophonique, 1937), 5, 6, 10.

one end of the scale, to the echoes of the infinitely distant at the other'.[12] She observed:

> You cannot see it, nor feel it, nor even hear it, except at the fleeting moment of its first projection into the ether. [. . .] [T]he total output is so vast that no one can keep track of more than a fraction of what is actually broadcast, even from one station, still less from all. At the receiving end there is no exact measure with which to gauge the individual response in each of the many million listeners.[13]

The printed press acted as radio's supplementary memory, and the journalism of the period is full of hidden riches, including illuminating discussions of radio's social and artistic roles.[14] Theorising about aesthetics remained a minority pursuit, however: the primary aims were to supply detailed radio programmes and teach listeners how to address common technical problems. Nevertheless, in the midst of programme listings, technical information and miscellaneous reviews, some gems of insight into aesthetic and cultural questions can often be found. The radio journalism that emerged in Weimar Germany, France, Britain and Italy took on different forms but followed broadly similar patterns: there were regular commentaries reviewing recent developments, often engaged in dialogue with other columns and publications; witty, impressionistic listening diaries; and essays seeking to define and conceptualise aspects of broadcasting that often pertained to radio drama and other radiogenic forms. These exploratory types of writing were erudite, quick to emphasise the considerable degree to which radio's immense possibilities had not been fully apprehended, and eager to debate how radio's prospects, as a medium of communication and entertainment, and as a technology and an art form, could be improved and augmented.

Radio's early history is often told as a story of firsts – from the first transmitters installed, to the first radio stations created, through to the first programmes transmitted. This anthology is interested in another way of thinking about history, through conversations, influences and debates unfolding not on a national but on an international scale, often diffusely, and through records and remnants of an evolving practice developed as part of vast, parallel and shared efforts. Understanding this foundational period in the history of radio also requires us to look beyond the canonical figures who spoke on the airwaves, and direct our

<hr>

[12] Hilda Matheson, 'Broadcasting: Implications,' *Observer*, 11 February 1934, 10.

[13] Hilda Matheson, 'Politics and Broadcasting,' *Political Quarterly* 5, no. 2 (1934): 179.

[14] See Lacey, *Feminine Frequencies*, 11; Simon Potter, *Wireless Internationalism and Distant Listening: Britain, Propaganda, and the Invention of Global Radio, 1920–1939* (Oxford: Oxford University Press, 2020), 7.

gaze at the long-forgotten authors, jobbing journalists, actors and producers who worked on and wrote about the medium on a regular basis – at the 'nobodies of radio art,' to borrow the phrase coined in another context by Gregory Whitehead; indeed, as Whitehead puts it, the history of radio is 'largely a history of nobodies'.[15] This is particularly true of the period spanning from the mid-1920s to the late 1930s: the distinctive and thought-provoking discussions about radio that emerged then were largely crafted and nurtured by the humble workhorses and enthusiasts who wrote for myriad publications furthering radio's cause.

The backgrounds, politics and activities of the men and women who wrote about radio were enormously varied, and the differences in their professional trajectories and fates after 1933 and after 1939 are striking, and often harrowing. Some belonged to a liberal elite, and others did not. Some published under their own names, while others published pseudonymously or anonymously. Ideas circulated, were reformulated and borrowed in a manner that was often anarchic, free-flowing and unpredictable. The celebrated writers who appeared punctually on the airwaves did not have as clear an understanding of radio's cultural worth: W. B. Yeats, E. M. Forster or Virginia Woolf, for example, may have written talks for BBC programmes, but they did not think about radio in meaningful depth, and their observations are at best anecdotal. For the most part, the genuinely innovative thinking emanated from individuals who lacked the cultural capital, the financial means or the contacts to pursue 'pure' literary and artistic careers, and often turned to radio journalism or broadcasting accidentally. The sheer abundance of manuals and guides published during the period, explaining how to make a career in broadcasting, speak at the microphone and write a radio play, bears testament to the fact that radio-related work chimed with the professional aspirations and experiences of a hidden, humble demographic, versatile by default, who needed to find ways to make a living.[16] This pattern was not unique to Europe: in Japan, for example, established authors were slow to turn to radio, and only did so after much encouragement from the radio press and other quarters.[17]

During the 1920s and 1930s, those who made radio hospitable to literary modernism and sonic experimentation included many aspiring or fledgling authors who saw radio as promising territory, actors and producers who

---

[15] Gregory Whitehead, 'Out of the Dark: Notes on the Nobodies of Radio Art,' in *Wireless Imagination: Sound, Radio, and the Avant-Garde*, eds. Douglas Kahn and Gregory Whitehead (Cambridge, MA: MIT Press, 1992), 253–64.

[16] Writing competitions focused on radio plays also became particularly common. The first book published in Britain on how to write radio plays was Gordon Lea's *Radio Drama and How To Write It* (London: Allen & Unwin, 1926).

[17] Kerim Yasar, *Electrified Voices: How the Telephone, Phonograph, and Radio Shaped Modern Japan, 1868–1945* (New York: Columbia University Press, 2018), 171.

had stepped into radio studios largely by chance, and radio journalists eager to sustain sideline careers, often in painting, theatre or poetry. This anthology offers a representative portrait of their efforts. Many early pioneers – notably, Paul Deharme, Hans Flesch, Carlos Larronde, Enzo Ferrieri, Hilda Matheson, Lance Sieveking and Tyrone Guthrie – had artistic as well as technical interests in broadcasting. Others – notably France Darget, Mabel Constanduros, Olive Shapley and Barbara Burnham – crafted new types of programmes and accumulated an extensive practical knowledge of how to structure radio performances. The anthology also features commentaries by avant-garde artists who made a living as radio journalists, such as the Dadaist Paul Dermée and the Futurist Guido Sommi-Picenardi; established writers who were fascinated by radio's social and cultural dimensions and gained a great deal of practical broadcasting experience over time, notably F. T. Marinetti, Ernst Toller, Alfred Döblin, Annette Kolb, Hermynia Zur Mühlen, Hermann Kasack, Rose Macaulay and Colette; less firmly established writers whose careers were rekindled by radio, such as Suzanne Malard and Fernand Divoire; accidental authors to whom radio offered a precious opportunity to write plays, such as Gabriel Germinet, Madeleine Montvoisin, René Christauflour and Rolf Gunold; artists and thinkers from other fields who were interested in the practicalities of radio sound, such as Walter Benjamin, Walter Ruttmann, Pierre Schaeffer and Kurt Weill; prolific journalists such as Egon Erwin Kisch, Kurt Tucholsky, Suzanne Cilly and Grace Wyndham Goldie; and other little-known or long-forgotten authors, radio commentators, producers and actors who penned insightful observations about radiogenic forms and contributed to the rise of a new literature for the wireless. Some of their ideas travelled far and wide, but in ways that are difficult to map and understand; for this reason, this anthology does not attempt to document in detail the tangible impact of ideas or the rationale behind their circulation, but is mostly concerned about their existence and the manner in which they were formulated. The French radio dramatist Madeleine Montvoisin, for example, about whom so little is known that even her dates of birth and death are not recorded anywhere, saw her ideas about radio drama – only ever published once, in *Comœdia* – radiate through foreign publications such as the Italian radio magazine *Radiocorriere* and the Brazilian radio magazine *Carioca*.[18] Similarly, the disabled writer René Christauflour, who turned to radio drama by chance, saw his concept of 'superhearing' and his radio play *L'Express 175* discussed far and wide, including in the Spanish radio magazine *Ondas*.[19]

The selections offered here span from 1924 (the year the BBC, Radio-Paris and the Südwestdeutsche Rundfunk in Frankfurt broadcast their first plays

---

[18] G. M., untitled article, *Radiocorriere*, 29 August to 4 September 1937, 4; 'Uma vitoria do "broadcasting" brasileiro!,' *Carioca*, 6 August 1938, 40.

[19] Francisco Ginestal, 'En París se estrena con éxito *El Expreso 175*,' *Ondas*, 9 February 1929, 26–7.

specifically written for radio: respectively, Richard Hughes's *Danger*, Pierre Cusy and Gabriel Germinet's *Marémoto*, and Hans Flesch's *Zauberei auf dem Sender*) to 1938. The anthology includes many texts published between 1929 and 1931, when particularly rich and intense debates developed around radiogenic forms, the radio play and radio's political dimensions. This time-frame reflects the fact that much of the intellectual life built around radio came to a sharp halt in Germany in 1933, after Hitler's accession to power, and elsewhere in 1939, with the beginning of the Second World War; it also accounts for the rich radio literature produced in Germany under the Weimar Republic, and for the debates about radio, peace and international politics that emerged around the pan-European pacifist movement, the work of the United Nations and the Spanish Civil War. Many of the ideas advanced in oft-cited texts about radio by Arnheim, Brecht and Schaeffer, in Theodor Adorno's *Current of Music: Elements of a Radio Theory* (drafted between 1938 and 1941), and in Donald McWhinnie's *The Art of Radio* (1959) have associations with this early radio culture, either originating directly from it, or summarising and rephrasing arguments developed during the interwar period.

The idea that radio could unite humanity in ways hitherto unthinkable is a leitmotiv in writing about radio during this period. This egalitarian rhetoric was very powerful. But in its functioning, and in the manner in which it was thought about, radio was far from egalitarian: the day-to-day running of radio stations, the production of radio journalism and the formulation of ways of thinking about radio were shaped by dynamics of class, wealth, gender and race and by social and political privileges that abided by extant political hegemonies. In an essay from 1927, Brecht – merciless as ever – highlighted how the continued emphasis on radio's potential had prevented a genuine reflection on its social results.[20] In conclusion, he hoped that 'the bourgeoisie would make a further invention that enables us to fix for all time what the radio communicates,' adding: 'Later generations would then have the opportunity to marvel how a certain caste was able to tell the whole planet what it had to say and at the same time how it enabled the planet to see that it had nothing to say.'[21] In an earlier critique approaching the politics of broadcasting from a different perspective, Siegfried Kracauer argued that radio was the organ of a new 'boundless imperialism' that proved impossible to escape:

> Since many people feel compelled to broadcast, one finds oneself in a state of permanent receptivity, constantly pregnant with London, the Eiffel Tower, and Berlin. Who would want to resist the invitation of those

---

[20] On the makeup of the German listening public, see Karl Christian Führer, 'A Medium of Modernity? Broadcasting in Weimar Germany, 1923–1932,' *Journal of Modern History* 69, no. 4 (1997): 738.

[21] Brecht, 'Radio – An Antediluvian Invention?' (1927), *Brecht on Film and Radio*, 37–8.

dainty headphones? [. . .] [T]he five continents are drawing ever closer. In truth, it is not we who extend ourselves out toward them; rather, it is their cultures that appropriate us in their boundless imperialism. It is as if one were having one of those dreams provoked by an empty stomach: a tiny ball rolls toward you from very far away, expands into a close-up, and finally roars right over you. You can neither stop it nor escape it, but lie there chained, a helpless little doll swept away by the giant colossus in whose ambit it expires. Flight is impossible. [. . .] [T]he Occident remains omnipresent, whether one acknowledges it or not.[22]

While many of Brecht and Kracauer's contemporaries were oblivious to these developments, large broadcasting organisations were not, and understood their cultural power in the context of their countries' colonial aspirations from early on. Celebrations of radio's geopolitical power are particularly common in magazines such as the BBC's *Radio Times* and *World-Radio*. An anecdote published in *World-Radio* in 1927 foregrounds radio's connection to imperialism in the most explicit terms: the Algiers journalist Michel Raineau, who occasionally contributed articles about broadcasting in the French Empire, related how an encounter with radio had led an influential Tuareg chief, whom he named Ameno-Sag (a clumsy phonetic approximation of the traditional title given to Tuareg leaders), to surrender his political power to the French. This chief had long been particularly recalcitrant, reminding everyone around him that the Sahara belonged to them and not to the French, and asserting that he preferred death to capitulation. After being captured by French soldiers, he heard a concert broadcast from Paris by Radio Tour Eiffel being played on their wireless set one evening. He listened too, silently; two weeks later, he returned and declared defeat, saying: 'Men who are so powerful as to make a human voice cross the airs on clouds are worthy to rule over the whole Sahara.' 'So submitted the most warlike Tuareg tribe,' Raineau concluded, 'thanks to a Parisian radio concert heard in the great African desert; and from that time onward caravans travel over its tracks with comparative security.'[23] What matters is not so much the veracity of the anecdote as what it reveals about the widespread perception of radio as a force for political conversion, able to further colonial expansion where everything else had failed.[24] The role that radio played as a 'tool of empire' – to borrow the term used by Simon Potter and Vincent Kuitenbrouwer – in the first half of the twentieth century was

---

[22] Siegfried Kracauer, 'Boredom' (1924), in *The Mass Ornament: Weimar Essays*, trans. and ed. Thomas Y. Levin (Cambridge, MA: Harvard University Press, 1995), 332–3.

[23] Michel Raineau, 'Radio in the Sahara,' *World-Radio*, 19 August 1927, 169, 171.

[24] This mission was previously ascribed to other sound instruments such as the phonograph; see Renée Altergott, 'Samori Touré and the Portable God: Imagining the Phonographic Conquest of West Africa,' *Nineteenth-Century French Studies* 50, no. 3–4 (2022): 151–69.

far-reaching, and the global history of radio and the global history of imperialism intersect in myriad ways, many still underexplored.[25] During the 1920s and 1930s, the empires served by radio were on the wane, and scholars have shown how ill-placed broadcasting systems were to fulfil their imperialist mission, owing to a paucity of resources and a poor grasp of the multilingual and multicultural realities of colonial societies.[26]

Although radio's colonial history remains beyond the remit of this anthology, which focuses on writings published in Europe, these dimensions are reflected in some of the texts included here – in their recesses, hollows and absences, in their assumptions and worldview. Indeed, visionary aspirations and the propensity to make broad, authoritative declarations about culture remained the preserve of radio journalism and essays published in large European cities, where the press was well-resourced and never short of cultural capital. What is available of the radio journalism published in the colonies – in French and British colonies notably – has an entirely different tenor; the colonial radio press was primarily in the business of supplying programmes and directing listeners to broadcasts of interest, that they could, in theory, hear, and had other priorities: wireless sets remained the preserve of the wealthiest, the numbers of sets were vanishingly small, the electricity supply could not be taken for granted, and those who benefited the most were rural settlers looking for ways to connect to the motherland.[27] When discursive journalism is included, it tends to point to the impact of low resources and staffing, and remains tied to guidance on how to resolve reception problems. This pattern recurs in a range of magazines, from the *Indian Listener*, the official publication of the Indian Broadcasting Service, to French radio magazines published in Morocco and French Indochina such as *La Radio Africaine et la TSF au Maroc*, *Radio Marocaine*, *Radio-Saïgon* and *Indo-Radio*, which were largely the work of white journalists interested in relaying ideas from the Paris and London radio press. Such publications often campaigned for better intercolonial radio provision and advocated for a vision of colonial broadcasting in which radio would satisfactorily bolster imperialism. It is not uncommon to see articles complain about the motherland failing to play its imperial role, failing to see how important broadcasting could be to

---

[25] Simon J. Potter, *Broadcasting Empire: The BBC and the British World, 1922–1970* (Oxford: Oxford University Press, 2012), 1, 11; Vincent Kuitenbrouwer, 'Radio as a Tool of Empire. Intercontinental Broadcasting from the Netherlands to the Dutch East Indies in the 1920s and 1930s,' *Itinerario* 40, no. 1 (2016): 83–103.

[26] See Potter, *Broadcasting Empire*, 14, 75; Scales, *Radio and the Politics of Sound*, 7; Rebecca P. Scales, 'Subversive Sound: Transnational Radio, Arabic Recordings, and the Dangers of Listening in French Colonial Algeria, 1934–1939,' *Comparative Studies in Society and History* 52, no. 2 (2010): 387.

[27] See Scales, *Radio and the Politics of Sound*, 214; Miquel, *Histoire de la radio et de la télévision*, 42; Potter, *Broadcasting Empire*, 26; Scales, 'Subversive Sound.'

the cohesion and endurance of the empire. This outlook reverberates in the texts included in this anthology in indirect ways, notably in the unshakeable confidence that many authors display in their cultural authority, in their deep faith that all stories are theirs to tell, in their vision of radio as an instrument ideally placed to conquer other territories and imaginations.

Across Europe, discourses exalting radio's universal reach and promotion of social harmony bolstered its spread throughout the 1920s and 1930s, in vastly different political contexts. Such discourses encouraged listeners to think of themselves as citizens of a new global, borderless 'radio nation,' to borrow Rebecca Scales's term, and foregrounded, as David Hendy argues, a 'language soaked in demotic values,' but radio during this period was not a medium in which a recognisably varied range of voices were represented in a democratic fashion.[28] Radio was both ahead of its time and behind its time, dominated by intractable tensions between its formal experimentalism and its deep social and political conservatism. Its political scope remained the stuff of paradox. Radio played a key role in peace campaigns on the one hand and bolstered Hitler's and Mussolini's regimes on the other, while remaining widely used for propagandist purposes elsewhere, including the Soviet Union, Spain and Portugal. It asserted its neutrality in contexts that were densely politicised and strictly policed, and commonly used censorship to do so. It was a prodigiously efficient means of communication, albeit one that was difficult to control and regulate, and its regulation remained a governmental priority across Europe, if not a question of law and order. Once again, radio journalism remains an important repository for these tensions, which sometimes manifested themselves in unexpected ways.

In this anthology, a great deal of effort has gone into attempting to represent women's contributions to thought on early radio; sadly, the scope of these attempts was sometimes curtailed by copyright issues, but the selections that are included represent a step forward: indeed texts written by women have been largely if not entirely left aside in previous anthologies of radio texts.[29] This

---

[28] Scales, *Radio and the Politics of Sound*, 6; David Hendy, *Radio in the Global Age* (Oxford: Oxford University Press, 2000), 195–6. BBC staffing and programming became more diverse during the Second World War, and thereafter enshrined dynamics continued to shift somewhat; see James Procter, 'Una Marson at the BBC,' *Small Axe* 19, no. 3 (2015): 1–28; Leonie Thomas, 'Making Waves: Una Marson's Poetic Voice at the BBC,' *Media History* 24, no. 2 (2018): 212–25; Daniel Ryan Morse, *Radio Empire: The BBC's Eastern Service and the Emergence of the Global Anglophone Novel* (New York: Columbia University Press, 2020).

[29] There are three German-language anthologies on early radio: Hans Bredow's *Aus meinem Archiv* (Heidelberg: Kurt Vowinckel, 1950); Gerhard Hay's *Literatur und Rundfunk 1923–1933* (Hildesheim: Gerstenberg, 1975); Irmela Schneider's *Radio-Kultur in der Weimarer Republik* (Tübingen: Gunter Narr, 1984). I have not found evidence of counterparts in other languages. Two English-language anthologies on radio have been published thus far; both cover a later period and have aims that differ from those of this anthology. Andrew

neglect reflects the fragile minority position that women occupied in relation to broadcasting, although special programmes were commonly developed for female audiences – notably, in the context of the German *Frauenfunk*. Indeed, broadcasting remained a masculine environment in which women mostly made inroads in secretarial and other behind-the-scenes roles.[30] At the microphone, their presence was never to be taken for granted, owing to deep-seated prejudices surrounding the female voice and women's abilities: indeed, the radio speaker was widely perceived as embodying the radio station's identity and values and, in Britain and the United States especially, various arguments were made against women's inclusion; their voices were thought to carry less well than men's, and were deemed to be less authoritative and less pleasant to the ear. In France, too, male speakers greatly outnumbered female speakers during the 1920s and 1930s; a provocative article published in *Comœdia* defined radio's main imperative as 'No Women!' and relayed the view that women brought unique harmony, grace and cheerfulness to radio broadcasts.[31] The problem was not universal, however, and Hilda Matheson was among the first to note the discrepancy of practice between Anglophone countries and southern and eastern continental Europe.[32] Female speakers and announcers were given a prominent role on the Italian airwaves, and listeners found Maria Luisa Boncompagni, Italy's first radio announcer and the voice of Roma-Napoli during the 1920s, and Lisa Sergio, called 'the Golden Voice of Rome,' particularly memorable. Lithuania, Switzerland, Denmark, Finland, Spain, Hungary and Poland also had radio stations in which female announcers had a high standing.[33] Women gained even greater prominence on the airwaves in Uruguay, with the feminist station La Voz del Aire and with Radio Femenina (celebrated for its all-women format, the first of its kind in the Western Hemisphere,

Crisell's three-volume anthology *Radio* (London: Routledge, 2009) prioritises contemporary academic essays; the first volume includes four essays from the 1930s to the 1950s by Brecht, Arnheim, Richard Hughes and Donald McWhinnie. Neil Strauss and Dave Mandl's *Radiotext(e)* (New York: Semiotext(e), 1993) includes essays by European and American theorists and artists, mostly from the post-1945 period.

[30] On the British and German contexts, see Kate Murphy, *Behind the Wireless: A History of Early Women at the BBC* (London: Palgrave Macmillan, 2016); Lacey, *Feminine Frequencies*. See also Caroline Mitchell, ed., *Women and Radio: Airing Differences* (London: Routledge, 2000); Maggie Andrews, *Domesticating the Airwaves: Broadcasting, Domesticity and Femininity* (London: Continuum, 2012); Christine Ehrick, *Radio and the Gendered Soundscape: Women and Broadcasting in Argentina and Uruguay, 1930–1950* (New York: Cambridge University Press, 2015); Justine Lloyd, *Gender and Media in the Broadcast Age: Women's Radio Programming at the BBC, CBC, and ABC* (London: Bloomsbury, 2020).

[31] A. Reader, 'Ce qu'ils disent . . .,' *Comœdia*, 2 September 1932, 3.

[32] Hilda Matheson, *Broadcasting* (London: Thornton Butterworth, 1933), 56.

[33] 'Eve at the Mike,' *Radio Pictorial*, 10 January 1936, 10.

launched in 1935), and in Argentina, where Radio Prieto in Buenos Aires nurtured female stars including the poet Silvia Guerrico. Similarly, in Mexico, the poet, author and journalist María Luisa Ross was a central figure in the early history of radio, as founder of Station XFX, and a relentless campaigner for educational programmes of quality.[34] Of course, speaking at the microphone or being employed by a broadcasting company was one thing; writing about radio for large readerships was another. The public discussion and conceptualisation of radio aesthetics remained privileges mostly enjoyed by men. If the number of women who created radio programmes or performed regularly on the airwaves was small, the number of women who wrote radio journalism was much smaller, and the number of women who wrote essays about aesthetics and theorised radio broadcasting was even smaller. Female radio journalists often specialised in anecdotal, in-the-moment chronicles rather than broader arguments about aesthetics and politics; Matheson was the exception in this regard. Many of the texts written by women, too, struggle with the concept of a plural audience, frequently envisaging the typical listener, the one who has taste and makes decisions, as a man, in keeping with the vision enshrined in radio journalism and essayistic writing. The misogyny of broadcasting as a working environment is everywhere evident in sources from the period, and the erasure of women's voices often manifests itself as a simple absence: for example, the landmark *Dichtung und Rundfunk* (Poetry and Radio) conference, which gathered major figures in German broadcasting in Kassel in 1929, featured one female speaker, the writer Ina Seidel, whose contribution is not recorded in the proceedings.[35]

Throughout this period, radio's greatest asset was not technology's rapid progress or the solidity of broadcasting networks, but the fact that those who worked in broadcasting truly believed in it and celebrated its potential, often in grandiloquent terms. In an early book from 1924, the BBC's founder John Reith described radio as the pinnacle of human achievement, claiming that the broadcast, 'as universal as the air,' was for everyone to enjoy.[36] Radio, he declared, 'ignores the puny and often artificial barriers which have estranged men from their fellows' and 'will soon take continents in its stride,' 'cast[ing] a girdle round the earth with bands that are all the stronger because invisible.'[37] These ideas, and the form in which they are cast, are aligned with a vast range of texts

---

[34] Joy Elizabeth Hayes, *Radio Nation: Communication, Popular Culture, and Nationalism in Mexico, 1920–1950* (Tucson: University of Arizona Press, 2000), 42; Elena Jackson Albarrán, *Seen and Heard in Mexico: Children and Revolutionary Cultural Nationalism* (Lincoln: University of Nebraska Press, 2015), 133, 144.

[35] *Dichtung und Rundfunk: Reden und Gegenreden. Als Verhandlungsniederschrift gedruckt* (Berlin: n.p., 1930), 5.

[36] John Reith, *Broadcast Over Britain* (London: Hodder and Stoughton, 1924), 217–18.

[37] Reith, *Broadcast Over Britain*, 219.

paying tribute to radio's possibilities, in ways that are surprisingly consensual and do not seem to have been swayed as radically as we might assume by personal, political or artistic creeds. Some avant-garde artists, particularly in Soviet Russia, argued that radio would change humanity profoundly, for the greater good. As early as 1920, El Lissitzky positioned radio transmission at 'the centre of collective effort,' presenting broadcasting as humanity's chance to 'throw off the shackles that bind us to the earth and rise above it'.[38] The following year, Velimir Khlebnikov penned a visionary manifesto anticipating the spread of broadcasting and celebrating radio as 'the central tree of our consciousness,' as 'the spiritual sun of the country, a great wizard and sorcerer,' as the means to 'forge continuous links in the universal soul and mold mankind into a single entity'.[39] Thereafter, Kazimir Malevich used radio as a metaphor for psychic life and the whole of human experience.[40] As exaggerated as these visions might seem, they nonetheless captured the dominant mood. Hyperbole was a sign of the times, as Pierre Schaeffer observed later, remembering the 1930s in particular as a time of intense experimentation, and recalling how 'the attractions, the enchantments of this miracle machine, this house of wonders' had sparked an intense 'juvenile enthusiasm'.[41] 'We are witnessing the apotheosis of the human voice,' Carlos Larronde reflected in 1930. 'Now is the reign of speech.'[42]

Many others with practical experience of radio work were persuaded that the early years were the golden years, and saw intense poetry both in the very architecture of the radio broadcast and in radio's ability to transform the mundane into something else entirely. 'Radio's great fortune,' Pierre Descaves declared about the early 1920s, 'is that its debut took place in an extraordinarily poetic atmosphere'.[43] 'One word goes through the microphone, and it immediately encircles the globe,' he observed. 'This voice that comes through our walls, bringing us a life we never suspected could exist, this magical rustling, have retained a quasi-miraculous character and grow in an atmosphere recalling that of the miracle.'[44] Literature and theatre often provided the frames

---

[38] El Lissitzy, 'Suprematism in World Reconstruction,' in *Russian Art of the Avant Garde: Theory and Criticism*, ed. and trans. John E. Bowlt (New York: Viking, 1976), 155.

[39] Velimir Khlebnikov, *The King of Time: Selected Writings of the Russian Futurian*, trans. Paul Schmidt, ed. Charlotte Douglas (Cambridge, MA: Harvard University Press, 1985), 155, 156, 159.

[40] Kazimir Malevich, 'Suprematism,' in *Kazimir Malevich: The World as Objectlessness*, eds. Simon Baier and Britta Tanya Dümpelmann, trans. Antonina W. Bouis (Basel: Kunstmuseum Basel, 2014), 195.

[41] Pierre Schaeffer, *Machines à communiquer I: Genèse des simulacres* (Paris: Editions du Seuil, 1970), 89.

[42] Carlos Larronde, 'Au film des jours,' *Lumière et Radio*, 10 January 1930, 31.

[43] Pierre Descaves, *Quand la radio s'appelait 'Tour Eiffel'* (Paris: La Table Ronde, 1963), 7.

[44] Pierre Descaves, 'La TSF et la paix,' *Lumière et Radio*, 10 June 1930, 7.

of reference through which radio's mission and form could be envisaged. Radio became the writer's medium early on, with writers who otherwise had little in common associating radio, often in similar terms, with the possibility of a new future for literature and theatre. Yeats described radio as an instrument that could 'change the oratory of the world' and help 'the dramatic art [to] come back in a new form';[45] Paul Valéry imagined that radio would give rise to 'a vast, purely oral literature' and 'replace the written literature familiar to us';[46] Anna de Noailles marvelled at radio's lyrical capabilities, greeting the weather forecast as the 'barometer of the universe'.[47] Jean Cocteau praised radio's 'marvellous vivacity and spirit,' describing his collaborators at Radio Luxembourg as 'the clockmakers of [an] invisible world, [. . .] experts in an unknown world where time and space have not only stopped existing but become enmeshed, overlapping and following new rules.'[48] Gertrude Stein remembered her experience of speaking at the microphone as a life-changing moment:

> It was it was really all going on, and it was, it really was, as if you were saying what you were saying and you knew you really knew not by what you knew but by what you felt, that everybody was listening . . . I was so filled with it. And then it was over and I never had liked anything as I had liked it.[49]

On the radio, George Bernard Shaw observed, one could speak to millions of listeners 'without risk of interruptions, missiles, stink bombs, patriotic songs, suffragettes, or having the platform rushed by a lynching mob.'[50] Even those who regretted radio's commercial aspirations shared this enthusiasm for its ability to reach everyone, everywhere. 'Radio can do anything, better than the printed press,' Maurice Maeterlinck announced, while denouncing publicity as a hindrance to radio's future.[51]

Throughout its history, radio has crossed linguistic and cultural boundaries as well as national borders; in Europe especially, radio was thoroughly European from the beginning, even before the formal advent of public broadcasting,[52] and

[45] 'A Poet Broadcasts,' *Belfast News-Letter*, 9 September 1931, 6.

[46] Paul Valéry, 'The Future of Literature: Will It Be a Sport?,' trans. Malcolm Cowley, *New York Herald Tribune*, 22 April 1928, 1.

[47] Cited in Descaves, *Quand la radio s'appelait 'Tour Eiffel,'* 9.

[48] Jean Cocteau, 'Radio Luxembourg parle au monde,' *Radio-Magazine*, 23 October 1938, 23.

[49] Gertrude Stein, *How Writing is Written*, ed. Robert Bartlett Haas (Los Angeles: Black Sparrow, 1974), 72.

[50] George Bernard Shaw, 'The Telltale Microphone,' *Political Quarterly* 6, no. 4 (1935): 465.

[51] 'Nos enquêtes: L'influence de la TSF,' *Lumière et Radio*, 10 March 1930, 19.

[52] See Maria Rikitianskaia, 'A Transnational Approach to Radio Amateurism in the 1910s,' in *Transnationalizing Radio Research: New Approaches to an Old Medium*, eds. Golo Föllmer and Alexander Badenoch (Bielefeld: transcript, 2018), 134.

its public was defined by wave frequencies rather than national borders. The ideal of radio as a public service, whose role was primarily educational and cultural, remained prevalent; radio could be variously described as 'a public utility service' catering for the public interest, or as 'a universal commodity, born at a time when it was already becoming natural for such a matter to be either guided or even controlled by the state, like traffic, light and water, and street-repairs,' to borrow Reith's and Arnheim's words.[53] This vision shaped the tone and register of much writing about radio – along with the sense of Europe as a broadcasting region, in which radio stations spoke to a large audience ready to welcome offerings from elsewhere. Radio stations across Europe collaborated with one another for landmark broadcasts and relays, and the concept of evenings dedicated to the culture of a particular country became particularly popular in 1929 and 1930. Radio magazines commonly reported on the innovations and equipment enjoyed by stations across Europe, and some of the earliest full-length studies on the broadcasting of drama and music – notably, Gabriel Germinet and Pierre Cusy's *Théâtre radiophonique: Mode nouveau d'expression artistique* (1926), André Coeuroy's *Panorama de la radio* (1930), and Enrico Rocca's *Panomara dell'arte radiofonica* (1938) – approached writing for radio as a pan-European endeavour. The radio press routinely foregrounded music and spoken word offerings from across the continent; in this respect, the *Radio Times* – with its programmes restricted to the BBC, unlike its cosmopolitan counterpart *World-Radio* – was the exception rather than the norm. The programmes of *Radio Wien*, the magazine of the Ravag, the Austrian broadcasting company, included radio stations from across Europe, while *Radiocorriere*, the magazine of the Italian broadcasting company EIAR (like its predecessors *Radio Orario* and *Radiorario*), featured radio stations from all over the world and commentaries on foreign programmes. Regional British newspapers, too, displayed a sustained engagement with European radio programmes. The reality was patchy, however, particularly when it came to patterns of wireless ownership: in central and eastern Europe, wireless sets were very unevenly distributed and numbers were low; in contrast, the number of private wireless set owners in Germany, France and the United Kingdom grew sharply during the 1930s, placing their number below the United States and above all other countries, whereas in Italy, ownership of wireless sets, initially affected by the lack of low-cost, industrially produced sets, remained less widespread.[54]

---

[53] Reith, *Broadcast Over Britain*, 57; Arnheim, *Radio*, 238–9. On the politics of Reith's conception of broadcasting, see Potter, *Broadcasting Empire*, 5, 9–10.

[54] Figures collected in September 1937 to map private wireless set ownership position the United States first (26,000,000 sets), then Germany (8,412,848), the United Kingdom (8,347,800) and France (4,018,000), and then (in order) the Soviet Union, Japan, Sweden, Czechoslovakia, the Netherlands, Belgium, Australia, Italy, Poland, Denmark, Austria, Switzerland, Hungary, Norway, Finland, the Union of South Africa, the Irish Free State, Lettonia, Yugoslavia, Algeria, Portugal, Egypt, the Dutch East Indies, British India, Estonia,

Although European broadcasting systems had little in common with the liberal and commercial American model which was reliant on a privatised network of stations, private enterprise and advertising, there was no standard model as such, but a mosaic of state-controlled systems: brought together by the work of organisations such as the International Broadcasting Union, they remained individually tied to commercial and industrial companies to various degrees, in arrangements that frequently relied, at least initially, on uneasy alliances between public and private interests.[55] The differences in terms of the structure, ethos and politics of broadcasting systems were considerable. At one end of the spectrum stood the Soviet Union, with a system entirely state-controlled, funded by public taxes, and a powerful network of state transmitters; at the other stood systems in which private organisations had a monopoly over broadcasting, and state involvement was limited, as in Luxembourg, Spain and Turkey. Poland, Romania, Czechoslovakia and Austria had radio broadcasting systems run by companies in which the state was a major stakeholder, while in Denmark, Norway, the Irish Free State and Hungary, state-controlled organisations had total monopoly. The Dutch system was organised around broadcasters of different political or religious affiliations. In Finland, broadcasting was controlled by a non-profit organisation; in Switzerland, it was handled by a central organisation gathering regional broadcasting companies; in Sweden, it was handled by the state and tied to the printed press; in Belgium, it was handled by a national broadcasting institute. In the United Kingdom, the BBC (and, prior to its creation in 1927, the British Broadcasting Company) had a monopoly over broadcasting, as part of licensing arrangements granted by the government and Parliament. Radio in Germany also developed within a state-controlled system, with a central national organisation, the Reichsrundfunkgesellschaft, exercising control over nine regional broadcasters and a national broadcaster based in Berlin, called Deutsche Welle.[56] France had a mixed

Danzig, Lithuania, Morocco and Bulgaria. See Benjamin Huc and François Robin, *Histoire et dessous de la radio en France et dans le monde* (Paris: Editions de France, 1938), 26–7. On Italy, see Franco Monteleone, *Storia della radio e della televisione in Italia: Società, politica, strategie, programmi 1922–1992* (Venice: Marsilio, 1992), 31–2, 45–80.

[55] See Suzanne Lommers, *Europe – on Air: Interwar Projects for Radio Broadcasting* (Amsterdam: Amsterdam University Press, 2012). For an overview from this period see Levering Tyson, ed., *Broadcasting Abroad* (New York: National Advisory Council on Radio in Education, 1934).

[56] These early regional broadcasters were Funk-Stunde AG, Berlin; Nordische Rundfunk AG (Norag), Hamburg; Ostmarken Rundfunk AG (Orag), Königsberg (now Kaliningrad, Russia); Südwestdeutsche Rundfunk AG (SWR/Süwrag), Frankfurt; Westdeutsche Funkstunde AG (Wefag), Münster, subsequently Westdeutsche Rundfunk AG (Werag), Cologne; Süddeutsche Rundfunk AG (Sürag), Stuttgart; Deutsche Stunde in Bayern GmbH, Munich; Mitteldeutsche Rundfunk AG (Mirag), Leipzig; Schlesische Funkstunde AG, Breslau (now Wroclaw, Poland).

economy of private and public broadcasters, and a vast range of unauthorised radio stations; the state retained monopoly control and had the ability to buy private radio stations. In Italy, the state was the principal shareholder in the URI (Unione Radiofonica Italiana, Italy's sole broadcaster from 1924) and its successor EIAR (Ente Italiano Audizioni Radiofoniche, formed in 1928), which had an exclusive right to broadcast; the rest of the shares were owned by private companies. Radio broadcasting became an integral part of the Fascist regime and its propaganda gradually, with propagandist efforts remaining confined to special public holidays until 1927; Italian radio was admired across Europe for the abundance and brilliance of its musical programming and cultural offerings, and occasionally hosted work in the Futurist vein until 1933, when efforts to align Italian cultural policy with practice in Nazi Germany put an end to such experiments. The daily management and daily life of Italian radio stations remained distinct from the political control exercised over broadcasting, while the Italian radio press often offered ample room for debating and theorising.[57] In the Italian context, as in other contexts, radio was not a medium in which realities, practice, aspirations and rhetoric mapped neatly and predictably onto one another, and the thinking about radio's technological and artistic possibilities could encompass a variety of incompatible political positions and outlets.

One of the characteristics that radio programmes shared across Europe was their strong cultural and artistic dimensions: music formed the bulk of the programming, then news and journalism, then talks (predominantly focused on literature, cinema and theatre), then literature and drama.[58] But radio, many believed, could do more than just disseminate culture, art and ideas: with the right resources and contributions, it could become the eighth art, as it was often called then. The degree to which radio could become an art in its own right, freed from comparisons with the cinema, was intensely debated – particularly between 1929 and 1931, as radio listening gradually evolved from a minority pastime, appealing mostly to the wealthy, culturally privileged and technologically literate, to a medium of mass communication deployed for public occasions and in public spaces. As early as 1926, the Expressionist

---

[57] See Philip V. Cannistraro, 'The Radio in Fascist Italy,' *Journal of European Studies* 2, no. 2 (1972): 127–54; Miquel, *Histoire de la radio et de la télévision*, 114; Cécile Méadel, *Histoire de la radio des années trente: Du sans-filiste à l'auditeur* (Paris: Anthropos Economica, 1994), 24–5; Margaret Fisher, 'Futurism and Radio,' in *Futurism and the Technological Imagination*, ed. Günter Berghaus (Amsterdam: Rodopi, 2009), 233; Margaret Fisher, '"The Art of Radia": Pino Masnata's Unpublished Gloss to the Futurist Radio Manifesto,' *Modernism/modernity* 19, no. 1 (2012): 155–6.

[58] This trend is clear from the information compiled by the International Broadcasting Office, Geneva, for May–August 1933, which was based on 15 European countries. See Tyson, *Broadcasting Abroad*, 41.

painter Hans Siebert von Heister, editor of Germany's major radio magazine, *Der Deutsche Rundfunk*, was using *Rundfunkkunst*, radio art, as a secure term and an established concept.[59] In *Radio* (published in English translation in 1936, long before the German original), Arnheim deployed just as confidently a larger vocabulary including 'aural art,' 'the art of sound,' 'the art of broadcasting,' 'the art of radio drama,' 'radio art,' 'spoken- or sound-art'. In France, two Congresses of Radiophonic Art were organised in 1937 and 1939; Germinet, Dermée and others conceptualised the new art of radio and campaigned for its recognition. The lexicon around radio drama was particularly varied, and sustained efforts were made to differentiate between a play written especially for radio and the transmission of a play not originally conceived for radio. French sources distinguished between *théâtre radiophonique* and *théâtre radiophoné*, for example, frequently deploying intermediary categories such as *radio-drame* or *radio-théâtre*; German sources differentiated between *Hörspiel* (the term coined by von Heister in 1924 to designate plays written specifically for radio) and *Sendespiel* (broadcasts of theatre plays), also employing terms such as *Hörfunk, Hörbühne, Rundfunkdrama* or *Funkdrama*. Other terms were invented to capture the concept of a voice, person or spectacle to be listened to without being seen; the most evocative include *auditocolo*, the term coined by the Italian Futurist Anton Giulio Bragaglia to designate the purely auditory counterpart of a *spettacolo* or spectacle,[60] and 'drama in sound,' which made a few appearances in BBC programmes. Discussions of radio's artistic power were not confined to small circles of radio enthusiasts or to specialised magazines, but reverberated in a wide range of publications and across a broad cultural and political spectrum. Many of the spoken word genres around which discussions of radiogenic possibilities crystallised are familiar to us today, and this anthology includes commentaries on the radio play, reportage, the documentary, the interview, the poetry broadcast, as well as discussions of other genres developed and widely debated during the interwar period, such as the news broadcast, radio talks, women's programmes, variety programmes and experimental categories such as the radio film.

The debates around the radiogenic potential of music, literature and theatre continued to gain momentum in the early 1930s, particularly in France and in Germany. The Weimar radio press discussed radiogenic forms early on, employing terms such as *Hörbild, Hörfolge, akustischer Film, Funkrevue* and *Funksketch*, while in Austria, terms such as *Radionovellen, Radiogedichte, Radioscherze, Radiolieder, Radiozeichnungen* and *Radiokarikaturen* also

---

[59] Hans Siebert von Heister, 'Rundfunkkunst: Gedanken zum Hörspiel,' *Der Deutsche Rundfunk*, 21 February 1926, 505–8.
[60] 'Inchiesta sulla Radio,' *Il Convegno* 12, no. 7–8 (August 1931): 373.

appeared.[61] The German lexicon for 'radiogenic' was extensive, and included *funkisch, funkgemäß, funkentsprechend, funkgerecht* or *funkgeeignet*; *radiogénique* and *radiogenico/a* were commonly employed in French and Italian publications. In contrast, 'radiogenic' remained an unusual word in English-language publications; somewhat belatedly, in 1929, Val Gielgud described radiogenic as 'a term recently coined in France, which may be translated as "good radio" – on the analogy of "good theatre".'[62] The term does not feature in the BBC's annual handbooks (neither does 'radiophonic') but makes sporadic appearances, again as a continental import, in the *Radio Times*, the regional British press and modernist magazines.[63] The radio play – the first radiogenic form to be explored in depth – was at the forefront of discussions, along with its relation to drama written for the stage and reflections on adaptation techniques. The crux of the matter was put across concisely by the literary critic R. D. Charques in *Vox*: 'Radio drama is a thing in the making; the broadcast play is a popularisation of the thing made.'[64] 'The first and last condition of radio drama,' Charques wrote, 'is complete disregard of the conventions of the theatre. It can never build up a technique of expression of its own without definitely scrapping all the rules and methods of the stage play.'[65] His argument reflects a developing consensus: the majority of those who wrote radio plays and commented on their approach described radio drama as a new form entirely, and argued that adaptation, if it was required, had to be radical. The interest in radio drama as a new form, which absorbed a great deal of energy and thought during the 1920s and the early 1930s, was shared far beyond Europe and the United States; in Japan, notably, radio pioneers discussed the advent of a theatre written specifically for radio in similar terms, while in Argentina the *novela radioteatral*, serialised radio drama, became a dominant form during the 1930s.[66]

[61] Literally, sound picture, acoustic sequence, acoustic film, radio-revue, radio-sketch; radio short stories, radio-poems, radio-jokes, radio-songs, radio-picture, radio-caricature. Peter Jelavich, *Berlin Alexanderplatz: Radio, Film, and the Death of Weimar Culture* (Berkeley: University of California Press, 2006), 55, 82–3, 264 n55; Antje Vowinckel, *Collagen im Hörspiel: Die Entwicklung einer radiophonen Kunst* (Würzburg: Königshausen & Neumann, 1995), 43, 44; see also Christine Ehardt, *Radiobilder: Eine Kulturgeschichte des Radios in Österreich* (Vienna: Vienna University Press, 2020).

[62] Val Gielgud, 'The Wireless Play – VI: A Practical Example,' *Radio Times*, 28 June 1929, 665.

[63] Some representative examples: 'Today's Broadcasting,' *Birmingham Daily Gazette*, 4 September 1928, 3; Anon., *The Era*, 11 January 1933, 2; 'The BBC's Language: The Official Thought Everybody Knew,' *Western Daily Press*, 9 September 1936, 8.

[64] R. D. Charques, 'The Difficulties of Radio Drama,' *Vox, The Radio Critic & Broadcast Review* 1, no. 3 (23 November 1929): 87.

[65] Charques, 'The Difficulties of Radio Drama,' 87.

[66] Yasar, *Electrified Voices*, 154–91, 161; Lauren Rea, *Argentine Serialised Radio Drama in the Infamous Decade, 1930–1943: Transmitting Nationhood* (Abingdon: Routledge, 2013), 1–22.

The intense debating and hyperbolic rhetoric often concealed other, more concrete challenges: listening to radio was never an easy task, and the problems posed by interferences and poor sound quality endured in spite of enormous steps forward (in 1931, Larronde remarked that it was still difficult to differentiate between a car horn beeping and a man blowing his nose, between plates falling on the floor and a hearse in motion).[67] In spite of efforts made by organisations including the International Broadcasting Union, interferences could have a severe impact, including for well-resourced broadcasting systems. For instance, in the late 1920s and early 1930s, the French stations Radio-Vitus (which used an unauthorised wavelength) and Radio-Toulouse, both of which broadcast advertising in English, caused interferences with the BBC's Cardiff station on British territory; for Parisian listeners, the broadcasts from Daventry often conflicted with those of Radio-Paris and the broadcasts from Langenberg with those of Paris-PTT, while in the French Alsace, listeners could mainly capture German stations, not French stations.[68] Discussions of tuning skills are common in the press of the period; entire magazines made it the core of their business to guide readers through the nitty-gritty of avoiding interferences, with some, such as *World-Radio*, offering detailed diaries of the broadcasting weather in terms that could be strikingly poetic. 'Either listen to radio, or don't listen to it; but if you listen, do it properly,' the radio journalist Pierre Keszler urged his readers, emphasising that listening to radio was an art in its own right.[69]

While ways of thinking and writing about radio remained strikingly diverse, some topics – such as the tensions between radio's technological and artistic dimensions, radio's political scope and social applications, the challenges posed by listening, the need to adapt old forms and invent new radiogenic genres (including a canon of radio drama) – remained obsessively present. This anthology offers representative insights into these prevalent concerns. Part 1, 'Radio as Technology, Radio as Art,' gathers longer essays as well as short reflections that advocate for the need to recognise radio's revolutionary aesthetics, and discuss technological achievements in light of radio's promise for artistic creation. Part 2, 'Behind the Microphone,' focuses on the practical challenges that the microphone posed to those involved in crafting and delivering broadcasts, and includes recollections and discussions of questions relating to performance. Part 3, 'The Art of Listening,' features powerful discussions of radio's capacity to engineer encounters with other languages, places and cultures, describing listening as a process that stimulates the intellect and the imagination. Part 4, 'Radio Genres,' focuses on the challenges inherent in writing for voices and

---

[67] Carlos Larronde, 'Le lyrisme de la radio,' *L'Intransigeant*, 23 March 1931, 10.
[68] Scales, *Radio and the Politics of Sound*, 127–9, 138–9, 142–3.
[69] Pierre Keszler, 'L'art d'écouter,' *La Liberté*, 6 April 1931, 4.

sounds whose origins are unseen, presenting a selection of texts reflecting on the new forms of expression generated by radio – including the radio talk and the feature programme as practised by the BBC, and reportage as practised elsewhere – and discussing what radio could bring to the interview, to comedy, to humour and to poetry. Part 5, 'A Theatre for the Ear,' focuses on radio drama – a genre developed by design as well as accident; the texts discuss how radio might move away from the broadcast play taken from the theatre repertory, and broadcast without fundamental modifications to its form, towards dramatic forms created especially for the microphone, taking into account the listeners' needs and radio's technical limitations. Part 6, 'Radio Politics and Radio Frontiers,' features texts describing the effects of radio on social barriers and frontiers, with some focusing on the dangers posed by radio as a tool for political propaganda, warmongering and censorship, and others wondering whether radio's potential for the promotion of social harmony, peace and cross-cultural understanding has been truly understood and realised.

Radio broadcasting was never monolingual or monocultural, but grew rhizomatically and anarchically during the interwar period, and thrived on linguistic and cultural exchange as well as political conflict. Yet thus far, transnational and transcultural histories of radio have largely remained minority endeavours,[70] and the multidisciplinary field of radio studies has been driven by a tendency to investigate the history of broadcasting from monolingual and national perspectives, separating national institutions and their cultural policies from one another. Our understanding of radio's history – which has shaped much of the twentieth century – has suffered from the paucity of transnational and multilingual approaches: scholars have long drawn attention to this problem, in publications ranging from Debra Rae Cohen, Michael Coyle and Jane Lewty's *Broadcasting Modernism* (2009) to Golo Föllmer and Alexander Badenoch's *Transnationalizing Radio Research* (2018), through to Simon Potter's *Wireless Internationalism and Distant Listening* (2020). Scholars including Kate Lacey, Daniel Gilfillan, Peter Jelavich, Rebecca Scales and Carolyn Birdsall have played a pioneering role in enabling cross-linguistic and cross-cultural approaches, and recent histories of broadcasting by Lauren Rea (Argentina),

---

[70] See Miquel, *Histoire de la radio et de la télévision*; Méadel, *Histoire de la radio des années trente*; Rudolfo Sacchettini, *La radiofonica arte invisibile. Il radiodramma italiano prima della televisione* (Pisa: Teatrino dei Fondi, Titivillus Mostre, 2011); Lommers, *Europe – on Air*. Global histories of radio in English published thus far do not deal with programme contents but sketch out broad administrative and systemic developments; see William E. McCavitt, ed., *Broadcasting Around the World* (Blue Ridge Summit, PA: TAB, 1981); James Wood, *A History of International Broadcasting* (London: Peregrinus, 1992); Alan Wells, ed., *World Broadcasting: A Comparative View* (Norwood, NJ: Ablex, 1996); Shaheed Nick Mohammed, *Global Radio: From Shortwave to Streaming* (Lanham, MD: Lexington, 2019).

Christine Ehrick (Argentina and Uruguay), J. Justin Castro and Joy Elizabeth Hayes (Mexico), Kerim Yasar (Japan) and Marissa Jean Moorman (Angola) demonstrate how foundational the 1920s and 1930s are to our understanding of radio's world history, and to our apprehension of radio's intimacy with political propaganda and imperialism.[71] In spite of this global turn, access to primary materials remains a problematic issue, and translations – translation remaining a tragically devalued art in the Anglophone world especially – are rare. The purpose of this anthology is to provide access to a new range of primary materials from a time often ignored, a time about which relatively little is known – and, hopefully, stimulate interest in radio's transnational history and long-standing ties to literary and artistic creation in a wider sense.

[71] Hayes, *Radio Nation*; Rea, *Argentine Serialised Radio Drama*; Ehrick, *Radio and the Gendered Soundscape*; J. Justin Castro, *Radio in Revolution: Wireless Technology and State Power in Mexico, 1897–1938* (Lincoln: University of Nebraska Press, 2016); Yasar, *Electrified Voices*; Marissa Jean Moorman, *Radio, State Power, and the Cold War in Angola, 1931–2002* (Athens: Ohio University Press, 2019). On radio after 1940, see also Morse, *Radio Empire*.

PART I
RADIO AS TECHNOLOGY, RADIO AS ART

1.1 HILDA MATHESON: FROM *BROADCASTING*

First published as *Broadcasting* (London: Thornton Butterworth, 1933), 14–18, 59–62, 71–2, 74–83.

The British radio pioneer Hilda Matheson (1888–1940) was the driving force behind the development of literary talks at the BBC. Her work was practical as well as conceptual, and she was one of a few people seeking to conceptualise radio's relation to literature and poetry. She became the BBC's first Director of Talks in 1927, after a brief period in the BBC Education Department, and worked with many prominent writers and artists. She favoured a conversational, intimate style of speaking over the established formal lecturing style, on the grounds that, with the right mode of delivery, radio could create intimacy like no other medium. Her BBC career was short-lived: she resigned in early 1932, in protest against John Reith's control over literary talks.[1] Thereafter, she wrote journalism for newspapers and magazines including the *Observer* and the *New Statesman*, and worked at the Royal Institute of International Affairs on Malcolm Hailey's 1938 *African Survey*, for which she was awarded an OBE. In 1939, she became Director of the Joint Broadcasting Committee, an organisation created to encourage pro-British propaganda abroad and partly funded by MI6, for which she had worked during the First World War.

● ● ●

[. . .] Broadcasting is not strictly speaking another machine; it makes use of apparatus (although the tendency is moving rapidly towards simplification); but fundamentally it is a harnessing of elemental forces, a capturing of sounds and voices all over the world to which hitherto we have been deaf.

---

[1] The focus of the disagreement was Reith's censorship of a talk by Harold Nicolson, but the episode had another dimension, to do with Reith's disapproval of Matheson's feminist and progressive politics. See Fred Hunter, 'Hilda Matheson and the BBC, 1926–1940,' in *This Working Day World: Women's Lives and Culture(s) in Britain, 1914–1945*, ed. Sybil Oldfield (London: Taylor and Francis, 1994), 168–74; Michael Carney, *Stoker: The Life of Hilda Matheson OBE, 1888–1940* (Llangynog: Carney, 1999); Kate Murphy, *Behind the Wireless: A History of Early Women at the BBC* (London: Palgrave Macmillan, 2016), 168–75; Todd Avery, *Radio Modernism: Literature, Ethics, and the BBC, 1922–1938* (Abingdon: Routledge, 2016), 44–52.

It is a means of enlarging the frontiers of human interest and consciousness, of widening personal experience, of shrinking the earth's surface. It is only possible to see it in its right perspective by seeing it in the scale already suggested – a milestone in the development of communications as momentous as its forerunners, and, like them, accompanying and assisting a new stage in civilization. Broadcasting as we know it, moreover, is in its infancy; it is comparable to the rudest scratchings on the cave-man's dark walls, to the guttural sounds which served the first *homo sapiens* for speech. It is not possible to pass final judgment upon its full significance; this is still wrapped in shadows. It is unreasonable, however, to regard it with distrust as a mechanical toy, as a new-fangled substitute for older and more familiar means of communication. For all we know, the first attempts to reproduce the sounds of speech and music by marks on stone or bark may have seemed as intolerably profane and mechanical as broadcasting seems to some to-day – robbing language of its beauty and confining it within the arbitrary limits of a few fixed symbols; and to reproduce those signs in quantities, by means of printing-presses, was, as we know, held at one time to be dangerous, if not impious. Broadcasting, and its allies, telegraphy and telephony, are only stages in the long process that began with man's existence some three hundred thousand years ago, and that may end in some form of thought transference of which we now have no conception.

It is of course possible that within the next few years we may see the end of an epoch; that, after a period of war, pestilence, and the breakdown of international commerce and finance, humanity will resume life as a small community living in primitive surroundings, with no machines, no wireless, and no broadcasting. Mr Wells' Fifth Age of Electrical Communications may be succeeded by a Sixth Age of no communications at all.[2] [. . .]

Each successive means of wider communication seems to have evolved in answer to some need in the developing world. Speech must have become necessary when ideas grew beyond primitive needs, and required expression more varied than gesture could supply. Writing must have accompanied the growth of social groups, of priesthood, of leadership, and the dawn of literature and speculation. Printing was the medium through which the Renaissance knowledge and spirit were spread abroad, and heralded the birth of what we call the modern world. Broadcasting and other forms of electrical communications have sprung up to meet the urgent requirements of a world which must perish unless it can devise an organization capable of expressing its human and economic unity. The need for rapid interchange of news and

---

[2]   H. G. Wells defined five successive stages of civilisation in *The Work, Wealth and Happiness of Mankind* (1931): before speech; speech; writing; printing; the age of mechanical transport and electrical communication.

views, for familiarizing each country with the ideas and habits of all other countries, and above all the need for an education which may fit men and women, literate and illiterate, for the complicated world of to-morrow – all these needs should find in broadcasting an instrument marvellously fitted to serve them.

This does not mean that it should be uncritically accepted. Broadcasting is a gift-horse which should be looked in the mouth. A reaction has set in against that religious acceptance of the marvels of applied science as inevitable signs of progress. We know now that they can play havoc in a world at war; we even begin to ask where science is leading us; we begin to wonder whether man was made for science or science for man. It is easy to write sentimentally and superficially about broadcasting – its elevating effects, its short cuts to culture, its universal message, its vast audience thrilled by one simultaneous emotion. It is not necessarily an advantage that the humble crofter in his lone shieling may hear sounds generated in Paris, Vienna or New York if those sounds are silly, or vulgar, or false. The ripples started by silly noises spread further and pollute more widely – that is all. Broadcasting may spread the worst features of our age as effectively as the best; it is only stimulating, constructive and valuable in so far as it can stiffen individuality and inoculate those who listen with some capacity to think, feel and understand.

[. . .] The most pervasive and the most powerful effects of broadcasting are seen, not in music, but in speech. [. . .] Broadcasting is clearly rediscovering the spoken language, the impermanent but living tongue, as distinct from the permanent but silent print. It is reminding us that speech is the basis of language; that writing and printing are only convenient symbols and as such invaluable accessories. It is making us conscious of the fact that writing and printing are incomplete symbols; they indicate words, but not accent, cadence or rhythm, which speech alone can show. Broadcasting is enabling complicated, difficult and novel ideas and experiences to be conveyed to people whose lack of literary education would ordinarily prevent or hinder them from getting in touch with those ideas and experiences direct from printed books. It is, moreover, providing a bridge, a connecting link between ear and eye impressions of words and sentences. Readings of prose and poetry, and plays, are giving them new life to many people who had missed the sound and significance of them in print. (It is, of course, true that reading aloud means rendering in a spoken form what was designed as written language. This raises yet another problem, which is not easily solved.) But, in addition, broadcasting is redressing the balance in favour of the vernacular. Early experiments with broadcast talks showed that it was useless to address the microphone as if it were a public meeting, or even to read it essays or leading articles. The person sitting at the other end expected the speaker to address him personally, simply, almost familiarly, as man to man. This led to further experiment. Should broadcasters speak impromptu? How else could this personal spoken speech be maintained? And yet, without a carefully prepared and timed talk, how could a speaker be sure of getting all he needed to say, in its right proportion, into his fixed space of time? These questions have been answered in different ways in different countries and on different occasions. Experience almost everywhere has shown that, though a few practised broadcasters, particularly if their speech is an informal accompaniment of music or reading, can speak impromptu with success, most speakers and certainly most novices need a prepared manuscript if they are to avoid tiresome hesitation or equally tiresome verbosity. A technique had therefore to be found for the writing, rehearsing and delivery of talks, which would avoid the pitfalls of impromptu speech and yet retain its atmosphere. Speakers, however eminent, welcome rather than resent preliminary discussion of the way in which to approach and present material; they submit with a good grace to voice tests to discover points of intonation, rhythm, articulation which may need correction; and they accept with thanks, if tactfully offered, criticisms of a manuscript which retains the form and flavour of an essay or a treatise instead of a talk. Many manuscripts submitted require something not unlike translation before they can hope to sound as if they were spoken to a person and not delivered to an assembly. Many speakers find it difficult, even with a manuscript in vernacular English, to retain a vernacular intonation, pace and emphasis. Conversational speech works upon a wholly different pattern, in all these respects, from platform speech, or from reading aloud. It is in attention to details of this kind that the success or failure of much broadcast talking lies. [. . .]

These considerations lead to the most absorbing and elusive puzzle of broadcast speech – the relation of voice and personality. What is their relation? Does it exist at all? Does a voice necessarily fit the personality it belongs to? Does a voice suggest the same kind of personality to everybody? How far is the success or failure of a broadcast talk due to the voice as distinct from the content? Is there any particular kind of voice which expresses personality more clearly than another? Can this kind of voice be taught? How far is the voice of the author of the talk an essential part of the broadcast, and how far can it be replaced by a substitute without loss and even with gain? These, and countless other questions, press urgently for solution upon the broadcaster; and even though solution may evade him, he must work out some kind of provisional answer on which to base his practice.

One might begin the enquiry with the voice alone, its timbre and quality and inflexion, quite apart from the words used – the voice of someone speaking a language of which we understand no single word. Is it possible to characterize a voice, and visualize its unseen owner, with only a meaningless sound to judge from? This raises questions too large to discuss here; but, since certain languages always sound as if their speakers were in a rage, and others as if they were in a state of utter misery, it seems unlikely that we should get very far in that direction. It is more to the immediate point to try to discover, if we can, how far voice is a reliable clue to personality when it is speaking words we understand. This at once makes the problem more difficult, since it means discovering also how far it is possible to dissociate the voice which speaks from what it says.

The whole subject is a new one, forced upon us mainly by broadcasting. A vague body of experience is gradually accumulating among broadcasters, but little or none of it is tabulated or co-coordinated. Valuable evidence lies concealed in the thousands of letters received over a period of years by regular broadcasters, a large proportion of which make specific reference to voice. [. . .] To most people, probably to everyone, every voice suggests some kind of social or occupational background, or its deviation from the social background to which it appears to belong. The effect of this recognition will be pleasant or unpleasant according to the point of view or the prejudice of each listener. Most voices, like most smells, start an immediate memory or association, which may consciously or unconsciously determine whether they are liked or not. A great deal of what is put down to voice will really be due to the vocabulary and the style of the speaker. Yet, when we have made this rough analysis, are we much nearer the inner truth? The share of impression which must be attributed to what the speaker actually says remains an unknown and variable quantity. What is it that makes some people, talking on the most unpromising subjects with no cheap tricks, welcomed as friends week after week, year after year, in every sort of household, rich and poor, educated and uneducated? Why is it that some people, with voices like corncrakes or like sparrows, can hold the breathless attention of a vast audience? Why should countless listeners write to a particular broadcaster to describe the help and comfort of her 'kind' voice? When all is said and done, we know at present little more than this – that a disembodied voice can act as a true reflector of a personality; that by luck and by diligence one may find speakers with personalities which can faithfully and acceptably reveal themselves in the same terms to an immensely large audience; that these successful voice and personality projectors seem to possess a particular range of personal qualities – they are human, sincere, unaffected and vital; that actual beauty of voice – though always welcome – is more important for reading than for talking, provided the voice conveys an acceptable personality; and that something vital, some indefinable virtue, goes out of the talk if it is read, however intelligently, by someone other than its creator. It is obvious from this that much of the personality is revealed in characteristic expressions, cadences, hesitations, stresses, change of pace, and general vocal gesture. It is important therefore that the training and rehearsing of speakers should never attempt to impose a uniform standard, and that, within the limits of intelligibility, speakers' idiosyncrasies of voice should be left to speak for themselves.

Broadcasting, then, is bringing a new consciousness of speech. By so doing it is influencing pronunciation and intonation, but it is also affecting the structure and composition of the language. It is not improbable that it may help to re-unite spelling and speech, and it is conceivable that it may encourage a critical scrutiny of the very words we use. A generation accustomed to relate much of its thought to spoken English may question whether even our words need remodelling as well as our spelling, if they are to be adequate for new purposes and ideas.

1.2 WALTER RUTTMANN: NEW COMPOSITIONAL MODES FOR SOUND FILM AND RADIO. PROGRAMME FOR AN ART OF ACOUSTIC PHOTOGRAPHY

Translated by Marielle Sutherland. First published as 'Neue Gestaltung von Tonfilm und Funk. Programm einer photographischen Hörkunst,' *Film-Kurier* 255, 26 October 1929, 1.

Walter Ruttmann (1887–1941) was a German film director. The arguments for a new kind of film that he advances here are connected to his conception of 'absolute film' and to the making of his only radio piece, *Wochenende* ('Weekend'), a sound montage portraying a weekend in Berlin. The work, commissioned in 1928 by Hans Flesch, then artistic director of the Berlin Funkstunde, was broadcast in June 1930 by the Berlin Funkstunde and the Schlesische Funkstunde, Breslau, and was also played in cinemas thereafter. *Wochenende* features no actors; it is an assemblage of sound and voice recordings from everyday life collected across Berlin. To make it, Ruttmann did not work with disc records but with an optical film system conceived for the film industry, which enabled him to cut and splice tape as he would have done for a film. He recorded the sounds of Berlin factories and trains using a mobile recording van, and supplemented these with studio recordings. *Wochenende* was categorised as a 'Film-Hörspiel' (film-radio play); Ruttmann variously called it a 'photographic radio play,' a 'blind film,' or a 'study in sound montage'.[1] It is one of several experiments with abstract composition for which Ruttmann became known during the 1920s. He also worked in advertising, and made numerous Nazi propaganda films after 1933.

• • •

Film has demonstrated how art can use 'natural' material.

Film uses (as material) neither constructed formulae and symbols (as in music) nor 'substitutes' (as in the theatre).

Even actors – in the context of film and its material – only become autonomous components once they have divested themselves entirely of their attributes as actors and transformed back into 'natural material'.

Film's intrinsic productivity lies in the selection, assemblage and montage of natural material.

Radio offers similar possibilities, but in the acoustic sphere.[2] It has the ability to transmit acoustic images of an event (whether this be a football match or a pilot's homecoming) – even as it is taking place. In so doing, however, what it offers is merely reportage, not composition.

[1] See Jeanpaul Goergen, ed., *Walter Ruttmann: Eine Dokumentation* (Berlin: Freunde der Deutschen Kinemathek, 1989), 131, 90; Antje Vowinckel, *Collagen im Hörspiel: Die Entwicklung einer radiophonen Kunst* (Würzburg: Königshausen & Neumann, 1995), 60–75; Michael Cowan, *Walter Ruttmann and the Cinema of Multiplicity: Avant-Garde – Advertising – Modernity* (Amsterdam: Amsterdam University Press, 2014); Andy Birtwhistle, 'Photographic Sound Art and the Silent Modernity of Walter Ruttmann's *Weekend* (1930),' *The New Soundtrack* 6, no. 2 (2016): 109–27; Dieter Daniels, 'Absolute Sounding Images: Abstract Film and Radio Drama of the 1920s as Complementary Forms of a Media-Specific Art,' trans. Annie Buenker, in *The Music and Sound of Experimental Film*, eds. Holly Rogers and Jeremy Barham (Oxford: Oxford University Press, 2017), 23–43; Christopher Williams, 'The Concrete "Sound Object" and the Emergence of Acoustical Film and Radiophonic Art in the Modernist Avant-Garde,' *Transcultural Studies* 13, no. 2 (2017): 239–63.

[2] In 1925, Kurt Weill predicted the emergence of an 'absolute radio art' that would 'extend the possibilities for acoustical expression' by taking the same path as the abstract films pioneered by Ruttmann and Eggeling. The main differences separating radio from film, he observed, were its 'pronounced dependency on other arts,' its use to disseminate music and literature, and its far-reaching educational power. Kurt Weill, 'Possibilities for Absolute Radio Art,' trans. Michael Cowan, in *The Promise of Cinema: German Film Theory, 1907–1933*, eds. Anton Kaes, Nicholas Baer and Michael Cowan (Berkeley: University of California Press, 2016), 587–8.

The radio-play,[3] which is the closest thing we have to this ambition for acoustic composition, sees its unity of effect impaired by the fact that it must remain restricted to a relatively accidental and improvised assemblage of materials – natural, artistic and imitative – that are inherently dissimilar by nature.

It erects signposts to experience without forging any pathways; it sketches anecdotally without offering any definitive formulation.

The true form and compositional assemblage of radio's natural material are dependent on the possibility of a montage that is – as in film – liberated from all contingencies and shaped by the creator right through to the last detail.

The technology of the sound film offers this possibility.

Here, the sound film is not to be construed as the combination of optical and acoustic photography, rather merely as the process of photographing phenomena that can be heard without stylisation and without effacing their specific spatial character. Now that sound can be photographed through the exposure of a film strip, acoustic montage is therefore afforded the same possibilities as film montage.

Everything audible in the whole world becomes material.

This infinite material can now be shaped to create new meaning in accordance with the laws of time and space.[4] This is because it is not only rhythm and dynamics that will serve the compositional impetus of the new radio-art, but also space, along with the entire spectrum of tonal variations emanating from it.

Thus, the pathway towards a completely new acoustic art – new in terms of both its means and its effect – is now open.

In its practice, it succeeds to, invigorates and expands the spheres of music and the radio-play.

It uses, above all things, the radio and the disc record.

[3] *Hörspiel* in the original: a play written specially for radio.

[4] The idea that time should be seen as artistic material is central to an essay from 1919–1920, where Ruttmann calls for an 'art for the eyes, which differs from painting because it occurs in time (like music) and because the artistic emphasis does not reside (as in painting) in the reduction of a (real or imaginary) process to a moment, but rather in the temporal development on the formal level.' This art, he concluded, would require 'a completely new type of artist,' 'positioned, as it were, midway between painting and music.' Ruttmann, 'Painting with Time,' trans. Michael Cowan, *The Promise of Cinema*, 451.

1.3 PAUL DEHARME: FROM *FOR A RADIOPHONIC ART*

Translated by Emilie Morin. First published as *Pour un art radiophonique* (Paris: Le Rouge et le Noir, 1930), 15–16, 18–22, 31–4, 37–42, 85.

Paul Deharme (1898–1934) was a French writer and businessman. He was among the first to advocate for an art of radio and theorise it. After training as a doctor, he was hired by Informations et Publicité, an advertising company that managed publicity programmes for Radio-Paris, the Poste Parisien and Radio Luxembourg and sold advertising far beyond; he directed the company until 1932, and also worked as an administrator for Radio-Paris. At Informations et Publicité, he created a new style of radio publicity that was creative and pleasant, and hired artists including Alejo Carpentier and Robert Desnos; Jacques Prévert, Antonin Artaud and Kurt Weill were also among the company's collaborators. In parallel, Deharme wrote celebrated radio plays including *Un incident au pont du Hibou* (based on Ambrose Bierce's short story 'An Occurrence at Owl Creek Bridge,' and first broadcast by Radio-Paris in May 1928) and *L'Ile des voix* (inspired from Robert Louis Stevenson's novel *Treasure Island*, and first broadcast by Radio Luxembourg in March 1935). His work was widely discussed in France and beyond during the 1930s. His book *Pour un art radiophonique* elaborated on ideas first presented in 1928 and 1929, in short essays for *La Nouvelle Revue Française* and *Radio-Magazine*. He had a strong interest in Freud's work, and was married to the Surrealist poet Lise Deharme (1898–1980).[1]

• • •

Radio, part of our way of life since 1919, has been the focus of many lyrical commentaries and many prophecies over the past ten years.[2]

[1] See Marie-Claire Dumas, *Robert Desnos ou l'exploration des limites* (Paris: Klincksieck, 1980), 194–8; Robert Desnos, *Mines de rien*, ed. Marie-Claire Dumas (Paris: Le Temps Qu'Il Fait, 1985), 188–90; Dominique Costa, 'Paul Deharme: Profils perdus,' France Culture, 1 and 8 July 1989, INA archives; Anke Birkenmaier, 'Surrealism for the Ear: Paul Deharme's Radio-Plays,' in *Europa! Europa?: The Avant-Garde, Modernism and the Fate of a Continent*, ed. Sascha Bru et al. (Berlin: De Gruyter, 2009), 423–33; Alain Chevrier, *La 'clef des songes' de Robert Desnos: Une émission radiophonique sur les rêves en 1938* (Lausanne: L'Age d'Homme, 2016), 83–101.

[2] Deharme's text is accompanied by occasional footnotes which have not been included in this translation because they are not footnotes in the common sense of the term, but separate texts which open up entirely new areas and are indirectly related to the chapter contents.

Once radio has decentralised our artistic, scientific, economic and financial life, once we begin to see light, smells and heat disseminated everywhere through radio-vision, and films that talk, in colour and in three dimensions,[3] there will be few intellectuals who won't be able to brandish something proving that they had predicted it all. The most sagacious writers will be able to show editions of their works bearing the following phrase, which was added sometime in the past few years: 'All rights of reproduction and adaptation including for cinema and radio are reserved for all countries.' This is more or less the only result of the attempts to encourage the so-called elite to dedicate a little of its time to researching radio broadcasting [. . .].

No matter what is done, the wireless transmission (or the wired transmission, as with the *théâtrophone*)[4] of the sound *part* of a theatre play, *or even of an opera, or even of a conference speech*, remains, by definition, an incomplete thing!

So why should we be satisfied with that; why should we stubbornly persist on the same path? The cinema has fumbled in all directions, but no one has ever tried to shoot *Around the World in Eighty Days* on the stage of the Chatelet Theatre!

Why is it so hard to understand that radio broadcasts – no matter whether we are talking about a well-chosen theatre play with simple dialogue and no action (such as *Le pain de ménage*), about a well-adapted play with preliminary indications and descriptions, cuts, condensed scenes and a musical part (such as *Barberine*), or about a play written especially for radio, hence populated with noises (such as *Marémoto*)[5] – all take the wrong starting point: theatre;

---

[3] Radio vision, the transmission of images through radio, was already discussed in the early 1920s; the first experiments on the radio transmission of photographs were conducted in 1923 by C. Francis Jenkins in Washington. This experimental form of television remained plagued by technical problems and interferences. An article published in the 1934 *Annuaire de la radiodiffusion nationale* – which also featured Deharme's last essay, 'Idées sur le radio-théâtre,' published posthumously – reviewed these developments in France; see P. Hemardinquer, 'La radiovision en France,' *Annuaire de la Radiodiffusion Nationale, année 1934* (Paris: Ministère des PTT; Service de la Radiodiffusion, 1934), 397–410.

[4] The *théâtrophone* – also called theatrophone and theatrephone in English – was a commercial service administered in France by the Compagnie du Théâtrophone from 1890 to 1932. It disseminated theatre and music performances by linking theatres to telephone lines. It began as a fee-paying service in Parisian hotels and cafés, and was later broadened to private homes as an addition to telephone subscriptions. Similar telephone relay services in Belgium, Portugal, Hungary, Sweden and Italy were very popular and had long lifespans. See Melissa van Drie, 'Know It Well, Know It Differently: New Sonic Practices in Late Nineteenth-Century Theatre-Going: The Case of the Theatrophone in Paris,' in *The Auditory Culture Reader*, eds. Michael Bull and Les Back, 2nd ed. (London: Bloomsbury, 2016), 205–16.

[5] Jules Renard's one-act play *Le pain de ménage* (1898); Alfred de Musset's comedy *Barberine* (1835); Pierre Cusy and Gabriel Germinet's radio play *Marémoto* (1924).

and all of them aim for something that is just as wrong: to compensate for the absence of vision *instead of trying to turn it to their advantage*. This is nothing but a replication of the mistake made by the cinema, where a machine would cleverly supplement with noise the photograph of a machine gun behind the screen until Eisenstein created the *visual metaphor*, by superimposing a tableau of the crowd torn to shreds by bullets and the staccato motion of a machine gun's silhouette.[6]

As a matter of fact, the history of the wireless up to now can literally be superimposed onto the history of the cinema. The pioneers in both arts were fascinated and intoxicated by the near-infinite number of possibilities that could be borrowed from the theatre. The theatre opened to the cinema an immense repertoire in the midst of which pantomime stood with open arms, offering a false impression of fraternity, just as musical comedy does with the wireless today. As absurd as it might seem now, nobody wanted to dismiss a *film d'art* featuring Le Bargy then, just as nobody wants to dismiss a radio performance of *Le chandelier* by the Comédie-Française now.[7] The cinema, engaged on the wrong path, produced 'adaptations,' by introducing outside scenes, quick set changes, subtitles; it searched for colours and photogenic make-up, etc. Sometimes, a camera (always fixed at ground level) would film a dancer on a rope or a football match whose attractiveness *seemed entirely transferable to the screen* [. . .]. The wireless, in turn, 'adapts' by introducing a playmaker, by adding some indications about the setting, by opting for operetta or for comedy (anything that is not radiogenic is left aside; if there are too many walk-ons, they become the hubbub of a crowd; secondary roles are cut or given accents from England or Marseilles in order to avoid confusion, etc.). At other times, too, the microphone captures the sound of a conference or a ceremony, and some believe that this is *directly transferable to the listeners' homes* . . .

Lastly, and most problematically, the wireless – in the fashion of the cinema – calls upon professional actors without trying to ask them to change their stage habits.

Those who are responsible for these mistakes are the public, more than the authors; the public, whose imagination is filled with suspicion, only has one instinct: to recreate the familiar, reassuring boards of the theatre stage. To reconstruct the stage, any landmark, any hint to focus on will do. [. . .]

The liminal problem posed by the radiophonic art is the following: why do a literary fragment and, even more so, a dramatic scene produce such different

---

[6] This is a reference to Sergei Eisenstein's silent film *October* (1927); scenes of crowds dying under gunfire also feature in *Strike* (1924) and *Battleship Potemkin* (1925).

[7] The silent film actor and director Charles Le Bargy (1858–1936); *Le chandelier*, play by Alfred de Musset (1848).

impressions when they are heard in a theatre and when they are heard on the wireless? (To this I would add: and when they are read – this will come later, but I am trying to pre-empt the absurd reply we hear all too often: 'Because it is not possible to see anything.' As if things were that simple! The cinema cannot hear, and yet it is somewhat more entertaining than the radio broadcast of *La mort de Pompée*!).[8]

It is because *the mind functions in different ways* when one is in a theatre and at the cinema on the one hand and, on the other, when one is listening to the wireless, listening to someone speaking on the telephone or reading something. In the first two cases, the mind is bombarded with *sensations*; in the other cases, the mind produces *images*.

In order to play on the word 'image,' used here in its usual sense and according to the terminology of psychologists, who oppose it to 'sensation,' let us agree that in the case of the wireless, the listener produces his own images, whereas with the theatre and the cinema the images are prepared for the spectator. The mind does not work through the action taking place on the stage or the screen, but works on a *subjective image*, which closely adheres to the image created by our senses when we watch a spectacle. (In order to illustrate the power of illusion of which the mind is capable, which varies according to the nature of perception and the different theatrical forms, let us recall that casting an ugly actress into the role of Yseult is completely unfeasible at the cinema, difficult in a comedy, commonplace in an opera, of no importance on the wireless.)

We can affirm, then,

1. That the physical images that make the theatre and the cinema what they are are essentially images that *produce sensations*;
2. That music, and *sounds*, mostly and above all, *produce sensations*. (Some music lovers partially transpose these sensations into images; the genuine musicians take offence at the idea);
3. That most words only *produce images*. (The study of language teaches us that this is not strictly true, especially with reading, but we can accept this as given for the time being, as one accepts that light propagates in a straight line.)

The common error has been to forget that *words are both sound facts and symbols; hence they produce images and sensations simultaneously* [. . .].

---

[8] A tragedy in five acts by Pierre Corneille (1644), featuring eleven main characters and two different crowds, representing exactly the kind of play that, for Deharme, was unsuited to radio.

Heard and mimed at the same time [. . .] words become almost all sensation, and what constitutes the image within them revolves around *belief* – the main characteristic of sensation. Heard only [. . .], they are no more than an image, and the main characteristic of the image is *the absence of belief*. The intonation changes nothing, for it comes with the risk of creating a sensation *alongside* the image instead of *within* the image [. . .].

At the theatre, at the cinema, subjective images – created by physical images *instantaneously* and effortlessly – are accompanied by sensations that make the spectacle believable. In the case of the wireless, it is more difficult for the mind to create and sustain images. Each word freshly heard, in itself and through its relation with the words that precede it, comes with the risk of capsizing everything that the imagination has built. Abstract words are destructive weapons: when they are employed *logically*, to articulate the word-images within a sentence, to reflect the thought of the author, they address neither our sensibility nor our imagination but our reason, and hence weigh down on and slow down the development and play of images.

If the fiefdom of the art of theatre, the art of mime, is the sensations; if the art of the speaking films is destined to be confined to the sensations too, and almost exclusively so (the cinema will soon understand that fiction needs a musical language in order to marry word-images to photo-sensations, and, if it continues to employ words, it will fumble for a long time before discovering how to use speech), then the radiophonic art is and will remain *the domain of images stimulated by words* (thus it may come to the rescue of the speaking films, at least in part), and its technique must consist of *bringing images to life*, taming them, shaping them. [. . .]

Before working on the study that I have just summarised – and which may enable the radiophonic art to make a step forward – I had sketched out, in 1928, somewhat intuitively, the broad outline for a new *method of adaptation* based on the deep instinct that makes us 'identify,' somewhat obscurely, with such and such fictional character we like, enabling us to become at one with that character and 'experience' their adventures, and making us likely, in turn, to 'step into' the action.[9]

It occurred to me that I could use that tendency, and I wrote a text that enabled each listener to believe that they are the hero – this, naturally, made me think of the dream.[10]

---

[9] This is a reference to his essay 'Proposition d'un art radiophonique,' *La Nouvelle Revue Française* 174 (1928): 413–22. For an English translation see Paul Deharme, 'Proposition for a Radiophonic Art,' trans. Anke Birkenmaier, *Modernism/modernity* 16, no. 2 (2009): 406–13.

[10] His radio play *Un incident au pont du Hibou.*

We dream when we sleep. Very well, but what then? We dream when it is dark outside, when we are alone, when we listen to music, when we hear the sound of the sea . . . *Why not dream when we listen to the wireless?*

As soon as we spend a few moments listening to a melody or a poem broadcast over the radio we are tempted to turn off the light, lie down and close our eyes; we are aware that these physical conditions are precisely those of the dream; and we see, with a singular facility and clarity, an abundance of images arising from the *collaboration* between the author of the piece we hear and our memory, revived by our appreciation; we feel, once we return to reality, that our mind has been better entertained and better distracted than by any other spectacle, by any other normal type of listening or reading: *it seems as though we have awoken* in order to be, in short, guided by experience. On this same path, the following proposition may guide us a priori:

The radio film[11] will consist of scenarios written and read according to certain rules that will facilitate in the mind of each listener, plunged in half-slumber, the automatic adaptation of these scenarios to his own personality: he will experience a directed dream. [. . .]

'Half-slumber' and 'dream' . . . Again? you might say. The fundamental basis of your project is nothing but a series of clichés from the past few years . . . That is true. But how I propose to employ the dream is new.

Indeed nobody (except doctors) – and not even the Surrealists, the mystics of our subconscious – has ever drawn on the psychological domain that remains the closest to us – dreams experienced in sleep or in half-sleep – to produce anything other than *inspiration* (be it literary, artistic, philosophical, political, etc.).

As a matter of fact, it is easy to demonstrate from a schematic standpoint that the Surrealist doctrine and my own conception of a new means of expression specific to the wireless are opposed wherever they intersect. [. . .] The dream is no longer the *origin* of the work: it is its *goal*. Slumber is no longer used as a *creative state*, but as a *receptive state*.[12] The automatic play of associations, the impregnation of subconscious materials with images created in preconsciousness are no longer the sole preserve of the author, but become the preserve of the public. Let the public play with the rotten apples and the crystal balls! [. . .]

The radiophonic art that I propose (who can say?) could become a frame for a new pedagogy, for a new maieutics that could give birth to the subconscious, and from which we could extract a solfège for the world's new harmony.

---

[11] *Film radiophonique* in the original.

[12] Deharme is here referring to what the Surrealists called 'the period of the sleeping fits' of the early 1920s, marked by experiments with dreams and automatic writing.

1.4 PIERRE KESZLER: IS THERE SUCH A THING AS A RADIOPHONIC ART?

Translated by Emilie Morin. First published as 'Existe-t-il un art radiophonique?,' *Comœdia*, 23 March 1934, 4.

The French journalist Pierre Keszler (fl. 1923–1939) had a special interest in broadcasting technologies and radio's applications for music. He started writing about radio in 1923. His journalism during the 1930s included articles for newspapers and magazines such as *Le Haut-Parleur*, *Excelsior* and *La Dépêche*, a column dispensing practical advice to radio listeners in *La Liberté* and regular articles on sound technologies, cinema and photography in *La Science et la Vie*. From 1932 to 1935, he was *Comœdia*'s special radio correspondent with Paul Dermée; his columns discussed questions pertaining to aesthetics and listening practice, often focusing on the broadcasting of music and the challenges posed by radio's technological limitations. He stopped publishing journalism after September 1939.

●　●　●

When the phonograph came into the world, when the first animated images shone on a screen, when the first loud speakers played something resembling music, we would regularly hear the same observation: this is strange; this will never be an art in its own right.

Today, however, no one is willing to question why the cinema is called the *seventh art*, and while no number has been associated with the phonograph, no one would dare to deny that there is such a thing as a *phonographic art*.

But today, still, some are reluctant to put the word *art* and the adjective *radiophonic* together. Yet it seems obvious that there is a relation between these two words.

All it takes to see this relation is to compare several radio programmes to one another.

If we simply put a microphone within a theatre or a concert hall, we may find that the sound quality is good, or that it is bad, but in that instance radio broadcasting is merely an instrument propagating the realisation of an artistic, dramatic or musical work; it is not in itself artistic, because creation has played no part in the process.

But if we take another view, and if the performance of a work only has one goal, to create a microphone performance that is as good as possible, then it becomes legitimate to say that radio is an art in its own right. An art it is indeed, for to succeed at it, it is necessary to possess a detailed knowledge of the physical laws that rule over the air waves and use this knowledge to create an illusion that is, from the perspective of the listener, as perfect as possible.

To this argument some have objected that they have never felt the slightest hint of emotion in front of their wireless set and that radio cannot be seen as an art for that reason. This absence of emotion can have several causes that are rigorously independent from the phenomenon of broadcasting as such: for example, a listening experience that takes place in poor conditions, a work that is poorly performed, a work that is totally unsuited to radio. Who would boast of having a perfect appreciation of music the first time they hear an orchestra playing? It is always necessary to get used to new sensations, and they are generally unpleasant to start with. Radio is no exception. It is only after a certain number of hours spent listening that the ear becomes able to discern subtleties, half-shades and nuances, just as it is only once the education of the eye has taken place that the amateur can recognise the talent of the painter.

There is other, more convincing evidence that shows us the path to take towards artistic and creative radio broadcasting. It is the path taken by microphone authors. Until now, serious efforts have only been made for radio drama. The necessity of establishing specific laws was felt more acutely than for music. The simple, unadorned broadcasting of a play generally turns out to be a disaster. It was, hence, necessary to study the rules of a new art, *the art of radio drama*. We know that this has produced valuable plays.

In relation to music such rules are less necessary, it seems. Indeed, the true music lover can be blind; in theory, music does not call upon our visual resources when it transmits musical emotion from the orchestra to the listeners' hearts. Nevertheless, we can affirm that, as a general rule, the generations whose appreciation of music has been formed by attending concerts tend to miss the sight of instruments being played.

The art of radiophonic music must take this fact into account and try, just as radio drama does, to capture the listeners' attention by using new effects, different from those employed in music concerts.

Once we have turned that corner, the last argument against radiophonic art will collapse.

1.5 PAUL DERMÉE: WILL WE HAVE A RADIOPHONIC ART?

Translated by Emilie Morin. First published as 'Aurons-nous un art radiophonique?,' *TSF Programme*, 26 August 1934, 5.

Paul Dermée (born Camille Janssen, 1866–1951) was a Belgian writer associated with Dada and Surrealism, founder of literary magazines including *L'Esprit Nouveau* (with Le Corbusier), and one of the most prolific radio journalists of his generation. He was married to the Dadaist poet Céline Arnauld (born Carolina Goldstein, 1885–1952). Dermée started to work for French radio in 1924, contributing to Radio Tour Eiffel's first news bulletins and acting as its literary critic during these early years. From 1925 to 1932, he wrote a weekly column for *La Parole Libre TSF* (a radio magazine founded by Radio Tour Eiffel's first director, Maurice Privat), first dealing with literature, then with matters including the sociology and aesthetics of radio. From 1932 to 1937, he wrote weekly and bi-weekly radio columns for *Comœdia*, a Paris newspaper dedicated to culture and the performing arts; some appeared under the pseudonym Polder, possibly because his columns were so numerous. He also wrote for other magazines including *Monde*, from 1928 to 1932, and *Le Haut-Parleur*, from 1931 to 1938. Dermée played a key role in French organisations set up in the service of radio broadcasting: during the 1930s, notably, he founded and led a professional trade union for radio journalists, the Association Syndicale Professionnelle des Journalistes de la Radio, acted as president of the Union d'Art Radiophonique (Union for Radiophonic Art, founded in 1934 to bring together radio authors, producers, actors, composers and technicians), and directed the 1937 and 1939 Congresses of Radiophonic Art in Paris. In his journalism, he reported on broadcasting in Europe, North America and elsewhere, and campaigned tirelessly for a better, internationalist radio and for truly radiogenic radio drama. He rarely wrote creatively for radio, but adapted some of his poetry into a longer lyrical work, *Aventure de mer: Oratorio radiophonique*, broadcast by Radio France in 1947, and created a radio film for Radio France in 1951 entitled *Deux mille ans au Quartier Latin*. With other French radio pioneers, Pierre Descaves, Georges Delamare and Paul Castan, he coined the French term that captures the radio producer's role: *metteur en ondes*, modelled after *metteur en scène*, theatre director.[1]

• • •

[1] *Mise en ondes* was the term they coined in 1924 to qualify the process of putting a radio programme together, after discarding other possibilities including *mise en studio*, *mise en auditorium*, *mise en micro* and *mise en antenne*. See Céline Arnauld and Paul Dermée, *Œuvres complètes*, 7 vols, ed. Victor Martin-Schmets (Paris: Classiques Garnier, 2013–2019); Louise-Marie Van Verdeghem, *Essai sur l'art de Paul Dermée* (Diss., University of Gand, 1957); Claire Chancel, 'La dramaturgie des voix,' France Culture, 27 October 1989, INA archives.

How could radio be an art in its own right? Many among the best and brightest will wonder at first, since radio can only transmit what the arts that have established personalities, such as music, theatre, etc., are willing to give to it.

It is easily forgotten that this logic doesn't account for what we all know: in order to be transmitted over the microphone without incident or obstacle, theatre, music, the spoken news, in short all radio activities must possess qualities that are very special indeed . . . and we can just about discern what these qualities are. We can no longer pretend that a radiophonic art does not exist, I think: if we follow the definition given in the Littré dictionary, art is 'a way of doing something according to certain methods, according to certain processes.'

This new art, I admit, is taking its first faltering steps. Only little by little are we discovering the psychological and aesthetic laws that shape the reactions of the wireless listener who is sitting comfortably at home. But let us not forget the physical laws of the microphone, and, more generally, the physical laws of the whole mechanical apparatus that makes transmission and reception possible. There is a considerable difference, for instance, between the value of some voices when they are heard directly and when they are heard on the wireless. It is by taking all these laws into account, and using them according to certain methods, certain processes, that radio will become an art.

The fact that radio uses material borrowed from other, older arts matters very little. Wagner has tried to create a synthesis between music, the action of speech, and the art of gestures, and has called this synthesis *orchestique*, but no one would say that Wagner's theatre does not deserve to be seen as a homogeneous oeuvre. The same goes for the cinema: since the advent of the talking films, it has created a synthesis of visual images, music and speech.

Thus, it seems to me, by analogy, that the radiophonic art will need to be an art of synthesis above all. But because it will only be able to use sound images – at least until television becomes a practical reality – it will need to create a synthesis of all the psychological effects that sounds can produce in the mind of the listener.

Let us consider the wireless listener immersed in the act of listening. The problem that radio broadcasting must address emerges clearly in the moment of listening: firstly, radio must ignite intense interest within him; secondly, radio must avoid wearing out his attention. Otherwise, he will stop listening quickly.

Let us see where this idea takes us.

In order to ignite *interest* it is necessary, if we follow the definition of the word, to communicate to the listener the elements that interest him, by which I mean the elements that matter to him, respond to needs within him that are more or less conscious; or it is necessary to enable him to witness conflicts that, in Aristotle's conception, purge his mind from dangerous tendencies, through aesthetic contemplation and in a peaceful way. Radio is thus obliged to call upon the listener as powerfully and as energetically as possible. Here, more than with anything else, we should distrust anyone who tries to duck these issues.

The spirit of decadence, by which I mean the celebration of individual sophistication and elitism, must be banished from radio; all listeners, without exception, must be able to hear radio's call.

But it is important to avoid creating fatigue, as the risk that the listener will stop listening is always present. It is hence necessary to keep everything short, and to permanently revive interest. How can this be done? By using all the elements of surprise available, by transforming all broadcast matter into dramatic matter regardless of the subject – even in a talk on the internal secretions of gallinaceans – and by ensuring that the radio programme becomes

> a comedy immense –
> Its acts unnumber'd and diverse,
> Its scene the boundless universe.[2]

Some have claimed that the radio style should be an elliptic style of images à la Giraudoux or à la Paul Morand.[3] I disagree. The style of these writers is far too refined for an exclusively oral literature. But it seems to me that the syncopated style of Blaise Cendrars ought to be studied closely by all the radio speakers of tomorrow.[4]

Radio will need to bombard the listener with compressed and short sentences, isolated words sometimes, images that are simple yet powerful, rough associations of syllogisms, no matter whether the broadcast is a political or a literary talk, a news bulletin or a radio-reportage.

Speed is essential, of course, as well as utmost clarity, the frequent repetition of essential words – for example *Paris* should not be replaced with *the capital of France* in order to avoid a repetition; all the effects available to create surprise should be used including changes of tone and changes of voice; finally – and this list is far from complete – one should create an atmosphere around each subject of discussion that is rendered through noises and gives the impression that the facts related are current and are genuinely happening before the microphone. *In short: this is about creating drama.*

All of this entails, of course, following a certain number of conventions, like anything that pertains to art. But the listeners will quickly forget and will collaborate in the illusion created for them on the radio, for their own enjoyment.

Radiophonic art, theatre's powerful offshoot, will be the great dynamic art of tomorrow.

---

[2] From Jean de la Fontaine's introduction to his *Fables*. The English lines are from Elizur Wright's 1841 translation.

[3] French authors Jean Giraudoux (1882–1944) and Paul Morand (1888–1976).

[4] The Swiss-French modernist poet Blaise Cendrars (1887–1961).

1.6 SUZANNE MALARD: RADIO, AN AUTONOMOUS ART

Translated by Emilie Morin. First published as 'La radiophonie, art autonome,' *La Revue de France* 4 (November–December 1934), 567–73.

Suzanne Malard (later known as Suzanne Cita-Malard, 1907–1982) was a French writer who specialised in radio drama and in poetry celebrating radio. She and her mother Cita Malard (Zoé Vandaele, 1884–1952) wrote popular radio plays, often informed by their Catholic faith and inspired by the Scriptures, as well as radio biographies of great figures and retellings of saints' lives. Some of their radio plays were experiments in form and structure, and were celebrated as such: notably, *Le Dieu vivant: Radio-reportage de la Passion en 4 journées* was a play styled as a documentary, which retold the Passion of Christ through the perspective of a reporter sent to Jerusalem. The play, broadcast by Paris-PTT in 1937 across four days coinciding with Easter, was subsequently translated and broadcast across Europe. Malard believed that radio would benefit the whole of humanity and outlined different possibilities for its future, maintaining that it ought to be seen as an autonomous art. At the 1937 International Congress of Radiophonic Art in Paris, for example, she presented radio as a refuge for lyric poetry, enabling not simply the revival of forgotten works but the creation of a new poetry adapted to radio's specific aesthetic.[1] The present essay was followed by a sequel in the literary magazine *La Revue de France*, where she argued that broadcasting should be used to facilitate encounters between nations, and called for a model of radiophonic montage that would enable listeners to travel across cultures and hear soundscapes from other places.[2]

●　●　●

Will radio, which yesterday was *nothing*, become *everything* tomorrow? Nothing is more capable of interfering with the affairs of the State than the invisible, breathtaking waves that are uniting the continents and are capable of setting the nations at odds. To spread panic across a whole region, all it would take would be to propagate false news on the air waves. It is easy to

---

[1] Suzanne Malard, 'Le lyrisme et l'art radiophonique,' Germinet-Vinot collection, Bibliothèque Nationale de France, box 8.

[2] Suzanne Malard, 'Le Théâtre Radiophonique (1),' *La Revue de France* 1 (January–February 1935): 188–9.

imagine how a furtive shock, once amplified and instantly multiplied, would bring about within the listeners' collective mentality the same lethal disorder that a points error can cause on the railways.

No one has forgotten how Hitler's putschists recently gained a stranglehold over the Ravag.[3] Twenty years after the premonitory anguish that dominated July 1914, a broadcast of Chancellor Dollfuss's funeral came to my ears in a garden in Brussels.[4] I keenly searched for the Munich station to see what it was broadcasting at that moment: it was jazz music. But on my wireless set only a few millimetres separated these dances, which were mixed with other international sounds and possibilities in the saturated space of the air waves, from the requiem being played in Vienna. Is it still a paradox to claim that radio is an art? Is it not the case that the duality between disorder and discipline lies at the origin of any aesthetic? In order to recreate a world, it is necessary to reduce it to a jigsaw puzzle first. The wireless gives us a new way of scattering the universal jigsaw puzzle of sounds and emotions . . .

It is up to the technicians to form alliances with inspired artists in order to enable the listener – our unknown collaborator – to connect and appropriate, without becoming too confused, the different perspectives that some altruistic pioneers have sometimes pursued . . . and would pursue more often if the passivity of the elite towards radio did not encourage those in control of the air waves to merely serve the scraps left over from other feasts to the anonymous guests from the ether . . . However, now that a fair tax has been imposed to fund the broadcasting budget and has transformed radio into a paying service,[5] millions of French listeners have become entitled to see fresh manna fall from the sky.

To enable our wireless sets to become something other than airborne information desks and excessively large vehicles for the popularisation and, occasionally, the distortion of information, we must do more than let the microphone swallow up pieces of music, demonstrations of eloquence and theatre plays – all this flotsam frequently left at the mercy of Hertzian waves, all too often riddled with interferences – and let the loud speaker drop them on the shores of listening. It will not even suffice to dye these samples with the indecisive colours of the ether through empirical and hasty adaptations. Music, oratory and theatre must agree to give birth to an autonomous art and let it

---

[3] In July 1934, the Vienna station of the Ravag, Austria's broadcasting company, was the site of the pro-Hitlerian July Putsch, orchestrated by a large number of SS; Engelbert Dollfuss, Chancellor of Austria, was severely wounded on that occasion and died from his injuries. The putschists took control of some parts of the building and broadcast a message announcing Dollfuss's death and a transfer of powers.

[4] Dollfuss, buried in September 1934, rests in the Seipel-Dollfuss Memorial Church, Vienna.

[5] This tax was first levied in May 1933.

grow from what they can each bring to it. I would like to suggest, here, a few of the metamorphoses through which this transfusion of sap and energy will enrich those who act as transmitters as much as the receiver.

Shall we talk about music? The mere fact that original scores have been written for the microphone by Mr Honegger, Mr Jean Clergue, Mr Flament, Mr Jacques de la Presle or Mr Tomasi is enough to demonstrate the interest that our best composers have shown towards this new mode of dissemination.[6] But there is more significant evidence, still.

Mr Eric Sarnette, a brilliant technician as well as a controversial aesthetician, has shown in a wonderful little book entitled *La musique et le micro* the opportunities offered by the new instruments he has developed in collaboration with Mr Adolphe Sax in order to 'suppress any harmonic whose frequency happens to be above the highest frequency that the best microphones and the human ear can capture, meaning 12,000, without modifying and, additionally, by purifying the timbre of the instruments from which they derive.'[7] A more supple use of brass instruments, which creates 'a sensation of power in the deep tones, saves space on the groove or the sound track,' and other advantages, too, show that the constraints seemingly imposed upon the art of music by the disc record and the aerial can also become the mathematical and controlled foundations for a truly organic renewal.

Some passages in an oral presentation delivered by Mr Sarnette last spring to the listeners of 'La Tribune de la Radio' have been less convincing . . .[8] Indeed, he compared the effects of music to a punch in the stomach, and wished to see installed in every town hall across France a large room especially fitted to enable subdued taxpayers to listen to live radio-boxing through a dictatorial loud speaker. This attempt to annihilate our most delicate and most individual reflexes through sound seemed to me to be far too Hitlerian for the

---

6   Arthur Honegger (1892–1955), Swiss composer and member of Les Six, who occasionally composed for radio; Jean Clergue (1905–1971), French composer and conductor; Edouard Flament (1880–1958), French composer; Jacques de La Presle (1888–1969), French composer; Henri Tomasi (1901–1971), French composer and conductor.

7   Eric Sarnette (1898–1993), prominent figure in film music and broadcasting sound, developed special 'microgenic' instruments with Adolphe Sax (son of the Belgian inventor Antoine-Joseph Sax, who created the saxophone and other instruments), and coined the term *microgénie*, the microgenic, on the model of *radiogénie* and *phonogénie*. See Eric Sarnette, *La musique et le micro, résumé et abrégé des travaux d'Eric Sarnette* (Paris: Office Général de la Musique, 1934).

8   'La Tribune de la Radio' was a series of debates on issues related to radio broadcasting. The first debate in January 1934 focused on the suppression of religious broadcasts from state-owned broadcasting and on the Lucerne Plan, which redistributed wavelengths across Europe.

French sensibility. It is true that, over the Rhine, such ideas have been pushed further by transforming the air waves into an instrument of denunciation: indeed, numerous listening posts are being built and secretly arranged in order to put any careless word under the dangerous threat of amplification.

Let me return to the advantages of a wireless made for the community; it is easy to underestimate them. They are mostly educational and perhaps political. Let us not forget the bar around the corner, which has been keeping a jealous eye on the abstemious loud speaker, and also dispenses euphoria, but by keeping the punters at home; we should fear the day when this bar regains its usual flow of customers at the beginning, at the end and perhaps even in the middle of the standardised programmes broadcast on the wireless . . .

The air waves, in my opinion, are essentially made to remedy isolation while respecting solitude. All too often modern life gives us the impression of being caught and confined in an impersonal agglomerate, so much so that the innocent freedom allowed by the wireless becomes more valuable, along with the ability it gives us to reunite with our families and tame the air waves, not in the way that others want us to, but as we please. [. . .]

If we consider, more briefly, how the Hertzian waves have transformed eloquence, it shall become clear that by dispensing with the redundancies, declamation and flourish otherwise supported by facial expression, gesture and the joyous excitation they provoke, the microphone – a school of impoverishment, condensation, instantaneity – humanises and rejuvenates the art of oratory. The listeners, be they Christian or not, who heard the talks by missionaries broadcast by the Poste Parisien during the autumn have been able to witness for themselves the qualities that microphone orators need to have. It is indeed curious that, by using a different timbre and different means, the priests and even the nuns who occasionally spoke at the microphone as part of these broadcasts all succeeded in igniting our interest, because they are people focused on deeds and action, people who have been accustomed to simplicity, clarity and cordiality through their apostolic experience.

In response to those who have expressed doubts about the efficacy of radio's invisible action, I would point to the prodigious growth of charitable movements initiated through the ether by Reverend Lhande in connection with the floods in the South, the red suburbs of Paris, French propaganda in India and in Madagascar, or disabled children and the unemployed.[9] But everyone knows that the only moment when wireless enthusiasts had the courage to stage a mass protest was when religious talks were banned.[10] Let us hope that they

---

[9] Pierre Lhande (1877–1957), Jesuit priest and pioneer of the 'radio-sermon' in the late 1920s.

[10] In early 1934, religious talks were banned from the programmes of Radio-Paris; they were subsequently reinstated.

will be coaxed out of their customary apathy by other needs that will be just as urgent though less crucial.

Now, turning away from eloquence to the theatre, let us consider another one of the 'sound décors' offered by radio's revolving stage: radio-reportage.[11] In this difficult genre sport seems to have secured the most remarkable successes. If more solemn occasions arise, perhaps the specialists will be spurred to choose other subjects.

Some time ago, we heard reportage about Marshal Joffre's funeral that was tiresome. Latterly, reportage about Marshal Lyautey's and President Barthou's funerals was dull.[12] The commentary on President Poincaré's funeral was better, but still featured overly detailed descriptions, of the garments worn by those in the procession, of the rainy weather.[13] It seemed as though we could see, floating through the air, a blank canvas that ought to have been embroidered with memories and good omens. What was it all about? It was about letting the immortality of a human being begin where his topicality ends. This is a perilous task that requires many talents, if not genius . . . 'The Marshal now belongs to history,' concluded the anonymous speaker reporting on the funeral from the Lorraine region. Allow me to correct this: the great hero of colonisation already belonged to history when he was alive. It would have been appropriate for the speaker, since he was speaking from the capital of one of our recovered provinces, in the shadow of Stanislas Leczinski, in the presence of our Head of State, of illustrious warriors, ambassadors and chieftains, over the sounds of French brass bands merging with traditional North African music, to let us hear the nascent wings of history fluttering while history turned into myth.

Mr Théo Fleischman succeeded in letting us hear, irresistibly, such a fluttering, along with the sobs of the people, as the whole of Belgium led the Knight King from the Cathedral of St Michael and St Gudula to the Laeken Church.[14] The Belgian poet, as he did in his *Soleil de minuit* and in other works in which the most precise realism is transfigured by creative emotion, was the best placed to take us out of an idle state of respect, which was the emotion we were supposed to feel, and let us embrace the events and be overwhelmed by them.[15]

---

[11] *Décors sonores* in the original.

[12] Marshal of France Hubert Lyautey (1854–1934), who had a long career in the colonial army and administration, particularly in Indochina, Algeria and Morocco. Louis Barthou (1862–1934), French politician and briefly Prime Minister in 1913.

[13] Raymond Poincaré (1860–1934), French politician who served as Prime Minister three times and as President from 1913 to 1920.

[14] Albert I of Belgium (1875–1934).

[15] In February 1934 the Belgian writer and radio journalist Théo Fleischman (1893–1979) broadcast much-celebrated reportage on the funeral. *Le soleil de minuit* was one of his radio plays.

During the funeral of King Alexander of Yugoslavia, Mr Jean Antoine succeeded at an even more difficult task: with only microphone and voice at his disposal, he succeeded in combining, with pathos and exactitude, the legendary history of Karadjordje's rebels and the heartbreaking cries coming from the procession.[16] This French success was a consolation after so much trial and error. However, once again, now that the universe is lending us an ear, we can, without deprecating anyone, hope to see a team of professionals with different aptitudes emerge, who will be able to grasp the vision and conscience of the nation, its memory and heart . . . And please, I beg you, let us not wait until another funeral takes place to fine-tune our innovations. If no public celebrations are forthcoming, let us create them, let the demonstration of our vitality bounce from border to border . . . Let us ensure that our acoustic fireworks remain bright by enrolling inventive and dexterous pyrotechnists. We in France have enough writers and public speakers whose reflexes have been honed through the practice of journalism and who can give form to the moments when our national emotions should electrify the air waves. Why are they not being called upon? Is it feared that they might display too much personality? Those in charge must take responsibility for creating and conveying the drama of great public events.

And now, permit me to express a profound wish: let us return, for a moment, to Marshal Lyautey, who has been laid in his final resting place in African soil. Only a poet I have never met could make my wish come true. There are episodes in the life of great men that could easily be resuscitated before the microphone, owing to their emotional power and their 'sound décor'. Are the heroes and witnesses of great events aware of the pathos that they could add to our listening experience if they agreed to bring them back to life? I am thinking of a night spent watching the front line; that night when, in order to fill the time until zero hour and keep minds alert and souls uplifted, Marshal Lyautey asked Captain Alfred Drouin to recite poetry to the sound of shellfire.[17] Would the mystery of the air waves not transform this lived fact for good, make it legendary? This, indeed, would be true radio drama.

[16] Alexander I of Yugoslavia (1888–1934); Jean Antoine (1900–1958), newspaper and radio journalist, who broadcast a reportage on the funeral on French radio stations in October 1934. Karadjordje (George Petrović, 1762–1817) led the First Serbian Uprising (1804–1813).

[17] Drouin was frequently asked by Lyautey to recite poetry to lighten the mood during the murderous 'pacification' of Morocco; his words, on that widely reported occasion in 1912, were 'Maintenant, mon petit, dis-nous des vers' ('And now, son, recite some poems for us').

1.7 PIERRE SCHAEFFER: THE PROBLEM CENTRAL TO RADIO BROADCASTING

Translated by Emilie Morin. First published as 'Problème central de la radiodiffusion,' *La Revue Musicale* 183 (April–May 1938): 317–22.

The French composer Pierre Schaeffer (1910–1995) created *musique concrète* and is widely seen as the inventor of electro-acoustic music. He led the development of artistic research on radio in France through various structures and institutions, such as the Studio d'Essai during the Second World War and the Groupe de Recherches Musicales thereafter, and published influential theories of sound and acoustics. His approach to composition was shaped by his deep involvement with radio broadcasting, which began in 1936, when he joined the Direction de la Radiodiffusion Nationale in Paris (the head office of the French national broadcasting service) as an engineer. He was tasked with improving the quality of sound capture for broadcasts made outside the studio, from the Paris Opera and other theatres. He put together a system to facilitate live broadcasting at the Paris Opera, which gave him privileged insights into the difficulties posed by the broadcasting of music. In the wake of an internal report he produced for the Radiodiffusion Nationale in 1938, titled *Vingt leçons et travaux pratiques destinés aux musiciens mélangeurs*, he was invited to contribute to *La Revue Musicale*, a periodical on music history and aesthetics, and he published his first two articles on radio broadcasting that year.[1] The present essay, the most substantial and visionary of the two, prefigures other reflections in Schaeffer's later writings.[2]

● ● ●

The problems of radio broadcasting are numerous and they are all-consuming. They are so numerous that, in the midst of such multitude, we sometimes fail to see the essential problem, the problem that is patiently awaiting its turn in the wings.

Preoccupied by their disputes, consumed by their daily work, the radio technician and the radio musician hardly have any time to think about it all.

---

[1] See also Pierre Schaeffer, 'Vérités premières,' *La Revue Musicale* 184 (June 1938): 414–15.

[2] See John Dack, 'Pierre Schaeffer and the Significance of Radiophonic Art,' *Contemporary Music Review* 10, no. 2 (1994): 3–11; Evelyne Gayou, *Le GRM, Groupe de Recherches Musicales: Cinquante ans d'histoire* (Paris: Fayard, 2007), 21–2; Martin Kaltenecker and Karine Le Bail, eds, *Pierre Schaeffer. Les constructions impatientes* (Paris: CNRS, 2012).

What are the real resources available to radio broadcasting? Does it offer the conditions in which an original art can be born? Or should it be – is it only capable of being – a faithful messenger relaying the classical works in the most perfect form?

Such are radio's many problems, both aesthetic and technical; these, up to now, seem to have only been glimpsed at, sandwiched between two pressing concerns, while every new day has brought a thousand new concerns.

The aesthetic of radio broadcasting takes its urgency and its provisional, indefinitely prolonged character from radio broadcasting itself.

For the cinema, things were different: an 'art' of the cinema created itself through force of circumstance. The existence of a 'radiophonic art' has been ignored up to now.

As soon as it was born, the cinema was welcome like a child who has arrived at the right time; a demanding child, to whom we could refuse nothing, whether we liked it or not. We had to bow down to its baroque demands.

At first, this child was mute; we clothed it with placards and adorned them with subtitles, to show what it was unable to explain clearly enough. It was mute, but it was noisy, and upon its beginnings music proved fairly good at covering that strange perpetual growl that encumbered its throat . . . Its disability demanded the most attentive care, as well as a tropical climate, blinding light and unusual installations. Born under the powerful light of the studio, the cinema could only be reborn in a dark building; for the first few years, the screen could only offer an incomplete reflection of all the light that had been bestowed upon its creation.

Nonetheless, within these selfsame halls, crowds congregated, marvelling at the miracle, and they watched avidly the marvellous image that had come out of the magic lantern, fulfilling a dream that had always been dear to their hearts!

For its sake, artists submitted themselves to the worst kinds of torture, remaining on their feet from dawn to dusk, wearing coarse make-up, perpetually waiting. When at last their turn came, they would be interrupted unceremoniously, with a clap, after they had uttered two or three lines, just as the most pathetic effect was being produced. They grumbled, and yet the cinema remained their darling child!

Soon we became aware that it was growing up and soon we could recognise its face. One day, it began to speak. We saw that it resembled its father, the theatre. But what a difference there was between them! Strangely, the cinema looked younger, sharper, more decided, more brutal. It had its own way – an entirely new way – of understanding life, and if it was sometimes lacking in finesse and education, what expressivity it possessed!

The magic of images was such that we sometimes regretted its silence, the time when it kept its deep power of evocation contained within itself, in its purest form.

The fairies who gathered around radio's cradle did not greet its arrival with the same benevolence. They had given everything to the firstborn – that imposter! – and its sibling had already fallen out of favour.

As soon as it was born, the radio, the sacrificed daughter, was put to work on the tasks that were the most thankless, the most difficult at a young age. And it was treated so harshly! While the cinema frolicked about freely, its every tantrum rewarded, the radio was forced to comply with the most exacting discipline and was asked to transmit, without making any errors, the most difficult pieces ever composed in the history of music; as for its modest demands, they were ignored, and the possibility that we might guess its presence from the humble shadow of a microphone suspended from a height was not tolerated.

Yet buildings were erected for it all the same – at least in other wealthy countries. Even in its own house,[3] it was never quite at home. Confidence took time to develop. At the beginning, the musicians would sulk, pretend that their habits could not be modified, that they had to keep on playing just as they did in their own abode, the concert hall, which had retained the same preferences as always.

The musicians did not want to hear any different, no matter how dismayed the servants of radio broadcasting turned out to be (they were sensitive to radio's humble extraction and modest manners), and no matter how often they stressed that this way of doing things ran against the ideal of faithful reproduction dear to musicians. It was impossible to attempt a rational arrangement for vocal and instrumental ensembles behind the microphone. What was commonplace in the cinema studio became inconceivable in the radio studio. The work was thankless, rehearsals were tense, and the technician was seen as a poor wretch, as an undesirable and unexpected obstacle.

Indeed, some orchestra conductors, including the greatest – who sometimes proved as inflexible as they were famous – could not understand how new constraints could be imposed by a medium that should have served them scrupulously and fearfully. In reality, they had failed to comprehend that their intransigence was sometimes tantamount to asking for the impossible.

Why such inability to understand that a new technique, placed at the service of an ancient art, needs to ask this art to adapt a little, in order to serve it better and remain faithful to it?

When the results are poor, it is all too easy to blame the instrument.

La Fontaine, whose work we know from childhood, has taught us to despise the worker who gives up unceremoniously.

---

[3] This is a reference to purpose-built buildings such as Berlin's Haus des Rundfunks, inaugurated in 1931, and Broadcasting House in London, inaugurated in 1932. Paris's Maison de la Radio was completed in 1963.

An instrument has the form that nature has given to it; it is what it is. In order to use it, it is necessary to know it well. Yet, at present, few people in radio broadcasting seem to have a precise idea of what their instrument is exactly or, above all, its limits – which matter a great deal, since we can only discover the possibilities and appropriate use of something through its limits.

Radio-audition, compared to direct audition, comes with incurable deformities. Have we understood this phenomenon well enough? The preoccupation that should have governed the development of radio broadcasting all the way through should have been precisely how to remedy such insufficiencies through a technique involving skill as well as artifice. It is from the whole realm of artifice, an 'art' in itself, that we can hope to hear a more or less correct transmission of sound, not in the form of an identical reproduction, but in the form of a *sound image* that is as close as possible to the original,[4] and that is original in itself.

Instead, the studio continues to be used like a concert hall or a theatre stage, in an approximative fashion. As for the listeners, they expect the sounds coming out of their loud-speaker to be identical to the sounds they would hear in a theatre or at a concert.

What a marvel, they say, radio broadcasting is! We no longer need to leave our homes. The Opera comes to us! Such bouts of lyricism and praise are often accompanied by a burst of anger that is just as ill-judged, and such zealous listeners complain bitterly about everything that they cannot hear *exactly*, in its entirety, everything that they would hear with their own two ears if they were sitting in a concert hall. Is an opera being transmitted? They hear the intolerable sound of footsteps. They forget that the selfsame footsteps are part of direct listening too, and that the reaction of their ear is psychological, complicit with their eye, prone to pushing the sound they hear into their unconscious. Are the singers moving to and fro on the stage? Do their voices inexplicably become weaker when they pass through the loud-speaker? These flaws would also arise in a concert hall, where they would be less apparent, admittedly, yet would seem perfectly justified. For the spectator, these fluctuations are not flaws, but an expression of life and action.

The richness of the sound perception that we experience when we listen to an orchestra with both our ears comes from our perception of contrast, among other things. With the loud-speaker, contrast disappears; the loud-speaker only brings to the listener a sound perception that is strangely impoverished, extremely confused sometimes, and disappointing for reasons unknown.

These are quotidian realities and yet they remain unrecognised; many of the 'flaws' for which radio broadcasting is blamed are, in reality, tied to impossibilities. The loud-speaker is still expected to perform a miracle that it is unable to craft. It is, more or less, as if the cinema spectator had started to make impossible

---

[4] *Image sonore* in the original.

demands, all of a sudden, and wanted to see the images he is watching step out of the screen, and actors of flesh and blood frolic around him.

Yet some radio broadcasts are pleasant; some radio broadcasts are good, even excellent. That is precisely the point.

It is the case that these very same limits, which play against the sound values and the artistry of a broadcast and partially destroy them, can also contain and produce an extremely clear, pleasant and even – if this is compatible with what can be achieved – faithful broadcast, if they are exploited judiciously. What the listener does not realise, then, is that the successful broadcast has been produced through various kinds of artifice. The most purist of the musicians, when he tunes in, may be charmed by the wares brought to him by his wireless set. The same musician, in the studio, would have thrown up his hands in dismay and been scandalised when liberties were taken.

In the same way, we come out of a photographer's studio satisfied when coarse tricks of lighting and framing have created a portrait that is strikingly true to life, even more real than life itself, as we might say.

What is it all about, then?

It is about a new problem, as new as the problem posed by the cinema, but never presented as such before, and on its way to becoming an old and unresolved problem.

Because the problem posed by the cinema was put in starker terms, it was resolved in good time. The problem of radio broadcasting remains to be resolved.

Why such a difference?

Perhaps because the ear is more accommodating than the eye, because the listening public is in a sense less demanding than the cinema's public. There is always something coming out of the loud-speaker. On average, the 'mainstream public,' who rarely has a feel for music, is easily satisfied if enough variety is provided and if listening is easy, whereas a film has to be shown to a public that is fully there, in the hall, and whose reactions are sharp. The public's physical presence comes with certain demands and keeps producers on their toes. As soon as it was born, the art of the cinema had to find its equilibrium, whereas radio broadcasting seems to have barely begun this process.

The cinema has taken into account, first and foremost, the limits imposed by technique, without speaking back. Without colour, without contrast, it has accepted its own limits and has placed its bets accordingly. It has enhanced these limits and done so magnificently. The effort necessary to produce simplicity, the multiple tricks that the camera demands, have ushered in a specifically cinematographic rendering of the world. Thus, technique has enabled a new art to be born, by preventing the cinema from imitating the theatre.

It seems that the opposite has happened with radio broadcasting. The limits of radio-audition have not led to the blossoming of a new art. Even before it existed, even before it took shape, radio broadcasting was in charge of transmitting an ancient art. As it tried to contain this ancient art, delivering it to the whole universe, it has remained at the mercy of its own limits, it seems – indeed, trapped by these limits.

The tragedy of radio broadcasting resides precisely in this difficulty and in this contradiction.

The cinema, born without good or bad forebears, did not have to contend with heredity. Radio broadcasting had the whole of music to contend with. This special difficulty was tied in with the fact that our cultural patrimony consisted of a wealth of musical riches acquired over time, since music notation has existed for a long time, whereas no such system of notation has been created for the image. Thus, radio broadcasting finds itself caught in the crossfire, as we might say. Radio needs to be admirably faithful to the music that it is in charge of transmitting and yet, at the same time, it has to be thoroughly original in the practice of its own means of expression, just like the cinema. But radio is about to ruin everything because such contradictory demands cause extreme confusion.

In fact, the only way out is to see clearly, to look the contradiction in the face, and to take either of the two separating paths that are opening up: one leads to the blossoming of a specifically radiophonic art that would be to sound what the cinema is to the image; the other path is more humble but nonetheless has the noble mission of transmitting traditional music as best it can to listeners across the world, its overall goal being not an ideal of perfection impossible to attain, but to render sounds as faithfully as possible.

Of these two paths, the latter is probably the most arduous: it demands the greatest sacrifices on the part of musicians and the most delicate precautions on the part of technicians. The limits of radio broadcasting will not recede, no matter how often the *Ninth Symphony* is broadcast.[5] The more the musical work is dense and loaded with meaning, the more its radio transmission runs the risk of coming across as flat and insufficient.

Compared to the cinema, the art of photography is, in the same way, the poor parent who cannot invent but can only reproduce. Yet by using its own limits, too, through its approach to the work that it transmits, photography tries to make a choice. It is an art that enables some elements to be enhanced. It can sacrifice a detail to the whole, or the whole to a detail; when necessary, it is not averse to using montage to enhance the object represented.

– Will you try, then, to interpret Beethoven's oeuvre in your own way?

– If I don't, the machines will, and they will not wait for me to do it. As a matter of fact, this is not about interpretation, but about knowing what is essential.

– But everything is essential!

---

[5] Beethoven's *Symphony No. 9*.

The conversation goes like this because no one is looking the problem in the face, owing to an overly scrupulous respect for form. Will we have to leave the venerable piece of music, the piece that has to be broadcast no matter what, to the laws of chance, the laws of broadcasting? Will these laws suddenly be suspended?

It is as though the photographer, saddened at the prospect of reproducing in two dimensions the ancient sculpture that he can see with both his eyes, in full volume, with the delicate detail brought by lighting, was looking away while handling the shutter, so as to avoid playing a role in the awful act of desecration committed by his camera!

From this we can see why radio broadcasting, which delivers to the listener a sound image that is entirely different from the image the ear would produce directly, should be analysed closely; it is so that we can find out exactly what it is capable of, and hence what we can demand of it.

Before tackling other problems, it is necessary for musicians and technicians to start 'thinking' radio broadcasting together, without burying their heads in the sand or pursuing the policy of ignorance that has all too often been theirs. After that, and only then, will we be able to discuss broadcasting in its quotidian details.

Some well-intentioned musicians have already tried to analyse the radiophonic necessities that the composer and the performer have to consider, based on what can be heard from behind a control loud-speaker.

Their intention, which remains entirely valid, has nonetheless caused alarm among technicians. By chance, and chance is always mischievous, many such attempts relied on equipment of disastrously poor quality.

How can these musicians continue to submit themselves to the strictest constraints in order to accommodate technical necessities when, to create the kind of work that ought to come with all possible guarantees, they are not even given the best equipment, the best microphones, the most perfect loud-speakers, irreproachable amplifiers?

Moreover, when the musician begins to undertake such work, he must be followed very closely by the technician, for the technique is constantly evolving, and what seems impossible today may be possible tomorrow. It would be appalling to see useless and often bizarre constraints imposed upon artists when the technique can make these constraints disappear very quickly. Only remarkably well-trained technicians can, in this domain, guide the artists and tell them, now that a mass of technical possibilities have opened up, which constraints will remain fixed for a given period of time – for a few years, a decade perhaps – and which constraints may evolve and change quickly. With radio broadcasting, it is impossible to conduct such an evaluation at present.

However, if such a conversation is to become possible, some preliminary work needs to be undertaken.

Up to now, the vocabulary used by the technicians and the musicians has not been the same. If they do not teach one another, if they do not look for equivalences, they run the risk of remaining trapped in perpetual misunderstanding.

It is the search for this shared vocabulary that matters once the groundwork begins, the work that we would like to see being undertaken in radio broadcasting.

This defined vocabulary could become the 'Rules of Art,' determined by both the musicians and the technicians as they help and assist one another.

The only aim of this short preamble is to open such a debate and to recall that there is an aesthetic problem specific to radio broadcasting that is not yet resolved, and one which we should not neglect while we argue over how fundamental it is!

1.8 ENZO FERRIERI: RADIO AS CREATIVE FORCE

Translated by Nicoletta Asciuto. First published as 'La radio come forza creativa,' *Il Convegno* 12, no. 6 (June 1931): 297–320.

Enzo Ferrieri (1890–1969) was a Milanese journalist, writer, theatre director, literary critic, editor, translator and prominent figure in Italian broadcasting. This essay-manifesto arose from his many radio activities. From 1929 to 1931, he was artistic director of the EIAR (Ente Italiano Audizioni Radiofoniche, Italian Institute for Radio Broadcasting), the Italian national broadcasting organisation under Benito Mussolini. Thereafter, he became artistic consultant for the Società Italiana per la Pubblicità Radiofonica Anonima (SIPRA, Italian Society for Anonymous Radiophonic Advertising, created in 1926). Later in the 1930s, he went on to become a radio producer and director of radio programming at the EIAR and, after the Second World War, he worked in the television industry, for the RAI, the EIAR's successor. Ferrieri's tenure as the EIAR's artistic director ended in March 1931 or shortly after, before the publication of 'La radio come forza creativa' in *Il Convegno*, the literary magazine he edited. This essay is widely recognised as Italy's first radio manifesto. It is one of several texts in which Ferrieri developed a distinction between radio as a medium able to educate, and bring music and literature within the reach of the general public, and as a creative force in its own right. The essay's various parts were originally articles published in the Milan newspaper *L'Ambrosiano*, for which Ferrieri acted as drama critic; the articles ignited debate, and Ferrieri decided to republish them together.[1] Although Ferrieri's broadcasting and journalistic career required him to work with, and for, the Fascist regime, he tried to keep *Il Convegno* at a distance from its cultural programme, and used his magazine during the 1930s as a vehicle for interrogating and countering Fascism – after 1936, notably, via subversive and coded visual symbols.[2] *Il Convegno* struggled to sustain itself during the 1930s and stopped appearing in January 1939.

For Senator Ettore Conti
For Professor G. Giacomo Ponti[3]

RADIO MANIFESTO

Whether its programmes be artistic or cultural, up to now the radio has been employed all over the world solely as a means of popularising ideas.

All over the world, radio is mostly used to disseminate news, just as printed newspapers do, to *transmit*[4] dramatic and lyrical works, as if in a theatre, and to let people hear music, as if in a concert hall. That most of what we might

[1] See Emilio Pozzi, ed., 'Dubbi e certezze di un pioniere,' in *La radio! la radio? la radio!* (Milan: Greco and Greco, 2002), 11–28; Angela Ida De Benedictis, *Radiodramma e arte radiofonica: Storia e funzioni della musica per radio in Italia* (Turin: EDT-De Sono, 2004), 4–5; Antonio Lucio Giannone, 'Radio e letteratura: Momenti di un (contrastato) rapporto,' *Quaderno di COMMUNICazione* 2 (2001): 100–9; Rodolfo Sacchettini, *La radiofonica arte invisibile. Il radiodramma italiano prima della televisione* (Pisa: Teatrino dei Fondi, Titivillus Mostre, 2011), 28–37; Rodolfo Sacchettini, *Scrittori alla radio: Interventi, riviste e radiodrammi per un'arte invisibile* (Florence: Firenze University Press, 2018), 10–11.

[2] Eric Bulson, 'Milan, the "Rivista," and the Deprovincialization of Italy: *Le Papyrus* (1894–6); *Poesia* (1905–9); *Il Convegno* (1920–40); *Pan* (1933–5); and *Corrente di vita giovanile* (1938–40),' in *The Oxford Critical and Cultural History of Modernist Magazines, vol. 3: Europe 1880–1940, Part 1*, eds. Peter Brooker, Sascha Bru, Andrew Thacker and Christian Weikop (Oxford: Oxford University Press, 2013), 519–27.

[3] Ettore Conti (1871–1972) and Gian Giacomo Ponti (1878–1939) were moguls in the Italian telephone and electricity industries. Conti was made Vice-President of the EIAR's Board of Directors in 1929 and was among the figures from whom Ferrieri solicited a response to this essay as part of the 'Radio Investigation' subsequently published in *Il Convegno*, partially translated thereafter. Ponti was one of the EIAR's foremost patrons and shareholders.

[4] In the original Italian text, Ferrieri frequently puts the terms he wants to emphasise between inverted commas and frequently uses italics, too, (sometimes, he does both). Some of these inverted commas have been kept; other words which appeared between inverted commas have been put in italics. Words italicised in the original remain italicised here.

call these disseminations of ideas and culture are produced in special auditoria, rather than in theatres or concert halls, is for technical reasons; never, or hardly ever, because we want to embrace new forms of radio-creativity. To be honest, the ambition of any auditorium director is always to compete with a theatre.

Beyond the odd, timid experiment, no country has begun to test the creative potential of radio for new journalistic or artistic forms, or to encourage new social habits (apart from that intrinsic to the medium of radio itself, of enabling reception at the furthest reaches of the transmitter, and hence in one's own home).

Radio will be able to assert itself as an original creative force in these terms:

1. As a fresh newspaper, not in contrast to but, rather, complementing the press and creating new forms of journalistic expression, in particular, a new *correspondent*: the special radio-reporter.[5]
2. By developing literary, theatrical and musical works suited to this new medium.
3. By integrating the future theatres, future concert halls and major artistic events in its own auditoria, where they will be transformed into broadcasts *transmittable from each city*, and by deciding what to offer to their spectators and what to broadcast to its public of listeners.

We have only just begun to broach the side streets of each of these big avenues, without any clear outcome in sight.

I summarise here the main considerations as we renew our methods for selecting broadcasts for the radio, with the intention of discussing them one after the other.

1. Radio must broadcast the most beautiful and most radiogenic voices.
2. The style best adapted to radio is quick, alive, ceaseless and economical, urgent, lyrical, typically Italian.[6]

---

[5] The debates about the relationship between radio, the news and the printed press predate the advent of public broadcasting and reverberated across the radio press. One of the first newspapers dedicated to radio was New York's *Radio News* (initially *Radio Amateur News*, which began circulating in 1919). Italy had a counterpart, called *Radio-Giornale: Rivista Mensile per Dilettanti di Radio*, based in Milan, while the French magazine *La Parole Libre TSF* was originally subtitled *Supplément du Journal Parlé* (supplement to the spoken newspaper). A 'newspaper without paper' was how Lenin first described radio: 'The matter is *of immense importance* (a newspaper without paper and without wires [. . .], all Russia will be able to hear a newspaper read in Moscow),' he wrote in 1921 to the construction chief of the first Soviet radio-telephone station in Moscow. V. I. Lenin, *Collected Works*, vol. 35, trans. Andrew Rothstein, ed. Robert Daglish (Moscow: Progress, 1973), 473.

[6] Ferrieri's ideas have many affinities with Futurist perspectives on radio; for the 'Radio Investigation' that appeared in *Il Convegno* in the wake of this essay, he solicited responses

3. Radio is the newspaper for immediate and dazzling news and instant description, presented by a reporter far, far away, who tells us about the arrival of a cruise, a football match, a meeting of important people, the great events happening in the world as they unfold, in the comfort of our own homes.

4. The only speakers allowed on radio should be either *special correspondents*, scattered across the capitals of the world, or authentic *maestros*. Radio should also be able to entertain. Because conversations are entertaining, theirs must be based on the new, the varied, the original, the unexpected.[7]

5. Only radiophonic plays conceived for radio and affirming its creative force shall be broadcast on the radio; alternatively, works of proven value, brilliantly executed by first-class artists, should be broadcast in order to affirm radio's power to popularise ideas and culture. All these will be broadcast from special auditoria, run by competent artistic and technical directors.

6. Music on the radio must be either composed especially for wireless transmission or selected according to the exigencies of radio broadcasting.

7. The radio shall only broadcast brand-new operettas or musical comedies, wherein a rapid, elegant, entertaining, spirited text, written in Italian and inspired by the modern world, will be matched by a musical accompaniment conveniently relying on the expedients most appropriate for radiogenic music.

8. Everything that continues to be transmitted from opera houses, concert halls and cultural institutions shall represent radio's miraculous contribution to the dissemination of authentically great works, authentically great artists from all countries, and authentic culture.

9. Radio is the first ambassador of any country; and, in the universal concert of voices, and with music now intersecting into space, the nation's radio also represents an assertion of one's own race. Italy will thus be the messenger of *bel canto*, of melodious women announcers, of the most daring correspondents, of musical maestros and lyric singers.

from the Futurists Anton Giulio Bragaglia and F. T. Marinetti, and from figures who had looser personal and artistic associations with Marinetti and Futurism like Massimo Bontempelli, Paolo Buzzi, Alfredo Casella, Alberto Casella, Gian Francesco Malipiero, Virgilio Mortari, Umberto Notari and Alceo Toni.

[7] Ferrieri's own broadcasting experience began in 1928, with evening programmes on the EIAR's Milan station entitled 'Nord e Sud,' which took on the form of conversations and travelogues around Italy and were tied to his work as literary and drama critic. This conversational model was also favoured by Arnaldo Mussolini (the EIAR's Vice-President), notably in the series he created on the Milan station in 1930, 'Condottieri e Maestri.'

Voice on the Radio

On the radio the voice is everything that is neither music nor 'noise'.

Announcers, readers, actors, lecturers reach us through space, through their voice.

With what nostalgia, then, shall we think of Helen's voice? Helen of Troy, for whom heroes would have lost their lives? When every evening, from every radio station in Europe, we tolerate the voices of not only relentless lecturers but also announcers, correspondents, that is to say the *technicians* of this new form of expression, who lack the least basis of authority?

The most important function of a broadcasting organisation, or at least the most delicate one, should be that of the researcher investigating voices. It should be exclusively devoted to selecting, from amongst the innumerable different voices available, the rare voice timbre that can immediately transform an announcement, a reading, a speech, into an auditory pleasure.

The voice coming out of the wireless set must represent the beauty, variety and suggestive force of the human voice.

All contributions that need not be improvised must be realised using radiogenic voices, and these voices cannot be found or trained other than with appropriate means and capable teachers.

The role of voice research and a school for voice and announcer training may seem like laughable matters; they are, on the contrary, extremely serious matters, and their roles are laughable only to the would-be experts who think it is enough to hurl a microphone at a random actor.[8]

Such institutions will soon represent the education and civilisation of their country, by way of these voices propelled into space and through their training and education.

There is no doubt that radio is our first ambassador abroad. Amongst the numerous letters sent by radio listeners, I remember a distinctive one from an Englishman. He was enthusiastic about Italy and our radio programmes, and especially the Teatro alla Scala broadcasts, but complained about the interruptions and handclapping re-transmitted in England during these musical performances, deeming it, rightly or wrongly, a sign of a poorly educated public.

The school for voice training must not offer a complex cultural education to its few students. It must select the most able students, stipulating specific entry requirements and unassailable testimonials. It must merely teach them the techniques of radio diction.

What happens with all other types of training will happen in this school for the voice. If the student is clever (in this case we might even call him an artist),

---

[8] A Centro di Preparazione Radiofonica (Centre for Training in Broadcasting) was created in 1936 in Rome to train radio technicians and performers.

he will quickly become a teacher himself; if not, it will never be possible to teach him the art of 'colouring' the news, the profound enigma of a pause, the delicate sense of opportunity, etc. And yet, this kind of training deserves a try.

A voice's different tones and expressions shall be especially useful in indicating which topics will be discussed. Every item of radio news over the air waves will be preceded by a spoken headline that is as explicit and engrossing as possible. A marked voice and a special pause to indicate the topic's title, just like a collocation of different fonts in a newspaper or a book, will highlight a heading or special item of news to the reader.

There is no doubt that the voice, thanks to its variety and modulations, has a richer range of tools than the fonts, margins, spacing and size of a page.

Just like a book printed in clear, harmonious, airy letters, radio diction shall be extremely neat, and yet always extremely natural, still, secure, with neat contours and astute breaks, sustained by the rhythm of a speaker aware that he is holding the attention of hundreds and thousands of listeners clinging onto this naked wire stretched in space.

Different modes of expression are suitable for the different kinds of radio-phonic materials to be announced or presented.

The tone of the *news reader* is different from the tone of the *advertiser* in wireless publicity. We do not need to be able to picture the features of the *news reader*. An utterly anonymous voice, it must bestow tranquillity and certainty upon the listener, who should not be disturbed with variations or with superfluous interventions. The news reader must be grave, but not professorial, capable, nonchalant and gentlemanly, and should speak like any good conversationalist, without descending into excessive familiarity with his own audience.

His different tones correspond to the various typographical fonts more precisely than anything else.

By contrast, the *advertiser* must have a voice able to create the richest variations, the most brilliant shades, and even the funniest ones; he is a more unprejudiced and ironic reader than the news reader, even though his purpose is to 'launch' a good-quality, trustworthy product onto the market. In the same way, the most effective publicity today is all somewhat casual and ironic, from the advertisement with bright electric liqueur glasses falling down the roofs of houses, to the advertisement projecting a name onto the glaringly white suit of the advertiser.

The financial journalist is a machine: complete assurance, precision, slowness. His listener is no layabout; he has invested money in such things, and this is always a very important matter.

The tone of the *sports announcer* is something else altogether. Everything must be precise, but also extremely quick, sharp, without too many comments or breaks, insistent, thrilling, lyrical at the right moments. Filling in pauses between results with nice, familiar topics, with colourful brush strokes, with bits of gossip, is puerile and against the principles of radio broadcasting.

Gossip and anecdotes have always been anti-radiophonic and only have value if they can be immediately comprehended as general symbols.

Little separates the announcer from the *sports correspondent*. The sports correspondent, sent across the world to report the events of the day, must be, first and foremost, an artist, like all other newspaper correspondents. He can then comment in the radiophonic style, give a more colourful rendering of the events, crack a joke, greet a cloud passing over the football pitch.[9]

But I shall say a lot more on the radio correspondent, the cornerstone of the radio of the future, later on.

Lastly, apart from being used in journalistic services and by correspondents, the voice will play a major role in radio's auditory economy, as we shall see, thanks to its distinct individuality.

WHAT MUST BE SAID

What must be said on the radio must be contemporary, immediate, previously unreleased, unforeseeable.

Soon the moment shall come when we give up on anecdotal lectures, encyclopaedia entries and generic digressions; at long last, we shall give up on all the *bric à brac* that everywhere, and all too often, makes up the paradoxical content of spoken programmes.

Some of the spoken content will be drafted in auditoria, according to the anonymous advice of expert readers.

The liveliest part of radiophonic conversation will have to be entrusted to the group of special correspondents, reporting directly, every evening, from their various cities in alternation.[10] Otherwise, only men of a certain reputation and authority must be at the microphone. No one would ever dream of welcoming reporters with little experience into big newspapers with millions of readers. This, however, is not enough. Using radio instead of a printed newspaper or a conference hall, for instance, can only be justified if what one has to say, apart from being of interest to the largest number of listeners, should gain value *by being said*. When does this occur? Either when the speaker has such capacities of expression that his words become a real pleasure for the listener, or when he speaks of topics requiring persuasion and moral authority in a way

---

[9] Two wireless and sports commentators from the early days of radio, H. B. T. Wakelam (BBC) and Edmond Dehorter (Radiola, known as le Parleur Inconnu, the Unknown Speaker), both said to have invented the live sports commentary, were widely praised for their capacity to do this.

[10] The EIAR's network in 1931 consisted of radio stations based in the larger Italian cities (Rome, Milan, Naples, Palermo, Bolzano, Genoa, Turin, Trieste) which were grouped together; the stations were called Roma-Napoli, Milano-Torino-Genova, Bolzano, Palermo, and Trieste.

that can seduce the wider mass of the listening public. In essence, when the speaker is a real force attracting other forces. Otherwise conversation would become a mere pastime, and it would be too costly, one would be tempted to say, for a medium such as radio – a medium which, in any case, must have all the essential features to amuse, attract and keep the public spellbound with its invisible spectacle.

We must not forget that the listening public, precisely because listeners are not distracted by any visual element, tends to be interested in what can create surprise and what has dramatic potential, even at the auditory level.

Unsurprisingly, two famous clowns have been delighting American listeners.[11] The clownesque style, with its suddenness, insolence, violence and grotesque tricks, is typically radiophonic. A listener constantly expects something new at every moment – a strange contrast or a *trouvaille* to break the monotony of the transmission.

Very rarely can a speaker alone hold the listener's attention for long on the radio. Dialogues are always the most appropriate form, and interviews, which are a specific form of dialogue, should also be used frequently.

A curious example of radiophonic dialogue is that which occurs between a speaker and other characters who are neither speaking nor visible (they do not exist); the speaker imagines that he is having a conversation with such characters. This is a canny way of precisely simulating the appeal of a dramatic scenario.

RADIOPHONIC STYLE

There is a requirement common to all materials transmitted on the radio, which accounts for the strength, range and temporal limitation of the medium: a strictly synthetic method should be adopted when creating, choosing and presenting all material – everything should be reduced to the essential.

For practical reasons, radio talks in all countries typically last ten minutes, and never sixty minutes; their rationale is, however, perfectly similar to that which governs the ordinary sixty-minute conference speech. It is not just that such radio broadcasts last ten minutes; the talk must abide by new rules; it must limit itself to what is significant, without any digressions, as in the architecture of a novella in comparison with that of a novel.

The first thing that springs to mind is certainly the analogy between new radiophonic modes of expression and the Futurist movement.

And not just in terms of their literary content, but also in terms of their critical and informative methods.

It is all about finding new spiritual syntheses through which reality can be expressed with maximum conciseness, but which also draw energy from

---

[11] It is unclear who these clowns may have been.

the element that typically dominates radio: silence (paradoxical though this may sound).

Silence is the limitless backdrop to all the voices coming to us through the radio – voices conjuring up images, landscapes, events, real and imaginary conflicts. These matters can be thrown into relief by the interjection of a pause, momentarily depriving our imagination of any props and then plunging it into a fearful abyss, from which only language can rescue it.

When we listen to some radio-plays, this sudden suspension (rigorously measured, because nothing is more dangerous than an injudiciously long pause) generates a shiver of anticipation and terror; we anxiously wait for some scenes to be over, as we do when we simply wait for some news to be gradually released to us.

When dealing with upsetting matters, the faraway correspondent, as well as the radio dramatist, will have to be reminded that radiophonic broadcasts will always gravitate in the speediest fashion in the direction of the imagination – towards the indeterminate, or rather the boundless – just as music otherwise does, the art that, based as it is on sound, is closest to the radiophonic medium.

Radio's mode of expression is also music itself, with the interpreter's voice as musical instrument; it makes use of words, silences and sounds chosen for their substance, their capacity to quickly become relatively open symbols, readily welcomed by millions of listeners.[12]

THEATRE ON THE RADIO

Those who think radio-plays are tedious are wrong.[13]

If traditional theatrical works have hitherto kept people interested and alert, then the new radio-plays, yet to be created, will excite them even more.[14]

Their character is difficult to predict.[15]

---

[12] In his 'Radio Investigation,' Ferrieri reasserted that comprehension is not based on words alone, and that there is more to the radiogenic voice than words. He related how he had tried to listen to a Russian radio station and heard the voice of a woman whose words he could not understand, which had such a tragic intensity that it became a symbol, a 'tragic mask.' 'Inchiesta sulla Radio,' *Il Convegno* 12, no. 7–8 (August 1931): 429.

[13] Ferrieri may have had in mind the radio magazine *L'Antenna*, which occasionally published satirical drawings deriding the EIAR and its aspirations. One of them presents a couple listening to Radio Torino-Milano at home, eagerly waiting for a comedy; they promptly fall asleep from sheer boredom (5 June 1930, 1).

[14] This is a disingenuous claim given how fast radio plays circulated across Europe, as original broadcasts or in translation. Radio drama began to be discussed as a specific artistic form in the Italian press in 1925, and *Radiorario*'s first radio drama writing competition (a popular exercise elsewhere, too) was organised in 1926.

[15] Ferrieri's ideas about *mise-en-scène* resonate with articles on radio and theatre he had previously written for *Radiocorriere*, the EIAR's weekly radio magazine, in June 1930.

I have already offered some observations about this above.

Drama, above all, will best express, in synthetic radiophonic style, a certain facet of reality, because the traditional techniques of comedy or tragedy are founded on synthesis rather than analysis, on the dynamic rather than the static, and are favourable to broadcasting.

Everything depends on the creation of this new economy.

Once radio-dramatists find a way to express in voice and sounds the spiritual dimension of situations which today are portrayed on the stage, through words, gestures, miming, movements and costumes, thousands of listeners will tune in with the same eagerness they feel nowadays when they follow words spoken on the stage.

A far too simplistic interpretation is that radio comedies should be based as far as possible on sounds, noises, whistles, hisses, moans, and so on and so forth. All this is a cardboard *mise-en-scène* for the ear, akin to a tawdry backdrop.

Successful radio-plays have been those based on the elements I have discussed under the rubric 'radiophonic style': involving silence as a source of sublime and fearful suggestion; the *boundlessness* of the backdrop. Here, it suffices to recall certain scenes from a shipwreck, where such elements effectively give the piece the highest evocative intensity.[16]

But what should permeate the transmission of a radio-play is the *individuality* of the different voices. Since it is vital that the invisible personages should not be confused with one another and should be recognisable from afar – often from abroad – these different voices will soon be so characteristic that they will actually come to represent specific states of mind and particular characters. Their various characteristics and techniques will be handed down by tradition. If critical expectations were not the worst omen for the development of a new art form, one might venture that we shall perhaps hear again, in a different way, something similar to the voice-masks of new actors in a hyper-modern *commedia dell'arte*, the voices of the Harlequins, Brighellas and Rosauras of the new mechanical comedy.[17]

To this should be added the enchanting power of improvised lines over the radio, improvised on the spot in front of the microphone. Attempts of this kind have already been made in other radio stations abroad.

The authentic energy of the new radio-plays will most certainly come from the individuality of the voices, their coming together and intertwining, their

---

[16] The shipwreck was central to the type of catastrophe play favoured by European listeners during the 1920s and 1930s. Ferrieri may have had in mind Cusy and Germinet's play *Marémoto* or Friedrich Wolf's *SOS . . . rao rao . . . Foyn – „Krassin" rettet „Italia"*, a play about the crash of Umberto Nobile's airship.

[17] The stock characters of the *commedia dell'arte*, often figured as puppets or impersonated by masked actors.

choruses, their pauses. Let us add in the effects specific to and typical of the radiophonic medium which should be deployed here, including the possibility of letting one voice suddenly dominate over all others, in a sort of improvised vocal close-up, similar to the cinematic close-up. Another very suggestive effect is the tone created by transmitting barely discernible voices, whispers, murmurs, dialogues in a low voice over the radio.

Naturally, radio comedy shall not be limited to the dramatic and *grand-guignolesque* style;[18] it can just as well be comical, upbeat and grotesque (styles that have proven especially popular in Germany).

If you turn the loud-speakers on one evening and let unbounded laughter suddenly take over the silence in the room, without even knowing where it is coming from, or certain simulated voices, certain gaps, followed by relentless dialogues, which you can barely recognise as fragments of a grotesque piece, probably transmitted by one German radio station or another, you will soon get an idea of how attractive such comedies can be.

They have already transcended the local and national character, the local and national interest, because their auditory principles offer certain attractions, even for listeners who do not understand the language.

That said, we should not be led to believe that radiophonic comedies are something exceptional, exquisite pieces of work somehow only reserved for few initiates. On the contrary, radio comedy, considering its extraordinary number of listeners, must appeal to the mass public.

An important observation that can be made at this point is that radio theatre's specific features (much more so than those of talks and news reports, etc.) arise from the specific condition that this theatre is, to an extent, a theatre for the blind.[19]

Ultimately, the arrival of television – not to be overlooked as the creative force of today and tomorrow – should mark the terminus of the typical radiophonic style. I do not believe this. Sound combined with visual transmission should, as in the case of sound and silent films, bring about a revolution in the sort of programmes transmitted, in so far as they would tend towards the kind

---

[18] French term to qualify a category of the horrific which is so exaggerated that it loses all verisimilitude. Ferrieri is referring to the Guignol show (the Punch and Judy show), which became popular in France in the early nineteenth century and involved travelling puppet shows and special puppet theatres such as the Théâtre de Guignol in Lyon and the Théâtre du Grand-Guignol, Paris. The central character, Polichinelle (Punch), was inspired from the Italian *commedia dell'arte*.

[19] Ferrieri may have in mind Tristan Bernard's essay from 1930, 'Pour des aveugles invisibles' (see 5.8), as well as other texts from the French radio press that developed the same argument: Italian radio magazines often featured summaries of articles published in France, sometimes reproducing parts of the French original. Bernard was often evoked in the Italian radio press, in *Radiocorriere* and *L'Antenna* in particular.

of realistic representation we hope shall remain the domain of documentaries or journalism.

But as soon as you wish to achieve an original effect – that is, make an attempt at a creative work – there is no doubt that optical transmission and auditory transmission will blend in unexpected ways, find their mutual gaps, help each other by mutual collaboration: occasions when the silence alone, voice alone and vision alone of a certain detail or a specific combination will become indispensable to giving the broadcast programme the completeness of a harmonious creative work.

The theatre of the future shall be built upon these foundations, in all phases of broadcasting. On the one hand, radio and television will be able to spread ideas by broadcasting plays and comedies just as they are performed in theatres today (if such art forms carry on existing), or realistic, photographic transmissions, mostly concerned with technique.

On the other hand, new works created in great new theatres – of which the modest auditoria of Italy and the more sophisticated auditoria of Germany and especially England are the first shoots – will provide families at home with their habitual evening entertainment.

We shall now turn our attention to the contrasts specific to radiophonic theatre.

The creative contribution that individual actors can make was mentioned earlier, as well as their contribution to radio-plays, which still remains to be imagined. This element of originality and spontaneity is not without its contradictions, however, and will need to be accompanied by another specific element: the necessity for absolute surveillance from the *régisseur* or the director.[20]

The time has now come for the youngest artists from the theatre to start acquainting themselves with these issues, and to prepare themselves for the radiophonic *mise-en-scène*. If doubt remains about the necessity for an all-encompassing and authoritative director in today's prose theatre; if some of our critics carry on believing more in the individual actor's ingenious creation and in actors' spontaneous harmony than in the contribution a *régisseur* makes to regulating their work, and if, taking into account the development of voice-masks and their direct impact on the play, we acknowledge the individual actor's vital and creative force, then it is clear that radio-plays will always require a specialist director, someone who can bring some discipline to the effects produced by the overall picture.

To gauge the importance of the radio *régisseur*, it suffices to think of the situation of radio actors with their tone *already modulated*, who cannot hear how their own voices sound, who do not know in what form their voices shall

---

[20] *Régisseur*, the French term that Ferrieri uses for radio producer, was also used in German (*Rundfunkregisseur*) and Dutch (*radioregisseur*).

reach the listener, who do not have, and perhaps will never have, an interaction with the audience, who ignore the exact contribution that sounds, noises and music bring to the work's total value (something which will become infinitely complicated in the television's *mise-en-scène*).

RADIO AS A NEWSPAPER

It took a few years for the idea of the radio as a newspaper to sink into the general public's consciousness – and not just theirs.

When you say *Giornale-radio*,[21] some people still immediately think of the journalistic organs of the various broadcasting organisations (i.e. *Radiocorriere, Rundfunk, Radio-Zeitung, Radio Magazine, Le Haut-Parleur, Radio Programme*, and so on)[22] or at best of that specific group of news bulletins broadcast by various radio stations at specific times under the name of 'Giornale Parlato'.[23]

This is not the only thing that makes the radio a newspaper: it is also the typically violent, totalitarian character of the radiophonic medium's speed and power of dissemination, given its ability to offer a picture of the greatest events around the world, and given its ability to report on events as they unfold – whether a competition, a concert, a meeting or a trial – from the furthest reaches of the world, *every day* or, rather, *every minute*.

---

[21] Ferrieri's ideas for the *Giornale-Radio* both reflected familiar realities and expressed hope for a new approach, as some of the respondents to his 'Radio Investigation' noted. Raffaele Calzini remarked that the news bulletin had been a reality in Soviet radio since 1925, while Carlo Linati pointed out that Ferrieri's model for a broadcast news bulletin replicated the ways in which the most technically advanced radio stations in Europe broadcast news. Indeed, some of Ferrieri's ideas anticipate procedures later employed by large broadcasting organisations such as the BBC; see, for example, 'How the News is Chosen,' *BBC Year Book 1933* (London: British Broadcasting Corporation, 1933), 177–80.

[22] The titles given by Ferrieri are approximations. By *Radio-Zeitung*, Ferrieri may have meant *Bayerische Radio-Zeitung*, and *Radio Programme* probably designates the French radio magazine *TSF Programme*. In this list, only *Radiocorriere* – the EIAR's magazine – was the journalistic organ of a broadcasting organisation. *Der Deutsche Rundfunk* was the first radio magazine in Weimar Germany; *Le Haut-Parleur* was a French radio magazine that mostly focused on electronics; *Radio Magazine* was the title of early French and American radio magazines.

[23] Literally, 'the spoken newspaper,' the phrase widely used to designate radio news across Europe. The EIAR had a Servizio Radio Giornale, a news service, by 1929. A new *Radio-Giornale* was created in 1929 at the Milan station, with a team of dedicated radio journalists, and the model was subsequently extended to other stations, taking on the name *Giornale-Radio*. Italy's first official tourism board, the Enit (Ente Nazionale per le Industrie Turistiche), also ran its own *Radio-Giornale* from 1929, providing information about travel and tourism to listeners in Italy and abroad.

Too many people used to believe and still believe it in their interest to oppose the radio as a newspaper. Even the printed newspapers believed for a time that the radio was their rival. This is not the case, except occasionally, and unavoidably, for irremediable reasons. But the great service radio will render the printed newspapers is to help them return to their traditional role of generating ideas, of gymnastics for the intelligence and for culture, of guiding the so-called public opinion on all fronts.

By contrast, radio is, or rather shall be, the great, the unique newspaper of immediate and shocking news, of description in real time, presented by the correspondent from afar, witnessing an event on the other side of Europe and discussing it in your own home.

Thanks to its core function, as an organ for the dissemination of news, the broadcast news bulletin presents news items in different ways (news and reports in situ,[24] radio-documentaries on events, including artistic events, and even those taking place far away, commentaries, etc.) and in the end makes up almost the totality of the wireless programming.

Only certain exceptional talks, radio comedies or music broadcasts from concert halls, and such radio-culture more generally as is not strictly tied to the current events of the day, can be considered to be beyond the remit of the broadcast news bulletin, constituting radio's literary, musical, cultural section instead.

For the rest, radio differs from the printed newspapers in how its services are organised, while retaining, owing to its origin in journalism, a certain kinship with them.

The whole of wireless programming, including shows broadcast from this or that concert hall or theatre, must be chosen according to criteria determined by current affairs and ultimately according to the widest possible conception of the new radiophonic journalism.

The proper *Giornale-radio* will have an editor-in-chief, as well as subeditors and reporters, just like a printed newspaper, but, even more than for the printed newspapers, all its functions will be ruled by the idea of speed because of the very fact that such rapidity is the true and original strength of the new medium.

Even though this new medium makes use of the same systems of information as the printed newspapers (such as capturing news through the radio and thus breaking free of telephone communications), it will always have the advantage of immediate transmission, and of bridging the gaps in the printed newspapers' circulation and reporting.

[24] The term used by Ferrieri, *informazione-cronaca*, was the term used in *Radiocorriere* for local and regional news (*informazioni-cronaca locale e regionale*).

In the future, rapidity will dominate every section of the radio-news, which will no longer arrange its architecture over the course of twenty-four hours, but rather over the course of every hour.

The foreign radio correspondent is not at leisure to collect his material for a set time, in order to align it with the best times for his newspaper to receive his telephone call; rather, he now knows that he has many more hours to contact his newsroom faraway, liberated from any typographic regime, and free to send his news out as a matter of absolute priority over any other means of dissemination.

On the other hand, the editor receiving the report is of the impression that the radiophonic style should sprout and grow directly on the page, because the more time it takes him to give the news a transmissible form, the more time is lost on broadcasting the actual piece of news; the little microphone, silent and implacable, awaiting the news reader's voice, is only a stone's throw away, much readier to release the news to the world than the talkative – and henceforth homely – linotype machine.

Which news should be broadcast over the radio?

First of all, the criteria employed when selecting news items differ greatly in the general economy of the 'programme of the day,' which corresponds to one or more – or indeed several – newspaper editions: likewise, many radio stations are connected to one editor-in-chief.

The editorial line taken is that only news of general interest will be chosen and will dominate the radio, due to the number of listeners living beyond the radio station's geographical location.

The number of marriages or births in a given city, listings of evening entertainments, a minor burglary or tram accident, cannot be of interest on the radio. Such reports are still broadcast in the news bulletins of every country, because they have yet to strike the right collective note when building their wireless programmes.

Generally, the local news bulletins hold no interest for the radio, because on the radio a local report necessarily loses its nature as news, turning instead into a kind of place description, i.e. a new *artistic composition* entirely dependent on the quality of the narrator, or into a radiophonic event aired for the interest of its live noises, sounds, speech and shouting.

News – from other cities or other countries – reaches us in exactly the same way as with the printed newspapers. This should suffice to convince us that radio has a major advantage when it comes to the news, since it can be broadcast earlier than it is printed, depending on its importance.

The new style of radiophonic news is born of the speed necessary in collecting and communicating news as well as the equally urgent need to express it as concisely as possible – after all, the minutes in a day cannot be multiplied like the pages of a daily paper.

This style is altogether different from that of the printed newspaper.

Just as the newspaper editor is handy and skilled in his craft – in so far as he can conjure up and 'make' a journalistic article from very few hints or telephone calls (often a piece succeeds to the extent that it fits the column inches of the paper), so with the radio editor: he is all the more handy and skilled in *his* new craft insofar as he can synthesise to the maximum and substantially compress his materials.

The editor of the radio-news must *not* try to take the newspaper editor as his model.

News over the radio must be delivered in all its clear, direct, metallic nudity: 'Facts, not words' is radio's motto, where every instant is precious and any commentary weakens the power of the news.

Precise nouns, exact definitions, suggestive and picturesque in their synthesis and capable of lightning-bolt expansion. Images immediately comprehensible by everyone – like common symbols.

In this sense, radio-news is a training in journalistic honesty, since only spotless credentials can entitle one to broadcast a piece of news.

Anything else is colour, clever commentary or criticism: all excellent things, but best left to the press.

As we saw in the case of local news bulletins, if at all possible, radio-news shall avoid giving news as information, in favour of delivering the *voice* of its special correspondent, or the distant event brought to the airwaves.

This is where we really enter new territory.

While it may be interesting, let's say, for a Milanese to follow from his own home a football match at the Arena or the latest automobile racing results from the Monza racetrack, it is of course more 'typical' to listen to the exact same football match but from Budapest or Vienna, or the exact same race but from the San Sebastián Circuit, or even from Indianapolis.[25]

At this juncture, radio-news comes into its own, at the same time as creating a new spectacle, new men, new social habits. In any case, what comes into play at this point is an artistic element, already a crucial part of the transmissions created by reporters, but expressed in new ways, full of possibilities.

All such transmissions of events over the radio are prepared, described or commentated on by a special correspondent. Often, however, the event does not lend itself to a radiophonic *mise en bande*, and instead comes to us directly through the correspondent's words. But when this is not possible, the documentary quality will quickly give way to the artistic, and the special correspondent will be forced to choose which noises, which sounds, which

---

[25] The Autodromo Nazionale di Monza is a racetrack near Milan. The San Sebastián Circuit hosted the annual Spanish Grand Prix car race; the Indianapolis Motor Speedway, the oldest racing track in the world, hosted the annual United States Grand Prix.

rounds of applause, which cries will be most likely to evoke the whole spectacle for us.

This is another way in which journalism becomes an art and perhaps one of the forms of radio drama; it is a new form, and one which shall no doubt adopt eminently popular features in order to establish its aim.

Even when the special correspondent has no event to broadcast – either to present or to comment upon –, he can still express himself radiophonically from the city he is in, about matters of general interest he has *witnessed*. The line-up of lecturers we hear every night from various European microphones must for the most part give way to a much more relevant, modern, timely and interesting group of talking heads, developers of *wireless lectures*.

Almost everything that is reported on the radio should be live, or should have been seen very recently, and then it should be introduced and reanimated in an original manner. An agile network of radiophonic correspondents will be scattered across the different cities interchangeably.

A new type of artist will thus be born – one created by the radio – with a rapid radiophonic vision and intuition, the right voice, a daring desire for travel and escapism, a totally contemporary spirit. Just like his own colleagues in the press, he shall select the big news, the event attracting the crowds; he will identify its key elements, and in just a few minutes will send them out into the ether again, in his own voice.

MUSIC ON THE RADIO

When we speak of music on the radio, we need to clearly distinguish what we do now from what we shall perhaps do in the near future. It may be that technological progress will render what we are about to say redundant, so that even the currently pressing necessity of creating music for the radio will be considered obsolete, perhaps with very few people caring about it in the future.

These days, the music transmitted on the radio, all over the world, is selected according to the shared repertoire of theatres, concert halls and small orchestras. The radio's work is thus, while very important, purely to popularise culture and ideas.

Within these limits, the radio must guarantee that what it transmits is rigorously scrutinised. Therefore, *given the current conditions* – since we have made no attempt yet to convince composers to write works for the radio, and since there are very few examples of radiogenic music – it is far preferable (at least ninety per cent of the time) that we should broadcast directly from theatres or concert halls, for all their shortcomings. These institutions are generally better equipped for transmission, whereas auditoria have always broadcast *the exact same music*, but with relatively more modest resources.

I already know what the dissenters on this issue are saying, but I am an enemy of half measures. Until a new repertoire of radio music comes into existence; until each and every country is able to solve the difficulties inherent in deciding which compositions can or cannot be broadcast (not by any means easy decisions); and finally, until the broadcasting conditions are perfect, it is better to be honest popularisers, allowing for deformations and imperfections, resorting to auditoria only in the face of timetable constraints and lack of other possibilities.

I find rather naïve the idea that we should be broadcasting on the radio forgotten or never-yet performed works, or works by the youngest playwrights. An eminently popular medium is not where we should attempt revivals or new experimental broadcasts, for these can only, at best, be exceptional performances for connoisseurs. In fact, as an educational medium, the radio should, rather, offer only the really 'authentic' to its hundreds of thousands of listeners.[26]

Besides, the absence of technological tricks (for the latter are not always achievable in the theatres and concert halls) is largely compensated by a sense of solidarity with thousands of spectators, which removes from the transmission itself that cold and artificial feeling, unavoidable when broadcasting from a room without an audience.

This might seem a merely formal argument. On the contrary, it is a fundamental matter for the radio.

Unlike the gramophone, radio is not a pleasure confined to the solitary, even though solitary people often make use of it. The moment either music or dramatic works issue forth in front of the microphone and are diffused everywhere by the loud-speakers, they call for sustained collective solidarity.

But soon the moment will come when radio will find its own independent path, at least for the most characteristic side of its musical activity, and will rigorously select music that best responds to the exigencies of broadcasting, by excluding the pieces considered non-transmissible, and by inspiring new pieces for the radio. New schools for radiophonic composition are already being established abroad. Paul Hindemith is training many novices at the Berlin Conservatory, for example.[27]

---

[26] Ferrieri is not thinking of didacticism in a revolutionary or Brechtian sense, whereby the ultimate purpose is to spur a realisation that the world must be changed for the better. He has a diffuse conception of how radio can disseminate ideas and educate, and a non-specific conception of the kind of ideas that it should disseminate.

[27] The composer Paul Hindemith (1895–1963) was renowned for his interest in mechanical music and for compositions featuring mechanical instruments. Berlin's Hochschule für Musik, where he taught composition for radio and film, had facilities and teaching dedicated to radio from 1928 onwards, and taught microphone performance technique as well as music composition for radio. Hindemith resigned in 1936, when his works, labelled as 'degenerate,' were prohibited.

It is even possible that as radio's social and economic strength increases, some new and great transformations will truly solve these difficulties – with more than modest palliatives – by way of broadcasts disseminating ideas from theatres and concert halls. By that time, technology too will have progressed far enough to ensure satisfactory transmissions with the least possible distortion.

It may not be a complete fantasy to think that in every country radio will enhance shows, concerts, etc. and that a great radiophonic organisation will arise, allowing radio stations to have venues for theatres and concerts alongside more experimental auditoria or studios for radiophonic music. The public will be admitted into these rooms, just as in today's public halls, but with ideal conditions for broadcasting.

This represents, then, a new conception of radio as a dominant force in all forms of musical organisation; this may come about for a number of artistic, economic and social reasons, and would also give the educational radio the most favourable conditions for disseminating our musical heritage.

The distinction between radio as creative force and radio as popularising force has a certain currency at present, since the right music for wireless broadcasting has specific features and exigencies. Obviously, some discretion should be exercised when considering these differences, but they should nevertheless be taken into account by composers.

The topic 'music for the radio' has rarely been debated in Italy. I remember one excellent article by Maestro Della Corte, some references by Giovannetti and, lastly, two articles by Maestro Gatti.[28]

In other countries, essays, talks and studies have already been devoted to this topic, and these are bound to produce many surprises. In bringing these to the attention of scholars and composers, it suffices to briefly mention what is already well known, i.e. that sounds undergo significant modifications in wireless transmission, that such modifications vary among the different families of instruments, and that the more complex and less differentiated the orchestral melodies are, the less the likelihood of a faithful reproduction.

To fulfil the exigencies of contemporary radiophony, music needs to be conceived with a very reduced number of musical instruments, with clearly distinct timbres, and with sharply resounding phrases.

It is worth considering that many typical features of radiophonic music coincide with specific characteristics and leading tendencies in modern music. As has happened abroad, and especially in Germany, this ought to attract to the medium of radio those composers who are most representative of the contemporary spirit.

---

[28] Sessions were dedicated to discussing radiophonic music at the first Congresso Internazionale di Musica (International Music Congress) in Florence in 1933.

From *Panorama* by Coeuroy, who has discussed this topic pertinently and knowledgeably, I have extracted a kind of *decalogue for the composer*, clear and persuasive as it is:[29]

1. Any orchestral piece whose melodies are not sufficiently differentiated from one another will sound different over the microphone;
2. Excessively rapid chords will become a 'chewing gum' for the ears. Composers who wish to write radiophonic music will thus be forced to adopt a new kind of score;
3. String instruments are well rendered by the microphone in the high and central notes, while low notes come across atrociously;
4. Woodwind instruments are admirably clear, but the piccolo drowns out all other instruments, especially in the high notes; we must accept this and leave it aside;
5. Horns, already the terror of orchestra conductors, sound catastrophically bad. Cruel microphone, you exaggerate every bug: because of you we can even hear the horn player salivating!
6. The trumpet, on the other hand, is benign. It bravely attacks any position, even when it is gagged by a muffler;
7. The harp retains all its graces, though more in the high notes than in the low;
8. The percussion is Pandora's box; the bass drum spoils everything; the snare is barely recognisable; the cymbals seem to ignore that reverberation that makes them so seductive over the phonograph;
9. The kettledrums are wonderful: short snaps? Excellent. Rolling? A complete disaster!
10. The xylophone is the king of the microphone.

From these brief and informative considerations, we can see that, up to now, except on rare occasions, radio critics and our composers have neglected these matters. Without offering arbitrary prophecies on the radiogenic music of the future, of which we already have some examples, we recommend greater prudence when transmitting music, more music, and still more music all over the world, at any time of day and night. A good idea, advanced by others in the context of theatrical repertoires, would be to compile a sort of list of works and compositions irreparably damaged by radio broadcasting, and which should be banned from being transmitted on the radio until technology finally resolves most of these difficulties.

[29] From André Coeuroy, *Panorama de la radio* (Paris: Editions Kra, 1930), 180–81. Coeuroy, a French musicologist, had a deep interest in the relation between music and radio. *Panorama de la radio*, one of the first histories of radio art, focuses on radio plays and radio music in France, Germany and Britain.

In the not-so-near future, radio, as the medium that can overcome the furthest distances, a medium which has precise technical exigencies and (perhaps!) can inspire new musical forms, shall attract the theatres and integrate them into its own auditoria. New types of building, new forms of spectacle shall arise from the new auditorium-theatre, and shall mark, in the history of entertainment, a new era, with new social habits.

1.9 FROM RADIO INVESTIGATION

After publishing his essay-manifesto 'La radio come forza creativa' (1.8), Enzo Ferrieri invited figures involved in journalism, literature, theatre and the arts across Italy to respond to his views, and published their comments as a separate 'Radio Investigation' in *Il Convegno* (the investigation of a radio-related question involving writers and artists was a popular exercise during the 1920s and 1930s, just like writing contests for new radio plays and short stories for radio). The contributions Ferrieri collated included replies he had solicited and newspaper articles commenting on his ideas. *Il Convegno*, which Ferrieri had founded in 1920, was an ideal platform for this exercise: it was an established literary magazine with a strong contemporary, international and modernist focus, around which he had long pursued other activities, including creating a bookshop, a publishing house, a lecture hall and a theatre during the 1920s. Many among Ferrieri's respondents discussed his project for a new kind of *Giornale-Radio*, which sought to define the future of news on the radio in light of extant practices in Italy and innovations elsewhere. Prior to the publication of 'La radio come forza creativa,' discussions of radiogenic modes of expression in the Italian radio press had been largely derivative, summarising articles from foreign radio magazines, mostly French and German. This tendency to look abroad for validation is manifest in the responses Ferrieri collected, which refer to Gabriel Germinet and Pierre Cusy, Tristan Bernard, André Coeuroy, Jean Cocteau and Max Reinhardt. The four commentaries selected here, however, envisage Ferrieri's suggestions on their own terms.

F. T. Marinetti: A Futurist Radio

Translated by Nicoletta Asciuto. First published as 'Inchiesta sulla Radio,' *Il Convegno* 12, no. 7–8 (August 1931): 416.

Filippo Tommaso Marinetti (1876–1944) was an Italian writer, editor and theorist, and the founder of Italian Futurism. He started to record discs in 1914 and first spoke on

Italian radio in April 1925, shortly after readings from his poems were first broadcast; the programme included a lecture on Futurist poetry and *parole in libertà* or words-in-freedom, and a performance of his poem 'Il bombardamento di Adrianopoli' ('The bombardment of Adrianople,' 1912). The following year, he spoke on Brazilian and Argentine radio. Thereafter, he featured regularly in Italian radio programmes until 1939. He gave talks, read or recited Futurist texts, and acted as live commentator on at least one occasion, for Italo Balbo's second transatlantic flight from the US to Italy in 1933. He wrote several *sintesi radiofoniche* or radiophonic syntheses, including pieces that toy with silence. His ideas on radio are developed in a more radical form in his 1933 manifesto, 'La Radia,' co-authored with Pino Masnata, which announced the birth of a Futurist radio predicated on words-in-freedom as its primary mode of expression.[1]

• • •

Radio has nothing in common with literary or artistic tradition. Any attempt to reconnect radio to tradition will therefore be useless and absurd. Like sound cinema, radio contains all the infinite Futurist possibilities of literary and artistic creation. Radiophonic plays must be aggressively Futurist plays – synthetic, quick, simultaneous, sudden, with no self-analysis, longueur, or psychoanalysis. Those quick, simultaneous, synthetic plays created by the Futurists, demanding throughout the speed of the revolving stage. Radio plays eschew traditional style. Words-in-freedom are their native language. Indeed, words-in-freedom, the offspring of the machine aesthetic, contain a whole orchestra of noises and noise chords (whether realistic or abstract) that, alone, can help the coloured and plastic word as it sketches out, fast as lightning, what cannot be seen.[2]

---

[1] See Lawrence Rainey, 'F. T. Marinetti and the Development of Futurism,' in *Futurism: An Anthology*, eds. Lawrence Rainey, Christine Poggi and Laura Wittman (New Haven: Yale University Press, 2009), 1–39; Margaret Fisher, 'Futurism and Radio,' in *Futurism and the Technological Imagination*, ed. Günter Berghaus (Amsterdam: Rodopi, 2009), 229–62; Jeffrey T. Schnapp, 'Radio Syntheses,' *Modernism/modernity* 16, no. 2 (2009): 415; Katia Pizzi, *Italian Futurism and the Machine* (Manchester: Manchester University Press, 2019), 75–8.

[2] The idea that radio is the ideal vehicle for Futurist words-in-freedom is reasserted in 'La Radia,' in a passage that echoes the present commentary: 'The words-in-freedom daughters of the machine aesthetic contain an orchestra of noises and noise harmonies (realistic and abstract) that can only help the shaped and colored word in the lightning-fast representation of what is not seen. If the radiast doesn't want to use words-in-freedom then he should express himself in the free-wordist style (derived from our words-in-freedom) which already circulates in avant-garde novels and newspapers that free-wordist style typically swift bursting synthetic simultaneous [. . .]'. F. T. Marinetti and Pino Masnata, 'The Radia: Futurist Manifesto,' trans. Lawrence Rainey, *Futurism: An Anthology*, 294.

If the radio dramatist does not wish to resort to words-in-freedom, he must at least express himself in that free-wordist style (derived from our words-in-freedom) already present in many novels by avant-garde writers: the typically quick, nimble, hyper-synthetic, simultaneous free-wordist style.

OTTORINO RESPIGHI: RADIO AND ART

Translated by Nicoletta Asciuto. First published as 'Inchiesta sulla Radio,' *Il Convegno* 12, no. 7–8 (August 1931): 422.

Ottorino Respighi (1879–1936) was a prominent Italian composer. He remained distant from Futurism: in the early 1930s he became part of an anti-modernist movement in Italian music, and signed a manifesto which protested against music consisting of '[a]tonal and multi-tonal trumpets blaring,' which 'does not wish to have and does not have any human content'.[3]

• • •

I have been meaning to say that thanks to special electrical waves, some inventor may recently have succeeded in producing a set of timbres able to then develop sounds with a completely new colour.[4] If this is true, I can well imagine that these new possibilities may inspire original musical pieces. Yet I do not think that the radio, a simple and still imperfect transmitter of sounds, with limited possibilities, should restrict my creativity – moreover, radio is too young an invention, still in development and capable of who knows what amazing improvements. And I trust radio – a marvellous tool for propaganda and culture – to act before Art as Mohammed did before the mountain.

EUGENIO COLORNI: RADIO'S ARTISTIC POSSIBILITIES

Translated by Nicoletta Asciuto. First published as 'Inchiesta sulla Radio,' *Il Convegno* 12, no. 7–8 (August 1931): 395–8.

Eugenio Colorni (1909–1944) was an Italian Jewish philosopher, political activist, socialist and staunch anti-fascist. He spent time in Berlin prior to 1933, and this essay is misdated 'Berlin, November 1931' in *Il Convegno*, although the issue appeared in August 1931. History hit Colorni at full force: arrested in 1938 for anti-fascist activities,

---

[3] See 'Manifesto of Italian Musicians for the Tradition of Nineteenth-Century Romantic Art,' December 1932, cited in Günter Berghaus, *Futurism and Politics: Between Anarchist Rebellion and Fascist Reaction, 1909–1944* (Providence, RI: Berghahn, 1996), 271.

[4] Respighi probably had in mind the *intonarumori* invented by Luigi Russolo, whose experiments were greeted with derision, fascination and uproar in Italy; see Günter Berghaus, *Italian Futurist Theatre, 1909–1944* (Oxford: Clarendon Press, 1998), 128–33.

he was imprisoned and confined on the island of Ventotene, where he contributed to the writing of the Ventotene Manifesto, which called for a socialist, federal Europe. He escaped in 1943 and was shot by a Nazi group, the Banda Koch, on the streets of Rome a few days before the city was liberated by the Allied forces.[5]

● ● ●

It is very difficult for me, as someone whose knowledge of radio is limited to Enzo Ferrieri's latest essay, to judge the value and feasibility of the suggestions and concrete proposals included within it. I shall say, however, as a true outsider,[6] that his essay seemed to me a typical representation of a widespread contemporary phenomenon, and, let me add, a universal one: it is art's attack against those new forms of technology that are making our society richer, little by little.

Such is art, with its unfailing tendency to stretch its arms towards everything, and take possession of everything initially created with a different purpose. At a certain moment in the development of an invention and in the progress of its influence on the way we live our lives, we see art's emotional disinterestedness usurping, or attaching itself, to the initial economic – or popularising, or educational – utility of the invention. Let us thrust our usual Vico aside: this has been, and continues to be, the course of events for both the press and architecture, for both the cinematograph and the radio.

Now, without a doubt, this is not just possible, but desirable: certainly, any new technological discovery can be of service to art as a means of expression. But it is interesting to observe how this takes place, and to what extent.

For this reason, it is dangerous to classify as art any consistent or totally effective advancement created by the new technologies. Nowadays it is a far too common whim to think that what technology produces is artistic if its products are faithful to their true nature, and if they achieve their goal in a manner that is immediate, that befits their contemporary purpose, through the tools that they employ. A car we call beautiful, i.e. a perfect, coherent, agile entity, with every part designed to fulfil its own purpose, gives pleasure when it is looked at, gratification when it is driven, and perhaps even evokes a deep emotion for the sensitive-minded who are well-versed in technology. But that does not mean that this pleasure, or gratification, or emotion, should be regarded as artistic in itself.

In these realms of life, as in all others, it is right to plead for the perfect adjustment and connection of means to ends: once this has been achieved, you

---

[5] See Piero Garofalo, Elizabeth Leake and Dana Renga, *Internal Exile in Fascist Italy: History and Representations of* Confino (Manchester: Manchester University Press, 2019), 195–6; Giuseppe Tramarollo, 'Eugenio Colorni, combattente della libertà europea,' *Rassegna Mensile di Israel* 40, no. 6 (1974): 230–4.

[6] *Outsider* appears in English in the original and between inverted commas.

will always have reached some degree of perfection. Such perfection may well be artistic, economic, technical, pedagogical, educational, or whatever you prefer. But the joy that art brings shall never be replaced by the joy you may feel from contemplating the harmony and cohesion of forces in action.

The same applies to radio: Ferrieri was absolutely right to define its force as creative rather than artistic. Radio is always creative, if we take the complete meaning of the word as intended by Ferrieri, because it is always capable of creating original, independent, autonomous values (of whatever kind they may be). Radio is only artistic when it *is* artistic: I mean when its line of action is directed towards that specific edge of emotion, creation, contemplation called – and it is not up to us to define it now – *art*.

What we have learned from Ferrieri's essay is this: the radio, whatever its ultimate purpose, is a form of expression demanding direct and linear methods; the radio has no real meaning except when it talks about things that can only be discussed, or only primarily discussed, through radio. Now, we cannot decide a priori whether this form of expression is artistic or not, whether it delivers information or education or propaganda rather than simply adhering to artistic tasks. All these functions are possible: when this work is accomplished with originality and propriety, you can, if you want, say it is beautiful. But 'beautiful' will come to mean 'perfect, consistent, autonomous'.

Ferrieri's essay tells us one more thing. If the radio is a new form of expression, on top of the ones we already know, and if it offers a new possibility for artistic action, its own artistic performances (insofar as they can only be performed through radio) will be able to present something new, bringing to light a new side of art and of spirituality more generally. In a way, radio will shape human sensibility, nurturing those emotions it is best capable of expressing.

Naturalism? Materialism? Not at all. I do not deny that art is a matter for the spirit, arising from the spirit. I only mean that to give man a new sense is to enable him to take his spirituality into his own hands and open a new portal into a sensibility hitherto ignored.

In a way, radio is now a new sense, an addition to all the other senses man the artist had at his disposal before. Without going as far as to say that each sense corresponds to a different kind of art, we cannot deny that the concrete and material form of each mode of expression has some relevance when searching for and describing the peculiar tone of an artistic emotion. Do we not talk about pictorial or musical tones, interior or exterior tones, and so on (meaning something not theoretically different, but more or less generically recognisable in the topography of the various artistic intuitions)? We can speak, then, of a 'radiophonic' style, which will mean, approximately, the specific artistic tone most appropriate for the radio as an expressive medium.

What this style might be, Ferrieri has begun to outline, mentioning speed, suddenness, surprise and, on the other hand, a tendency towards indeterminacy, and hinting at analogies with some Futurist tones, the role of silence, and so on. Very likely, it will be possible to be even more specific still, once radio, in its concrete development, displays more clearly its possibilities for artistic expression.

LUCIO D'AMBRA LIFE: POETRY, RADIO

Translated by Nicoletta Asciuto. First published as 'Inchiesta sulla Radio,' *Il Convegno* 12, no. 7–8 (August 1931): 398–400.

Lucio D'Ambra (pseudonym of Renato Eduardo Manganella, 1880–1939) was an Italian novelist, comedy writer, screenwriter, journalist and theatre and cinema critic, renowned during the 1930s for his comedies and remembered for novels celebrating Italian Fascism. His plays began to be broadcast in 1927 and he started to contribute regular broadcasts on literature and culture to the EIAR's Rome station in 1929. He wrote regularly for *Radiocorriere*, the EIAR's magazine, and his name and works featured frequently in Italian radio programmes throughout the 1930s.[7]

●　●　●

In the marvellous and incredibly dense pages he has dedicated to the radio, so rich with facts and ideas, Enzo Ferrieri, like all apostles, is able to look beyond the horizon; perhaps even into those distances which can only be reached by venturing, by ever more ambitious leaps and bounds, into the unreal and the impossible. Nevertheless, he sketches out extremely well the features of this new technology of communication between human beings, which is also, once the initial feelings of fear and wonder are overcome, turning out to be a new way of disseminating art and poetry. God bless Enzo Ferrieri for his propaganda; his aim is to let into Italian houses as much of our national art and intelligence as possible![8] In Italy, too many houses never let a book cross their threshold and the only art form they are prepared to accommodate within their walls is the fox-trot. Left out of the door, art comes back in through the windows and walls. For such a miracle we shall thank the radio and the EIAR.

---

[7] See Enrico Tiozzo, 'Dissidente in felucca: Lucio D'Ambra,' *Belfagor* 61, no. 3 (2006): 245–55; Philip V. Cannistraro, 'The Radio in Fascist Italy,' *Journal of European Studies* 2 (1972): 127–54; Francesco Casetti, Silvio Alovisio and Luca Mazzei, 'Lucio d'Ambra,' in *Early Film Theories in Italy 1896–1922: The Little Magic Machine* (Amsterdam: Amsterdam University Press, 2017), 462–63.

[8] Margaret Fisher observes that Ferrieri used his own essays on radio to give a 'rational and more thoughtful' form to the fervid articles published in *Radiocorriere* by Arnaldo Mussolini, Benito Mussolini's brother, appointed as the EIAR's Vice-President in 1927. See Fisher, 'Futurism and Radio,' *Futurism and the Technological Imagination*, 233.

But if the aim is really to enter all Italian houses, and stay there, we need to know exactly what is wanted. We should not forget that, if radio speaks in every place, and anywhere, with a turn of the dial, it is also extremely easy to reduce it to silence. Thus, to entrust radio with the explorations and ambitions of a new art, with its efforts and experiments, is at present to ask too much of it. The crowd appreciates finished products and does not care for attempts or sketches. Best then to consider radio not as the tool for a new art, but as a new medium broadcasting art from across the ages, so long as that art is clear, genial, solid, understandable by everyone. Cinema and radio – the sight and hearing of the masses – will intuitively reject, by definition, enigmas, exceptions, singularities. And radio's influence – whether in music or theatre – will naturally benefit the restoration of eternal art to forgotten and ancient beauties. More and more, the musical art transmitted through the radio will need harmony and melody and, more and more (since noises and sounds are merely background events and details), radiophonic drama will have to restore to its full worth the kind of dense and full dialogue that is perfectly self-contained, without needing gestures or captions: that stage dialogue which was always the classical dialogue of theatrical masterpieces, from Shakespeare to Musset, from Molière to Goldoni . . .

At the invitation of the EIAR and its dynamic and supportive Directorate General, I am currently writing two cheerful radio comedies which are all about action, movement, scenic progress and evolving situations, but their dialogues are completely different from the dialogues of visible and traditional theatre.[9] One of the biggest mistakes one can make when writing radio comedies is to watch theatre plays. Instead, you should only watch – and listen to – life . . .

Life *and* poetry: yes, because poetry and music will find expression in the great silence of radio. Maestro Giuseppe Mulè and I will attempt to compose a 'radiophonic poem,' where imagination and harmony will compete to let dreams of fantastic and infinite things through the closed doors of our domestic lives . . .[10]

---

[9] Ferrieri's 'Radio Investigation' spurred the EIAR to invite a group of writers to contribute new broadcasts, but the results were mediocre; see Sacchettini, *Scrittori alla radio*, 10–11. D'Ambra may be referring to his radio plays *Il bridge delle signore mature* and *Ritratto di fanciullo*, broadcast by the Roma-Napoli station in June and December 1932.

[10] Giuseppe Mulè (1885–1951), Italian composer and conductor who oversaw the broadcasting of literature as member of EIAR's Superior Committee of Vigilance, created in 1928 to monitor radio's adherence to the Fascist cultural programme. Mulè conceived a large number of broadcasts for the EIAR in 1932. There is no trace of this particular radiophonic poem, but a number of works bearing the title 'radiophonic poem' were broadcast during the 1930s – notably, Carlos Larronde's *Le douzième coup de minuit*, broadcast by Paris-PTT in 1933, musical *radiopoemetti* (short radio poems) by Angelo Nizza and Riccardo Morbelli, broadcast on all EIAR stations in 1936, and Théo Fleischman's *Archibald le danseur de corde*, broadcast by Radio-Paris that same year.

PART 2
BEHIND THE MICROPHONE

2.1 ANON.: ON EMOTION AND LIFE BEFORE THE MICROPHONE

Translated by Emilie Morin. First published as 'De l'émotion et de la vie devant le micro,' *Annuaire de la Radiodiffusion Nationale, année 1933* (Paris: Ministère des PTT; Service de la Radiodiffusion, 1933), 235–7.

The anonymous author of this piece worked for the French state-owned radio network, probably for the station Paris-PTT. The *Annuaire de la Radiodiffusion Nationale* was an official handbook which aimed to provide a yearly overview of achievements in French broadcasting. It only appeared twice, in 1933 and 1934. It was similar in scope and spirit to the handbooks published by national broadcasting systems elsewhere: the BBC published annual handbooks from 1928 onwards, the EIAR published an *Annuario* from 1929, albeit less regularly, and the Reichsrundfunkgesellschaft published a *Rundfunk-Jahrbuch* from 1929 to 1933.

● ● ●

[. . .] The microphone is a rather strange little instrument. Standing before its nickel ear, singing sweet nothings, screaming dramatic lines with vehemence, or whispering tender secrets: all this will always be intimidating when we think of the tens of thousands of ears – be they troubled or cheerful, critical or quietly ironic, appreciative or deceitful – that are listening to everything that is uttered by the singer's or the speaker's mouth.

In a public hall, the artist incarnates the emotions he feels, in front of people he can see, with their attentive faces stretched out before him, their eyes fixed on the expression of his face. When he holds the room, as we say, he feels it . . . And he can feel, instantly, the spectators' reactions to his performance, lines or singing. Of course, if the reactions are favourable, they help him a great deal. The applause that greets his performance gives him faith in his qualities, in his worth. To him, applause is the most powerful form of encouragement, and it supports and enables his success.

With the microphone, none of this applies. For the innumerable listeners whose sensory perception is reduced to hearing alone, there is nothing to animate the performance. Before the little metallic disc, the artist feels alone: he sings, plays in front of a blind listener whose eyes remain stubbornly closed, a paralytic whose face and limbs remain immutably still . . . If singing is involved, then the pianist will be playing at a distance of five yards behind him, against all custom; he will have to make do without the reassuring closeness of his musician. If he is performing in a comedy, he has to pay attention not only to his text but also to the volume of his voice, which means that he has to change position at every instant and modify his delivery at the most dramatic moments in order to remain comprehensible at all times.

Why, then, should we be surprised that many artists – even the greatest – should suffer terribly from nerves when they face the microphone, although they never suffer from stage fright when they are performing in public? You can rest assured that this is not in any way an exaggeration. [. . .] We could give the names of many artists who are cherished by their public each time they appear on a theatre stage and yet, once they found themselves waiting for their turn at the microphone in the corridor outside the studio, were shaking with emotion. Recently, a well-known singer arrived full of self-confidence – a confidence begotten by his craft – in the waiting room of a radio station, an hour before a concert; after asking for all sorts of information about what it feels like to speak at the microphone, after a trial run, after taking off his tie and detachable collar . . . he walked out, five minutes before his performance, and he apologised, saying that he was not in good voice. It was the atmosphere, purely and simply, that had led to this; nervousness drove him away. And we also know artists who now refuse to leave the stage to sing on the radio . . .

Other artists are not so easily intimidated and become accustomed to radio broadcasting fairly quickly, once they have worked through their initial instincts and emotions. These artists are the most interesting to watch when they are performing. Inside the studio, there is generally a box that is especially well situated – a box behind bars, we might say, from which one can watch the broadcasting 'patients' without being seen. From the amplifying room adjacent to the studio, where the operator is, one can watch the artist performing at the microphone from one or two metres away, unbeknownst to him. No gesture goes unnoticed and, because we are dealing with someone who is no longer intimidated by the microphone, personality comes to the fore naturally. And this is very instructive sometimes! When we watch a celebrated artist, well-known to us, sing a comic opera in the studio, and when we see how he makes his company sing it, we also see how much will-power is involved in the art of extracting as much as possible out of a voice, no matter whether it is beautiful, good, middling or weak. This manager we know gesticulates to pull the notes out of the singers' chests – if they do not appear to come from further away! This is a spectacle in itself, consisting of silent calls and gesticulations, of threatening yet inoffensive punches into the air, of jaws open far and wide, coming to the rescue, albeit silently, of notes sung . . . by others; it is a vertical ascent, we might say, above the ground, with both arms lifted towards the ceiling, whenever a comrade must give a perilous A: before us stands a man perspiring like a horse, drowning in sweat, red, unrestrained, throwing himself fully into the effort . . . And when his own turn comes, he handles himself like a stage artist singing to a spell-bound hall and gives you a sample of his beautiful voice, his face animated by a great ardour, his body outstretched . . .

Here is another fact: before the microphone, artists do not know how to prevent themselves from adopting the attitude dictated by their text, and they do so unwittingly. Actors capable of moving listeners to tears know all about this: their own faces also become bathed in tears, for real. We often hear about one artist who, one evening, became stranded, as we say, in the middle of a performance of *Le rosaire*[1] after letting his tears flow out freely; eventually, he became unable to see his text and had to stop in order to wipe his eyes . . .

To conclude, performing at the microphone, once one's nervousness has been overcome, is like the prolongation of a stage performance. It is behind this motionless little device, no doubt, that we find the best actors – those who can envisage the innumerable listeners absorbed in their performance and let themselves respond to what their imagined public feels.

2.2 PAUL DERMÉE: MICROPHONE RUDIMENTS FOR RADIO ACTORS

Translated by Emilie Morin. First published as 'L'ABC des comédiens parlant devant le micro,' *Comœdia*, 15–16 July 1932, 5.

A biographical sketch is included with 'Will We Have a Radiophonic Art?' (1.5).

• • •

Many famous actors greet with some impatience the advice dispensed by the microphone's obscure servants.

---

[1] This could have been a broadcast of André Bisson's adaptation of Florence Barclay's novel *The Rosary*, previously staged numerous times at the Odéon Theatre in Paris.

How could a nobody who is not even a professor at the Conservatoire be presumptuous enough to teach illustrious members of the Comédie-Française the secrets of their art?

Thankfully, my subject here is not the art of acting on the stage, but how to adapt the art of acting for the microphone, that singularly demanding and tyrannical instrument.

When we speak into its ear, the microphone is an extremely sensitive instrument. But as soon as we move away from it, its sensitivity diminishes much more quickly than that of a human ear. Moreover, it captures little beyond the sounds that hit it directly, at full force. This is why one should avoid veering to the right or left of the microphone's cone of capture, which is rather narrow.

The impact of these unique conditions upon acting are immediately noticeable: even over the course of the most violent and animated play, the actor must stay still, and the radio producer, who is listening in the next room, must control the sounds created by the slightest movement.

It is through the movement of the voice alone that one must convey the movement of the performance. Performance tricks are no use, since the listeners cannot see and, moreover, such tricks can be dangerous. To borrow the phrase aptly coined by Mr Roger Dathys, one of our best radio artists, 'microphone theatre is verbal pantomime.'[1]

Should the actor try to gesticulate at the microphone, try to act in costume? These are controversial questions because they can only have individual solutions. Above all, verbal acting must remain animated and colourful. If gesture and a costume can help, use them.

Microphone beginners must also ponder this very simple notion: the position of the microphone is not by the footlights, but on the listener's armchair. Thus the microphone ought to be thought of as the average spectator who needs to be able to hear. In some American studios this fact has been made obvious and visible, by dissimulating the microphone in a sculpted wax head that looks as authentic as the statues of the Musée Grévin. It is to the microphone that one must speak or sing, to the Lord Microphone who wants to bring comedy into his abode.

No need to project one's voice as one would do at the opera or on the stage of the Odéon Theatre. Just sing and perform as you would do in a drawing room.

But the drawing room is dark, and your listeners cannot see you . . . We know how difficult it is to follow what an orator is saying when we cannot even see a silhouette! For this reason one should spare the wireless listener any fatigue by enunciating as perfectly as possible, and bringing nuances to one's speech as skilfully as possible.

---

[1] Roger Dathys (Emile-Paul Meunier, fl. 1910s–1950s), theatre and radio actor and radio producer.

Now is the time to talk about silences at the microphone. In the manner of Théodore de Banville,[2] we could say: 'Silences at the microphone? There are none and there cannot be any.' Nonetheless, silence must be used to add rhythm to one's delivery, to emphasise the periods, the commas and the ellipses above all. Limit yourselves to making silences, pauses and necessary moments of suspension half as long as you would make them in a theatre. Never forget that radio listening transforms a crotchet into a minim and a minim into a semibreve.

On the other hand – and this may seem contradictory – it is important not to increase the speed of the voice, not to cut corners with the microphone. Indeed, the wireless listeners must be able to hear every single word, and every word you utter should reach their ears with the maximum level of intelligibility and according to a distinctive rhythm, so that the listener has time to recognise and understand all the words, one after the other. This is also true of disc records: we have all been irritated when we found ourselves unable to follow a comic monologue delivered at breakneck speed.

Although I am offering here the mere rudiments of a very complex art that is still far from being fully formed, I must insist on the importance of remaining natural at the microphone. One should avoid pretending that one is in a theatre, and one should avoid like the plague certain mannerisms, certain tricks, which are horribly magnified and seem outrageously uncouth over the radio.

To conclude, in order to become a good radio artist, it is important to know the microphone and submit oneself to its exigencies, which is relatively easy, and be an excellent actor, which, frankly, is far from everyone's reach.

2.3 FRANCE DARGET: HOW TO ACT IN FRONT OF THE MICROPHONE

Translated by Emilie Morin. First published as 'Comment jouez-vous devant le micro?,' *Comœdia*, 21 September 1934, 3.

France Darget (1886–1965) was a French writer. She published her first volume of poetry at the age of fifteen, to great acclaim, and developed an interest in acting and

---

[2] Théodore de Banville (1823–1891), French poet and leader of the Parnassian movement.

performance at a young age. In the 1920s, she turned to theatre, wrote plays in verse and started exploring performance techniques. From 1932, with her theatre company Le Coryphée, she developed techniques for performing verse drama in different contexts: in Parisian theatres, on the radio and in open-air performances. In 1935, she started to produce and adapt plays and other works for radio. She believed that verse theatre provided the way forward for radio drama and discussed its value for radio in many settings, including at the 1937 International Congress of Radiophonic Art in Paris. 'Comment jouez-vous devant le micro?' (How do you act in front of the microphone?) was one of *Comœdia*'s special investigations into the world of radio broadcasting, for which Paul Dermée approached theatre and film actors and radio producers. Earlier in 1934, Darget had initiated a similar survey for *Comœdia*, but on verse theatre and radio.

● ● ●

I, a novice at the microphone (although I have followed its creations since the first hour of its life), have had the pleasure of contributing to the establishment of a new form of verse theatre for radio, towards the realisation of which I have been working for years through open-air readings, through my *Inédits* and through public talks.[1]

I shall write only about this particular art form here.

Verse theatre (dramatic theatre, heroic theatre, or even classical theatre) needs a new lease of life, more than any other art form. What has kept the public away from verse theatre for some time is, I believe, the fixed formula to which it has been confined by the actors' conventional delivery, by inexplicable prejudices – such as the idea that acting in a tragedy requires standing upright! – by the uniformity of the stage sets and the mediocrity of the *mise-en-scène*; in short, all the mutilations from which poetry has irremediably suffered.

This is why, above all and out of a concern for what is in the listener's interest, I have been trying to reconstruct behind the microphone the total atmosphere of the work *on a stage*. Finding the perfect equilibrium between stage performance and radio transmission is difficult; yet it can be achieved, and it requires trial and error.

Together with the members of my Coryphée who have joined me, armed with all our good faith and good will, I chose to subordinate the visual elements of the work to its purely auditory dimension, but I remain persuaded that the possibilities of stage performance can enrich the work's auditory elements by adding other sound perspectives, a sense of the differences between planes, a synchrony between acting, memory and diction, and an invisible yet no less real communion with the public.

[1] The *Inédits* was a monthly event organised by France Darget and Mrs Lemoyne-Darget at the Cercle d'Iéna in Paris between 1932 and 1934, which featured performances of unpublished dramatic and musical works.

It remains the case that working in an auditorium is easier: there, our work benefits from the experience and knowledge amassed over time, and from equipment especially conceived to facilitate radio broadcasting.

The ideal auditorium should feature a stage as well as an audience. If this proves impossible, let us look for a stage that could become an auditorium.[2]

And, on this stage, let us discard all the false conceptions that had threatened to extinguish verse theatre, to which radio seems to have brought salutary changes.

Listening to radio, we are told, cannot accommodate what is known as emphasis. Must we take away from verse theatre its music, its rhythm or even its *style* – a style that will never become familiar or indeed vulgar, since verse theatre grapples with the great themes of humanity? Not in my opinion. Indeed, what the listener often perceives as emphasis, and what causes his boredom, is the monotony of the vocal range used by most of our actors – including the greatest! – as soon as they turn to verse.

Hence, I have been trying to preserve the infinite suppleness of prose within verse and to create variation within rhyme; indeed, rhyme is all too often the speaker's stumbling block!

Furthermore, listening places paramount importance upon the choice of vocal timbres. In my work for the stage I have always looked for voices that have the capacity to create conflict while maintaining harmony, for I am convinced that verse drama must be ordered musically, just like an opera.

Finally, the demands of listening will necessitate what we might call a background of sound[3] that evokes nature, suggests figuration and offers a happy equilibrium between musical expression and verbal expression, with the latter becoming 'linked by a sovereign idea and elevated to a supreme degree by their own significant energy,' to cite d'Annunzio.[4]

Add to this equation the need to adapt the duration of the verse play performed at the microphone (listening time, in my opinion, should not exceed an hour and a half, or two hours at most) and the need to add a presentation by the author describing the work's essential meaning, and you will have an idea of how I approach my task behind the microphone – a fascinating task, due to its sheer difficulty, and the new and marvellous possibilities that it affords.

---

[2] Darget's call for a new kind of space was attuned with developments elsewhere; in the Soviet Union, for example, 'radio-theatres' were created in the late 1920s, and doubled up as studio spaces allowing actors to perform before an audience and as venues for ordinary theatre productions, concerts and meetings. See Stephen Lovell, 'Broadcasting Bolshevik: The Radio Voice of Soviet Culture, 1920s–1950s,' *Journal of Contemporary History* 48, no. 1 (2013): 90–1.

[3] *Fonds sonore* in the original.

[4] The original citation is adapted from G. Hérelle's French translation of Gabriele D'Annunzio's *Le feu* (1924). The citation above is from Kassandra Vivaria's English translation of d'Annunzio's *The Flame of Life* (1910).

2.4 ANON.: THE SPEAKER'S QUALITIES

Translated by Emilie Morin. First published as 'Les qualités du speaker,' *Annuaire de la Radiodiffusion Nationale, année 1933* (Paris: Ministère des PTT; Service de la Radiodiffusion, 1933), 219–24.

The author of this piece is unknown, and is likely to have worked for the French state-owned radio network. See also the biographical sketch for 'On Emotion and Life Before the Microphone' (2.1).

●　●　●

Among the invisible characters who contribute to the making of a radio broadcast, there is one who plays a decisive role, whether we like it or not: the speaker, also designated as announcer, presenter, herald, radio-reader, etc. by those who are eager to break away from tradition.

The very nature of his functions seems, at first sight, to relegate him to the same status as the voices we hear in the background when we listen to a radio-concert. Is he not, in effect, a neutral character, charged with the simple task of being *useful*? Moreover, should we not consider that his announcements are comparable, if we want to establish a correspondence, to the subtitles of the silent films of yore, which were admittedly useful for comprehension yet by no means indispensable to the animated scenes projected onto the screen? And, after all, why should a voice that does nothing but read through a programme peppered with news and announcements – a task within the reach of anyone who can read without mumbling – be the focus of so much interest and seem so important? Now, as we have affirmed earlier, the speaker – and by this we mean the good speaker – plays an essential role, a capital role, in any radio broadcast. He personifies the concert for which he is acting as a spokesperson, gives character to it. His voice and his 'style' form an acoustic whole that is one of the representative features, we might say, of the radio station in which he officiates. Soon enough, this invisible and mysterious character becomes our friend, a familiar presence whom listeners living close by or far away – those who live far away most of all – await at the same time every day and welcome into their intimate world. To those who live far away, the speaker brings an echo of the intense life of the great cities and a distraction from the calm and monotony of a provincial existence. This is why one might instinctively greet the beginning of a programme with a cordial 'hello' when one hears the speaker's voice, and greet his 'good night' with a friendly reply at the end of the day. If he has a good ear and becomes the listeners' favourite, genuine success beckons, and innumerable listeners try to imagine what the owner of that moving voice, the voice that radiates through space, that the loud speaker picks up, looks like in his physical form.

But if the voice of the speaker is unpleasant, or his art defective, the listeners will stop listening to the radio broadcast, rightly or wrongly.[1]

What, then, are the qualities that a speaker must possess in order to show off the programmes of his radio station to their advantage and in order to court the attention of its immense audience? Indeed the wireless public is more likely to listen to radio-concerts that are presented well – and this well-known fact indicates the importance of the publicity that a good speaker can do for his radio station.

Before going further, let us return to the basic facts. What is a radio broadcasting station? It is an organisation that serves the general interest and believes its duties are to entertain and, sometimes, to stir feelings, to inform or educate the listeners who have tuned their wireless sets on its wavelength.[2]

And what kind of public does it deal with?

With the kind of public that is the most difficult to satisfy. Here is why: the wireless public is inherently partitioned, composed of listeners or units isolated from one another and, as a consequence, unable to respond to one another. Such a public does not abide by the laws described by Gustave Le Bon in his *Psychology of Crowds*. The confined spectators of the wireless, beyond the fact that they are only concerned about 'receiving' and, as such, remain resolutely in favour of what we might call the least effort, share another essential feature: they are blind, and their hearing, the only sense that is called upon, becomes intransigent; their propensity to criticise, as a consequence, increases to an extraordinary degree.

Indeed, woe betide the speaker who mispronounces a word, or who, when reading a text without preparation, pauses – even for a split second – before uttering a word whose meaning escapes him, shying away like a horse before an obstacle!

Woe betide the announcer who adds too much emphasis to his speech, or who comes across as excessively affected or precious!

---

[1] An anonymous BBC author made a similar argument in 1931: the 'personality, that rare and indefinable quality which alone can always be counted upon to bridge the gap between loud-speaker and listener, is even more elusive in the broadcasting studio than elsewhere. [. . .] The famous author may stammer through his manuscript in a cockney voice; the well-known actress, radiating personality and perfume through the Studio, may sound on the loud-speaker like a tired school-marm; the famous explorer [. . .] very possibly can't put two sensible words together before the microphone; and, by way of contrast, the unexpected nobody delivering a talk on slugs or dustbins reaps a thousand appreciative letters. [. . .] Listeners are quick to recognise those who can, as it were, enter their room as a friend might enter it, and talk to them as a friend might talk.' Anon., 'Personality in Speakers,' *The BBC Year Book 1931* (London: British Broadcasting Corporation, 1931), 211–14.

[2] This echoes the BBC's motto as set by John Reith: 'inform, educate and entertain.'

Tremble, all speakers who fail to repress a faint Parisian accent, or anything resembling a northern or southern accent!

To all the radio-readers who have a deathly voice oozing boredom, and whose cheerfulness feels laboured: the ears of your *dear listeners* are already turning away!

From all this we can establish which qualities the speaker needs to have to exercise his art.

These qualities fall into two different categories: on the one hand, those that are innate; on the other, those that have been developed over time or still need to be developed.

The gifts that cannot be learned include a voice with a radiogenic timbre, both warm and round; a deep voice or a baritone voice, devoid of a regional accent; a good visual acuity; and a certain vivacity of spirit, with excellent and sharp reflexes, which will serve the speaker marvellously well whenever he needs to understand unknown texts in the blink of an eye and interpret them appropriately.

But these gifts will remain sterile and useless without other qualities, themselves requiring a judicious psychological and physiological training for every speaker wanting to excel at his art. These are: an impeccable and clear diction, simplicity, naturalness, ease, and a cheerful and amicable tone, which nonetheless always remains measured.

Here is a good piece of advice: the speaker, like a good boy who wants to please and be understood, will need to imagine that he is speaking to a confidante, someone he knows and who he thinks may be listening to him speaking. This is an excellent way of animating the flow of words, of making speech feel responsive and alive, for words are always vulnerable to the influence created by the intimidating atmosphere of the auditorium, an empty and often deserted space, where the speaker remains alone with an inexpressive microphone.

And that is why the speaker's craft is tiring, despite what appearances may suggest. Indeed, the announcer must constantly remain in a state of animation and constantly call upon what we might call his internal dynamism. He is always 'living on the edge,' to borrow the popular expression.

He must know how to speak fluently and without hesitation, have a good general education, and know at least the basics of English, German, Italian and Spanish pronunciation. He may also need to know how to improvise in order to offer impromptu explanations to listeners, but this is not within everyone's reach . . . Finding oneself in front of this little machine, so silent, so sensitive to the ears of the tens of the thousands of people who are listening, is an entirely insignificant experience, which nevertheless sets even the most assured minds in turmoil – even those who are accustomed to speaking in public and are confident about it.

Let us add that, given the very particular conditions in which the speakers employed by our state-owned radio stations have been working and sometimes continue to work, it is appropriate to acknowledge that speakers need to be operators, first and foremost, meaning that they must possess the knowledge necessary to set up a voice-amplifying installation, address any breakdowns, arrange the microphones judiciously in every one of the very diverse places in which they find themselves whenever they broadcast outside the studio. They must be conversant with sound installations and telephone lines; on occasion, they must show off their acrobatic skills and attach suspended microphones to the arches of circus tents, to the top of a tree, to the bell tower of a town hall, to belfry towers.

On top of that, the speaker must also be gifted with that indefinable quality known as *vocal charm*.

This charm, this je ne sais quoi, this distinction, this chic, this ease, which sets the high-class speakers apart from their disciples, is infinitely scarcer than we might think.

And its scarcity allows us to affirm, like Mr Popence [*sic*], that 'Not everyone makes a good speaker. A speaker is born, not made; a good speaker is a rare person.'[3]

2.5 SHEILA BORRETT: SCENE – AND UNSEEN!

First published as 'Scene – and Unseen!,' *Radio Pictorial*, 16 February 1934, 3.

Sheila Borrett (née Graham, 1905–1986) was a British actress and the first female announcer on the BBC National Programme. She started to feature in BBC radio

---

[3] C. B. Popenoe, manager of New York stations WJZ and WJY. This is a reference to a *Wireless World* article in which his name was misspelt as Popence. Elsewhere, Popenoe had expressed views aligned with those of other American radio station directors and with common myths: he dismissed the use of female speakers, arguing that 'in no case does the female voice transmit as well as that of the man' and that it 'does not carry the volume of the average male voice'. See Jennie Irene Mix, 'The Listeners' Point of View: For and Against the Woman Radio Speaker,' *Radio Broadcast* (September 1924): 393; A. Dinsdale, 'American Radio Showmanship,' *Wireless World and Radio Review* 10 (January 1927): 18; J. Godchaux Abrahams, 'Voices of the Night,' *Wireless Magazine* 5, no. 29 (June 1927): 430.

plays and musical comedies in 1932, and was appointed as announcer in July 1933 under her married name, Mrs Giles Borrett. She was dismissed after three months following the ten thousand letters of complaint that the BBC received from the British public (90 per cent of them, it was said, were from female listeners). When Borrett recalled this experience in *Radio Pictorial*, she asked whether her dismissal was an expression of 'racial prejudice against woman playing a speaking part in the affairs of the world,' and wondered whether her career would have taken a different turn if she had 'slipped unobtrusively into Broadcasting House and the programmes' to enable listeners to become accustomed to a female announcer.[1] After her dismissal, she continued to act in BBC plays and present entertainment programmes as Sheila Stewart. In 1942, she was hired as BBC announcer again, under her new married name, Sheila Cox, and presented programmes for the BBC Overseas Service and the Forces Programme. In 1952, she moved to New York, then to Florida, where she worked as a presenter for the Tampa station WUSF until the end of her life.[2]

●　　●　　●

When first I went up to Broadcasting House to act in a play, I was rather depressed by the cold-blooded atmosphere attached to studio rehearsing.

I was used to the bustle and friendly excitement of stage rehearsals. I hadn't expected the complete and businesslike calm which I found in the studios.

People sat silently round the walls, waiting for their cues; the producer was just a voice coming through a loud-speaker; and, of course, all the waiting for little flicking red and green lights just terrified me.

I arrived for the first performance, wondering how I was going to get up enough enthusiasm and excitement to be able to act at all – in this quiet, unhurried atmosphere.

And then suddenly, as I stood waiting for the light – waiting to speak for the first time over the ether – I realised the unseen audience: millions of listeners of all ages and descriptions, to whom my voice had got to bring some message, if only a small and unimportant one.

As this realisation swept over me, I found that my knees were shaking and my heart bumping at about 120 to the minute.

It was a very great moment!

It is this vision of the great listening crowd that radio actors must keep always fresh in their minds if they are to give really good performances.

---

[1] Sheila Borrett, 'Why I Came and Why I Went,' *Radio Pictorial*, 9 March 1934, 27.

[2] See Cheris Kramarae, 'Censorship of Women's Voices on Radio,' in *Gender and Discourse: The Politics of Talk*, eds. Sue Fisher and Alexandra Todd (Norwood, NJ: Ablex, 1988), 243–54; Murphy, *Behind the Wireless*, 241–5; Charlie Connelly, 'Women Against the Tide: The Ballad of Sheila Borrett,' in *Last Train to Hilversum: A Journey in Search of the Magic of Radio* (London: Bloomsbury, 2019), 120–36.

Actors and actresses on the stage will tell you that they frequently 'forget their audience.'

By this they mean that they get so wrapped up in their part they do not consciously think about it. But the audience is there just the same; giving them fresh inspiration, creating atmosphere which enables them to give of their best, night after night.

With radio acting it would be fatally easy to forget that silent public, who can neither applaud nor criticise, if one had not felt the thrill I have described. It is more difficult, too, for radio actors to keep their interest fresh and keen, because they never see the play as a whole.

On the stage the actors can watch the progress of the play; they can see if it is running smoothly and note how the audience is reacting to it . . . they can tell, in short, if it is a good or a bad performance.

In radio plays the cast may be divided between two or three studios. The music comes from another, and the noise effects somewhere else again.

The individual actor can only be responsible for his own little bit. He must leave the knitting up to the producer, who 'sits up aloft,' doing what I always think of as a cross between making a gigantic Christmas cake and playing an organ! Taking all those little bits, mixing them, and welding them into the perfect and finished whole, which goes out over the air.

Only the producer and the listeners know if it is a good performance, as a whole, or not.

Now let us take the point of view of the audience for a moment.

Of the three great media of expression which the stage actor uses – voice, face, and gesture – the radio actor can use only the first.

The listener has, therefore, to concentrate far more intently on the play than any theatregoer if he is not to lose the thread. It is easy for a listener coming as a stranger to these voices to get hopelessly bewildered by the similarity between two, particularly if they are men, which to the producer, who knows them, sound totally different.

It therefore behoves radio actors to use their voices very carefully, making use of any characteristic inflexion they may have in order to impress their personalities on the listeners.

A very brilliant actor I know, in playing the leading part in a radio play some time ago, gave to his character a slight stammer.

This effectively fixed him in one's mind each time he spoke, and took away a great deal of the strain of listening.

Without doing anything as definite as that, the idea might well be extended.

Again, because the radio actor has only his voice as a means of expressing emotion, it is all too easy for him to find himself exaggerating, using too much emphasis.

He cannot study his part and then become mechanical in it, as he can on the stage.

He must be thinking of his words all the time if his voice is to express to his unseen, unseeing audience, each inflexion of the words is speaking.

For this reason it is a good thing that radio actors have to come to the microphone with their scripts in their hands. It is much easier to concentrate on putting the full significance of your part over if you have the printed word before you.

2.6 MABEL CONSTANDUROS: MY FIRST BROADCAST

First published as 'My First Broadcast,' *Radio Times*, 9 October 1925, 99.

Mabel Constanduros (née Tilling, 1880–1957) was a celebrated British actress who pioneered new performance styles on the radio and had a particular gift for comedy. This article relates her initial audition with the BBC's first Radio Repertory Company in 1925; thereafter, she became a household name as a BBC entertainer. She was also a prolific writer of children's books and novels, and her radio creations were numerous and varied, including plays, adaptations, sketches and serial programmes about women's work and class in Britain. She appeared in radio plays such as Tyrone Guthrie's *Squirrel's Cage* (see 5.11), did some film acting, and contributed to the BBC's Children's Hour until the end of her life. Her most popular creation was *The Buggins Family*, a radio series about a fictional Cockney family that ran from the 1920s through to the postwar period, for which she originally performed all the female characters as well as the young son (a collaborator, Michael Hogan, later took on the male parts). Constanduros saw herself, first and foremost, as a careful listener: 'The chief quality needed for work like mine is an intense sympathy for other people, which enables one to enter into their troubles and understand their point of view,' she observed in a later article for the *Radio Times*. 'I am always listening to other people's points of view, and always learning, and while they are talking to me every trick of voice and manner is registering itself upon my mind.'[1] She does not appear to have

---

[1] Mabel Constanduros, 'Where I Found the Bugginses,' *Radio Times*, 8 February 1929, 312.

been invited to reflect on her radio work often; although the *Radio Times* and *Radio Pictorial* – a magazine for radio fans, in which women's interests and female radio personalities were prominently represented – published occasional interviews of her, these pieces often focused on innocuous topics. During the Second World War, *The Buggins Family* was harnessed to serve the war effort; the BBC's collaboration with the Ministry of Food on the food economy campaign led to the creation of a radio series titled 'On the Kitchen Front,' in which Constanduros played a key part. From 1942 to 1945, and from 1947 to 1949, she contributed a regular food column to the *Listener*, offering recipes using wartime ingredients, rations and substitutes.[2]

● ● ●

First came the audition – a typewritten postcard on my breakfast-table one morning, inviting my attendance at 2, Savoy Hill.

With what difficulty did I force myself up the first flight of stairs towards 'Enquiries,' and little did I guess how familiar the face of the kindly uniformed official who directed me, was presently to become! Shrinkingly, I entered the ante-room, among a most heterogeneous crowd, where women who might have been duchesses' daughters out for a lark, mingled with pathetic ex-music-hall and concert artists hoping for a new field of activity now that age had made the old one impossible.

BENUMBED!

All the terror of the Unknown was upon me when my turn came to enter the heavy studio door, and I found myself in a drab-hung empty room, and was told, 'There is the microphone; will you please begin?'

Begin! But where should I stand? How loudly must I speak? And what should I say? For by this time every word that I had ever learned by heart had oozed from my benumbed brain.

However, I pulled myself together, and tremblingly addressed a box which stood in front of me. I found myself smiling at it, pleading with it, addressing it in melting tones, throwing arch glances at it; all the time feeling bitterly conscious that there were seventeen different kinds of fool and that I was being all of them! At intervals a delightful masculine voice came down a loud speaker with startling suddenness, giving me directions and curt thanks.

I went home sadly, feeling that broadcasting was not for me.

Nevertheless, I was wrong, for the wonderful day did arrive, upon which I was to make my first attempt at broadcasting. I tottered up the steps of 2, Savoy Hill, one night, and sank into one of the comfortable chairs in the Artists' Room.

---

[2] See Mabel Constanduros, *Shreds and Patches* (London: Lawson & Dunn, 1946); Jennifer J. Purcell, *Mother of the BBC: Mabel Constanduros and the Development of Popular Entertainment on the BBC, 1925–1957* (New York: Bloomsbury, 2020).

The strains of the orchestra were issuing from the loud-speaker in the corner, and a charming young man was soothing the very natural apprehension of an old lady who was to give her first 'Talk' through the microphone that evening.

A LOVE-MAKING VOICE

I timidly asked if I might listen to my predecessor, so as to get the hang of things a little, and receiving a gracious assent, I sidled into the studio in the old lady's wake. The silence was one that might be felt.

I suppose the talk preceding my 'turn' did not last for hours, but I felt that it did. I could scarcely remember the time when I had not been sitting in that studio, waiting to begin. At last, I had the shock of hearing myself introduced by name to over a million people, by a young man with a voice like honey and cream. Even in the panic which fell upon me instantly, I could not help thinking that it was a voice which should be exclusively used for making love, or crooning poems on moony nights, not for uttering bald announcements through a microphone – such a waste! But my turn had come, and a cold horror was upon me. If I could only fall through the floor, wither and die on the spot, do anything, in fact, but walk up to that horrible unresponsive box and be funny to it!

I approached it with a sickly smile, and began. The announcer was noble. To my dying day I shall remember that he smiled. Twice. It was a striking example of pure benevolence. Ten terrible minutes, and it was over.

2.7 VICTOR MARGUERITTE: FACING THE MICROPHONE

Translated by Emilie Morin. First published as 'Devant le micro,' *Lumière et Radio*, 10 April 1930, 1–2.

Victor Margueritte (1866–1942) was a French novelist, poet and playwright born in Algeria, who turned to writing after abandoning a military career. He was renowned for his writing advocating for women's freedom and became a prominent advocate of pacifism in France, a position which led him during the 1930s to argue, like many others, that occupation and collaboration with Hitler were preferable to war. Margueritte did not write for radio specifically, but some of his theatre plays were adapted for radio during the 1930s. He made his debut at the microphone in March 1930, as guest of the novelist and critic Frédéric Lefèvre, who hosted a series of 'radio-dialogues' on Radio-Paris; these were transpositions of the written interview format Lefèvre had previously used in *Les Nouvelles Littéraires*. *Lumière et Radio*, which commissioned this piece, was a short-lived monthly magazine aimed at a small, elite public interested in discussions of radio's artistic and social potential.

• • •

I have spoken before many an audience, lectured in France, Belgium and Switzerland on fifty different occasions, and given a great many speeches in solemn circumstances. Never before had I experienced the kind of agitation I felt the other day, just before my first encounter with the microphone.

An orator who is about to speak and a writer who is about to read sentences previously rehearsed in the silence of his study are all too aware of the kind of doubling that unfolds within the mind once they begin to speak to an attentive and generally favourable audience.

As soon as the first words are uttered, a mysterious power circulates between the person serving as the transmitter and the public serving as the receiver. You are not speaking in a void, that much is clear, and you become aware that speech, the echo of thought, has entered in direct contact with your listeners and is sustained by their willingness or their refusal to bestow attention and sympathy, so to speak. The current circulates. What ensues is either fusion or a clash of feelings, but there is only one electrical current, vibrating from one pole to another.

Speaking before the microphone is something else entirely: it means speaking to hundreds of thousands of invisible listeners, at distances that can vary infinitely.

You abandon the domain of relativity and the tangible to enter a kind of absolute and ungraspable truth. You find yourself before an abyss inhabited by a mysterious life form. You confront a void simmering with invisible and dimly felt presences, who wait silently before edging closer, tighter, to form a magical circle around you.

I confess that I was somewhat intimidated when I arrived at Radio-Paris.[1] The sensation lasted until I was ushered into the auditorium alongside my interlocutor, Frédéric Lefèvre, whom we all know as one of our best contemporary critics and essayists . . . Already accustomed to the exercise, he was as calm as I was nervous. Everything is an apprenticeship; that much is true.

---

[1] A large private radio station which went into public ownership in late 1933. The studios were then located on rue François 1er, Paris.

Once the bell rang and once our dialogue was announced, I had to throw myself resolutely into the precipice opened up before me by the metal rectangle and the sensitive plate – a narrow frame opening onto the elemental field,[2] the empire of the air waves, that fabulous electro-magnetic domain.

Then – seized by the sense of dissociation that grips the mind at decisive moments and splits us into a thinking being and an acting being – I realised that my preperception was correct.

It seemed to me that the voice coming out of my mouth no longer belonged to me – that it had been snatched away, along with the ideas that it carried, and sucked up by an unknown force. I was like a swimmer who, although he knows all the secrets of breaststroke and crawl, can suddenly no longer do anything except automatic movements, in a water that has become as soft as cotton wool . . . There is nothing to hold on to. You swim because you must, until you can feel the ground again – until that second when you hear the speaker ring the bell again and announce the end of this perilous exercise.

What a relief. You step back on firm ground, pleased to be liberated from that feeling of being suspended in a void . . . This is a void created by the immensity of space as well as the reverence emanating from the faraway crowd touched by your own energy, with whom reciprocal communication remains impossible.

I felt happily reassured by the responses I received the following day – messages of congratulations from wireless listeners, letters from women living in provincial towns who said that they were happy to listen to my thoughts, although they did not know me personally. And, instantly, the sense of wonder I experienced from having been present in such diverse places over the course of the same evening turned into a surge of admiration for radio; into an act of faith for this magnificent discovery that, just as it shatters the old world and its narrow limits, opens up to our dreams and our amazement the perspectives of a new Community, of a new Society.

Ours is a fabulous era: we have seen speed leap from the wheels of the bicycle onto the wheels of the automobile and then onto the aeroplane, and we have seen light grow at vertiginous speed, from the oil lamp to the enchantment of electric incandescence! We are, still, merely at the threshold of revelations that are so miraculous that the mind cannot even imagine them.

Does not light, by its very nature and texture, already add endless possibilities to the physical world, through its corpuscles and waves? Who knows – soon we might see the speaker on the wireless stand before us, close enough to touch, just as easily as we perceive his voice today from thousands of miles away.

And, beyond the subject of radio broadcasting, if we think about all the ways in which pure thought can be transmitted (by telepathy, through the materialisation of the otherworld), we allow ourselves to dream about the

---

[2] The condenser microphone, with its two metal plates and circular casing.

metaphysical and parapsychological planes from which life's radiance originates, such as those described in the hypothesis advanced by Georges Lakhovsky last year.[3]

When it comes to science, nothing is ever impossible. Camille Flammarion – as I recalled in my preface to *Chant du Berger* – once told an entertaining story about how, in 1878, during the session of the Academy of Sciences at which the physicist Du Moncel presented Edison's phonograph, a member of this learned assembly called Mr Bouillaud, who could not believe what he had heard, hurled himself upon his colleague, crying out: 'Wretch! We shall not be duped by a ventriloquist!'

What would this fossil say if he heard the wireless – a miracle that no longer surprises our children, unfazed by progress?

Let me add that such a miracle should under no circumstances be handed over to the pontiffs preaching political or religious sectarianism, no matter their walk of life. In their hands, the wireless could become nothing more than an instrument of domination, oppression and stupidity.

Used correctly, the wireless may acquire magnificent social utility and bring the greatest good across the world, serve people's civic education, their professional learning – or it may be used to simply entertain, since entertainment is also good for our health. But once again, this can only happen on the condition that the gear levers of progress, by which I mean the wireless sets, remain private property, submitted to the free play of competition and its benefits.

If the wireless – evidently an agent of progress – were ever to become a state-owned privilege, then it would turn into the most formidable brainwashing machine. We, who only know the slow action of print, can only imagine the power that oral impression would gain, the devastating influence that false news would reap, the reiterated lies that would pass as eloquence.

Radio broadcasting, that ductile form of international speech, would turn into what is worst about humankind, just like the tongue of Aesop. Yet it is becoming increasingly clear that radio can also become what is best about humankind – but only if impartial leaders use it to disseminate accurate information and new ideas, as a radio news bulletin that is unafraid of controversy would do, in a spirit of great tolerance and as part of an ingenious process of popularisation.

Educate, teach and entertain at the same time.[4] What a mission! We have the organ for this. All we need is an organisation, and the virtues that turn an organisation into fertile ground: a sense of measure and sincere love for the public good.

---

[3] A controversial scientist and inventor (1869–1942).

[4] A reference to BBC motto coined by Reith, its founder and first Director-General: 'inform, educate and entertain.'

The most dreadful thing is that, although these two virtues are necessary conditions, partisanship all too often ruins the former, while the latter can be understood in as many different ways as there are political parties. I would like to see a learned group of philosophers and artists, which would exclude all politicians, no matter their party, act as advisors to the kings of finance who control the workings of industry today in ways that are more or less visible, here and elsewhere.

This is a simple suggestion in response to *Lumière et Radio*'s investigation.

2.8 WALTER BENJAMIN: ON TIME TO THE MINUTE

Translated by Marielle Sutherland. First published as Detlef Holz, 'Auf die Minute,' *Frankfurter Zeitung*, 6 December 1934, 2.

Walter Benjamin (1892–1940) was a German philosopher, literary critic and translator. He wrote prolifically for radio, including many radio plays for children; he also delivered regular talks, conversations and readings on German radio stations between 1927 and 1933. His broadcasting career began with a talk on Russian literature for the Südwestdeutsche Rundfunk (Frankfurt): 'Junge russische Dichter,' broadcast on 23 March 1927. He recalled this first experience at the microphone in the text that follows – the last text he wrote about radio, which he saw as 'a little filler joke'.[1] It appeared in December 1934 in the *Frankfurter Zeitung* under a pseudonym Benjamin commonly used, Detlef Holz.[2] By that point, Benjamin, who was Jewish,

[1] Benjamin to Gerhard Scholem, 26 December 1934, *The Correspondence of Walter Benjamin, 1910–1940*, eds. Gershom Scholem and Theodor W. Adorno, trans. Manfred R. Jacobson and Evelyn M. Jacobson (Chicago: University of Chicago Press, 1994), 470.

[2] See Lecia Rosenthal, ed., *Radio Benjamin* (London: Verso, 2014), 377–86; Robert Ryder, 'On the Minute, Out of Time: Reading the Misreading of Time in Walter Benjamin's "Auf die Minute" (1934),' *Germanic Review: Literature, Culture, Theory* 91, no. 3 (2016): 217–35. For another full translation of 'Auf die Minute,' see Walter Benjamin, *The Work of Art in the Age of Its Technological Reproducibility, and Other Writings on Media*, eds. Michael W. Jennings, Brigid Doherty and Thomas Y. Levin (Cambridge, MA: Harvard University Press, 2008), 407.

had left Germany. He settled in Paris, was stripped of his German citizenship in 1939 and became stateless, was incarcerated by the French regime, and took his own life at the Spanish border with France in 1940, while attempting to flee from persecution.

• • •

After soliciting for work for several months, I was commissioned by the station director of D . . . to entertain listeners for twenty minutes with a report from my specialist area, literary criticism. I was promised that if my talk met with a positive response, I would be invited to contribute regular items of this kind. The departmental director was kind enough to point out that it is not only the structure of such a lecture that is crucial here, but also the manner in which it is delivered. 'Beginners,' he said, 'mistakenly believe they are giving a lecture to a relatively large audience, the only difference being that the audience happens to be invisible. Nothing could be further from the truth. The radio listener is almost always an individual, and even if you reach several thousand people, you are always only reaching thousands of individual people. You must therefore behave as if you were speaking to a single individual – or to many individuals, if you prefer; but on no account to a large assembly of people. That's the first thing. And now for the second: you must keep exactly to the allotted time. If you do not, we have to do it for you, which means we have to pull the plug on you indiscriminately. Any delay, even the slightest, has – as we know from experience – the tendency to multiply itself over the course of the programme. If we do not intervene immediately, our overall programme comes apart at the seams. – So, don't forget: informal lecture style! And finish on time to the minute!'

I followed these instructions very strictly; ultimately, a lot depended on the reception of my first lecture. I took the manuscript with me to the radio station at the agreed time. I had recited it aloud to myself at home, and I had also timed the lecture. The announcer welcomed me obligingly, and I took it as a sign of trust that he refrained from monitoring my debut from an adjoining chamber. Between being announced and signing off, I was my own master. For the first time in my life, I was standing in a modern broadcasting studio, where everything was arranged for the complete comfort and convenience of the speaker, and to encourage the unconstrained elaboration of his skills. He may step up to a lectern or sit down on a sizeable armchair; he may choose from among a host of very different light sources; he may even walk up and down, taking his microphone with him. Last but not least, a grandfather clock with a clock face marking only minutes – not hours – conveys to him how much value is placed on the moment in this sealed-off chamber. I had to have finished by the time the hand was showing forty.

I had read over half the manuscript, when I glanced at the clock again and saw that the second hand was circling around the same circuit set out for the minute hand, but at sixty times the speed. Had I made a mistake in the arrangement at home? Had I now made a mistake with the pace? One thing was clear: two thirds of my allotted speaking time had elapsed. As I carried on reading my script with an affable inflection, I was silently but frantically trying to find a solution. A bold decision was needed; whole sections would have to be sacrificed, and I would therefore have to improvise the reflections building up to the conclusion. Departing from the text was not without its risks. But I had no choice. I summoned all my strength, skipped several pages of the manuscript – thereby cutting out a long period of time – and finally touched down, contented, like a pilot on his airfield, within the configuration of ideas in the final paragraph. Breathing a sigh of relief, I immediately gathered up my papers, and feeling elated by my par force performance, I stepped back from the lectern and began to casually slip on my coat.

Indeed, the announcer should have entered at this point. But he made me wait, and I turned to the door. In so doing, my eyes came to rest once again upon the grandfather clock. Its minute hand was showing thirty-six! – another full four minutes until forty! What I had hurriedly registered a short while ago must have been the position of the *second hand*! I understood then why the announcer was staying away. At the same instant, however, the silence, which only moments before had felt pleasant, enveloped me like a net. In this chamber, devised around the technology and the human being at the centre of it, a new kind of shudder, yet related to the oldest kind of shudder we know, crept over me. I attuned my ear to myself: and now it was suddenly picking up nothing but my own silence. This I recognised, however, as the silence of death, which was at this very moment, simultaneously in a thousand ears and a thousand parlours, seizing me and carrying me off.

An indescribable fear came over me, and thereupon a ferocious determination. Save what can be saved, I said to myself. I wrenched the manuscript out of my coat pocket, took the first best of the pages I had passed over, and carried on reading in a voice that felt like it was drowning out the thudding in my chest. I could no longer expect to come up with any new ideas. And because the section of text I had grabbed was short, I stretched out the syllables, increased the resonance of the vowels, rolled the r's and inserted pensive pauses into the sentences. In this way, I once again reached the end – this time the right one. The announcer came and released me as obligingly as he had welcomed me before. Yet my sense of unease persisted. The next day, I met up with a friend I knew had heard my performance. I casually asked him what his impression of it was. 'It was very good,' he said. 'It's just that there are always faults with the receivers. Mine stalled for a whole minute.'

2.9 EGON ERWIN KISCH: WOE BETIDE THE ONE WHO SEES

Translated by Marielle Sutherland. First published as 'Weh' dem, der sieht!,' in *Funkköpfe: 46 literarische Porträts*, ed. Karl Wilczynski (Berlin: Funk-Dienst, 1927), 47–51.

Egon Erwin Kisch (1885–1948), born in Prague to a German-speaking Jewish family, was a Czech writer and journalist. He was a militant pacifist, active in Communist organisations, and fiercely opposed to Hitler. He moved to Berlin in 1919 and became renowned for his reports and travel journalism on Soviet Russia and Europe. It is unclear how much practical radio experience he had by the time this text appeared, but from 1929, and for an undetermined period of time, he was in charge of Radio Moscow's German-language programmes, and occasionally contributed talks and reportage. Radio Moscow, which started to broadcast in German in October 1929 (and, subsequently, in English, French and other languages), soon became a platform for German anti-fascists. Its first German-language broadcast included reportage by Kisch on the festivities organised for the 1929 anniversary of the October Revolution on Red Square. In 1933, Kisch was in Germany; after the Reichstag fire, he was arrested, imprisoned, then expelled to Czechoslovakia. He moved to Paris, where he continued to contribute to the work of anti-fascist organisations, spent some time in Australia, where his presence ignited a scandal and attempts were made to expel him, and travelled to Spain, where he acted as reporter for the International Brigades. After 1940, he left Europe for Mexico, returning to Prague in 1946.[1] The present text is a portrait of the 'Control-Room Man,' who ruled over the control room – 'the "Nerve-centre" of a broadcasting station,' to borrow the BBC's definition.[2]

* * *

[1] See Christian Ernst Siegel, 'Abschied vom neusachlichen Flaneur: Anmerkungen zu den Reportagen Egon Erwin Kischs,' in *Literatur und Rundfunk 1923–1933*, ed. Gerhard Hay (Hildesheim: Gerstenberg, 1975), 319–25; US Foreign Broadcast Information Service, 'Anniversary Brings Praise to Moscow Broadcasting,' *Daily Report*, 25 October 1989, 91; Ken Slater, 'Egon Kisch: A Biographical Outline,' *Labour History* 36 (1979): 94–103, Terrence O'Keeffe, 'Egon Kisch: Supplementing and Correcting the Biographical Record,' *Labour History* 110 (2016): 161–71.

[2] 'Glossary of Technical Terms,' *BBC Handbook 1929* (London: British Broadcasting Corporation, 1929), 431.

Among the hundreds of thousands of people who listen to radio broadcasts through headphones or in front of the horn of the loudspeaker, only one of them, only a single one, can see the people producing the sound. This person occupies the *amplifier room*, right next to the performance room, which he can see through a window. Just a few feet away from the microphone, he sees the conference speaker addressing the masses (by no means dressed formally, rather quite the contrary: his lounge suit is protected by a linen smock); just a few feet away, he sees the orchestra conductor (in shirt sleeves) haranguing the members of the philharmonic orchestra (sitting in unbuttoned shirt collars) up to fortissimo; and just a few feet away from the (ancient) adolescent singer opening her mouth, ready to screech, and from all the other acoustic performances; he sees it very clearly – yes, he sees it – the needle jumping on the voltmeter scale – the force of the sound. Yet he hears no sound. More precisely, he hears no sound *directly*. His room is soundproof, separated from the performance chamber; the window he is looking through is a tightly closed double window.

What he sees before his eyes travels to his ear by way of a detour. He has a long conduit: there he sits, high up in the broadcasting centre; in the next room people are speaking, singing and playing into the microphone, but the sounds do not come straight to him. First of all, they travel out of the Potsdamer Straße to the transmitter on Magdeburger Platz, or through to Witzleben, or even to Königswusterhausen, forty kilometres away, and from there they turn around and come back to him, to the man sitting right on the edge of the performance chamber, the man who only learns from the loudspeaker what he is seeing.

'*What he is seeing?*' Should this not be in the past tense? Didn't we learn at school that sound travels significantly slower than light? So, isn't it the case that the sounds that have had to make a detour of many kilometres can only tell the man at the window in retrospect what he *has seen*?

Wrong. Sound, as we learned in school, ambles along slowly – its regular pace is thirty-three metres per second. However, electric waves hold quite a different record. In one second, they spread out three hundred thousand kilometres – which is as much as saying that they can travel *seven times around the globe in one second*. The man at the window, who has a long conduit, therefore simultaneously hears what he sees, despite being separated from the radio-performers by a soundproof wall, and despite the detour via Magdeburger Platz, Witzleben, Königswusterhausen or Stettin.[3] In fact, he even hears it *faster than he would if he heard it more directly*. If, for instance, as part of the broadcast performance, a trumpet call should sound, then it is blown outside in the corridor, and our man in the amplifier room hears it, after he has heard it via Königswusterhausen, *for a second time half a second later: from the corridor, in natura.*

---

[3] German radio transmitters.

Incidentally, he can adjust all the transmissions even at the beginning of the long conduit, and that is actually why he is there. He fastens the receiver directly to the amplifier and turns the screw so that the acoustic energy – which, in the next room, travels into the microphone and from there by wire into the black box, translated into electrical energy – is sufficient to steer the radio transmitter. If anyone listening cannot hear the sound properly, a local disturbance is to blame, and by no means our esteemed friend here. He is a functionary of the Telegraphentechnische Reichsanstalt [*sic*],[4] and this institute has propriety over the soundproof area, which is separated from the realm of the radio corporation. A marble control panel facilitates the dissemination of the performances to all German radio stations, and the steering of all German transmitters. The Hamburg Naval Observatory announces the time by telephone; the cables for the transmission are freed up by telephone, but the telephones do not ring in the room. They merely vibrate discreetly; otherwise, despite the soundproof wall and despite the tightly closed double windows, the tinkling would travel to the microphone, and any radio listeners who are also telephone subscribers would rush to their telephones in the midst of the broadcast, believing someone was calling them.

Our man is present at the rehearsals; he gives the director or conductor a signal if there is too much or too little emphasis, and, as the technician, he is the highest authority, although he is not permitted to engage in any artistic criticism. Furthermore, as regards the performance, he is the sole representative of an audience numbering hundreds of thousands, *he is the sole representative of a truly incalculable – because invisible – mass.* And the radio-performers, who of course are otherwise regular actors, must now present their art to an empty house – can we hold against them the fact that only their mouths are directed at the suspended microphone, whilst their eyes, anxious, mistrustful, enquiring, begging for applause, peer at the window, where the man from the Telegraphentechnische Reichsanstalt sits, like a King Ludwig of Bavaria, filling the stalls, the loges and the galleries . . .? His smile bolsters; his nod gladdens the heart – all for one and one for all.

And yet, readers, listeners, performers, do not believe that he, the only one who sees and hears, is to be envied, or that he is the best critic, or even merely the leading representative of the public. No, he is not enviable; no, he is not in a position to judge the effect; in fact, he is the worst representative of the auditorium. Why? Because he not only hears but also sees! All illusions are lost on him. He sees that, to the distant listeners, a *shower of water over a bathtub* signifies, on one occasion, *sea surf*, and on another, a *waterfall*, here the *stroke*

---

4   Telegraphentechnische Reichsamt (Telegraph Engineering Bureau of Germany), the government department of the Weimar Republic in charge of telegraphy and telecommunications, which was reshaped in the late 1920s, and whose domain included radio.

of the oar of a boat, there a *cloudburst*, while *peas shaken on a tambourine* evidently represent a *downpour*;

he sees that the *thunder* of the furious sky is produced by a fat, phlegmatic man on a *kettledrum*;

he sees that it is not a *steamboat* setting sail, not a *factory* shrilly announcing the end of the shift, and not a *locomotive* departing when we hear a little gas flowing from the *carbonic acid bottle* into the metal pipe;

he sees that there is no *railway train* travelling through the landscape, rather merely that someone is playing a *broken gramophone record*, and it is this that is producing the clattering rhythm; he sees that the noise of the *automobile* being driven away by the rich uncle is provided by an *idling motorcycle*, placed in the corridor so that it does not stink out the performance chamber;

he, who not only hears but also sees, can see that the rolling *farm cart* is not there at all, but is represented by a piece of *corrugated tin*, bent and creaking in the hands of the stage manager, and that the lovers, who, the happy listeners believe, have just begun to embrace, have already left the chamber, and that the blissful *kiss* is made passionately *on his own hand* by the radio play director;

he sees that the farmers in Tolstoy's 'The Power of Darkness' or Anzengruber's 'The Worm of Conscience' are not trudging clumsily through the parlour in their heavy boots;[5] rather, the assistant director is stamping on a platform of planks he has constructed himself, and the *church bells* are nothing more than *suspended metal tubes clashing together*;

he sees that all the animals involved are non-existent: an *electric piano* (going by the nickname 'bleating machine' at the broadcasting centre) chirps like a cricket, crows like a cockerel, whinnies like a horse, twitters like a nightingale, moos like a cow, clucks like a hen and yaps like a dog, and a pasteboard rattle – a box pulled by a cardboard tube with the aid of cords – provides the frightening groan of the lion; it is only occasionally that an *animal sound imitator* is used for individual animal roles;

he sees wind machines, rain machines and other theatrical props, and new inventions for the radio stage; he sees even-tempered faces in passionate scenes, ugly performers in beautiful roles, carelessly dressed performers in elegant roles, the agitated people of old Genoa in modern lounge suits muttering 'rhubarb rhubarb,' and the conspirators sitting around, bored, whispering the terrible-sounding secret 'peas and carrots'. Alas, he sees, and sees through the whole sham; he *sees*, and to make matters worse, he sees what others only hear.

---

[5] Two plays about peasant life by Leo Tolstoy and Ludwig Anzengruber.

2.10 FLORENCE MILNES: A DAY IN THE LIFE OF THE BBC LIBRARIAN

First published as 'Miss Florence Milnes, the BBC Librarian, Reveals a Day in her Life to Godfrey Winn,' *Radio Pictorial*, 13 March 1936, 29, 31.

Florence Milnes (1893–1966) was Head Librarian at the BBC for over thirty years. She first joined the BBC as an Information Assistant in 1925, conducting background research for a wide range of programmes, and became the BBC's librarian in 1927. She created a much-admired reference library, which by 1952 included 50,000 books and 100,000 illustrations, and provided research assistance, bibliographies, book lists and help with listeners' queries to BBC staff across all departments.[1]

● ● ●

8 a.m. – Awake, reluctantly, but awake, and without any of the usual methods of alarum. I do not need them. Have I not tapped on my heels eight times last thing before I went to bed? To friends, who refuse at first to accept the efficacy of this childhood's habit, I say: Try it yourself, before you smile at me.

8.15 a.m. – There are alarums, nevertheless – unasked for, needless to say. I had always heard how hard musicians worked, but I had no practical experience of their labours till I went to live in a musical corner of St. John's Wood. Studio to left of me, studio to right of me. From one, there now emerges an everlastingly unsuccessful attempt to reach top C, from the other, scales and scales and still more scales.

8.30 a.m. – Can they hear each other as well as I can hear them both, I wonder, as I dress and have my breakfast.

9 a.m. – Catch a communal car. A nice ordinary 'bus takes me to work!

9.10 a.m. – As I pass Lord's, I find myself thinking not for the first time, what a myriad of different worlds inhabit this globe of ours. What is cricket to me? What is the BBC's library to them? What is Hecuba to either of us?

9.15 a.m. – Someone is quite likely to ask me that, I remind myself, or something equally inaccurate in the course of the day, and expect me to give

---

[1] See Murphy, *Behind the Wireless*, 123–4; Florence Milnes, 'A Library for Broadcasters,' *BBC Year Book 1952* (London: British Broadcasting Corporation, 1952), 66–8.

back the *correct* quotation, plus its context, in return. You see, it's part of my job to have half lines of poetry hurled at my head all day long, with a request for *accurate* information. Lots of other questions, too, they ask me, and sometimes they know the answer as well as I do. Then why ask? Why look it up in one of my reference books all over again? For this reason. The BBC library has tried to build up a reputation for giving the ultimate authority. Ask the library, they'll know, they'll find out. And we do, somehow, however complicated and vague the reference, but we take just the same amount of trouble over checking the easy queries as the difficult ones. We must, for the sake of our reputation.

9.15 a.m. – I'm here! Up in the lift and along the corridor to the library with its green book-cases, its friendly atmosphere. Books: touching them, reading them, handling them. Some people have to work to live, others live to work, I only know that as far back as I can remember, I wanted to be among books. Well, now that I am, I am one of the lucky ones. And I am only too thankful to admit it!

9.30 a.m. – Have a quick look at all the leading newspapers, in turn, which are placed on reading stands, for the convenience of the staff, in one corner of the room. There is a comprehensive selection of weeklies and monthlies, too. All through the day the different department chiefs will come and go. Some, of course, are more regular visitors than others. Val Gielgud, for instance, hardly ever misses a day.[2]

9.50 a.m. – A heap of press cuttings lie on my desk. I don't pretend that I have time to read everything that anyone has written anywhere about the BBC, but I notice to-day from a swift survey that, as usual, the critics cancel themselves out. In other words, the old saying about one man's meat, etc., might have been specially created for broadcasting reviews.

9.53 a.m. – My telephone rings. Is that the library? We're off . . .

9.54 a.m. – Who was Israel?

9.56 a.m. – Have I got a book on Maya customs?

9.58 – Where are the Kaieteur Falls?

10 a.m. – Then there are the correspondence queries that have to be answered. They are usually of a far vaguer nature, even, than those that have their source in the building. For instance, to-day there is a letter from a lady that begins – 'I rather think that in a wireless talk (I can't remember its name, but it was sometime last autumn) there was a book about wild flowers mentioned. I would like to know its name.' I daresay she would, I think, as I turn to the next which is an enquiry about the title of a poem which (apparently) has as its theme, King Alfred, and an old sea captain, who brought back a walrus tooth. Do you know the answer? Longfellow's *Discoverer of the North Cape*.

---

[2] Val Gielgud (1900–1981) was an actor, speaker, writer and a key figure at the BBC, who steered the ways in which radio drama in particular was produced as well as written.

10.20 a.m. – Can you exactly describe a Palanquin?

10.24 a.m. – Can I let So-and-So know what General X's decorations are?

10.26 a.m. – Can I suggest an old book print of Lyons Cathedral? Many of the times that my telephone rings, it is to hear a programme builder the other end, seeking information or reassurance about the exactness of his knowledge, or asking me for a list of books, dealing with some special subject, person, or period of history. Indeed, the resources of the library are undoubtedly of enormous assistance in the concocting of programmes. It is true that it is not a large library, consisting, as it does, of only 5,000 volumes – in fact, it is as remarkable for what it does *not* possess, as what it does – but every one of those volumes has been carefully chosen as a link in the armour of knowledge. Naturally a lot of research must be done with outside libraries, too.

10.42 a.m. – What is the Latin name of the tobacco plant?

10.50 a.m. – What is clause 19 of the Covenant of the League of Nations?

11.00 a.m. – Can I provide some information about sixteenth century trade with Spain? Can I also let them have some books on Mediaeval Spain *immediately*? I smile at the urgency in their voice. Doubtless, in three weeks' time, when I ring up, in turn, and enquire whether I can have the books back, I shall be told they haven't started using them yet! I shall be fobbed off with 'Next week, Miss Milnes.'

11.10 a.m. – What was the date of the foundation of the Canadian Mounted Police?

11.15 a.m. – When did So-and-So retire? He hasn't yet, I reply, as I turn over the pages of a catalogue of second-hand books, seeing if there is anything I want for the library. Bargains mean nothing to us, unless they are the right ones. We don't collect books, rare or valuable, we aren't interested in bindings or printing, as some libraries. All we care about is expanding our knowledge and making it more complete.

11.24 a.m. – Can I produce the date of the Rymill Expedition?

11.28 a.m. – A misquotation – thought to be from Henry the Fifth. After some time and trouble, the right context is discovered by one of my assistants in Henry the Fourth.

11.40 a.m. – What's this year in the Mohammedan calendar?

11.43 a.m. – Origin of saying 'To heap coals of fire,' etc.?

11.45 a.m. – Who were the teams in Cup Final of 1927?

11.50 a.m. – Do I know of a book of General Gordon's Letters, in connection with the Siege of Khartoum?

11.55 a.m. – Have I got a book to describe Everyman, the Morality play?

12 noon – What is the acreage of Rutland?

12.5 p.m. –What was the actual time of Galsworthy's death?

12.8 p.m. – Age of Tobias Mathias?

12.11 p.m. – Date of the Derby in 1880, and the winner?

12.14 p.m. – Can I find a description of the opening ceremony of London Bridge in 1831?

12.35 p.m. – Who was the music critic of a literary weekly, under a particular editor?

12.40 p.m. – Date of the Storming of Quebec by Wolfe.

12.45 p.m. – What's the name of the submarine, sunk July 9, 1929?

12.55 p.m. – Is it correct to say dice is, or dice are loaded against you? At the moment my chief thought is, that they seem loaded against my getting away to lunch!

1.15 p.m. – Lunch. A breathing space and I linger over my coffee, loth to set off in the heat to Somerset House, where I must search out the birthplace of a certain famous modern poetess. [. . .] All my reference books say that she was born in Devonshire, but reference books are not *always* infallible! Somerset House, in this case, is the ultimate authority.

2.30 p.m. – The journey was worth while. I find that the query was justified. The Devonshire poetess actually first saw the light of day in Manchester!

2.50 p.m. – Arrive at the British Museum, where I proceed to do some research work for one of the production chiefs. This is always interesting to do, sometimes excitingly so. For instance, I shall never forget the extraordinary coincidence that occurred on one occasion when Lionel Fielden had asked for some 'dope' on the old houses of Portland Place,[3] a century ago. He was planning, as a Christmas programme, a story he had made up himself about an old man who lived in Portland Place, and had invented a time-machine. As a background he was using the interval-signal, which at that time you will remember was a ticking clock. In the story this was the ghost of the man who had tried to invent a non-stop clock. Well, you can imagine my excitement when in the course of my research, I came across an old book, which was the story of a certain Mr Cayzer who had lived in Portland Place a century ago, and spent his life trying to invent such a clock himself! In fact, the book was illustrated with the different models of Lionel Fielden's 'Time Machine.' Extraordinary coincidence, wasn't it?

3.15 p.m. – Back in Portland Place. Find that a series of inquiries have accumulated on my desk in my absence. Somebody apparently wants the dates of the deaths of Gogol, Jules Verne, and Mark Twain.

3.45 p.m. – Does a Gadfly bite or sting?

Many of the queries are out of the ordinary, but this one makes even me gasp for a moment. However, my official self quickly regains control over my

---

[3] Lionel Fielden (1896–1974) joined the BBC in 1927 as Talks Assistant, seconding Hilda Matheson, and wrote, produced and acted in various BBC programmes. In 1935, he became India's first Controller of Broadcasting, then Director General of All-India Radio.

sense of humour, and I stretch out my arm for the right book of reference. It's extraordinary how *automatic* this gesture becomes after a time.

4 p.m. – A description of the ballet, *The Gods Go A' Begging*, please.

4.15 p.m. – What was the date of Mussolini's march on Rome, and is the date still celebrated in Italy?

4.30 p.m. – Yet another date! What are the dates of the first Electric Light Supply, and of the first electric railway?

This reminds me of my Anniversary Index, an elaborate affair to be the last word in such concoctions, that I have been planning for a long time already.

4.40 p.m. – One of the announcers arrives, in search of some information about the music programme that he has to introduce later in the day. As soon as he has been shown where the book lodges that he wants, I have to attend to the needs of an engineer, who wants a technical work on studio acoustics. Or someone else drops in to ask my advice about a reading list for the holidays. Of course, we don't stock any fiction ourselves, but at the same time, it is part of my job to keep up to date with all the reviews in the principal papers so that I am in a position to recommend some new novels, if my aid is invoked. Incidentally, I also study the publishers' advertisements very carefully.

5 p.m. – And so it goes on for the rest of the afternoon, questions, answers, office routine, dictating letters, ordering books, supervising the catalogue, helping with suggestions for winter programmes (on a hot September afternoon) or summer programmes (on a bleak February morning), more questions, more answers, until, at

5.50 p.m. – A distracted Empire official rushes in, demanding 'What do I know about CORRUGATED IRON!'

PART 3
THE ART OF LISTENING

3.1 FERNAND DIVOIRE: THE ZONE OF THE STORMS

Translated by Emilie Morin. First published as 'En écoutant . . . La zone des tempêtes,' *Lumière et Radio*, 10 February 1930, 4.

Fernand Divoire (1883–1951) was a Belgian-French modernist writer, and a member of the French Simultaneist group during his formative years. A prolific critic and journalist, he served as editor-in-chief of *L'Intransigeant* and *Le Journal Littéraire*, and contributed to many other publications, including Carlos Larronde's literary radio magazine *Lumière et Radio*. He worked with many artists, notably the 'theatre laboratory' Art et Action directed by Edouard Autant and Louise Lara, who performed his simultaneous poems 'Naissance du poème' and *L'Exhortation à la victoire*. 'Naissance du poème,' an early experiment with sound poetry, was widely celebrated and became a mass-produced gramophone record in 1919–1920. Divoire wrote a substantial number of radio plays, the most interesting of which include *Les voix amies et ennemies* (first broadcast in 1934 on Radio-Paris) and *Marathon* (an adaptation of one of his stage plays, first broadcast in 1931 on Radio-Paris). He occasionally gave talks on Radio-Paris, including a talk on sound scenery in radio drama in 1932. From 1941 until the liberation of Paris in August 1944, he contributed a daily column on cultural matters to *Paris-Midi*, then characterised by its fervid collaborationism and anti-Semitism, and acted as the newspaper's editor-in-chief.[1]

●　●　●

Sometimes, when I am tired of listening to music, tired of moving from one frequency to another, I seek refuge in the zone of the storms.

It is the obscure zone that rules over the radio between 600 and 1,000 meters. We are all aware that, over there, at 600 meters, lies the wavelength used by ships, but I don't know Morse code and, to me, telegraphic messages are a secret language. I can hence *imagine* orders issued by the fairy stock exchange, messages from lone hearts crossing the air towards each other, calls from sinking ships . . .

---

[1] The fullest account of Divoire's life was given in a radio tribute: 'Dixième anniversaire de la mort de Fernand Divoire,' France 3 Nationale, 18 July 1961, INA archives. On the broader context of Divoire's radio journalism, see Rebecca P. Scales, *Radio and the Politics of Sound in Interwar France, 1921–1939* (Cambridge: Cambridge University Press, 2016), 114–50.

Imagine. Is that not the great pleasure gifted to us by the wireless?

But the ships are not alone. There is also the storm.

As soon as you plunge below Hilversum, where everything was utterly quiet, you fall into virgin territory in your wireless log.[2] There, you should be able to hear faraway Moscow or the vague Swiss wireless, but you have been caught in the hurricane.

A whole volley of demons hiss, sing, scream. Sometimes they imitate sirens and sometimes they imitate the whistle of locomotives. At other times, they take pains to modulate their cries. A concert performed by the most improbable birds ensues. Then, all of a sudden, your wireless set shakes and crackles as though it were about to break. Storms . . . Storms . . .

Those who enjoy good music depart from the zone of the storms straight away. They travel up towards Hilversum or down towards Budapest. For my part, I enjoy wandering in the midst of these radio storms. Why is it so? Simply because they bring *unreal* noises to the listener.

These noises are less expected, less familiar than the music created by composers.

Once again, *I imagine* . . . What I am holding is no longer a wireless set: it is a black cloud, or it is the ocean. It is a space populated with living noises that I cannot name, cannot identify, cannot track, cannot convert into a list.

And it broadens my horizons and enriches my world even more. 'Anywhere out of the world':[3] there.

I wouldn't pretend that I spend hours there, in the screams raging through my zone of the storms. I even confess that I move away rather quickly. But when you have long felt immensely proud to belong to the civilisation that has domesticated the air waves, as I have, it makes you happy to listen, every so often, to what you *imagine* as inhuman waves, as rebel waves . . .

There is nothing to prevent you from identifying a voice, every so often, in the midst of all this racket . . . And this voice could be, for example, an interference from Radio Tour Eiffel, which will bring you back to us, your contemporaries, and remind you of all those marvels you can buy, like that paste that can clean copper and sharpen your razor.[4]

---

[2] In the early days particularly, some radio enthusiasts kept records of what they had heard and when, in the fashion of maritime wireless logs. The practice endured over time; its popularity is clear from two long-standing columns in the BBC magazine *World-Radio* and its precedessor *The Radio Supplement*: 'Which Station Was That?,' which identified foreign stations and programmes for listeners wanting to know what they had picked up, and 'Last Week's Log,' which commented on interferences and the quality of transmissions from major foreign stations in a mode resembling that of the weather forecast.

[3] From Charles Baudelaire's prose-poem 'N'importe où hors du monde.'

[4] Radio Tour Eiffel, the first French radio station, took its name from its location: its antennas were situated at the top of the Eiffel Tower.

3.2 FERNAND DIVOIRE: THE DON JUAN OF THE AIR WAVES

Translated by Emilie Morin. First published as 'Le Don Juan des ondes,' *Lumière et Radio*, 10 October 1929, 1–2.

A biographical sketch is included with 'The Zone of the Storms' (3.1).

• • •

Everyone experiences the joys of radio differently depending on their personal tastes. For some, radio is about listening to comedians singing clumsy café-concert songs; others want to hear opera or symphonies. But the true radio lovers have their hearts set on one station: the unknown station . . .

Remember your beginnings: first you 'picked up' Radio Tour Eiffel, Radio-Paris or Radio PTT,[1] and you picked them up so well that you feared your wireless set would explode. Then you searched for something else and you stumbled upon Daventry.[2] You turned to your family triumphantly and said: 'I am in England!'

This seemed absolutely miraculous to you. But just as automobile drivers are crazy about speed, radio lovers are crazy about distances. After England, you found Germany. Then the problems started: there are so many German broadcasts; where were you?

At first, the joy of 'being in Germany' swept everything else away. Then you found yourself trying to distinguish one radio station from another, for each of them was saying the same thing at the same time; only one thing made you happy: identifying one of these stations before bedtime. But perhaps there were some that you still had not managed to identify. Your

---

[1] Radio-PTT, a state-owned radio station set up in 1923, had different names over time: 'Poste de l'ESPTT,' 'Radio PTT,' 'les PTT' and, once its regional network started to expand, Paris-PTT. The PTT (Postes, Télégraphes et Téléphones) was the organisation administering the postal services, telegraph and telephone in France.

[2] 5XX Daventry was the BBC's first short-wave international station. The station, which began to broadcast in 1925, had the world's first long-wave transmitter.

wireless magazines gave you some indications: a chime here, some trumpets there, some metronomes here and there . . .[3] But who can differentiate a metronome set at 170 beats per minute from a metronome set at 210 beats per minute? Then, just when everything suggested that you were in Berlin – for example – you heard words that did not correspond at all to what your radio magazine said you should have heard. A gentleman announced: 'Deutsche Rundschau!' and this did not correspond to anything laid out in the list in front of you.[4]

One day, the realm of your delights expanded even more: the gentle voice of a woman spoke to you – to you personally, you knew that much! And the voice said to you: 'Hello! This is Bratislava.'

Such a soft voice, so nicely modulated . . . Did you not feel that you were falling in love, just a little, with Bratislava's charming voice?

And once Bratislava came along, you managed to recognise the other Czech radio stations: Prague, Brno, Moravska-Ostrava . . . And then you started searching for Spain and for Italy.

Milan: another female voice, low-pitched and clear, very different from Bratislava's charming voice. You tried to persuade yourself that the figures stamped on ancient Roman coins would have spoken that way. Then you picked up Milan, Turin, Genoa and perhaps Rome. But Naples eluded you. Then you picked up Barcelona and Madrid, too. And you – that same you who made a brutal exit from the French stations when they praised certain makes of soap or automobile accessories – took great pleasure in how funny Barcelona's male voice became in the Spanish publicity announcements . . .

And you kept on searching. One day, a big debate erupted at home. Your wife claimed: 'This is German, I am sure of it!' With authority, you replied: 'It can only be Dutch or a Scandinavian language, and you know nothing about it all.'

In your mind, 'a Scandinavian language' made you likely to win on three counts, since it could be Norwegian, Swedish or Danish. And when it was proven that it was Dutch, the prestige that you enjoyed at home grew even more.

One day, you finally managed to break your listening habits. Was that Motala you found, perhaps, over there, with 'the Scandinavians'? Or was it Poland? After that, you had only one ambition: to hear the bells of the Kremlin . . . But that is unlikely to happen anytime soon.

---

[3] Divoire is referring to the sound signals which differentiated radio stations from one another. Radio magazines and handbooks occasionally published tables with brief descriptions of these sound markers, especially in the late 1920s.

[4] A long-established German periodical.

After that, when you had money to spend, you tried to make a short wave set work, and you promised yourself that you would hear Nairobi and Java that day.

Your wife asked: 'Where is Nairobi?'

And your prestige grew even more, because you were able to say: 'In Africa, near the Indian Ocean.'

Now you are, in your abode, the man who can distinguish Spanish from Italian, German from Dutch. And, the other day, after hearing bagpipes on the radio, you affirmed that the speaker had a Scottish accent. Which station was that? It did not feature in your magazine programmes, and every so often you return to it, still, to try and fathom its secret.

All this knowledge was not built in the space of a day, nor indeed in the space of a month. Some evenings, you got lucky and found three or four of 'them'; on other evenings, you listened to jazz for three hours without hearing any clues as to where you might be. According to the wavelength, it might have been here, or there; but where?

One day you began to think that, soon enough, radio would no longer interest you.

'With my wireless set,' you said, 'I think I have picked up just about everything I can.'

And that evening you found a new radio station. You heard aeroplanes in conversation with Le Bourget airport; you found something, somewhere in Italy, Switzerland or Germany that may have been a radio station, if it wasn't a simple interference – you couldn't tell. Then, you searched for all the stations that you ought to have been able to pick up but had not been able to find yet; it took you some time to find Budapest, and you kept on circling around Poland without managing to pin it down.

The radio lover always has an unknown station still to pick up: the unknown station that he chases without cease, without ever finding it.

The radio lover is like an insatiable Don Juan: anything that he has come to 'know' stops being of interest to him instantly, and he is always attracted to novelty, always searching further ahead. Will this Don Juan ever reach his limits? Never. The unknown station will always be there. And when he is finally on the cusp of picking it up, a new Prague Plan will burst his sky open.[5]

And everything will start anew, once again.

---

[5] The Prague Plan, implemented in June 1929, dealt with wavelength allocations across Europe.

3.3 GUIDO SOMMI PICENARDI: MURMURS FROM THE ETHER

Translated by Nicoletta Asciuto. First published as 'Susurri dell'etere,' *Radiocorriere*, 19–25 May 1935, 15.

Guido Sommi Picenardi (1892–1949) was an Italian musician and avant-garde composer interested in Futurism, and a radio critic who wrote for the EIAR's weekly radio magazine *Radiocorriere* throughout the 1930s, contributing a weekly column entitled 'Susurri dell'etere' from 1931 to 1936. He is often mistaken for his cousin Gianfranco, a militant Fascist and notorious anti-Semite, and little is known about him beyond his wealth and aristocratic origins, his marriage to Princess Pignatelli d'Aragona Cortez, a sculptor, and the portrait that Tamara de Lempicka painted of him in 1925. He became seen as an opponent to Fascism during the Second World War and was tortured on that account in 1945.[1]

* * *

One of my occasional treats in the evening is to sit alone in front of the radio with the lights turned off, and roam blindly through the ether, searching for unknown waves until I receive a fleeting gift of music and words from each one of them, as if bestowed by an unknown woman who ventures into my house singing, and leaves still singing, without introducing herself. I often recognise a programme by the tone of the broadcast, by the sound quality of its pauses, or by the voice of its announcer: yet, for as long as the mystery lasts, the search for errant harmonies spreading across infinity makes for such a generous yet intangible treasure trove of unexpected possibilities that the imagination never wearies of it.

Tonight, during one of my aimless wanderings, for instance, from the magic box that renews the daily miracle of making harmony out of the silence of the world, I suddenly picked up a voice. Like a melodious spring suddenly welling up, a feminine voice of rare beauty flowed out of the loudspeaker, so pure and so soft that I could have imagined her as a creature from heaven, had she not spoken human words.[2] Sweetly grave, warmly vibrant, the voice filled my dark

---

[1] See Serena Benelli, 'Le sculture della collezione Sommi Picenardi,' *Concorso: Arti e Lettere* 11 (2018): 11–12.

[2] Sommi Picenardi's feminisation of radio dovetails with Futurist practices, notably with Marinetti and Masnata's manifesto 'La Radia.' Masnata explained that they gave radio 'a

and solitary room with its presence, turning into a passionate soul echoing and reverberating: then it switched off and vanished, swallowed up, perhaps, by the nocturnal monster the technicians, so apt at coining barbarisms, call 'fading'.[3]

Where did you come from, amazing voice, found by chance, and lost by chance, singing prodigy of only a few moments? To whom did you belong? Turn the electric light back on, look at the micrometre, check the daily schedule in *Radiocorriere*: it would have been easy for me to find out . . . I shall never know. Or I will only know this: that charming voice came from the depths of space, travelled marvellous distances on its silent pilgrimage, crossing paths with a hundred other voices, equally muted, and was suddenly captured like a fleeting shadow, offering me a moment of emotion, caressing my spirit with the wing of a dream woven with accents of melody.

In our present age, abundant in Doubting Thomases – each of us priding ourselves on being practical and shrewd, unwavering in our determination never to fall into the error, celebrated in the famous fable, of deserting one's prey for a shadow – how bizarre this phenomenon of being enchanted by shadows arising out of the screen projections of the most popular theatres, and out of the invisible world introduced into the intimacy of our homes through the radio!

At the cinematograph, you shall see the crowd get excited by the reflections of absent characters – moving shadows on the screen. The crowd loves them, pursues them, is happy to find them again. They breathe life into the memories of the crowd; they invigorate its reverie; for the young boy, the Rudello[4] of the twentieth century, the Hollywood star is his faraway Princess; the young girl copies the clothing and hairstyle of said princess, mimics her posture and even her gestures of seduction and love. Spurred on by enthusiasm, the audience calls divas by their Christian names: Greta, Joan, Brigitte; the audience applauds them as if they were present and not simply reflections of shadows.

For the cinema spectators, entertained, moved to tears, instructed, admiring with reverent familiarity, these figures basically represent models of an exemplary

---

name with a feminine ending because that is the gender of almost all the arts, from painting [*la pittura*] to sculpture [*la scultura*], from architecture [*l'architettura*] to poetry [*la poesia*].' Margaret Fisher, '"The Art of Radia": Pino Masnata's Unpublished Gloss to the Futurist Radio Manifesto: Introduction,' *Modernism/modernity* 19, no. 1 (2012): 155–8.

[3] Fading was defined in BBC glossaries of the period as the 'variation in strength of a signal received from a distant station, assumed to be due to changes in the Heaviside layer altering the angle of reflection of the transmitted ray in an irregular manner.' Technicians also had at their disposal a 'fade unit or mixing unit,' which connected a potentiometer to the microphone-amplifier circuits and enabled them to modulate signal strength. 'Glossary of Technical Terms,' *BBC Hand Book 1928* (London: British Broadcasting Corporation, 1928), 268.

[4] The fate of Rudello, hero of Vincenzo Ferroni's tragic opera *Rudello* (1890), is shaped by his all-consuming love for Countess Melisanda.

and enviable humanity. Yet, I repeat, they are nothing but reflections of shadows: they are simple images magnified hugely, passing on the screen, elusive, non-existent, just like the black-and-white flight of a swallow in the azure sliding over the waters, its reflection only visible for a brief moment.

In front of the loudspeakers, the realm of shadows comes to the fore and takes on a completely different form. We hear it; we no longer see it. For those of us stepping into the aesthetic circle of the blind, the shadows are now sounds, and their guise is music and words . . . Beings we cannot glimpse come in, come near us, talk to us, sing, weep, swear, beg, shout, sigh so close to our ears that we cannot elude the weakest or most fleeting note. Yet speakers, actors, musicians, singers have neither gestures nor face, and the whole expression of their soul is collected in words and sounds, so that nothing, other than an echo and an interval, fills the void created by silence opening and stretching between one word and the next, between one set of notes and the next.

We might believe at that moment that we are communing with spirits in a wholly esoteric realm, as if every word were not, more or less, part of the everyday language currently in use, and as if music did not belong to a well-known repertoire . . .

But gradually we realise that we have formed particular relationships and have virtually become accustomed to these 'absent' and 'invisible' people entering our home and living in our rooms. We picture them according to our inspirations and our fancy: not out of a whim however, but on the basis of probable identities and auditory suggestions. Likes and dislikes spontaneously grow. Our imagination opens for us a workshop of wizards, producing characters, landscapes, scenes: faces are being drawn, forms cut, attitudes formed. For the theatre of the blind, the radio, we create the actors, we make them move, dress them, and make them live in a physical, yet simultaneously fantastic, reality . . .

Thus, dreams – expelled from contemporary life, alongside poetry, proscribed by men who merely seem to wish to rest their minds, eyes, hands and desires on solid materiality – return from exile and defeat banishment.

Dream and poetry are reborn in our most popular and most modern forms of entertainment, cinema and radio: what do they represent if not the eternally seductive mystery which encircles our inner life with a halo of unspeakable beauty?

Indiscernible mystery before us, play of visible and invisible spirits, of visual and acoustic forces, what else are you if not the revenge of illusion over the heart of man, if not another, however temporary, victory for emotional attitudes once believed to be lost? What are you, if not a mysterious revelation of the unknowable world, a glimpse of the magical sphere of hopes where the best in us thrives, a harmonious revelation like that sweetly grave, warmly vibrant voice that invited me to pause in the ether a while ago, during my adventurous nocturnal hunt, the voice that briefly took me out of the realm of real things, that embraced me for a few instants, almost as if the device before me, interlaced with electrical valves, mechanical tricks, wheels and metallic wires, were an instrument of witchcraft . . .?

Science, in the pride of its early conquest and its power to dispel the atmosphere that once produced and nurtured our beliefs in magic, is now, in its shiny laboratories and through the rapid churning of laws regulated by dry mathematical formulae, recreating that very atmosphere, and it is even going so far as to draw on those zones of psychology and human consciousness that science had previously denied to itself and to others!

3.4 ROSE MACAULAY:
THE ARM-CHAIR MILLENNIUM

First published as 'The Arm-Chair Millennium,' *Radio Times*, 14 January 1927, 97–8.

Rose Macaulay (1881–1958) was a British novelist and literary critic, and a prolific journalist who wrote for magazines including *Time and Tide*, *Good Housekeeping*, *The Spectator* and the *New Statesman*. She wrote regularly for the *Listener* from 1934 to 1957, contributing witty articles about literature and culture, and gained preeminence as a radio critic and broadcaster after the Second World War. During the 1920s and 1930s, her contributions to radio programmes were occasional but varied: she gave readings, contributed to debates and general knowledge games, and readings from her works were broadcast. Her first BBC appearance was in 1926, for a debate titled 'Must the Novel Decline in Vogue?'. In 1937, she was invited to serve on the BBC's Talks Advisory Committee (the only other woman invited was Megan Lloyd George). She served on the BBC Spoken English Committee's Permanent Specialist Subcommittee from 1938 until its formal suspension in early 1940 (she and Cynthia Asquith were the only women).

• • •

A bright millennium (why do we thus limit our expected felicities to periods of a thousand years?) seems to be rapidly approaching. It is to be a millennium of comfort and ease; an arm-chair millennium.

What preachers have, for the last several centuries, called 'this age of hurry and unrest' is drawing to a close. Already we need not leave our happy homes in order to hear music, for we have music pouring into our sitting rooms, bedrooms, or wherever we elect to hear it. No more, either, need we go out to dance, for dance music fills our passages and parlours and we can Charleston round the dining-room anyhow until midnight.

Nor is it necessary to sally forth in search of oratory (if we chance to have a taste for this pleasure), for ever and anon, and quite often enough to suit most of us, the sonorous voices of eloquent speakers declaim into our drawing-rooms. Nor need Sunday evening services any more be attended in person, for those of us who have a fancy for these can join in prayers, hymns, psalms and sermons sitting on our own sofas. Many persons, indeed, do this who never dreamed, nor ever would dream, of being found within a church.

As to the drama, the arrangements for its transmission to an arm-chair audience are not yet completed; at present they can only hear it, which is unsatisfactory, if economical and comfortable; but one understands that before long television will give us quite a good view of the stage and performers. That, for many of us, will be the millennium. To see and hear a play every night, without further trouble and expense than one's own wireless set entails, without the tedium of going out and coming back and the discomfort of being surrounded by other people as noisy and tiresome as ourselves (for those in our homes we should be able, with a little firmness, to keep in order) – here indeed is bliss, only a little marred by the fact that we cannot choose what play we see, but must accept what is given us. And, if our taste is rather for the Silent Drama, we shall doubtless be able soon to behold that too, captions and all.

All the same, we shall not even then have attained perfect convenience. There will still be life to be lived, and I, for one, feel strongly that we ought not to have the trouble of living it. *Everything* ought to be done for us by what is, oddly enough, called wireless, and what I, observing the tangle, as of nests and vipers, which crawls profusely about my own set and runs down my passage, prefer to call wires.

Yes; everything should be done for us; why not? It is rumoured that we may soon have rushing into our homes over the wires all kinds of domestic help; unseen power will come at our need, and will clean our rooms, wash our dishes, cook our food, run up meals to our arm-chairs on electrically propelled tables, make our beds, turn on our baths, divest us of our clothes and dress us again, shave us, wash us, do our hair, fling us into bed.

And as to our recreations, why should we not have dinner parties by wireless of an evening, instead of sallying out from our homes to the homes of others? Turn us on to any dinner party where there is jollity, wit, the feast of reason and the flow of soul, transmit to us the taste of savoury viands (this should be a simple business) and let us sit and enjoy the evening without trouble.

It may be objected that, if everyone thus sat at home, there would be no dinner parties to be broadcast to them, but to provide these should, of course, be the task of the staff at Savoy Hill. As for the public-houses, they may as well, when these arrangements are completed, close down, for every sensation they provide of liquor imbibed will be conveyed to us, and even, if desired, the sensation of having imbibed too much.

But broadcasting will have to become also more selective; each set owner must be able to call for what he wants and get it; he will set his wavelength for a Scotch and splash, or a small lager, or a large raspberry syrup, without necessarily inflicting these beverages on others.

Indeed, this matter of individual selection is the most important of the points which the broadcasting authorities must see to. In a world with so many million different tastes and desires, it is not to be expected that we should all want to see and hear the same things. At present there is nearly always someone in each home ready to say 'turn that nonsense off' just when the others are enjoying themselves. There is no reason why one listener should not enjoy 'Who's My Baby?' while others listen to Bach, Debussy, or Sir Oliver Lodge on the atom.[1]

In the millennium, those of us who have a whim to see a little country landscape, without the trouble of taking a walk or a journey, will be shown vignettes of fields, woods and lanes which would cause others to expire of boredom. Those who wish to do so will be able to enjoy country scenery without the tedium of 'living in Kent and being content,' or of 'going to Surrey and living without worry,' while those more urban souls who find the home and other counties distasteful, and prefer Art to Nature, will instead look at picture exhibitions from their chairs (but Heaven forbid that those who lack this taste should have to do so).

And for those with a taste for literature there will be reading aloud of infinite variety, so that never again need we trouble to wear out our eyes by studying print. As to those of us who desire to write, the gift of words will rush into us along the wires, and we shall be electrically impelled to fluency, if not to intelligence. Our pens will be propelled over the paper as if planchette pushed them, and page after page will rapidly be filled with dashing electric thoughts.

I should like all this to occur. I hold that there has always been too much action and initiative in this world where all things travail together. We have made of it a restless, untranquil place, in which created beings, human and other, hurtle about from spot to spot, hectically intent on their private ends. Why, for instance, go forth to see doctors, dentists, osteopaths, and other healers, when the same treatment could be so much more restfully meted out to us

[1] The British physicist Oliver Lodge (1851–1940) gave frequent talks on BBC programmes from 1924 onwards, and delivered weekly talks on the atom on 2LO London in 1926.

as we sit at home? We should be able to press a button and be – well, not healed, for to heal human ills is usually beyond the skill either of human or electrical physicians, and can only be done by the processes of time – but anyhow, treated.

I contemplate starting a Society for Not Taking Any Trouble. Most societies seem rather to have been started with some other end in view than this; it is quite time that mine got going. As to most of the societies now functioning, a short and convenient way with them has been suggested, which would suspend their activities and hasten the advent of the arm-chair millennium; they should each pair with some society of opposed tendencies, as do Members of Parliament on opposite sides of the House. Thus, the Anti-Vivisection Society should pair with the Society for Anatomical Research, the Vegetarians' Guild with the Butchers' Union, the Birth Controllers with the More Men for the Empire League, Fascists with Socialists, the Miners' Federation with the Coal Owners' Association; and the newspapers might do a little pairing too; and as to that, and while we are on the subject of pairing, and not wishing to be in the least offensive, what about a little of it among private persons? We all know some people who would be better paired than actively functioning; perhaps most of us would.

But here we are on delicate and controversial ground. This paper started with an exaltation of the marvels of science and the pleasures of inactivity, and an exhortation to keep both of these going, only more so; let it end on the same note – that of perfect peace.

3.5 FRITZ ZOREFF: RADIO DRAMA AND THE INNER VISION

Translated by Emilie Morin. First published as 'Le théâtre radiophonique et la vision intérieure,' *Comœdia*, 22 July 1932, 5.

Fritz Zoreff (also spelt Zoref, 1893–1948) was an Austrian author from Vienna with a background as theatre director and musicologist. He wrote comic operas, screenplays and scenarios for silent and musical films in the late 1920s and early 1930s. He turned to radio in 1932, adapting Carl Millöcker's operetta *Der Bettelstudent* ('The beggar student') for broadcasting, and writing a radio play about blindness entitled

Das andere Land, which associates the disability of its main character with radio's lack of a visual dimension. These works were broadcast by Radio Wien (Vienna) in January and July 1932 respectively. The present article appeared in the French press in 1932; that same year, Zoreff published an essay in *Radio Wien*, the Ravag's weekly magazine, highlighting the needs and specificities of radio drama, and the differences between radio and stage performance.[1]

●　　●　　●

The listener should not accept the image presented to him: instead, he must be able to create that image himself.

Radio drama requires a new approach to dramaturgy.

Some have said that pure radio drama, that is to say the domain of the spoken word and music, descends directly from the epic, which in turn originates from the dawn of culture, and is intimately tied to the sensibility and the thought of the people. The epic was born within the people, and, through this very fact, it remains familiar to the people, preserving within its living form the memory of the glorious past, the image of the present and a glimpse of the future.

But the epic, while it calls upon the imagination of the listener and asks him to assemble images within his mind (and this is precisely how the epic has opened the way for the radio drama of today, with its focus on hearing, apperception, figuration and visual images), is in essence epic, and for that reason it inhibits the feeling of spontaneity that the experience of immediacy can create. This is the abyss that separates the epic from radio drama. We do not want to be *told* the story of what happened; we want to *live* through it as spectators, in the narrow sense of the word, even if we can only do so through the images that we create within ourselves, inside our minds, from reportage presented to us by our ears.

Such a synthesis of apperception, epic poetry and nature, which is a synthesis of dramatic meaning and dramatic effect, forces dramaturgy to venture onto uncharted paths. The ideal radio drama, whose theoretical exigencies are much easier to define than its form, should prevent the listener from feeling the absence of something or someone to look at, and should stimulate the imagination to such a degree that the images invoked by one's inner vision replace 'theatricality' as the principal characteristic of the drama, and take over.

The description spoken by an eye-witness – that is, reportage in its elementary form: also an approximation, also a primal form – will not suffice. It is only suited to the broadcasting of news when it is accompanied by an acoustic

---

[1] Fritz Zoreff, 'Millöcker's *Der Bettelstudent* als Hörspiel,' *Radio Wien*, 15 January 1932, 4–5.

illustration that evokes the atmosphere of the place where the event is unfolding: the hubbub of a crowd, the sound of applause, the noise of a racing car.

In a tragedy, the background of sound can be used to animate the acoustic scene and, through speech or song, it can invite the imagination of the listener to create visual images. The intimate events that define the drama properly speaking can only be exposed through the telling of the action in a way that makes the listener feel as though the characters' movements and feelings have become tangible.

This 'reflected' form is less cumbersome and less intrusive than spoken description.

The reflection within the human mind of the action or the psychological evolution of the drama that is created through speech alone can develop more delicately, more artistically, just as a raw image taken from real life can become sublime once it is placed under the play of shadows.

It is through acoustic means alone that radio drama must explore the full scope of any dramatic action of great magnitude. It remains necessary, nonetheless, to take into account the technical factors, which sometimes prevent the play from reaching the desired intensity and greatness. Differences of sensibility and imagination between individual listeners endowed with very different personalities can give rise to different dramatic possibilities when it comes to exploiting the value of the same plot, and can channel the creative work done by the listener in different directions. For example, a catastrophe in a mine cannot be fully rendered through acoustic means alone, but through the conglomeration of isolated and individual facts – by presenting the different reactions triggered off by this event, including those of the mine's owner, the employee in charge and the wife of a victim.[2] From all this a mosaic can be composed to convey the atmosphere and create a powerful play.

Such a form remains bound by the intangible law of the radio play: the characters should be opposed to one another and their lineaments should be sketched out as clearly as possible. If the author succeeds in delineating his characters so that their reflected images arise in the mind of every listener spontaneously and effortlessly, while still assuming a form specific to every individual listener, then many unnecessary words will fall away from the most laboured of the dialogues created by the new radio dramaturgy. The goal is to create dramas whose composition, structure and dramatic palette are so persuasive that they force the listener to become a creator himself, by drawing on his inner vision, instead of accepting the image presented to him as he would do in a theatre.

---

[2] This is a reference to Richard Hughes's *A Comedy of Danger*, commonly seen as the first BBC play written especially for radio.

3.6 ENRICO ROCCA: FROM A GEOGRAPHY OF THE INVISIBLE

Translated by Nicoletta Asciuto. First published as 'Geografia dell'invisibile,' *Panorama dell'arte radiofonica* (Milan: Bompiani, 1938), 17–18, 20–1, 22–4, 26–7, 28.

Enrico Rocca (1895–1944) was an Italian journalist and literary critic, and a translator renowned for his translations of Stefan Zweig. He was Jewish. He worked for various Fascist periodicals and newspapers including *Roma Futurista*, for which he acted as editor, *L'Impero*, which he founded with Emilio Settimelli and Mario Carli, and *Il Lavoro Fascista*. He became associated with Futurism after the First World War, just as he became interested in Fascism; he joined the Futurist Political Party in 1918 and the Fasci di Combattimento created by Mussolini in 1919, becoming one of the few Futurists to be recognised as 'Fascists of the First Hour'. His direct involvement with Fascism was short-lived, and he lost interest in politics after 1922. During the 1930s, he became involved with radio broadcasting, giving occasional talks on EIAR programmes and contributing to the judging of writing competitions; he taught classes on radiophonic genres and directed the Centro di Preparazione Radiofonica, a centre founded in Rome in 1936 to train radio journalists, announcers and other radio professionals. Thrown into precarity by the Italian Racial Laws of 1938, Rocca became increasingly disillusioned with Fascism. He continued to write under a pseudonym. In 1944, he worked for Radio Napoli, then an American radio station, delivering daily radio broadcasts in May and June. He took his own life that year, feeling that his position, as an Italian Jew who had worked for and against Fascism, had become untenable.[1] His book *Panorama dell'arte radiofonica*, published in 1938, is a transnational history of radio writing that primarily discusses developments in Italy, France, Germany and Britain, while also briefly considering Northern and Eastern Europe, China, Brazil and Mexico.

• • •

---

[1] See Enrico Rocca, *Diario degli anni bui*, ed. Sergio Raffaelli (Udine: Gaspari, 2005); Günter Berghaus, 'The Futurist Political Party,' in *The Invention of Politics in the European Avant-Garde (1906–1940)*, eds. Sascha Bru and Gunther Martens (Amsterdam: Rodopi, 2006), 163, 168; Selena Daly, *Italian Futurism and the First World War* (Toronto: University of Toronto Press, 2016), 230 n4.

The empire of radio encompasses the extent of the universe and its depth, nearly all the domains of the spirit.

For those of you who are not easily satisfied by words and who only believe – as if in pious surrender to an oracle – the often treacherous verdict of numbers, we shall add that this invisible empire radiates from more than 2,000 transmitters, it speaks from 68 millions of devices, and influences 270 millions of listeners scattered across the most familiar and the most unlikely parts of the world.

But did some philosopher not say that the minute you start counting, you stop understanding? Even without these figures, the miracle remains: a prodigy of the most Italian of brands, whereby the world is translated into sound, becomes volatile, defies space and, shedding earthly substance, achieves ubiquity.[2] This is, however, an enchantment available to all, no more amazing than rain or shine, no more than sunset or sunrise, no more than the leaves turning green on the trees, no more than the thousand wonders the world offers us – every one of which, if we pause to think about it, is marvellous. With the essential difference that, where it is our spirit alone that has made nature seem banal, radio's magic has been diminished far too early by man's incorrigible mediocrity, subduing this newest instrument to repeat what are too often paltry and hackneyed things. [. . .]

What happens, exactly, when we are listening to a loudspeaker? A voice comes out of God knows where, makes its way to our ears, reaches our brain directly, and summons up the intended concepts or images. Typically, though, the world sneaks into us in auditory form, devoid of its visible substance, and yet somehow enriched by this lack, which stimulates the possibility of a collaborative integration. [. . .]

[A] noise heard in isolation can suggest any number of things. The droning of a propeller in the air reveals an aeroplane, suggests the act of flying, gives a fading or intensifying sense of distance (and even, in non-radiophonic situations, the idea of direction), and with its duration provokes an awareness of time. Obviously, an undifferentiated thud from upstairs or a distant explosion (which may be a gun firing or a tyre bursting) are less richly indicative acoustic perceptions; the stamping of a horse, the horn of a car, the sound of a bell speak

---

[2] Rocca is alluding to the Italian inventor and entrepreneur Guglielmo Marconi (1874–1937). Marconi's scientific experiments were conducted outside Italy, as were most of his business activities; the Marconi Wireless Telegraph Company and its subsidiary companies were primarily based in London and North America. Marconi was a staunch supporter of Mussolini from the early days; although their friendship ebbed and waned, Marconi remained for Mussolini a critical ally and a key link to Britain and North America. See Marc Raboy, *Marconi: The Man Who Networked the World* (New York: Oxford University Press, 2016), 461, 455–626.

such a flatly intelligible language that it is unsurprising to find them at the top of the list of the most banal sound effects. An equally well-known fact is that sounds, as well as noises, sometimes have the power to stir sentiments both grave and gay: let us leave aside the sacred ringing of the bronze bells, with their expressive and varied language, or the overdone example of the pendulum, suggestive of the ineluctable passing of time or destiny; let us think, rather, of that sense of fervid activity we get from the fury of hammers boisterously beating the anvil, or the unnerving obsession that the rhythmic dripping of a badly closed water tap or leaking gutter can convey.

In short, let us say that if sight speaks to us through things, then hearing speaks to us through the noises which are the voice of things; through the sounds which are noises made transparent; through the yells and screeches which are the language of animals; through the cries and shouts which, expressing joy, rage, grief, are the most elementary and most eloquent expressions of an emotion; and, finally, through words, the articulate evolution of a cry and the verbal equivalent of things. [. . .]

For the sake of clarity, shall we add that this alphabet of sounds, too, is made up of vowels and consonants; of emancipated sounds that can be perfectly well understood alone and that stroll around nonchalantly in the radiophonic world, and of consonants that need the support of vowels to stand up? Our clever reader has already understood that vowels are the ancient languages of word and music, and without whose timely intervention noises and sounds, clear and expressive though they be, would constitute (one readily imagines) a rather squalid radiophonic programme. When the ring of a telephone suddenly breaks the silence, it indicates someone is calling, but does not specify anything else. We need the intervention of a voice for the call to acquire radiophonic meaning. If nothing follows a dull roar from the loudspeaker, the listener will be perplexed. If, on the other hand, cries of pain and someone shouting 'Stretcher-bearer!' follow the explosion, it will be clear that a war scene is being transmitted. Rings and rumbles are radiophonic consonants, while cries are semi-vowels. Taken separately, they have, at best, less expressive value than the facial expression of a deaf-mute. Their random succession would mean little or nothing. In order, then, for a radiophonic action, whether real or artistic, to acquire some principle of meaning, noises and sounds need to be coupled with voice. What all the isolated or collected noises of the world would vainly try to trace – that is, the elementary sketch of a situation or the basic lineaments of a play – a single voice, or two contrasting voices at most, would easily manage. Only radiophonic theatre in its infancy could have believed that radio should revolve around noises and should therefore be in need of an abundant and naturalistic backdrop of sound effects. This is a crass mistake, not just in radio-drama. Nowadays everyone knows that the world begins with the human being, even radiophonically speaking: it starts with human speech.

If, however, there do exist autonomous acoustic elements able to create meaning by themselves, we should not deem less significant those other elements which, as we have observed, serve an auxiliary function. We should note that with radiophonic listening the ear becomes more sensitive to pairs of sounds as an extraordinarily effective means of conjuring up reality in a formless world. However, such pairing does not occur through ordering syllables, as this over-extended metaphor of the alphabet may well have let you suppose, but almost by way of a chemical law deeply affecting the balance between elements in a new compound. [. . .]

An ambiguous noise, perceived together with its cause, makes up a complete perception. Immersed in invisibility, detached from its source, it drowns in waves of generality. Over the radio, unless someone points it out to me, I will find it difficult to distinguish the droning of a swarm of flies from the buzzing of bees. On the other hand, invisibility, which is like atmosphere for the radio, is at times enough to make evocative noises which would not otherwise be so, and to make a part stand in for the whole. Some Morse code tapping, to which more tapping in a different timbre responds, evokes dialogues between ships and the coast, between boats and ships, between islands and continents; at the same time, it creates a sense of immensity. The bell, a way of simplifying a familiar optical-acoustic complex, stands for the church, the siren for the steamer, the crowing of a cock for the dawn. The capacity of hearing to perceive two noises or two sounds simultaneously frames the mountain cottage between bells ringing and cows bellowing, and the ballroom or café between a chamber orchestra and a hubbub of voices.

Even more than sounds and noises, however, the word undergoes the effects of invisibility on the radio. The word begins, so to speak, to lose its specific weight and tends to evaporate. In its printed form, the word is there, ready to be read again and again. Spoken by someone we can see, it is completed by facial expression; even when we are in a theatre, gesture and expression help us to understand the meaning of a sentence, which we may have partly missed. [. . .]

Radio, then – contrary to all that the common, exasperating definition of 'blind art' leads us to believe – is exercised by people with the ability to see for other people with the ability to see, and its ultimate aim is to stir what we shall call auditory sight in the listener. This faculty of seeing through the brain and the imagination can even plot with the necromantic powers of invisibility to exceed the permitted limits of common sight. [. . .]

It is to this extent that invisibility has turned the word into something other than what we know: extremely volatile, but extraordinarily protean; devoid of its optical attire, but full of unusual suggestive power.

3.7 ROLF GUNOLD: THE SEVENTH SENSE

Translated by Marielle Sutherland. First published as 'Der siebente Sinn,' *Funk*, 25 January 1929, 16.

Rolf Gunold (born Rudolf Gumbinner II, 1884–1949) was a German theatre actor who was among the first to experiment with writing radio plays. He was interested in the practical as well as the symbolic and mystical dimensions of radio. His play *Spuk* ('Ghost apparition'), subtitled *Eine Gespenstersonate in fünf Sätzen nach Motiven von E. T. A. Hoffmann* ('A ghost sonata in five movements based on E. T. A. Hoffmann'), broadcast by the Schlesische Funkstunde (Breslau) in July 1925, is commonly described as one of the first plays written specifically for radio in Germany, along with Hans Flesch's *Zauberei auf dem Sender*. Prior to that, Gunold had written another radio play, *Bellinzona: Eine funkdramatische Studie* ('Bellinzona: a study in radio drama'), which dealt with a railway disaster, and was presented as a kind of 'noise symphony' in the press. *Bellinzona*, published in *Der Deutsche Rundfunk* in 1925, was not broadcast until 1978, but Gunold's other plays – *Radiobolo, der Funkdeibel* ('Radiobolo, the radio-devil'), broadcast by the Westdeutsche Funkstunde (Münster) in 1926, and *Das pochende Herz* ('The beating heart'), broadcast by the Berlin Funkstunde in 1929 – had greater success. A note accompanying the present essay celebrated Gunold's international success, and stated that the manuscript of *Das pochende Herz* had been greeted with interest by radio stations in Lithuania and Norway, where translations and further performances were planned. A Jewish artist, Gunold was struck by a professional ban by the Reichskulturkammer, the Nazi Chamber of Culture, in 1934. How he went about living and surviving thereafter remains unknown.[1]

• • •

We have come to the conclusion, I believe, that we have six senses. I have a vague feeling that I possess a seventh: an acoustic sense. I recall very well that, even as a child, anything connected with sound, tone and noise made me disproportionately happy; in those days, a hissing locomotive was an acoustic revelation for me. Later on, it was music that captivated me; I nourished my

---

[1] Irmela Schneider, ed., *Radio-Kultur in der Weimarer Republik* (Tübingen: Gunter Narr, 1984), 238; 'Urteile über das erste akustische Drama,' *Schlesische Funkstunde*, 31 July 1925, 6; 'Das erste deutsche Funkdrama,' *Der Tag*, 7 June 1925, 12. Gunold's papers are held at Berlin's Jüdisches Museum; see https://objekte.jmberlin.de/object/jmb-obj-557598/ Sammlung+Familie+Gumbinner, last accessed 1 April 2021.

sense, in a manner of speaking, with the sound of the notes. And this world of resounding symphonies was soon enhanced by the world of technology with its manifold sounds, that symphony of work. I listened to the acoustics of the cosmos thundering through my ear; every sound within this strange, visible and invisible world, even the smallest, most inconspicuous sound, unheeded by thousands of people passing by in their hordes, would, like an alarm clock, trigger my seventh sense.

As beautiful as I found this gift that had been bestowed upon me by nature, as often and as deeply as it made me happy, it seemed to me entirely useless; but when I left school and went into the acting and directing professions, my 'acoustic gift' became an essential means of grasping the world of theatre and the art of speaking connected with it. In the beginning, there was the word in the theatre: it was there that I could systematically enrich my phonetic knowledge and develop my sense of sound; it was there that I learned how to translate the primordial sounds of nature into something artistic and spiritual. I experienced theatrical thunder, landslides, wind and rain machines in the same way, and to the same intensity, as I experienced the hissing locomotive of my childhood. Walking through heaven, earth and hell, treading the boards that signified the world, was of immense importance for my later pursuits

Despite this, my acoustic sense was only passively engaged; yet there was a deep urge within me to shape my sound visions creatively and put them to use.

Once the war ended, it took almost ten years for acoustic art, which had been so neglected, to awaken from its deep slumber. It was radio that achieved this miracle; it needed this new art form. It also meant that my moment had arrived. At long last, I could apply my 'seventh sense.' In 1924, rapidly, and without inhibition, I wrote my first radio drama 'Bellinzona.' The hissing locomotive of my childhood, the mysterious resounding and ringing of the railway track, acoustically so rich and vivid, came alive within my heart and mind; my pen ordered the chaos of sounds into the acoustic symbol of a new, emerging art form: the 'radio drama.'[2]

The rest was empirical progression. I conquered the noisy, external world of sounds, and tried to find a way to sublimate them. For me, this sound material had become 'acoustic symbols' of a new dramatic genre that had the highest level of intellectual discipline, yet was conveyed solely to the ear. Nowadays we call it 'the radio play.'[3]

And, in the final stage of this refinement of my seventh sense, I wrote 'Das pochende Herz,' which I hope will prove its worth across the air waves, 'everywhere.'

---

[2] *Funkdrama* in the original.
[3] *Hörspiel* in the original, the term coined in 1924 by Hans Siebert von Heister to designate a play conceived specifically for radio.

3.8 ELLA FITZGERALD: WIRELESS AND WOMEN

First published as 'Wireless and Women,' *Radio Times*, 30 November 1923, 330.

Ella Fitzgerald (b. 1887) is one of the oft-forgotten female architects of BBC programming. After an early career as a Fleet Street journalist, she was hired by the BBC in 1923 as a Talks Assistant with special responsibility for women's programmes. She was in charge of Children's Hour from April to November 1923; from April 1923 to March 1924, she oversaw the ill-fated Women's Hour (an early predecessor to the BBC's long-standing Woman's Hour, still running today), which consisted of two talks, six days a week, on topics pertinent to everyday life and often educational in nature; she contributed two talks to the series every week. She wrote for the *Radio Times* on at least one other occasion, to comment on Women's Hour lack of success.[1] After the suspension of Women's Hour, she continued to produce talks for women on other programmes. In 1926, she joined the BBC magazine *World-Radio* as Assistant, later becoming Assistant Editor. When *World-Radio*, which dealt with foreign broadcasting stations and BBC services across the British Empire, ceased publication in 1939, she became the BBC's Overseas Press Officer.[2]

* * *

THE NEW ANGEL IN THE HOUSE.

Little more than a year has passed since wireless first invaded the home. In that short space of time it has become, if not man's 'whole existence,' then the more important part of it, so far as his evenings at home are concerned.

And what of us women – the 'wireless widows' at whose expense cartoonists make merry? Have we come to regard our winged visitor as ally or antagonist?

Before we can decide it is necessary to make a comparison between *then* and *now*. It isn't easy to reconstruct a pre-wireless evening except by force of contrast, so I propose to begin with *now*, despite my husband's *sotto voce* imploration of the gods to enlighten him as to why no woman ever begins at the foundations of her argument!

---

[1] Ella Fitzgerald, 'In Reply to Mrs Belloc Lowndes,' *Radio Times*, 17 October 1924, 145.
[2] See Murphy, *Behind the Wireless*, 195–200; Kate Murphy, '"Brightening their Leisure Hours"? The Experiment of BBC Women's Hour, 1923–1925,' *Women's History Review* 29, no. 2 (2020): 183–96.

The Husband's View.

Wireless, according to my husband, is the wonder of all ages. It has, he says, taught woman to listen. Subtle, of course, but, like most sweeping assertions of masculine origin, it misses the corners. Wireless isn't wonderful because it has made woman listen. Woman always could, and sometimes did, listen. Wireless has made her want to listen. A distinction with a difference.

But is she encouraged by her household to cultivate this supposedly rare virtue? Well, any woman who is the possessor of a receiving set plus a family will recognize the following as a description, more or less accurate, of an average evening at home.

4.55 p.m. – Having settled the children down to tea at 4.30, 'mother' tunes in, and waits with what patience she can command for the cheery, 'Hallo, everybody! Blank Station calling.'

Listening Under Difficulties.

It comes at last. 'A talk on careers for women will now be given by – .'

'Mother! John's put three pieces of sugar in his second cup.'

'. . . now that practically all vocations are open to woman, educational opportunities equal to those of her brother are demanded by her, and – '

'Mother, quick! Sheila's choking! She's swallowed something.'

Having retrieved an adventurous plum-stone and restored order and apparent serenity among the older children, 'mother' is just in time to hear 'Blank Station closing down till six o'clock. Good afternoon.'

The Supreme Test.

At 5.57 the procedure is somewhat like this. Marshal children to their appointed places; settle heated dispute of the 'those are my head-phones' order (or turn the dog out and the loud-speaker on, as the case may be); proceed to enjoy the 'Children's Hour.'

Like all good things, this comes to an end. The children are put to bed, and at seven o'clock the magicianly powers of the stranger within our midst are put to the supreme test.

The head of the house, arrived home wearied and with temper slightly frayed at the edges after an 'off' day at the office, attacks the evening meal with the light of battle in his eye.

'Will he notice that the mutton is hashed?' is the question which grips the mind of his wife what time she casts beseeching glances in the direction of the loud-speaker.

'. . . Ipecuanas, 5 7/8ths; Montana-segrados, 2 11/12ths.'

So far all is well. The head of the house has forgotten that he is eating at all.

In the lull that follows the News Bulletin, the mistress of the house asks demurely, 'What *are* Ipecu-segrados? And why are they 5 11/14ths?' And man, ever ready to be guide and mentor to the sex which it was wisely ordained should look to him for information upon those matters which require the deeper understanding, first corrects her inexactitudes, and then proceeds to explain.

No Boundaries.

A 'Criticism' provides a sympathetic outlet for the master's pent-up irritation: and then, 'music hath charms' – undoubted charms! Thus soothed, each of a separate disquiet and attuned in harmony, the Head and the Heart of the House settle down to their nightly arm-chair adventures.

That is the great romance of wireless. It knows no boundaries. I may do my morning shopping in a New York emporium; lunch in Paris after a stroll along the boulevards, and in between that and tea in Japan amid mimosa and mousmés, my husband and I may sandwich in a big-game hunt in the heart of Africa and an expedition to the Arctic.

Consolations.

And if 'X Station closing down' brings us back to a sense of possibilities unprobed, there are consolations.

On the whole, the case for broadcasting is easily made. The receiving set may safely be regarded by woman as a collaborator rather than a competitor for the subduing of man to domesticity.

3.9 CAMILLA: THE WOMAN LISTENER

First published as 'Vox Angelica: The Woman Listener,' *Vox, The Radio Critic & Broadcast Review* 1, no. 1 (9 November 1929): 23.

Vox, The Radio Critic & Broadcast Review was an independent Scottish radio journal created by Hugh MacDiarmid (pseudonym of Christopher Grieve, 1892–1978) and Compton Mackenzie (1883–1972), two of the founders of the Scottish National Party; it appeared between November 1929 and February 1930. Mackenzie, then a regular BBC guest and *Radio Times* contributor, acted as the magazine's leading voice. *Vox* remained closely tied to the *Radio Times* and the *Listener* but offered sharp criticism of the BBC from a Scottish perspective, with articles denouncing the BBC's centralising impulses, its use of Standard English and the impact of the Regional Scheme upon the variety and accessibility of programmes. It also featured regular articles on radio genres, radio aesthetics and radio stations abroad.[1] The identity of Camilla, who contributed a regular column titled 'Vox Angelica' discussing programming from women's perspective, is unknown, but her assured and caustic tone invites speculation. It seems possible that Camilla was a pen name invented by the British author Faith Compton Mackenzie (1878–1960), who was then writing a great deal of journalism and specialised in gramophone music. She had been heavily and invisibly involved in her husband's publishing ventures – particularly his better-established magazine *The Gramophone*, for which she wrote under a pseudonym, F. Sharp.[2]

• • •

I have been reading a great deal in the papers recently to the effect that women who are at home during the day do not listen to wireless programmes. Several reasons have been given for this abstention, most of them existing, I imagine, in the minds of the men journalists who put forward the suggestion.

The first was that women cannot listen if they object to the colour and design of the receiving set. I find this a curious libel on feminine mentality. A woman who has to put up with man's comic idea of labour-saving houses, of gas-stoves, of suitable locations for old slippers and of the importance of the litter he calls his 'private papers,' will not boggle over a little thing like the line of a loud speaker or the colour of the mahogany cabinet.

The next objection was that women do not know how to work wireless sets. Most modern sets are so simply controlled that this statement is a further libel. There are, however, men who have devised sets so complicated that none but the makers can tune them, and even they spend nearly the whole evening over the process. There are such men. I am married to one of them. But these men can easily be persuaded to carry their technical skill a little further and provide a controlling plug which the most untechnical woman can attach or detach at will.

The third objection has something in it. It is that so much noise is made in the home already by children that the ear-weary mother will not consent to add wireless to the din. This is presuming the presence of at least three to four strong-lunged children in every home, figures which are not borne out by statistics. Nor does the journalist seem to know that between the hours of at least 10 and 3 p.m. these children, if they are over five, will be making, or attempting to make, their din in another place. There do remain, however, the mothers of children under five to whom this condition does apply, and who therefore, as I

---

[1] See Birgit Van Puymbroeck, 'Compton Mackenzie's and Hugh MacDiarmid's Early Broadcasting Critique: *Vox*, Modernism, and the BBC,' *Modernist Cultures* 14, no. 4 (2019): 522–42.
[2] See Faith Compton Mackenzie, *More Than I Should* (London: Collins, 1940), 136, 150, 214.

see, have no opportunity to listen during the day. If there are women who are clever enough to manage both their young children and a certain amount of listening, I hope they will write and say how they do it.

The fourth objection is that many women have so much to do that from the time the last member of the family goes out to the time when the first returns, they have not a single moment to themselves. I have no doubt that there are still devoted women of this kind. But if they see the wisdom of devoting one half-hour of the day to themselves, let them take the opportunity to declare that there is something for them in wireless, and that Dorothy must iron her own bits and pieces and Derek get up ten minutes earlier and tackle his untidiness.

The last objection, the one which is my chief concern and which I hope to make equally yours, is that there is nothing in the programmes suitable for women at home and, if there is, that they do not know about it.

The *Radio Times* is certainly not as helpful as it might be. It makes no mark between the day programmes, for which the audience must be mostly women at home, and the evening programmes, for which the audience may be anybody. A woman in a hurry might find it of assistance to have a column, 'For the Woman at Home,' giving at a glance the programmes of the week that she might be likely to find interesting. I have made such a column for myself from this week's *Radio Times*. I confess I do not find it enthralling. There is usually light music from 5XX between 1 p.m. and 2 p.m. There are concerts which seem very pleasant from 5GB every afternoon from 3 p.m. to 5.30 p.m. An odd talk or two from Manchester and Glasgow sound interesting and may be profitable if one can get these stations. Most of the afternoons from London are taken up with transmissions to schools. The matter of these talks is probably inviting. The manner, as probably, does not attract the woman who is already being educated by her husband, her young sons, her elder sisters, and her husband's relations. There are, further, the morning talks from London which are addressed specially to women. Three of these are housekeeping talks, two offering recipes. The fourth is a series of comments on the week in Parliament, to be given by various women Members. Two lines of treatment seem possible here. One is to give an outline of actual happenings, the other to stimulate interest in Parliament and its personalities so that women will be led to read the full newspaper reports for themselves. I wonder which line will be taken and which would be the more acceptable. Mrs Strachey, in her now concluded series of commentaries, seemed to presuppose an interest in affairs, but did not provide, to my mind, much to feed it.

The final series of morning talks is on defects in children's speech. As the speech-forming age is roughly between one and five, these talks can only be available and of use to those few particularly clever women whom I mentioned previously. If there are many more than I counted on, I hope they will contradict me to their full number.

All of these talks, I notice, are by women. I wonder if the women at home are as appreciative of this as the BBC thinks they ought to be. On the one hand there are the many writers who assert that women dress, cook, read and tune their minds to and for men. On the other hand the BBC, which infers that women desire efficiency and knowledge for their own sakes. Who can say which is right? Only, of course, the women who listen.

I have been looking through the columns of '*Listeners' Letters*,' and find that most of these are from men, or possibly from women, masquerading under masculine *noms-de-plume*. 'Aha!' says Mr Journalist, 'what did I tell you? Women don't listen and, when they do, they use no critical faculty!' That is masculine and foolish boasting. Every capable housekeeper spends half her time criticising. She criticises the efforts of the butcher, the fishmonger, and the greengrocer. She criticises still more the efforts of the laundry and the charwoman. She criticises, though more silently, the efforts of her husband to make a budget and of her children to grow up in next-to-no-time. And she can criticise radio programmes just as easily and as helpfully if she gets the habit. An odd letter to the BBC may not, she perhaps feels, achieve much, but many letters to me, each carrying its own particular piece of wisdom, may provide such a body of criticism as the BBC would not, indeed could not, ignore. If you are anxious to listen, to know what you want for the programmes, and to express your will, I hope that in these columns I may be your voice.

3.10 ERNST HARDT: THE ECHO OF THE LISTENERS' NEEDS

Translated by Marielle Sutherland. First published as 'Das Echo der Hörerwünsche,' *Die Werag* 2, no. 7 (1927): 25–7.

Ernst Hardt (born Ernst Stöckhardt, 1876–1947) was a German poet, novelist, playwright, theatre director, translator and radio producer. After directing Weimar's National Theater and the Schauspiel Köln, Cologne, he was appointed director of the Werag (Westdeutsche Rundfunk AG, the West German Radio Company, Cologne) in 1926. This text was published in the Werag's magazine *Die Werag*, created that year.

Alongside his administrative duties, Hardt directed radio plays, gave radio talks and readings, wrote essays about radio, and did a great deal to promote literature and the arts through his broadcasting work. In 1933, he was removed from his post by the Nazis, and was arrested and imprisoned alongside other prominent broadcasters of the Weimar era. Thereafter, he eked a meagre living from translation, odds and ends of literary work and journalism, working under a pseudonym.[1]

• • •

I would not wish to end this discussion with you without having considered, from a general point of view, the concept of radio and radio programming fostered by the intellectual and artistic directors of the Westdeutsche Rundfunk.

Radio! We have all now become accustomed to this word; we pronounce it like an everyday word. We have become accustomed to the thing itself, and we handle it like an everyday thing. And yet the technological invention of the wireless is surely one of the greatest miracles to come out of this recent period of miraculous technology. However, whereas the other miraculous gifts of the technological age have been barely capable of changing or perfecting the intellectual and spiritual face of humanity, the invention we call radio is one of those inventions of the millennium that is slowly, day by day, re-shaping the human soul and intellect, just as radio's sister invention – the printing press – has done. This miraculous power inherent in radio, which unconditionally affects anyone who enters into its sphere of radiance, enables us to discern the enormous amount of responsibility borne by those who work with it. It is their duty to bring to an almost immeasurable number of listeners, encompassing all ages, social classes and stages of human maturity, a sense of the vividness of life and a living culture, both their own and that of all peoples of the world; it is their duty to offer them emotional elevation, intellectual development and entertaining diversion. The labourer, the workman, the clerk, the salesman, the craftsman, the sick person confined to his bed, the blind man, the young boy the young girl, the housewife, the mother, the civil servant, the doctor, the farmer, the scholar, whether they live in solitude, close to nature in the country, or packed in tightly between iron and concrete in the big cities – it is to all of them that radio must bring new life in terms of intellect and entertainment and yet, at the same time, it should also *educate* the listener *in his own strengths, in his own tastes*, and how to *enhance* them. It should awaken a sympathy for

---

[1] See F. K. Richter, 'Ernst Hardt, 1876–1947: Ein Beitrag zur deutschen Neuromantik,' *Monatshefte* 39, no. 3 (1947): 190–4; Heide-Erika Koppe, 'Von der Mission des Rundfunks: Ernst Hardt,' *Literatur und Rundfunk 1923–1933*, 121–3; Karl H. Karst, 'Ernst Hardt (1876–1947),' *Geschichte im Westen. Halbjahres-Zeitschrift für Landes-und Zeitgeschichte* 7, no. 1 (1992): 99–116.

and receptiveness to things of an ever higher nature, on an ever higher level, for this is how it creates ever more happiness in ever more beautiful ways. The superior number and composite nature of the listeners, however, should never lead to the belief, for instance, that the intellectually or artistically cheap common denominator is good enough in terms of the product that is supplied to so many people. Instead, radio should always, as far as possible, aim to deliver a product of quality that will make the listener receptive to something better, that will awaken a desire for the best. Any other approach to radio would entail committing the same sin that would have been committed if the printing press had been used to disseminate cheap, shallow amusement rather than, primarily, the world culture we possess today. Let us not forget, ladies and gentlemen, that German workers make up a very large percentage of those who listen to German radio. Walter Rathenau, that great authority on world industry, said that listening to the wireless had made him into the most educated worker in the world.[2] He achieved this by seizing – *passionately* seizing – every available opportunity to educate himself and raise himself higher. If only for his sake, radio must be a vehicle of culture, otherwise the German worker will refuse to engage with it.

If we try to define the functions of radio more precisely, we find there are two distinctly separate spheres of activity. Within the first, radio must strive to make audible the greatest abundance of vivid life in terms of its intellectual, ethical, economic or artistic value or sensuous appeal, as we did, for example, with the broadcast from the Westfalenhalle.[3] As hundreds of letters testify, this one hour generated more interest in the sport of boxing than would otherwise have been possible over many years. This is how radio brings all corners of the world together, builds bridges between social classes, clans, nations, creating for each person and everyone reciprocally – like nothing else before – that great foundation of judicious life: knowledge of the world.

Radio's second sphere of activity is more autonomous and more creative. It takes upon itself the responsibility not only for selecting the content it provides but also for how it provides this, i.e. it strives to relate the sounds and reverberations of the content it provides directly to the technical characteristics of remote transmission and to the fact that the recipient can only receive the material via a single sense – the solitary ear.

One half of this second sphere of activity, the educational lecture, can be fully addressed by selecting a good scientist and speaker who is, at the same time,

[2] The Jewish writer, businessman and politician Walther Rathenau (1867–1922), who served as Foreign Minister in the early years of the Weimar Republic, was widely remembered owing to the circumstances of his assassination by a far-right group.

[3] The Westfalenhalle (Hall of Westphalia) in Dortmund regularly hosted major sporting events.

someone with humanity and soul, for there is nothing stronger than personality in radio broadcasting, and there is no sound in radio that is hollower or emptier than the absence of a human being.

The other half of this second sphere of activity consists mainly of any kind of art that can be made audible.

The actual intellectual laws of radio broadcasting, its fundamental laws, need to be explored further. The one thing we have already learned is that radio requires variation and diversity, for every one of the hundreds of thousands of listeners must be satisfied, and only variation can prevent the ear from becoming paralysed with fatigue. Nonetheless, this principle and this diversity must not lead to the kind of senseless cluttering we find in a warehouse; rather, this muddle must make sense.

So, ladies and gentlemen, what are the dangers faced by the programme builder? The greatest and most terrible danger is surely something you have not yet anticipated. He could make the fatal mistake of thinking he is more educated, more knowledgeable or more cultivated than his audience, extracted from a broad range of social classes, to whom he wishes to bring serious delectation, enhancement or amusement. His misapprehension may then easily cause him to lose all emotional intelligence and to believe he may not present his underrated audience with the same words, the same ideas, the same beauties, the same works he would present to those he himself holds in high regard. His misapprehension may lead to the foolish idea that these things are too elevated for a varied audience, that they will never ever be understood or appreciated. If, when talking to a manual labourer instead of a doctor or a civil servant in the top tenth income bracket, he fancies he must speak on a different intellectual and emotional level, he is forgetting that, ultimately, only a human being can talk to human beings. And so he ploughs on, collecting – in all honesty and with great effort – bronzed, tawdry nuggets, claiming his audience desires these and not the real golden nuggets he himself loves.

Woe betide the programme builder who falls foul of this error, for human dignity inexorably abides by the following principle: the more varied the audience is, the more respectfully it should be treated, which means the presiding artistic, aesthetic, scientific, musical, moral and ethical conscience should be all the more scrupulous and rigorous. This alone should be the programme builder's guiding principle.

Ladies and gentlemen, whoever you may be, in whatever life circumstances you may find yourselves, let us enter into a faithful pact of friendship with one another: the Westdeutsche Rundfunk aims to meet all your needs in terms of edification, enhancement, instruction, entertainment and diversion, as well as your irrepressible need for escapism and levity in these difficult times. The Westdeutsche Rundfunk is profoundly and earnestly committed to this task but it wishes to execute it as a faithful servant who understands his master as a fellow human being. This servant wishes to subtly guide his master if, weary with work, he embarks upon the wrong path and is on the point of unconsciously going astray. And do not be afraid to speak your mind to this servant as often as you wish, either with sincere politeness or sincere rudeness – however you may be inclined –; he will always answer you willingly, as he is obliged to do by the nature of his task: to be a faithful and wholehearted signpost and guide . . .

3.11 ANNETTE KOLB: FROM
BOOK OF COMPLAINTS

Translated by Marielle Sutherland. First published as *Beschwerdebuch* (Berlin: Rowohlt, 1932), 9–22.

Annette Kolb (born Anna Mathilde Kolb, 1870–1967) was a novelist, essayist and biographer. Born to a German father and French mother, she had attachments to both Germany and France, and was a staunch and indefatigable pacifist. Struck by a travel ban, she spent the First World War in Switzerland, returning to Germany in 1923. In 1933, her work was banned in Germany, and she left for Ireland, where her sister lived; she then emigrated to Paris, becoming a French citizen in 1936, and continued to visit Ireland regularly. In 1941, she moved to the United States, where she felt, in her own words, 'grateful and unhappy';[1] in 1945, she returned to Germany. She had a keen interest in radio broadcasting, and gave readings from her work on the Stuttgart, Frankfurt, Leipzig, Langenberg, Munich and Berlin stations at various points between 1926 and 1933. In August 1932 and February 1933 in particular, she read excerpts from *Beschwerdebuch*, a collection of witty fragments published in late 1932 from which the present text originates, on the Frankfurt and Langenberg stations. Thereafter, she was no longer heard on German radio but continued to engage with broadcasting nonetheless: she read from her work on two occasions in 1937, on the Swiss Beromünster station and on Radio Wien (Vienna), and gave a talk on Wagner on the Irish station Radio Eireann in 1947. She was an excellent pianist, and gave

---

[1] Cited in Jean-Michel Palmier, *Weimar in Exile: The Antifascist Emigration in Europe and America*, trans. David Fernbach (London: Verso, 2006), 494.

piano recitals on Radio Athlone, Radio Eireann's precedessor, during stays in Ireland in 1937 and 1938.[2]

• • •

Radio Pleasures and Radio Pains I

For someone who lives on the edge of a forest, or even in a desert, radio forms an almost indispensable bridge to the outside world. To guard himself against interruptions from a storage battery going flat, a hermit such as this does not hesitate to acquire an electrical device; in so doing, he finds himself experiencing all weathers, as otherwise only pilots do. It whirs and whistles and rattles in his box, gusts of wind surge into a Caruso aria,[3] and there is nearly always something like a sewing machine to be heard, working away in the background. Nonetheless, this connection does have some excellent advantages. Whereas the car is incapable of any further refinements, so the experts assure us, radio is still in the initial stages of its development – almost as much so as the talking picture, which inflicts such brutality on the ear. Hence, the tireless gentlemen inventors of radio should welcome any criticism. A young lady announcer at a certain station recently lamented, unjustifiably, that radio listeners 'expect too much for their two Deutschmarks per month, and complain far too often.'

First of all, radio does not cost two Deutschmarks, and a good-quality loudspeaker is expensive too. Good progress has already been made in the development of this piece of equipment, which means, one hopes, that the bell horn – horrible in both shape and sound – will soon have disappeared altogether.

The radio station really ought to bear this in mind: the radio owner is defenceless. When he finds his radio blaring, shrieking, yelling, trumpeting, pealing, crackling and howling, instead of simply sounding, and when he leaps to his feet in despair, no one bats an eyelid. All he can do is switch it off. For days on end, at least in the country, no pure sound can be sustained, and this is what is referred to as bad reception. This does not make it any better. The 'dear listener' can get as annoyed as he likes. And admittedly, he is twice as irritable

---

[2] See Johannes F. Evelein, *Literary Exiles from Nazi Germany: Exemplarity and the Search for Meaning* (Rochester, NY: Camden House, 2014), 42–3; Gisela Holfter, 'Marginalised Voices: Women in Irish Exile,' in *Exile and Gender II: Politics, Education and the Arts*, eds. Charmian Brinson, Jana Barbora Buresova and Andrea Hammel (New York: Rodopi, 2017): 224–46; Gisela Holfter and Horst Dickel, *An Irish Sanctuary: German-Speaking Refugees in Ireland, 1933–1945* (Berlin: De Gruyter, 2017), 15–16.

[3] The Italian opera tenor Enrico Caruso (1873–1921), who continued to enjoy international fame long after his death, owing to the large number of phonograph records he made in the last two decades of his life.

because of course he can find no outlet for his anger anywhere. If he bangs the table and cries, 'Faulty!', that's his business. The poor devil.

So, it is now time for a full critical appraisal!

Stuttgart is nowadays considered to be the wealthiest and most thriving city in southern Germany; well, it is certainly not the most musical. Its promenade concerts from the Schlossplatz are nothing to write home about.[4] They seem – if I am not mistaken – to be ringing out noisy tidings. They may well have good tidings in Stuttgart, but they certainly do not have any decent instruments; Munich, decried as a 'big village,' would not suffer such hornblowers for any length of time.

Then there are the speakers' bad habits, which really do hammer the listeners' nerves. [. . .]

Stuttgart (the station I depend on) has both excellent pianists and likeable announcers. But why do they say 'the English capital' London, the 'Austrian capital' Vienna, the 'southern French seaport' Marseille, the 'Italian capital' Rome and the 'American city' Chicago? In Paris they say 'à Londres,' 'à Berlin' and 'vous venez d'entendre l'ouverture des Maîtres Chanteurs,' while the Württemberg capital Stuttgart considers it its duty to announce that the Meistersinger are by Richard Wagner. [. . .]

Now, what about the radio listeners' taste? Of course, it will often be bad.

But that is no reason to pander to it. Oh! Having to listen, over and over again, to people singing 'Duljöh, Duljöh'[5] at this or that 'popular' afternoon concert, relayed from the Excelsior and Cafasö pavilions![6] One of the manifold duties of radio is surely also to educate its underdeveloped listeners. More often than not, of course, these people are underestimated, and they do not necessarily deserve to be fobbed off with the 'Mühle im Schwarzwald'.[7]

To prove my point, let me tell you that recently, some people who had missed their train went into a tavern called Zum Lamm or Zum Ochsen. It only had a bar parlour: on the right sat a few farmers, and on the left were some empty tables and a piano. Sheets of music were lying on top of the piano; one of the travellers fished out a Haydn sonata and started playing it to pass the time. Before long, the room had fallen silent and two old men had drawn closer to the piano to listen.

Since we are talking of the beauty of Haydn, still conveyed despite a mediocre or even bad performance, I must say that Mozart arias are one of the most acute pains of radio. I would a thousand times over prefer to hear a waltz

---

[4] A large public square in Stuttgart from which promenade concerts were often relayed.

[5] Kolb is alluding to popular waltz tunes.

[6] The Excelsior Hotel in Cologne and the Cafasö Café in Mannheim, renowned for their dance music concerts.

[7] 'Mill in the Black Forest' (1887), a popular composition by Richard Eilenberg.

performed beautifully by the Marek Weber Orchestra.[8] I am petitioning for a ban on Mozart arias for anyone who is a beginner in musical appreciation.

Oh yes, and I also wanted to say this: this daily fanfare of birthday greetings! We are embarrassing ourselves here! –

And now to the pleasures.

If fortune is smiling down upon him, the listener will hear pure music emerging, with no interference from any storm, snow or lightning; or he will hear Else Lasker-Schüler, if she is well disposed, reciting her poems.[9] This, then, is more than pleasure – this is bliss bestowed on the lonely radio owner; this is when everything is forgotten. This is when he believes he has won the match, that he and his pains are quits.

Radio Pains and Radio Pleasures II

The preceding essay has drawn a reaction from the 'Drahtloser Dienst, Aktiengesellschaft Berlin,'[10] which has now made a number of statements. They say that a certain punctiliousness is justified when naming cities because consideration must be given to the 'tired listener,' who might, in the German pronunciation of the vowels, mis-hear Berlin as Vienna, or vice versa. May I ask which other cities are in danger of being mistaken for one another? It seems rather as if the medium of radio was already anticipated when these cities were founded and named, and if the tired listener is so tired that he is no longer able to distinguish Tokyo from Madrid or Buenos Aires, then believe me, Drahtloser Dienst, he must be unhinged.

That is to say, the Drahtloser Dienst prefers to focus all its beneficence on the inattentive and ignorant listener; the nervy listener, on the other hand, is granted not an ounce of goodwill. The announcers are issued so many directives; only one is missing: names that are used day in, day out should be pronounced correctly. It is useless if millions of Germans learn to say MacDoooonald, when the name is actually MacDonald: with a short, open 'o'.

We quite rightly Germanise certain foreign words; we say Venedig instead of Venezia, Florenz instead of Firenze.[11] The French say Munich instead of München. Whoever says Draesden instead of Dresden, though, should be fined.

---

[8] A popular orchestra renowned for its disc recordings.

[9] The German writer Else Lasker-Schüler (1869–1945), who was regularly invited to read her poems on German radio.

[10] The Wireless News Service, known as Dradag, was a partly privatised company formed in 1926 in charge of supplying news to radio stations for their news bulletins. Stations were free to choose which news items to broadcast; they could change the wording of the news bulletins but had to abide by the meaning and intention of the messages supplied. See Peter Jelavich, *Berlin Alexanderplatz: Radio, Film, and the Death of Weimar Culture* (Berkeley: University of California Press, 2006), 43–4.

[11] Venice and Florence.

And why should it only ever be the tired, ignorant and inattentive listener who is taken into consideration? Why does he deserve the honour? Incidentally, even the most stupid among them deserves someone to take up the cudgels on his behalf. Nowadays, even he knows that Marseille and Toulon are seaports in southern France. A simple survey would prove it. Why should Germans in particular be so slow on the uptake that the same piece of wisdom must be constantly hammered into them? It really makes us stick out like a sore thumb! Because let me tell you: neither the French capital Paris nor the English capital London employ these demeaning methods!

And why, gentlemen, is it always the tired listener and never the sensitive one?

Many months ago, the poem 'Lieber dot als Sklav' by Liliencron was recited so beautifully in Stuttgart or Frankfurt that the sensitive listener would have been on the point of crying out, 'da capo'.[12] If anyone decides to set up an Association for the Protection of Sensitive and Irascible Radio Owners, I will join!

RADIO PAINS

January 1932

I was already feeling triumphant. I was already thinking I'd won the match, since things like the daily congratulations for birthdays (Herr Matuschka has one too!),[13] name days, silver, golden or diamond weddings had been done away with, the 'Mühle im Schwarzwald' had stopped clattering, and 'Groß-mütterchen' had stopped chirping her song.[14] I had already stuck an imaginary feather in my cap because, in particular, the midday concerts from certain palace squares had fallen silent. All it took was for someone who liked them to utter – recently, in a radio magazine – their hankering for them to be brought back, and here they are, back again!

And as if that wasn't enough, now they've added in, at this time of day, Oskaly [*sic*] and cinema organs, and those organs they play in radio adverts![15]

For the civilised listener, however, this destroys the only hour in which he is granted, via the disc record, relatively pure, noble and consoling music.

There will come a time when our children and our children's children will smile pityingly at the present state of our radio devices (and our sound films!), just as we smile pityingly at the smoking petroleum lamp of past decades, or even the tallow candle of our ancestors. Unless – and there is perhaps a very serious risk of this happening – we become accustomed to a surrogate music in place of real music, and we mistake the one for the other. [. . .]

---

[12] 'Better Dead Than a Slave,' by the German writer Detlev von Liliencron (1844–1909).
[13] It is unclear whom Kolb has in mind.
[14] Granny. This may be a reference to Gustav Langer's *Grossmütterchen*, Op. 20.
[15] The Oskalyd-Orgel was an organ for theatres and cinemas.

The German Language

is, however, not only endowed with an inexhaustible magnificence; it is the most hospitable language there is: as a true world language, it is also a refuge for foreign tongues, which sometimes unquestionably coax new melodious sounds, new pitches, new charms out of its golden lyres. Yet it is unrelentingly severe in its anticipation of any transgressions against its wonderful structure: it is a born pacifist on the greatest scale, ruling over its empire before its own gates, true to the spirit of the grand finale, and even here with unrivalled liberalism: allowing in dialects such as the Rhenish, the Austrian and a moderate Bavarian, but on no account permitting any Couronian, Saxon or Swabian in an official lecture.

Radio Music

We do not wish to be too stringent. Light music, which the Frenchman calls 'la musiquette,' performed with verve and talent, is like a really ripping yarn in literature. If someone is completely exhausted, it might even be pleasant to listen to a tearjerker, as this does not require one's full attention, rather merely conforms to the respective mood, just like musical accompaniment, table music or the plucking of a zither. But no dross, please! I'm begging the vice police for an emergency decree against Tawdry and Filthy Cacophonies. What has happened to the much-talked-of 'improvement of the people'?[16]

On the Protection of Minorities

S.O.S.!

After 7pm, we find ourselves giving up the fight anyway.

Oh beautiful, breezily striving Stuttgart, on which I am dependent for my radio, start up your promenade concerts and mass-produced organs by lantern light! That is when chaos is thriving anyway, when there is no prospect of the waves parting for us. That is when a traditional Viennese folk music trio (mere imitators at that – and from Feldmoching! not even from Vienna!) hacks straight through an Amar Quartet; that is when, instead of an interesting programme by Rosbaud, a wild barking announces: 'Mei Schatzl is a Millimadl'.[17]

Why, oh why, we ask, from the depths of our shredded nerves, why do the radio stations not pool their music, so that we may listen to either the

---

[16] In reference to the 1926 'Gesetz zur Bewahrung der Jugend vor Schund- und Schmutzschriften' (Law for the Protection of Youth from Tawdry and Filthy Writings). See Kurt Tucholsky's 'Free Radio! Free Film!' (6.5), which also alludes to this law.

[17] 'Ma Darlin' is a Milkmaid'. Feldmoching: a surburb of Munich; the Amar Quartet, or the Amar-Hindemith Quartet: an ensemble founded by Paul Hindemith, who gave concerts of classical and contemporary works in Germany and abroad from 1921 to 1929; Hans Rosbaud (1895–1962), Austrian conductor.

one or the other. If there is ever a mention of 'affiliated stations' and the words 'Berlin-Wusterhausen' are proclaimed, oh, how our pain is permeated with hope![18]

Admittedly, we are hysterics; we are prone to fits of screaming – everything you say is true. But it is not only the robust mainstream that deserves to be taken into consideration – we do too, and not only us! Because it is not they, but we, who are grateful, we who never forget a beautiful performance, and we who praise and celebrate radio's every advancement!

3.12 CARLOS LARRONDE: RADIO DRAMA

Translated by Emilie Morin. First published as 'Le théâtre radiophonique,' *Lumière et Radio*, 10 September 1930, 21.

Carlos Larronde (1888–1940) was a French writer and journalist born in Argentina. He had many interests: in education, craftsmanship, theatre and, later, radio. He began to write about radio when he became editor of *Lumière et Radio* (1929–1931). After the magazine's demise in 1931, he joined *L'Intransigeant*, a large-circulation evening newspaper, and ran its radio columns alongside reporter Jean Antoine, gradually becoming the main radio critic. He began experimenting with reportage then, producing programmes for Paris-PTT and the Poste Colonial (the broadcasting service for the French colonies). With prominent reporters such as Antoine and Alex Virot, he created reportage on sports, the arts and culture, led the team of radio reporters at *L'Intransigeant*, who were involved in innovative live broadcasts, and gave talks and presented programmes on various French radio stations. In 1935, he joined the private station Radio-Cité, and directed its literature and theatre sections until 1937. In 1938, he became director of reportage at the Radiodiffusion Nationale, the French national broadcasting service. He held other roles in parallel, notably as president of the French trade union for radio authors, composers and producers (Association Syndicale des Auteurs, Compositeurs et Réalisateurs de la Radio, founded in 1934, later known as Association Syndicale des Auteurs et Compositeurs de la Radiophonie et de la Télévision). He saw radio reportage as an art form in its own right, equal to theatre ('an improvised spectacle, a spectacle

---

[18] The Berlin-Königswusterhausen radio station. The Königswusterhausen transmitter near Berlin transmitted the first German public broadcast in 1920.

for the ear, extracted from life itself'),[1] and campaigned for it to be recognised as such. He wrote numerous texts for radio, experimented with genre, sound and atmosphere, and collaborated with foremost composers and theatre practitioners, notably for his 'orchestral poem' *Le douzième coup de minuit* (first broadcast in December 1933 by Paris-PTT with music by Arthur Honegger and starring the Art et Action theatre laboratory) and his radio play *Le chant des sphères* (first broadcast by Radio-Paris in March 1936 with music by Nikolai Obukhov).[2]

• • •

With my ears shut to all noise, I adjust the optical tube of my astronomical telescope.

I have only one desire: to catch an image. To aim for one of the stars and reach it. To perceive as much as possible of the luminous spot that is a star, of the tiny disc that is a planet, of the scarcely defined cloud that is a nebula.

The astronomer is an eye at a standstill. The night around him is mute.

There is a kind of occult training that advocates the shutting down of the senses. To make oneself deaf, there is no better exercise than chasing a star.

When I handle the condensers on my wireless set, my thoughts turn, in spite of myself, to my nights at the telescope. Once again, there is a dial to turn delicately, in order to bring things further away, closer, *into focus*. This time, however, I am blind. I am just an ear. Capturing sound. Tuning in. My whole being is striving for this goal, like the hunter in the high mountains looking for izards and chamois, holding his breath.

When a fine artisan or a skilled mechanic wants to evaluate the precise strength of a tool, examine an engine, he tends to look away. We do this, too, in a well-lit room when we are truly affected by the music, or when we listen to a voice coming out of the wireless from beyond the seas.

Living through the eye or through the ear: these are similar situations, requiring concentration, either visual or auditory.

With astronomy, one is always fulfilled. The lunar mountains with their shadows, the gaseous nebulas showing the internal movement stirring the substance of a future Milky Way: these are images that always exceed the memory they leave behind and the intensity we expect.

Is this true of the world of sound too? Indeed it is, insofar as human emotions are concerned. Travelling across the planet, feeling as though one is both in Germany and in America, following a football match and a concert of the Orchestre Lamoureux:[3] all this procures an impression of freedom, a joyful

---

[1] Carlos Larronde, 'La radio est le royaume des voix,' *L'Intransigeant*, 28 March 1931, 10.
[2] See Christopher Todd, *Carlos Larronde (1888–1940): Poète des ondes* (Paris: L'Harmattan, 2007), 105–7, 211–30, 231–56.
[3] A Parisian symphonic orchestra created in 1881.

feeling of communion that has often been celebrated. But that impression wears out. That joy wanes. Why? Because we become saturated with art and with the very best, and we are quickly disappointed when we discover that something is lacking in quality. Without art, the wireless is nothing but a toy, a marvellous toy, but it should be more than that: a casket safeguarding new wonders.

I am thinking about radio theatre mostly: at first we find it enchanting to follow a dialogue between actors speaking in a faraway place. We experience the same enchantment again, strengthened by greater emotion this time, when we follow the relay of a sports event or a public gathering. We can follow these events all the more intensely whenever distance prevents us from being there since our eyes cannot warn us of the surprises to come. Emotional tension, becoming a kind of divinatory power, replaces sight. Who can forget this unique moment: the arrival of Costes in New York?[4]

A bad radio play simply makes us wish we were at the theatre (and that is always achievable).

But how could radio drama up to now be anything other than poor?

Radio plays have purely and simply (and here I am speaking about France) transported the stage before the microphone and deprived it of everything that makes the actors shine and confers prestige upon their performance.

Radio drama will only find its raison d'être once it becomes a genre in itself, a new genre without analogy, or with few analogies to theatre as such. I know that, in this domain, some works have been created especially for the microphone in Germany, according to a particular aesthetic and drawing on appropriate artistic means, and a new form of art has been unveiled for the listeners' benefit.

In France, up to now, we have attempted nothing in this domain, so to speak. Alexandre Virot, Pierre Descaves, Jean Antoine and Paul Dermée have deplored this fact, too.[5]

I am speaking here about authors and am not dismissing the efforts made by Paul Castan, Georges Colin, Louis Cognet or Lugné-Poë.[6] If plays are written for them, they will broadcast them. Tristan Bernard has given us a precious model, but he has done so as a playwright who writes for the theatre.

---

[4] This is a reference to Maurice Bellonte and Dieudonné Costes's first non-stop flight between Paris and New York on 1 and 2 September 1930, which gave rise to a celebrated broadcast aired publicly in central Paris. Fernand Divoire describes it in powerful terms in 'En écoutant . . . Le jour de gloire,' *Lumière et Radio*, 10 September 1930, 4.

[5] Jean Antoine (1900–1958), a prominent radio reporter, who also worked as a press journalist for *L'Intransigeant* and other newspapers.

[6] The radio producer, broadcaster and actor Paul Castan (1899–1987); the radio actor and producer Georges Colin (1880–1945); Louis Cognet (fl. 1920s–1930s), director of a theatre company that specialised in radio broadcasting; the theatre actor, director and stage designer Lugné-Poë (1869–1940).

During a debate at the Faubourg,[7] I said that, in my opinion, writers should create works for radio even without the immediate guarantee of broadcasting and payment, and that these works would undoubtedly make their way through our great stations.

It is customary to accuse broadcasters of never trying anything new, and it is fair to do so to a degree. But for this accusation to gain its full might we would need to know for certain that our station directors are keeping original manuscripts locked away in their desks.

It is not the case.

I know perfectly well that the particularly harsh times in which we live rarely allow the artist or the writer to create something without expecting anything in return, or to be poorly remunerated. But the faith in art, the need to express, the power of inspiration have always been irresistible to the few men who are truly talented.

Do you really believe that economic concerns intervened in the conception of *Hamlet* or *Parsifal*?

There are the pages that one writes out of professional obligation and in order to earn a living; such pages will never be masterpieces even if they have been conscientiously written. And there are the masterpieces that come into being because nothing was powerful enough to prevent their authors from giving birth to them.

Don't get me wrong. Only a small number of creators will ever be able to give the wireless, that marvellous instrument, its total significance.

What will this microphone theatre be?

We already have a visual art – the cinema, whose evolution has been much delayed, and still is, by its attempt to imitate theatre.

We have an auditory art – the radio, which suffers from exactly the same ailment.

Yet the theatre, the radio and the cinema have something in common: *an atmosphere*; that is, the particular quality, the kind of vibration that make the work come alive wherever it is performed.

There is a *visual* atmosphere on the screen, just as there is a *psychological* atmosphere in the theatre (here I am not even talking about the décor). The good radio works will be those that have an *acoustic* atmosphere. Which means not only that they will employ the possibilities provided by noise with skill and to the right ends, through what we could call the work's auditory fabric, but also – since art is never imitation – that they will preserve, within

---

[7] The Club du Faubourg, a debating club founded in 1918 which met at the Salle de Wagram in Paris, organised a special debate on radio at the Théâtre de la Gaieté-Rochechouart in May 1930; the event was staged as a 'tribunal of the people' cross-examining the offerings of Parisian radio stations, and Larronde was one of the speakers.

their own truth, within their comic or tragic force, and independently of noise effects, the power to *prolong* the imagination; without this, any line will lack in dynamism even when it has been perfectly formulated.

I am thinking about the voice. About the magic of the voice!

My main grievance against the sound and talking film is that, up to now, it has robbed language of this prestige, this music, this force of contact and penetration that is the hallmark of the Word.

The same criticism could be levelled against the wireless: those who are the most gifted at speaking remain the least gifted artists. Their voices don't reach us to our core.

Only with a rebirth of the marvellous, as Pierre Descaves rightly says, will the wireless be renewed just like the cinema, albeit through different means. Through this same process, sound reportage will earn its place alongside visual reportage.

I believe that the simultaneous poetry that Barzun, Divoire and Voirol were the first to create will produce microphone masterpieces of the highest significance.[8]

Some of the texts that they have already written could be broadcast right now.

Henri Vermeil is due to stage *Commentaire du Pater* by Fernand Divoire in October. There is no doubt that he will do something wonderful with this poem.[9]

I would also like to see this work presented to us in a purely auditory form.

We all remember how Darius Milhaud's *Choéphores* worked wonders.[10]

Spoken choruses, the orchestration of voices, the mixture of timbres, the subtle science of inflexions can bring much to radio; if not the tragic form we are waiting for, then, at the very least, the purest lyrical form.

But this task will require sustained preparation and special education on the part of the performers. My friend Robert de Souza, a master of phonetics, would find here a vast mission to fulfil.[11]

When I directed the stage performance of Fernand Divoire's *L'Exhortation à la victoire* at the Théâtre des Champs-Elysées,[12] I wanted the monologists to stay still at the beginning. Madame Lara of the Comédie-Française, who was playing the leading role, argued that gesture should be added to the recitation.[13] I believe she was essentially right and gave in to her arguments. Yet, in truth,

[8] Henri Martin Barzun (1881–1974), founder of the French Simultaneist group, which Fernand Divoire and Sébastien Voirol (1870–1930) joined.

[9] The theatre director and radio producer Henri Vermeil (fl. 1920s–1960s).

[10] Milhaud composed music for Paul Claudel's *Les choéphores* (1915), part of Claudel's translation of Aeschylus's *The Oresteia*.

[11] Author of studies of rhythm, poetry and the French language.

[12] *L'Exhortation à la Victoire*, written in 1913, was dedicated to the dancer Isadora Duncan and was subtitled *Chœur tragique* ('Tragic chorus').

[13] Louise Lara (1876–1952), who led the theatre laboratory Art et Action with her husband Edouard Autant.

what did the ability to see add to this poem? It would have been preferable to listen to it with our eyes closed, the way we listen to Wagner whenever the singer's corpulence, the cardboard swan, the inflatable dragon and the Bengal fires become tiresome to watch.

Radio is the art of the *voice*. The richness of the voice is infinite. No need for another conclusion.

3.13 ANTON KUH: FEAR OF RADIO

Translated by Marielle Sutherland. First published as 'Angst vor dem Radio,' *Der Querschnitt* 10, no. 4 (April 1930): 243–4.

Anton Kuh (1890–1941) was an Austrian writer, journalist and public speaker. A pacifist and anti-fascist, he wrote for magazines such as *Der Querschnitt* (a Berlin modernist magazine which dealt with literature, performance and the visual arts) and *Die Weltbühne* and, after 1933, for German exile publications such as *Die Neue Weltbühne* and *Der Pariser Tageblatt*. Kuh lived in Prague, Vienna and Berlin; as a Jewish writer, he was unable to remain in Berlin and moved to Vienna in 1933, subsequently leaving Austria for the United States in 1938 to escape persecution. He spoke on the radio occasionally between 1927 and 1933, appearing on the Berlin Funkstunde, the Südwestdeutsche Rundfunk (Frankfurt) and Radio Wien (Vienna), and in 1938, in a programme broadcast by the New York Yiddish radio station WEVD, which hosted German-language programmes and talks by German émigrés. He died of a heart attack in New York in 1941.[1]

• • •

I am afraid of radio.

People of a humanist disposition (in contrast to electrical engineers) find it difficult to become acquainted with new inventions. Yes, brother tinkerers, you may well be astounded, but their imagination – no matter how noted it may be for its poetic power and lightning speed – just cannot keep up! New technical innovations linger in their minds for a long time, like Trojan

---

[1] See Walter Schübler, *Anton Kuh: Biographie* (Göttingen: Wallstein, 2018), esp. 251–2.

horses that the gods have slipped into their lives in order to tempt them. They stand at the threshold of a miracle, while others are already deftly availing themselves of it; they have an accursed habit of asking the meaning of things before putting them to use. Or, to put it differently, and perhaps more uncannily: their thoughts turn first to the apocalypse and only then to human development.

But as regards the subject of 'radio', to what extent is a Trojan horse a threat here? What do the gods have to do with engineers? What kind of devilish temptation is inherent in transmitting and receiving?

My superstition replies: I do not like leaving traces. No matter how desirable it would have been for me to have written 'Hamlet' or to have triumphed over the Persians at the Battle of Marathon, in other words, to have left a trail of light behind me in this or that form – I do not like engraving myself on the earthly realm with my earthly paws. There are people who, without any timidity or inhibition, scratch their names into their school desks with pocket knives, transform trees into monuments to previous misadventures in love, leave their signature on park benches, sign guest books, and even, in political fervour, immortalise themselves on the wall of a public convenience. I admire these people; I envy their fearlessness. Are they not afraid of having pledged their soul here on the site of their notches, their written record of themselves? Are they not troubled by an apprehensive presentiment that all these signatures and other inky traces of their existence might bear witness to their earthly life? . . .

One day, I was visited in my hotel room by the Bohemian engineer P., a figure who could have come from a Meyrinkian borderland between farce and nightmare, full of delusional ideas that oscillated between the humdrum and the scientific.[2] He presented his new hypothesis: that radio destroys life. Humans, he said, are themselves antennae, as is already written – for those who know how to interpret the legend of the Jericho trumpets – in the Holy Scripture. Whereupon he deduced – to-ing and fro-ing between technical terms that on the whole sounded Chinese to my ear – that, in the end, exponentiated wave amplification would result in the disintegration of that living antenna, the human being. It was Pallenberg physics.[3] But all of a sudden, I was convinced. It echoed my superstition! . . . Now I understood everything: why the music from Stuttgart seeped through my headphones like whining phantoms; why the spectral, droning, slurping, vaporous, enmeshed and rattling voices echoed through the loudspeaker as if half dead; why the air in a radio-filled chamber

---

[2] Gustav Meyrink (pseudonym of Gustav Meyer, 1868–1932), author of fantastic novels and tales.

[3] It is unclear what Kuh is thinking of. He may be referring to the animal sculptor Josef Pallenberg (1882–1946), who undertook challenging work on volume and gravity with his bronzes, which often represent bulky animals with thin legs.

sounded strained and artificially inflated. The language of mundane life, which thus far has merely drifted away into a corner, is now charging like a hurricane across the globe; ephemera dart above our heads like giant bluebottles, clattering like aeroplanes; the universal realm of waves has become a single school desk and a scribbling wall where the little runt of the Earth leaves its phonetic trace. Humanity has debased outer space; it has turned it into its gramophone. What shall become of all this? . . . Whatever is written and printed – indeed anything that is depicted – crumbles away, and this is of great comfort to us; what might be the Library of Alexandria today, is scrap paper tomorrow. But the voice is living energy. It cannot die; it amplifies in outer space; it swells and circles and rampages and . . .?

The promotion and acceleration of the end lie, for the time being, in the hands of the radio producers. They are the mediators between the ephemeral and the eternal; their weekly programming is based on the principle of turning a single day into something infinite and – God forbid! – not the other way round. To this end, they compete – if the radio station is located in Berlin – with the newspapers; they are constantly ladling the latest sound from the cauldron of time with a fervid hand, extracting every last drop out of the day as swiftly as they can, exonerating themselves through the glut of counter-voices that are, in reality, no such thing. And deafening the poor human ear with the flood of talk – which they call reportage, improvisation, discussion.

Yet by turning radio into the acoustic sister of the newspaper, they fail to notice that they (like film professionals who turn the screen into theatre) are rendering its invention futile. In so doing, they entirely forget the meaning of the invention. Its meaning is the discovery of the human voice. Just as the meaning of film was the discovery of the human face – or rather, it should have been. But in the same way film has betrayed its purpose, radio has forgotten its purpose; and therefore radio, like film, has also forgotten the discrepancy between apparatus and spirit, the oppressive apparition which demands the maximum level of technology whilst offering only the minimum in reality. Ultimately, the impression film gives is that of the gigantic head of a gigolo (or a mannequin) eyeballing humanity until it gives up the ghost. Radio gives the same impression, but in an acoustic sense. Yet, instead of in the first instance annexing the so-called 'realm of art,' both film and radio needed only to restrict themselves to what suited their nature best in order to fulfil their potential.

Face and spirit are one and the same; tone of voice and spirit likewise. Only the spirit could look the way Voltaire looked; only the spirit could sound the way Mirabeau's speeches sounded. It would make sense to transmit this spirit, amplified thousandfold and millionfold, into the ether. But radio takes as little notice of voices as film of physiognomies; it does not choose between tones of voice, rather between names and subject matter. It transmits, uncritically and in all variations, the tone of vulgarity into the universe . . . and instead of it being the spirit of the Earth who speaks, even though this may be through the mouth of an actor, it is a phonetic runt who takes to the skies, spitting, hissing, slavering and muculent, on infinite waves.

May only the voice of God resound from Mount Sinai.

3.14 COLETTE: AN INTERVIEW ABOUT THE WIRELESS

Translated by Emilie Morin. First published as Pierre Keszler, 'Colette nous parle de la TSF,' *La Liberté*, 11 April 1932, 7.

Colette (born Sidonie-Gabrielle Colette, 1873–1954) was a celebrated French writer. She was never quite the radio novice she claimed to be in this interview with Pierre Keszler; in 1924 already, she was part of the jury created by the newspaper *L'Impartial Français* for the first French radio drama contest (a joint first prize was attributed to Pierre Cusy and Gabriel Germinet's *Marémoto* and to a monologue that was never broadcast, *Agonie* by Paul Camille). Her work was often read and discussed on French radio, and her broadcasting experience was extremely varied. She gave various talks from 1935 onwards, including talks celebrating the animal world on Radio-Paris in 1935 and 1938; she contributed to the women's programme 'La demi-heure de la femme' ('Woman's half-hour') on the Poste Parisien from April to December 1936; she participated in a radio debate about the novel on Radio-Paris in October 1937 and a radio fundraising event in January 1938; she held her own radio show, 'Colette vous parle' ('Colette is speaking to you'), from February 1937 to May 1940, first on the Poste Parisien, then on Radio-Paris; she gave regular talks on Radio-Mondial, France's international station, between November 1939 and June 1940, which were broadcast to American listeners.[1] Her involvement with radio continued until shortly

---

[1] Colette's second husband Henry de Jouvenel (1876–1935), a journalist and politician, held various roles at Radio-Paris and in French broadcasting from 1929, eventually becoming President of the Conseil des Emissions, which oversaw programming on the state-owned radio network, and President of the Association des Auditeurs de la Radiodiffusion Française, an influential association of radio listeners. See Colette, *Paysages et portraits* (Paris: Flammarion, 1958), 231–60; Jeannie Malige, *Colette: Qui êtes-vous?* (Lyon: La

before her death. A biographical sketch of Pierre Keszler is included with 'Is There Such a Thing as a Radiophonic Art?' (1.4).

• • •

When it was in its infancy, radio broadcasting was willfully ignored by artists, by people of delicate and refined taste.

But each day brings progress, and today those who refuse to acknowledge the wireless seem as misguided as the sycophants of the young radio science who argue, with their usual excess of enthusiasm, that other forms of expression have gone bankrupt.

To anyone who enjoys deep thinking, radio broadcasting raises a question, poses a problem. Georges Duhamel formulated this well when he expressed his fear that the new inventions would disrupt our peaceful and reasoned lives.[2]

I asked Colette what she thought of the air waves and their literary prospects. She answered and kept our conversation focused precisely on that question. She asked:

– What is the place of silence, now that the disc record and the wireless have taken over?
– What is your fear exactly? That an excess of enthusiasm for these machines may force silence to disappear, the silence we nonetheless need to be able to think?
– I do worry about that. All these processes that have been invented to entertain us are anaesthetics for the spirit. While someone listens, no matter how distractedly, to the phonograph or the loud-speaker, he forgets about his worries, and unconsciously this is what he is looking for.

  Oblivion has the effect of a drug and can make the intelligence insensitive, lazy, useless. The more the century progresses, the more people throw themselves at all the things that a few enterprising minds have created for the intellectually lazy. There is more to this than we can account

Manufacture, 1987), 137–88; Christian Brochand, *Histoire générale de la radio et de la télévision en France, tome 1: 1921–1944* (Paris: Documentation Française, 1994), 250; Claude Pichois and Alain Brunet, *Colette* (Paris: Editions de Fallois, 1999), 403–4, 546 n17.

[2] This is a reference to Duhamel's *Scènes de la vie future* (1930), a novel based on a trip to the United States which denounced 'la téhessef' as a major threat to civilisation ('la TSF,' standing for *transmission sans fil*, was the standard French term for wireless). The same hostility towards the mechanised dissemination of culture and towards radio characterises Duhamel's later texts and talks; ironically, in September 1939, he was made overseer of programming on French radio. See Christopher Todd, 'Georges Duhamel: Enemy-Cum-Friend of the Radio,' *Modern Language Review* 92, no. 1 (1997): 48–59.

for here . . . How can we, in our cities, resist the invasion perpetrated by the sounds of our neighbours' machines? There is nothing we can do against this invasion. Soon it will be impossible to find somewhere to retreat, somewhere that is quiet enough to work in peace . . . But this is beyond the remit of our interview.

– Not at all, and no one could possibly argue that the development of the wireless will not give rise to serious questions . . . Your comments echo some of the objections that have naturally arisen against the hasty dissemination of modern scientific processes . . . What about the listener who wants to keep on thinking? Do you believe that the air waves can bring him new elements of culture?

– Certainly. When it comes to music, I believe that the wireless is an admirable thing. Nothing is better able to reveal all the beauty of music. Although, even today, I do not own a wireless set, I have often listened to excellent radio-concerts with friends, in their homes, and I would say without hesitation that the music was perfectly reproduced. Nonetheless, anyone born long before the apparition of indirect music will always be bothered by the lack of a visual sensation, but we cannot hold the machines responsible for that.

Our brains, which always associate a sound to its physical occurrence, are baffled when one of these two elements disappears. Our education, which has been entirely visual, has certainly prevented us from experiencing purely auditory joys. The younger generations, my daughter's generation for example (she is eighteen), have, on the contrary, received an education that almost entirely takes place through the ear and addresses the ear.

– When it comes to literature, do you think that lectures broadcast on the wireless will expand the listeners' knowledge, and encourage them to go and read a book from which they have heard a few excerpts?

– This is possible, but it is difficult to ascertain. I am persuaded, however, that the reach of a literary talk depends directly on the manner in which it is delivered. I do not mean that content ought to be sacrificed for form, but I am persuaded that form is of capital importance. The art of speaking, be it in public or in front of the microphone, consists in attracting and retaining the listener's attention. On the wireless, the conference speaker is deprived of the help of gesture and must add to his voice a whole gamut of inflexions to give life and movement to his sentences.

In order to overcome the impression of monotony that will arise without fail, one needs to add clarity, warmth, timbre to the other qualities that the speaking voice must possess, and a great variety of nuances, feeling and modulation, as in music. Finally, and above all, the speaker must remain concise, since the listeners' attention cannot remain focused on the same topic for a long time.

– Have you gained this in-depth knowledge of the radio-speaker's craft in the auditorium?

– I have never spoken before a microphone . . . But I have listened!

– We hope that this serious lacuna will soon be remedied, and that we will hear you soon.

– Someone will come and find me when I am needed . . .

– Let us conclude this discussion. What are your views on radio's future?

– Radio broadcasting is an inevitable thing. It will spread everywhere. I have, personally, resisted it for a long time. But I spend long periods of time in the countryside, and I have thought about everything that a wireless set would bring me. When I return to my country house in the spring, I will bring a wireless set in my luggage . . . The telephone, too, has overcome our resistance; it is everywhere now, and no one feels that it is a disgrace to pick up the receiver. People used to laugh at taxis. But who has never taken a taxi? The same will happen with the wireless, for better or worse.

PART 4
RADIO GENRES

4.1 HANS FLESCH: THE FUTURE SHAPE OF RADIO PROGRAMMING

Translated by Marielle Sutherland. Talk from 1930, first published as 'Zukünftige Gestaltung des Rundfunkprogramms,' in Hans Bredow, ed., *Aus meinem Archiv: Probleme des Rundfunks* (Heidelberg: Kurt Vowinckel, 1950), 121–4.

Hans Flesch (1896–1945), a German radio producer, was a leading figure in Weimar-era radio. He collaborated with Walter Benjamin, Bertolt Brecht, Arnold Schönberg, Alfred Döblin, Kurt Weill, and his brother-in-law Paul Hindemith, among others, and facilitated their turn to radio. From 1924 to 1929, he was artistic director of the Südwestdeutsche Rundfunk (South West German Radio Company, Frankfurt), a post which enabled him to commission music and plays for radio. He wrote for radio, too, and authored one of the first radio plays: *Zauberei auf dem Sender: Versuch einer Rundfunkgroteske* ('Magic on the air: attempt at a radio grotesque'), broadcast by the SWR in October 1924. Thereafter, from 1929 to 1932, he was director of the Berlin Funkstunde, and became renowned for his experiments with recording, editing and archiving sound. He directed the new Haus des Rundfunks until 1932. Flesch also wrote widely about radio, using his radio journalism to define and theorise the possibilities and aesthetics of the medium. A progressive figure, dedicated to a democratic ideal for radio, Flesch came under threat before the Nazis took power; he was dismissed from his post at the Funkstunde in August 1932 after being submitted to anti-Semitic attacks and after new, restrictive radio legislation was introduced. In August 1933, he was arrested alongside other major figures in Weimar radio and was detained in the Oranienburg concentration camp. He was released in 1935 and banned from exercising any kind of cultural activity, having been branded as a 'half-Jew' by the Hitlerian laws. Having initially trained as a doctor, he returned to practising medicine during the Second World War. He disappeared in mysterious circumstances in Berlin in the spring of 1945 and was never found.[1] The present piece is the script of

---

[1] See Jelavich, *Berlin Alexanderplatz*, 84–85; 241–3; Daniel Gilfillan, *Pieces of Sound: German Experimental Radio* (Minneapolis: University of Minnesota Press, 2009), 46–66; Solveig Ottmann, *Im Anfang war das Experiment. Das Weimarer Radio bei Hans Flesch und Ernst Schoen* (Berlin: Kulturverlag Kadmos, 2013); Hans Flesch, *Magic on the Air: Attempt at a Radio Grotesque*, trans. Lisa Harries Schumann, *Cultural Critique* 91 (2015): 17–31; Carolyn Birdsall, 'Radio Documents: Broadcasting, Sound Archiving, and the Rise of Radio Studies in Interwar Germany,' *Technology and Culture* 60, no. 2 (2019): 96–128.

a talk delivered at a radio conference organised in Vienna in September 1930, gathering leading figures in German and Austrian broadcasting.

•　•　•

Radio has existed in Germany and Austria for six years now. For almost seven years, on a daily basis, every person has had this strange and marvellous opportunity to listen to music, hear news, receive teaching, and witness large-scale events happening hundreds of kilometres away. On the other hand, the radio corporations face the question of taming and mastering the enormous amount of material and turning it into a full programme plan. The material is inexhaustible. Programming means selecting and shaping.

It is not my role to comment on the ideas and principles upon which the selection is based; I am more concerned here with formal matters.

After almost seven years of programme development, I no longer need to point out that not everything that lends itself to acoustic perception is also suitable for radio broadcasting. It was different at the beginning: music could be broadcast in any form, books read aloud, plays performed with allocated roles, the content of educational books imparted; in short, radio was seen as the instrument of dissemination par excellence; its invention was compared with the art of printing, and parallels were drawn with the book, the gramophone, cinema and the newspaper. There are still foreign radio corporations who call themselves 'Radio-journal' and their full programme plan a 'spoken newspaper'.[2]

Radio is undoubtedly a disseminator, a mediator, vividly and rapidly reproducing and propagating in ways that are true to life, capturing the movements and actions of vast numbers of people. But that is just one of its possibilities. When, for the first time, the microphone left the broadcasting studio, so that instead of delivering pre-prepared pieces presented on site, it could communicate an actual process, an event happening elsewhere – whether this was a festivity that could now be followed by a hundred thousand instead of only a thousand people, or a sporting event described, as it unfolded, by the speaker –, something fundamentally new was happening: radio was making it possible to

---

[2] *Radiojournal* and *gesprochene Zeitung* in the original, between inverted commas. This may be a reference to Radiozurnal, the national broadcasting company in Czechoslovakia, or to Soviet radio: in the Soviet Union, the *radiogazeta* (radio newspaper) had been the dominant radiophonic genre since 1924 and, by 1930, there were over 300 different types of *radiogazety* in various languages spoken across the Soviet Union. See Stephen Lovell, *Russia in the Microphone Age: A History of Soviet Radio, 1919–1970* (Oxford: Oxford University Press, 2015), 72–5. 'Spoken newspaper' was then commonly used to designate radio news bulletins outside of the English-speaking world: *gesprochene Tageszeitung* in Germany, *journal parlé* in France, *giornale parlato* in Italy.

share in the experience. Its communicative ability was incomparable: what it was disseminating was no longer arranged and prepared; instead, it was bringing the course of an actual event, simultaneously, as it unfolded, within the reach of an unlimited number of people, from a great distance away. This is where the parallels end: as long as there is no television, only the wireless can do this; this is its most intrinsic function, and any comparisons with the book, the cinema, the newspaper or the gramophone collapse when considering the simultaneity of events, communication and reception experienced by the listeners.

There are therefore two very different types of radio: it disseminates pre-prepared pieces, selected and delimited according to the will of the artistic director, but it also disseminates actual events, the course and outcome of which are unknown and unrepeatable.

In both cases, it reproduces. This raises the question of whether radio might not also produce, whether it might not create rather than reproduce: whether radio might not be able to execute its own characteristic work. The radio play as an art intrinsic to radio, music intrinsic to radio, where the definition of such is based not on secondary and technical grounds but on valid stylistic considerations – is there such a thing? It is not my intention to discuss, rather only to mention, this question – which I, personally, would answer in the affirmative – because it centres on a third type of radio. We can easily classify it in this study; the work of art conceived for radio, whether this be a radio play or music, will always belong to the category of pre-prepared, self-contained pieces.

The recognition of this two-sided nature of radio should influence the programming. In accordance with the artistic director's fixed programme plan, the individual pieces should follow one another; the explicit pursuit of achievable perfection means they should be coordinated with one another, balanced and well arranged.

The event – life itself – grabs the microphone with no regard for the programme plan, temporally autonomous, dependent only on the artistic director's selection. When society comes together to carry out a deed, to celebrate, to grieve, to enjoy, radio makes it possible for those who cannot be there to share in the experience.

If the programming has responded and adapted to this recognition, the next question is whether the form, too, has been modified. I am thinking of the pre-prepared pieces within the programme plan, and I believe radio should aim for the highest perfection in terms of the pieces it presents itself. These programmes are certainly rehearsed extensively before they are broadcast. I remember that, once, a single-act modern opera broadcast by the Berlin station needed fifteen long orchestra rehearsals.[3] However, it is not about the number, rather about

---

[3] *Berliner Sender* in the original. The first German broadcasting station, which began to broadcast in October 1923, named Funk-Stunde (Radio Hour) in 1924.

whether radio should not go one step further in terms of technology when preparing its pieces, and adapt what it has to offer to the technical instrument. This is because the listener demands the highest perfection from his device; if a real event is being broadcast, then it should be as true to life as possible so that the listener feels he has been transported there; however, if radio contributes something itself – music or a radio play – then only the most perfect technical precision can make an artistic impression on the listener. And this can only be achieved if the piece is prepared, right through to its fixation, on some kind of medium, whether this be a phonograph disc record, film, or Stille's magnetic steel tape.[4]

There are many objections, and many purely intuitive aversions, to a radio piece – even a concert – being so extensively prepared that it is recorded onto a medium, whether this be a phonograph record or film, and then being brought to the listener in that state. What are these objections? First of all, there is a fear that radio might become a slave to mechanisation, and that those who advocate this are sinning against the idea of live radio. I do not entirely agree with this, for I do not understand wherein the danger of 'mechanisation' is supposed to lie if a pre-prepared piece is broadcast one hour earlier or later. What I am advocating here is by no means the broadcasting of purchasable phonograph records, rather the broadcasting of a radio station's own programme – one that it has prepared down to the last detail. The idea is no longer to rehearse everything ten times over, consider that the performance is ready the eleventh time around, and then broadcast this in the evening, despite all the contingencies to which it is exposed. The idea is rather to use this eleventh time to fix the material onto phonograph record or film; this then allows us to transmit a truly perfect, flawless broadcast to the listener. Already, programmes are prepared differently to how they were prepared in the past. We are no longer content to rehearse and try to ascertain whether the performance will be good enough to broadcast; we now prefer to record our rehearsals onto wax discs and afterwards listen to, review and improve them on the basis of scientific methods (in cooperation with the technician) and artistic impression (in cooperation with the bandmaster). Once the technicians and bandmaster have come together and agreed that the optimal performance has been achieved, we are merely one step from recording

---

[4] The steel tape recording machine patented in 1924 by Kurt Stille, a German engineer, gave rise to the steel tape recording machines used in radio studios during the 1930s. The Blattnerphone, also referred to as 'Stille Machine' – a recording machine installed in BBC studios in 1931 – was commercialised in 1925, and the Marconi-Stille magnetic tape recorder was commercialised in 1934. Magnetic steel tape was notoriously heavy and dangerous to handle; edits had to be made by welding or soldering the tape. Sound recording remained a rare practice: at the BBC, even in the mid-1930s, sound recording was only possible in the London studios, and only for material judged to be particularly significant. See Paddy Scannell and Peter Cardiff, *A Social History of British Broadcasting vol. 1: 1922–1939: Serving the Nation* (Oxford: Basil Blackwell, 1991), 145–6.

this optimum piece and bringing it to the listener in this form. I know the objection to this is that listeners need to have the feeling: someone is singing here for you; someone is here for you. There is certainly something in this. Yet in artistic terms, is the listener's need here in fact not the very same in every respect if he knows that this performance was perhaps fixed an hour beforehand and is now being broadcast for him? What, in actual fact, is the aesthetic difference between a dead studio broadcast (dead because an orchestra is playing without a direct audience; the artist does not receive any response) and the same process, the same effect, if there is now a time delay between process and effect? Simultaneity is only a condition of sharing in the experience in the case of a real event. So, what is the nature of the 'event' taking place in the broadcasting studio?

I would like to clarify this by offering an example. It is surely the case that, in future, the only possible way of representing our attempts to create an art intrinsic to radio, i.e. the radio play, will be on another medium, on a phonograph record or on film. Allow me to introduce a utopian idea here. Imagine you are chosen as the director of a radio corporation with the ability to broadcast not only acoustically but also optically; imagine television has been perfected as a medium to the point that it can somehow transmit everything just as it is presented to the lens of a photographic device or the lens of a camera. What would your programming look like in this case? You would undoubtedly broadcast, above all, occasions, sporting events, celebrations and gatherings. But what would the plan for non-news programmes look like, those compiled with your particular intentions in mind? I am thinking here of your ambition to create an audio and visual play for the new audio and visual radio. Do you think you could prepare such a visual play in your studio and simultaneously broadcast the performance? This would not be possible, for you would wish to make use of the same possibilities that are open to the motion picture film: continually switching scenes, cross-fading, achieving particular affects by cutting the film. You could not do any of this if you were performing and broadcasting at the same time. Neither would you wish to do this, for of course you would not have a theatre with an audience immediately present. You would absolutely have to adapt a visual or an audio-visual film, produce it in the studio and then broadcast this film to the listener.

Already, the very same is also true of the radio play. The self-containment of an event seems to make it adaptable to technology.

In terms of the future shape of radio programming, I believe that, much more than has been the case thus far, real life will be brought to the listener via radio. And again, much more than ever before, every event in the life of the community and the individual – gatherings, celebrations, public concerts – will be broadcast directly to the listeners so that they can stay connected with what is happening in their time. On the other hand, the pedagogical and artistic portion of the programming will be developed in accordance with a more stringent plan. And I believe that this educational and artistic side of radio, in as far as it takes place in the broadcasting studio, ought to adapt to technology and, in pursuit of the highest perfection, make use of all the available technical means to a greater degree than it has done thus far.

4.2 HERMYNIA ZUR MÜHLEN: RADIO PROGRAMMES FOR WOMEN

Translated by Marielle Sutherland. First published as 'Radiosendungen für Frauen,' *Der Wiener Tag*, 7 September 1934, 6.

Hermynia Zur Mühlen (née Countess Folliot de Crenneville-Poutet, 1883–1951) was an Austrian writer and translator, who translated over a hundred works by Russian, French, English and American writers into German. She wrote novels, short stories, autobiographical texts, politicised fairy tales, as well as radio plays and radio broadcasts. This essay from the Austrian daily *Der Wiener Tag* accompanied the broadcast on Radio Wien's women's hour programme of her 'Märtyrerinnen der Liebe' (Martyrs of love), a series of portraits of royal mistresses Inês de Castro, Louise de la Vallière and Victorine von Wolfsberg. Born to a family of Viennese aristocrats, Zur Mühlen – sometimes called 'the Red Countess' – became committed to social equality and social justice early on. She was a member of the German Communist Party until 1931 or 1932, and became an outspoken critic of the Nazi regime. In 1933, she left Germany for Austria, then left Austria in 1938 for Slovakia, then England, where she lived until her death. During the Second World War, she made a precarious living from her writing, mostly by publishing short stories in German émigré and Swiss newspapers; she occasionally wrote radio plays for the BBC's German–language broadcasting service, then newly established.[1]

• • •

---

[1] See Deborah Vietor-Engländer, 'Hermynia Zur Mühlen and the BBC,' in *'Stimme der Wahrheit': German-Language Broadcasting by the BBC*, eds. Charmian Brinson and Richard Dove (Amsterdam: Rodopi, 2003), 27–42; Ailsa Wallace, *Hermynia Zur Mühlen: The Guises of Socialist Fiction* (Oxford: Oxford University Press, 2009); Lionel Gossman, ed., 'Remembering Hermynia Zur Mühlen: A Tribute,' in *The Red Countess: Select Autobiographical and Fictional Writing of Hermynia Zur Mühlen* (London: Open Book, 2018), 407–34.

If it were up to me, there would be no distinction at all between radio programmes for men and women.[2] For although I am by no means a feminist, as a woman I find it mortifying that a member of the male sex should tap me on the shoulder patronisingly and cheerfully say, 'Now, dear woman, just go and turn on your radio and listen to what I have written for you and your fellow females on the women's hour programme'.

Why does the station director appeal to us as women and not to us as human beings per se? If his women's hour programme conveys artistically distinct values, should these not have a human appeal in the broadest sense? Yet by no means do I wish to cast doubt on the institution of the weekly women's hour broadcast. It is a rostrum that has given many creative and practising female artists the opportunity to have their say. Thus far, the aim has been, on the whole, to re-introduce great historical female figures to the public and, likewise, poetry by women, read out by women. However, no radio station has yet found a suitable means of bringing the ordinary, unknown woman of our times to the microphone so that she may tell us about the immediate reality of her life, her hopes and fears, without any reticence or inhibition.

Since this is not so easy to put into practice, we cannot disapprove of the current method of evoking the memory of the great female figures of the past. Yet there is still a pressing need to ensure that any historical destiny we would wish to represent and emulate is a clear reflection of our times, our very own struggles, feelings and fears; it must move us inwardly if it is not to drift away from us like flotsam.

There is a whole host of great female figures who fully satisfy this requirement. I am thinking here, for example, of the figure of the great German theatre manager and director Neuberin,[3] whose impact on her epoch is conveyed with such immediacy by her letters and by the writings of Gottsched;[4] the organiser of the Red Cross, Florence Nightingale, the magnificent biography of whom has been penned by Lytton Strachey;[5] and finally, the great Austrian writer, Marie von Ebner-Eschenbach, whose superb novellas 'Lotti die Uhrmacherin'

---

[2] Radio Wien broadcast *Frauenstunde* (Women's Hour) programmes twice a week from 1930 to 1937. Women's programmes were common elsewhere, too – in Weimar Germany particularly, where the *Frauenfunk*, encompassing a network of departments dedicated to women's programming, broadened its offerings, from initial broadcasts restricted to domestic economy to varied programmes dealing with literature and the arts, politics and history. See Kate Lacey, *Feminine Frequencies: Gender, German Radio, and the Public Sphere, 1923–1945* (Ann Arbor: University of Michigan Press, 1996).

[3] Friederike Caroline Neuber, known as Die Neuberin (1697–1760).

[4] The German philosopher, critic and dramatist Johann Christoph Gottsched (1700–1766), the first to call her 'Die Neuberin,' saw her approach and methods as models of the reformed theatre that he wanted to develop on German stages.

[5] In *Eminent Victorians* (1918).

and 'Der Muff' would surely make for a very special kind of radio experience.[6] Is there, ultimately, any instrument that is better than radio at building bridges between time and space? How compellingly the microphone would convey women's experience in its broadest and most universal sense in a programme in which several female figures from the same period, but different countries, were able to speak to us through the mirror of poetry?!

4.3 ALFRED DÖBLIN: LITERATURE AND RADIO

Translated by Marielle Sutherland. First published as 'Literatur und Rundfunk,' in *Dichtung und Rundfunk: Reden und Gegenreden. Als Verhandlungsniederschrift gedruckt* (Berlin: n.p., 1930), 7–15.

Alfred Döblin (1878–1957) was a German novelist and a doctor whose practice of medicine reflected his socialist persuasion. This essay was originally a speech delivered at the opening of the *Dichtung und Rundfunk* (Poetry and Radio) conference held in Kassel, Germany, on 30 September and 1 October 1929, which gathered prominent radio producers and writers including Hans Flesch, Walter Bischoff, Ernst Hardt, Hans Bodenstedt, Alfred Braun, Hermann Kasack, Hans Kyser, Alfons Paquet and Ina Seidel, the only female speaker. The conference was organised by the Reichsrundfunkgesellschaft (the German National Radio Company) and the Prussian Academy of Arts, with the aim of attracting talented writers to radio. Döblin was a keen radio listener; he enjoyed building his own radio sets, and his broadcasting experience was extensive. He presented his first broadcasts on the Berlin Funkstunde in 1925 and 1926 and, after a brief hiatus, gave regular talks and readings from 1928 to 1931 on the Berlin Funkstunde while also contributing to the offerings of the Leipzig, Cologne and Frankfurt stations. His broadcasts included conversations with foremost writers, an experimental storytelling programme with Rudolf Arnheim, Hermann Kasack and Arnold Zweig, and imaginative talks about thinkers and authors across history. He wrote for the German radio press regularly. His radio play *Lusitania*, an adaptation of

---

[6] *Lotti, die Uhrmacherin* ('Lotti the clockmaker,' 1881) and 'Der Muff' ('The muff,' 1883), by the Austrian writer Marie von Ebner-Eschenbach (1830–1916).

a previous stage play, was broadcast in late 1929 and, in 1930, he wrote a radio play based on his novel *Berlin Alexanderplatz*, entitled *The Story of Franz Biberkopf*; its broadcast was cancelled following the rise in anti-Semitism concurrent with Hitler's electoral success that year. In 1933, Döblin, who was of Jewish descent, left Germany for France to escape Nazi persecution, becoming a French citizen in 1936; between 1939 and 1940, he worked for the French Haut-Commissariat de l'Information (High Commission for Information) and produced a memorandum discussing how radio and other modes of communication could be harnessed for propagandist purposes against Nazism in Germany. He emigrated to the United States in 1940. He returned to Germany in 1945; between 1946 and 1952, he worked for the Südwestfunk in Baden-Baden, writing radio essays and producing a regular radio programme called 'Kritik der Zeit' (Critique of our time). He settled in Paris again in 1953.[1]

• • •

I would like, gentlemen, to pick out a select group of questions to examine with you. These are the questions that are the most important for both authors and radio professionals from a practical and technical point of view, namely questions regarding the formal nature of literature and the formal nature of radio. After determining the nature of these two fields, I would like to explore with you how they relate to one another in terms of their nature, whether there is a real possibility of a connection between the two, and to what extent a connection is possible at all.

We literary authors have reason to reflect on this because, from a negative point of view, it may save us from fruitless endeavours, and from a positive point of view, we need to understand what kind of literary possibilities radio may offer us. [. . .]

In the first instance, the lyrical genre, the epic genre and the essay have a particular formal characteristic: they are printed in books. They are either not spoken, or they are spoken only in exceptional cases. The majority of our literature is therefore characterised by printing type, and the organ through which this literature enters our heads – and we must note this well – is the eye. The dramatic genre has a special status here: its products become real on the stage, where they are heard and simultaneously seen in three dimensions. Yet if this is

---

[1] See Erich Kleinschmidt, 'Döblin's Engagement with the New Media: Film, Radio and Photography,' trans. Detlev Koepke, in *A Companion to the Works of Alfred Döblin*, eds. Roland Dollinger, Wulf Koepke and Heidi Thomann Tewarson (Rochester, NY: Camden House, 2004), 171–5; Jelavich, *Berlin Alexanderplatz*, 75–8, 82–3, 94–7, 114–25; Cyril de Beun, 'The *Dichtung und Rundfunk* Conference: Medial Configurations of Speech Networks,' *SoundEffects* 4, no. 1 (2014): 67–89; Dagmar von Hoff, 'Rundfunkbeiträge 1946–1952,' *Döblin-Handbuch: Leben – Werk – Wirkung*, ed. Sabina Becker (Stuttgart: Metzler, 2016), 246–9.

the case, we might also consider the fact that radio is an acoustic instrument of dissemination for words, tones and sounds, whereas the majority of our literature thus far is silent; it is under the spell of printing type, written for the inner sense. Dramatic literature, indeed, is written for the ear, but at the same time for the eye – so, how can literature and radio come together? This question immediately sheds light on the difficult, indeed almost unhappy role of literature within radio, not to mention the many thousands of people who perhaps understand nothing of literature (we are talking here only about the difficulties with regard to radio in and of itself). We need to look at this more closely. To come straight to the point, the situation is this: for music and journalism, radio is on no account a fundamental innovation; it is merely a new technical means of dissemination. For literature, however, radio is a transformative medium. Literature would have to undergo a formal transformation in order to adapt to radio; how should, or indeed how can, literature respond to the demands radio places on it? [. . .]

Radio does not return us to an original and natural situation. It is indeed the oral language, the living language, that is spoken on the microphone, yet radio has immediately proved to be an artificial, a very artificial technical tool; this is because our oral language thrives on the contact between speaker and listener. Furthermore, living language is never spoken in isolation but is always accompanied by facial expression, by a variety of gestures, by eye contact. Radio cannot recreate this situation. It is true that we know, because we are told as much, that nowadays there are many thousands of people listening when we speak, but in actual fact we are sitting in isolation in the recording studio, and these thousands of people exist at best in our imagination. Yet even then, we do not experience the resonance, the audience's reaction to us; and this is why radio lacks the energy and life that language and the spoken word really bring in the first place; ultimately, it lacks the impetus and elements of moderation that characterise the interaction between speaker and listener. So, perhaps radio does not return us to the natural human situation of the speaker, the narrator, but it nonetheless creates a less artificial situation.

At all events, radio provides literature with a vocal language once again; this is a great asset, and we really must understand its value. It is an advantage we must now capitalise upon. We must now create things that are spoken, things that make a sound. For anyone who writes, it is clear that this will change the substance of the literary work.

A further element that defines radio is this: radio involves speaking before a large mass of people which, although not visible, is real and present. This formal characteristic of radio – that of reaching an indefinitely large number of people – may bring about an important change in a positive sense. [. . .]

Having considered these two formal characteristics of radio, and having acknowledged the demands they place on literature, I would now like to briefly turn to the four literary genres and explore how their intrinsic characters relate to that of radio, whether it is possible to marry or unite them in some way, or whether there can perhaps be only a brief liaison between them.

So, the prospects are good for the essay. The only demands radio places on the essay are that it be short – because it is not possible to follow long, spoken essays, especially not for an ordinary person – and that it be simple. These are desirable and achievable aims, which suggests the transition from essay writing to radio will be a smooth one. Incidentally, it is a much easier transition to make than many speakers giving talks on the radio believe: the speaker must convey to the mass of listeners the sense that the talk, even if it is a scientific lecture, has the character of an essay, a literary product, that it is neither too tedious nor too difficult. Radio directors may wish to give their speakers some training in this kind of essay writing. Nietzsche wrote about a 'gay science,' and the speakers may do well to bear this expression in mind. Of course, a huge amount of essay writing cannot be used at all in radio; it remains reserved for books and newspapers.

The lyrical genre can be absorbed into radio just as easily as the essay – which, incidentally, through reportage, may become a powerful component in radio presentations. Poetry is particularly suited to translation into vocal language. Brevity is intrinsic to its nature; all that remains is to select works characterised by simplicity and poignancy and to concern oneself with the purely technical question of their arrangement within the overall programme. I am, incidentally, of the opinion that poetry should be allocated much more space within the overall radio programme, for poetry is very close to music – it speaks directly to the listener, addresses itself to the emotions; it engages. Beyond that, all that is important is correct arrangement and selection in conjunction with musical performances. I wish to note here, as a matter of principle, that I believe authors themselves should only perform their work if it is poetry, not if it is from another literary genre. To do so would be a crime, and in actual fact, it would make no sense, for authors have nothing more to do with the finished work, and the performance of the work would come under a different artistic genre: the art of speaking or singing. I can only endorse an author's presence in the radio broadcast of his works if he is giving a brief introduction, offering a brief personal comment or sketching a radio portrait.[2]

Whereas it is possible to bring together radio and literature both effortlessly and productively in the essay and the lyric due to their essentially analogous relation to the character of radio, it is dangerous, and potentially even catastrophic to attempt to combine radio with what today are the broadest fields

---

[2] Döblin is here referring to a popular genre, which he also practised: the vocal portrait or *Stimmporträt* – a biographical sketch written especially for radio, focusing on a great figure from the past or the present.

of literature: the epic and the dramatic genres. Here, we encounter the utmost difficulties, difficulties that are indeed absolutely insurmountable.

The novel of today has been created, in part, by the format of the book. It is silent and, to a greater or lesser extent, long; not to mention whether or not it is difficult. Now let us examine radio: it requires speech, brevity, vivid simplicity. Language, it seems, is its advantage – I argued this earlier. Yet this is only true in the case of a future epic literature, a narrative literature purely created for radio. I have emphasised to authors the desirability of such writing. The novel of today, however, is a bookish novel, and to give an oral performance of it would be an error. Epic novels, from Don Quixote to the penny dreadfuls we read today, would die a death if they were subjected to an oral rendition, for this would contravene the basic intentions and therefore the nature of these works. Breadth, extensiveness and flow are essential to the novel and the epic work. To take in this breadth, extensiveness and flow, we have at our disposal our eyes, which glide across the pages and enable us to experience, within a matter of a few hours, a narrative for which a potential listener would need to set aside many days, if indeed he could endure it at all. Our eyes are the fast riders, the express trains that take in this extensiveness, allowing us to apprehend what we call tension. The slow vehicle of spoken language chews up and decimates the tension holding these greater contexts so tightly together. [. . .]

Oral language is actually bad for the epic literature that has been produced thus far. Vocal language does not add anything positive by lending sound to the novel; rather, it restricts the imagination through the timbre of the voice, the particular type of voice and the intonation – none of which the author intended as part of the work. In actual fact, it is the imagination that is the undisputed site of the novel, that intellectual and sensory imaginative engagement, and reading is infinitely better at stimulating it. Our concentration reaches deeper in the act of reading; we are less distracted, which means the author of the novel can more easily orchestrate the necessary self-hypnosis.

This means that the extremely important, great epic genre – at all events, in its current form – must, without doubt, be omitted. I am disregarding occasional short stories here; these are not an important component in our literature.

And the situation is no better in the case of the dramatic genre. It is possible neither to read novels nor perform dramas on the radio. I believe any assertion to the contrary is erroneous – many of the radio performances I have heard have convinced me of this. The eyes differentiate between the persons presented in a normal drama, and this is the author's intention. Facial expression, gesture and dumb-show are arguably essential in all plays, and in many plays there are also specific stage actions. Think of situation comedy, which cannot be attempted on the radio, as radio can only offer sound. The plays broadcast on the radio are reproductions in the manner of a black and white print taken from a colour image. They are readings of plays from the script, but they never become performances, and they can certainly never be theatre, for theatre has become something that radio, for a particular reason, is entirely incapable of becoming. Theatre is a collective experience. In the theatre, a drama is performed in front of a mass audience, and in fact together with it. Theatre only becomes real, as any audience member would agree, in the communal experience. Theatre, like any large gathering, has a fundamental social function. Radio lacks this function in the way it is constituted; radio does indeed address itself to a hundred thousand people, and yet – and we should not understate this – it speaks to a hundred thousand individuals. And just as, for instance, the author speaking on the radio is sitting in isolation, encountering these hundred thousand people only dimly in his imagination, or perhaps not at all, and not picking up on any living reaction, so here the mass audience is carved up and divided by this magnificent but murderous instrument; the mass audience is not there, which is why theatre is not possible on the radio, rather only its surrogate: the broadcast play[3] or the transmission of a performance from a theatre. Now, none of this is meant in any way as a reproach to radio, rather merely as a way of determining its limits and its nature.

So, whether we write books or for the theatre, we authors are only marginally, and by no means profoundly, excited by what radio has to offer, and it is unlikely we will become any more excited about it, despite all the incentives. Radio has too many deficiencies in comparison with the status of literature today, deficiencies that it does not at all possess in relation to music and journalism. So, if we as authors do choose to engage with radio not only out of good will but also out of a sense of responsibility, we and the gentlemen who work in radio, the actual radio professionals, must ponder and take into account the arguments presented here. It is possible to combine the lyrical genre and the essay effortlessly and productively with radio. There is a good chance that the gentlemen in radio can work together with those in literature to make advances in this area. If we say to radio, with regard to epic and dramatic literature, as far as possible: hands off; or: carry on with your broadcast plays and transmissions from theatres, but these cannot be called art, for they are nothing more than poor copies of art, fragmented torsos or reproductions – if we say this (and of course, we may), we must, at the same time, supplement this with some other, positive idea. It is true that radio cannot simply absorb epic and dramatic literature, yet it need only return, like Antaeus, to its own ground, whereupon it may assimilate the epic and dramatic genres in its own way and develop its own popular radio art, a highly important and interesting artistic genre. This genre would have to accommodate the features of radio – audibility, brevity, concision, simplicity. Radio must absolutely develop its own radio plays – a task that, almost without exception, has lain in the hands of the dramaturgs thus far – by

---

[3] *Sendespiel* in the original: a play taken from the theatre repertory and broadcast without modifications to its form.

means of real literature, for a radio play requires language and poetic imagination. Radio is indeed making efforts in this direction, but it needs to give greater consideration than it has thus far to the idea that the age-old distinction between epic and dramatic literature is suspended in radio. These are the familiar distinctions that separate literature into the book and the theatre. I am certain that, in future, real radio plays will be created, plays that will also adapt the other possibilities of radio – music and sound – to their own purposes. This will, however, only be possible if lyrical, epic and even essayistic elements are employed in a wholly unconstrained manner. Incidentally, I can also imagine that it will be possible to broadcast episodes of radio plays in instalments on the radio like novels; this serial form would otherwise be impossible.

4.4 BARBARA BURNHAM: ADAPTATIONS

First published in 'Sidelights on Radio Drama,' *Radio Times*, 30 August 1935, 6.

Barbara Burnham (d. 1974) was a celebrated British producer who had a long and uninterrupted career adapting, producing and translating works for radio. Her name first appears in BBC programmes in 1929, where she is credited for arranging George S. Kaufman and Marc Connelly's play *Beggar on Horseback*. Adaptations of Robert Louis Stevenson's *The Strange Case of Dr. Jekyll and Mr Hyde* and Shakespeare's *The Winter's Tale* followed in 1930, marking the beginning of a prolific career adapting stage plays and novels for radio. She had an interest in German drama and translated and adapted various German plays for BBC broadcasting during the 1930s, including Friedrich Wolf's *The Sailors of Cattaro*. She was first credited as producer in 1933, and a lauded adaptation of Anton Chekhov's *The Seagull* the following year launched her career as producer. She collaborated closely with the novelist James Hilton during the 1930s on radio adaptations of his novels. After the Second World War, she extended her focus to theatre and television production, but continued to produce radio programmes.[1]

• • •

[1] See Cecil Whitaker-Wilson, '"Simple Radio Plays Are Best" Says Barbara Burnham (the BBC Woman Producer),' *Radio Pictorial*, 17 July 1936, 18; Murphy, *Behind the Wireless*, 101–2, 134–5.

There are no rule-of-thumb methods to guide you in radio adaptation, and this is what makes the work fascinating. For each novel, play, or story in question makes its own intrinsic demands on your care, judgment, taste, and common sense. Each fresh piece of work calls for an individual treatment, and the recognition of this need is the only working principle that should guide you in adapting any and every kind of material for the microphone.

How do we start the work? To begin with there's the choice of material. Sometimes you are able to choose this yourself: at other times it is chosen for you. Perhaps one of us reads a book, gets keen about it, and (with the author's permission, of course!) we decide to turn it into a radio play. *Lost Horizon*, for instance, I happened to read myself by chance.[2] And everything about the story struck me as being essentially 'radiogenic' (if you will forgive that rather highbrow word we sometimes use in our Department to describe something that strikes us as having distinct broadcasting possibilities). In that case, as with all the others, the job was to try to keep the essential charm and atmosphere of the novel while making it equally effective in its new medium. In this particular work I had the advantage of the author's collaboration. When we can do this, it is best. And the same applied to our joint adaptation of *Goodbye, Mr Chips*.[3] The choice of suitable material, you see, is quite half the battle. I think we are only beginning to realise the importance of this.

How much adapting is necessary? That depends, of course, entirely on the nature of the original. In a stage play such as *The Circle*, which you will hear broadcast in October, or in *Eden End*, which will be heard over the air about a month later, the adaptor's job is a comparatively light one. These are both plays in which the dialogue is telling to the point of brilliance, and brilliant dialogue is of even more value to the radio play than it is to the stage one. In these two plays our aim is to give the quality of the play with as little interference as possible. No stunts for stunts' sake, you see. That would be pointless and unfair to the author. In plays such as these, it's merely a matter of cutting out – however reluctantly! – certain parts of the play that depend upon visual effects and, if you must, substituting dialogue (though it *should* be the author's *own* dialogue!). As in the novel adaptation, it's getting the story and the atmosphere across that counts: if you haven't, you've let the play down.

And the Narrator? Here opinions differ. But the same principles should guide you. Don't, on the one hand, sacrifice simplicity or clarity for stunts: but on the other, don't let the quality of the play or the story be missed through

---

[2] *Lost Horizon*, radio play by James Hilton and Barbara Burnham, based on Hilton's novel, first broadcast on the BBC Regional Programme in June 1934, in a production by Burnham.

[3] *Goodbye, Mr Chips*, radio play by James Hilton and Barbara Burnham, based on Hilton's novel, first broadcast on the BBC Regional Programme in January 1935, in a production by Burnham.

lack of invention or resources. I myself can never see the necessity for a bald narrator. There is nearly always a good way out. Very often, in adapting a book, you can make one or more of the characters tell his or her own story. And in a play careful timing (the producer's job, as well as your own), music, and sometimes a preliminary introduction of the characters, is in nearly all cases just what you need.

4.5 ANON.: THE BROADCASTING OF POETRY

First published as 'The Broadcasting of Poetry,' *The BBC Year Book 1931* (London: British Broadcasting Corporation, 1931), 222–4.

This text, published anonymously, was a sequel to another piece from the *BBC Handbook 1929* bearing the same title, also anonymous. The writing style and concerns in both essays suggest Hilda Matheson as the most likely author (see 1.1 for a biographical sketch).[1]

• • •

The broadcasting of poetry probably arouses the critical, indeed the combative, instinct in listeners more acutely than any other part of the programme. This fact seems to be an additional proof – if additional proof be needed – that poetry has very deep and therefore very individual roots in the English character. People usually get angry about things in proportion as they care about them. It may be argued, therefore, that there is a strong case for the reading of poetry.

Broadcasting, however, may seem on the face of it a wholly unsuitable medium. It has of necessity a more or less universal appeal; how can it be brought to serve a peculiarly individual art like poetry? The loud-speaker

---

[1] Early radio and BBC scholar Kate Murphy has confirmed the likelihood of Matheson being the author in personal correspondence.

sends out what it receives in whatever company it may find itself – a noisy street, a busy kitchen, a living-room containing half a dozen people of different ages engaged in different occupations. How can an English lyric, however lovely, find the right reception in such circumstances? The answer, of course, is that it cannot; poetry, possibly more than any other kind of programme, demands some degree of co-operation on the part of the listener. It is a fact that much of the criticism of poetry reading does come from those who are waiting for the news or dance music to begin, for whom the reading is merely an annoying interlude. For such critics switching off must remain the only remedy.

But the important part of the problem concerns those who genuinely love poetry – or some poetry. Among these, the diversity of taste is clearly endless. There are those who have a strong prejudice against all contemporary poetry; there are others who are wearied by readings from poetry written in what seems to them archaic English. There must be many whose enjoyment of the poetry is marred by a feeling that they are not getting its full meaning – that they know too little about the poem, or the circumstances in which it was written, or the poet, or the point of the allusions. There are others, again, with a wider range of knowledge, who are irritated by any attempt at comment or explanation, which seems to them academic and tiresomely informative. Another set of controversies centres round the kind of poetry to be read. Some maintain that dramatic poetry or narrative poetry is the only poetry suitable for broadcasting; others, that these sound either too rhetorical or require too sustained an effort for broadcasting, and that lyric poetry, pure poetry, can make a more direct and more certain emotional appeal.

So much for the poetry; what of the reader? At one end of the scale are those who admire the manner and delivery of the trained elocutionist, the manner of the platform or of the stage. At the other end are those who feel strongly that the reader's voice should be entirely neutral and impersonal, letting the poetry speak for itself. In between, so far as one can judge, comes the large public which has no cut-and-dried theories, but which knows what it likes when it hears it. The available evidence seems to show that those who like, on the wireless, the elocutionary style are a small minority, and a dwindling minority; that the school of the ultra-monotone tradition is also a small one, and that for the largest public which listens to poetry it is important to avoid the extremes at both ends and to look for the following essentials: –

1. The reader should have the kind of voice which has a compelling quality of tone – the kind of voice one would want to listen to no matter what it said – a voice, therefore, without mannerism or affectation. Moreover, it must be of a kind which preserves these qualities even through the microphone.

2. He must understand the nature and structure of poetry, so that he can strike the right balance between bringing out the rhythm of the poem, the value of the words, and the meaning of the content, neither unduly obtruding his own personality nor repressing it by any trick.
3. He must be chosen specially for the poetry to be read. No one 'poetry reader' would serve for all kinds of poetry. He (or she) should have the appropriate timbre of voice, as well as a personal interest in, and feeling for, the poetry in question. In proportion as the reader is soaked in the poetry and has been able, as it were, to get inside the poet's conception, is the reading likely to be a success.

It will be seen, therefore, that the broadcasting of poetry demands quite special qualities and quite special study. Wireless is a universal medium, yet it makes its appeal to people, not in crowds, not as collected audiences, but as individuals. Poetry broadcasts must aim at something which will give the illusion of a reader at one's own fireside, *i.e.* a reading, not a performance. The reading must combine the right voice (and this means a voice which shall seem right to a very great diversity of listeners) and an understanding of the poetry – it cannot, in fact, be a perfunctory business. The most sensitive readers, therefore, are often those most vividly aware of the difficulties and most liable to suffer from a peculiarly paralysing kind of self-consciousness, which is not only a severe strain in itself, but which makes it difficult to continue to read poetry with success for long at a time. It is rare indeed that the poet himself is the right person to read his own poetry, because it is rare to find the poet's gifts combined with the right qualities of voice and diction, and unaffected by the conditions of studio and microphone.

All that can be said with certainty is that, since poetry was written not to be read only, but to be heard, broadcasting must surely continue to study the problem of how to let it be heard to the best advantage, so as to give pleasure to the largest number of listeners. There is no cut-and-dried theory of broadcast reading; but concentrated study and research during the last two years have enabled members of the BBC staff to learn at least some of the difficulties, some of the things to be avoided, and a few of the qualities which are essential. There is room for much experiment in presentation – from the occasional short reading of ten or fifteen minutes, to the half-hour talk illustrated by reading. The size of the present-day audience means that some degree of specialisation is inevitable in this as in other kinds of programme; no one kind of reading can hope to please everybody. But the aim should be, and is, to ensure that listeners should hear some of the finest poetry in the world read in a manner worthy of it, and that this should include the best of both old and new.

4.6 KURT WEILL: ON THE 'MUSICAL RADIO PLAY'

Translated by Marielle Sutherland. First published as 'Zum Thema „Musikalisches Hörspiel,"' *Der Deutsche Rundfunk*, 15 February 1929, 196.

Kurt Weill (1900–1950) was a German composer who wrote music for theatre, film and radio, and used music as a tool for political critique. His collaborations with Bertolt Brecht, with whom he worked from 1927 until the 1940s, are particularly well known. He wrote prolifically about radio too, and from 1925 to 1929 he was the chief music and drama critic for *Der Deutsche Rundfunk*, the leading German radio magazine edited by the Expressionist painter Hans Siebert von Heister. Weill was also the magazine's Berlin correspondent, contributing regular articles marked by his concern for radio's social responsibilities. Under threat as a Jewish artist, he left Germany for Paris in 1933; in 1935, he moved to the United States, where he wrote music for theatre and film, worked for Broadway theatres and in Hollywood, and continued to compose music for radio.[1]

* * *

Whereas there is currently much interest, among entrepreneurs and the general public, in developing literary radio plays, whereas people have already carried out important preliminary work in creating a dramatic poetry for the radio – using a broad range of methods, such as competitions, commissions, direct engagement of the most valuable personnel in active collaboration –, thus far, in actual fact, as good as no progress has been made as regards the *musical radio play*. The opera divisions of the various radio stations have limited themselves to exclusively presenting existing opera and operetta literature. In most cases (and presumably always in the case of smaller stations), this involves works that form part of the permanent repertoire of the opera houses and for which the stations need only find singers who have studied the respective roles, meaning that rehearsals are almost always used

[1] See Douglas Jarman, *Kurt Weill: An Illustrated Biography* (London: Orbis, 1982), 18, 110; Jürgen Schebera, *Kurt Weill: An Illustrated Life*, trans. Caroline Murphy (New Haven: Yale University Press, 1995), 63–4, 131–2; Nils Grosch, *Die Musik der Neue Sachlichkeit* (Stuttgart: Metzler, 1999), 226–39.

merely to refresh and consolidate the musical material. In more propitious, yet extremely rare, cases, an unknown new opera or a long-forgotten musical play from an earlier period is broadcast on the radio; by nature, such works require a new production of the solo parts, the choir and the orchestra, i.e. a considerable investment in rehearsals that may perhaps seem somewhat excessive for a single performance. Now, it is often said that a good radio performance of an opera is not only an adequate substitute for a broadcast from an opera house but often, in its effect, takes the listener beyond any impression that the performance was created in a broadcasting studio. This is certainly understandable if we consider that an opera performance in a broadcasting studio differs only slightly from such a performance in an opera house. The work of the person who arranges opera for radio is in most cases limited to dramaturgical condensation and clarification of the setting and the dramatic situation. Apart from that, the emphasis in the broadcasting studio too is on the effect of the music; this effect is naturally much stronger in the opera house, for of course greater tension is achieved there through the presence of the audience, through costume and scene, and through the indeterminable charm of the scenery.

The performance of opera on the radio, which differs only very slightly from a concert performance of a musical play, has only contributed significantly to the further development of radio itself in the sense that the intention has been to use it to pave the way towards a musical-dramatic art within radio. Thus far, however, there has been no progress in the creation of a musical radio play, and it looks as if the radio stations would be willing to make this preliminary stage permanent.

Recently, however, the development of opera has gone down a route which, in all likelihood, will also lead to a new genre of radio opera. Today, music in operatic theatre is beginning to play an entirely different role to that in previous decades. It no longer serves to accompany and enhance the action, to characterise the protagonists, to intensify the mood, the atmosphere of the play; rather, it takes up its own, specific space in the course of the action; it is only introduced where it can have an effect in and of itself, indeed where it can have absolute predominance. I strongly believe that this is the same task that will fall to music in the 'radio opera' of the future. Here too, music will only be introduced where the course of realistic events is interrupted, where articulation must take place on a higher level, where the language of music cannot be replaced by anything else. Indeed, such purely musical moments will arise much more fluently and frequently in a purely acoustic work of art than in a theatre. And so, it seems the prerequisites for a musical radio play have been created within musical theatre; it is now up to the broadcasters to take the necessary steps towards the creation of a work of art such as this.

4.7 PAUL DERMÉE: THE BROADCASTING OF SILENCE

Translated by Emilie Morin. First published as 'La radiodiffusion du silence,' *La Parole Libre TSF*, 16 December 1928, 3.

A biographical sketch is included with 'Will We Have a Radiophonic Art?' (1.5).

• • •

Yes, radio should care more about silence, the part of speech that is so conspicuously laden with pathos and so cruelly lacking in our civilisation. The plea for silence written by an anonymous English listener, which I endorse with conviction, should be put up on the walls of radio studios all over the world.[1]

How things contrast with their surroundings is what enables us to see them. Some animals are always on the lookout, are only governed by the impulse to fight or flee, and cannot distinguish between their prey and an enemy standing still. Although human sensations are better differentiated, we only notice things through their contrast with the larger picture: for example, the inhabitants of the great industrial cities can no longer hear the noise constantly rumbling around them. Yet it is within our cities that the minute of silence marking the anniversary of the Armistice became immensely dramatic, without other symbolic representation. Contrast is what brings art to life! Cézanne used to say that a good painting needs to have light and darkness in equal proportions. In the same vein, one should note how valuable silences are to music and to the diction of great actors.

---

[1] This anonymous plea could not be found, but similar appeals acknowledging the value of silence were made regularly. As early as June 1924, John Reith wrote a *Radio Times* article on 'The Broadcasting of Silence.' In the French press, discussions of silence were not unusual. Notably, the actor Denis d'Inès argued that 'radio theatre is not the art of noise but the art of silences. The attempt to produce special effects through sound is a big mistake and has stopped the progress of radio drama!' Likewise, Carlos Larronde identified silence as a key ingredient in radio drama: 'Radio drama, the theatre of space, wants space between the words.' Denis d'Inès, 'Comment jouez-vous devant le micro?,' *Comœdia*, 7 September 1934, 4; Carlos Larronde, 'Notes d'écoute,' *L'Intransigeant*, 27 June 1938, 5.

Radio must use silence as one of the most powerful means of enhancing sound. Silence should spread itself behind the voice or the instrument like a heavy velvet curtain. The sounds transmitted by the microphone should remain shrouded in silence, except when it is necessary to compose an arrangement of background noises *deliberately*. In some studios, whispers and people moving to and fro are barely heard, but even faint noises are enough to pollute the immaculate whiteness of silence – and that, the listeners can feel too.

We must make sure that our speakers, all those who deliver conference speeches on the radio learn the value of silence between words, between propositions, and above all between sentences. These are the rudiments of microphone diction, shall we say. Another reason, then, not to underestimate silence (as has been done all too often).

Lastly, silence has an enormous role to play in radio drama. Up to now, silence has been looked upon with suspicion, on the grounds that the microphone does not show all the things that a spectator sitting in a theatre, who can see the actors' gestures and facial expressions, will find moving. Without a doubt, and this is also part of the rudiments to learn, we should do better than attempt a brutal transfer of stage techniques onto the studio. When, for example, in the darkest sort of tragedy the murderer edges slowly towards his victim, it is silence, laden with emotion and the vision of what is happening, that creates dramatic emotion. And it is frequent to hear a spectator cry out at that precise moment because he is unable to control his emotions. I remember de Max[2] playing Nero and Lugné-Poë's performance as Rosmer in Ibsen's tragedy.[3] The violent internal debates tearing these characters apart were mimed *silently* by these great artists. And we could *see* them writhing as though their bodies had been set to burn on an invisible pyre. This is what the wireless cannot show. This is why the moments of silence that the wireless transmits should be carefully laden with meaning through the words that are uttered before each pause.

This reflection on a simple psychological impression has led us back to the subject of theatre on the wireless. It is impossible to stop thinking about it. It will be the great achievement of our era and it will reflect the present state of our civilisation.

Every day new blocks, more or less roughly trimmed, are being carried to the building site from which the temple of radio drama will eventually arise. Today, let us contribute a small white stone: silence.

---

[2] The Romanian-French actor Edouard de Max (1869–1924), who specialised in tragedies.
[3] Lugné-Poë directed productions of Ibsen's *Rosmersholm* in which he played the role of Jean Rosmer.

4.8 ALEX VIROT: REFLECTIONS ON RADIO-REPORTAGE

Translated by Emilie Morin. First published as 'Réflexions sur le radio-report-age,' *La Parole Libre TSF*, 25 October 1931, 1.

Alex Virot (1890–1957) was a celebrated French reporter. He started out working as a newspaper cartoonist, and gradually turned to radio broadcasting and radio journalism, writing for publications including *Paris-Soir*, *La Parole Libre TSF* and the sports weekly *Match L'Intran*. From 1930 onwards, he contributed to *L'Intransigeant* as a radio journalist, writing columns on diverse matters including radio plays. His radio journalism frequently discussed reportage techniques; he was persuaded that live reportage would not be supplanted by prerecorded content, and became renowned for his adventurous approach to the techniques and practicalities of live reporting. In 1929, he collaborated with reporter Jean Antoine on the occasion of the first live coverage of the Tour de France, using new equipment including one of the first mobile recording structures: a van fitted with a short-wave transmitter (sports reporters had previously used a fixed microphone positioned wherever the event was taking place, in a stadium or boxing ring, without any possibility of movement). Virot became a familiar voice in contexts far beyond sports: in 1935, notably, he covered the Italo-Abyssinian war and broadcast an exclusive interview of Haile Selassie on the Radio-Journal de France; in 1938, he covered the arrival of Nazi troops in Vienna for Radio-Cité. He worked for a range of radio stations, including Radio-Cité from 1935 onwards, and the Radiodiffusion Française and Radio Luxembourg after the Second World War. During the war, he joined the Maquis, resuming reportage work in 1944. He died in a road accident while covering the Tour de France for Radio Luxembourg.[1]

• • •

Radio-reportage is an activity worthy of the highest praise, because it addresses fresh themes that also draw attention to the difficulties posed by technical execution.

[1] H. de Peslouan, 'Les secrets du radio-reportage,' *Lectures Pour Tous*, July 1936, 72–80; Cécile Méadel, 'De l'épreuve et de la relation. Genèse du radio-reportage,' *Politix* 5, no. 19 (1992): 87–101; Felix Lowe, 'The Remarkable Tale of Alex Virot, the Tragic Tintin of the Tour de France,' Eurosport, 2017, https://www.eurosport.co.uk/cycling/tour-de-france/2017/the-remarkable-tale-of-alex-virot-the-tragic-tintin-of-the-tour-de-france_sto6242316/story.shtml, last accessed 7 September 2021.

Although the technique of radio transmission is indubitably making progress, the task of the radio-reporter remains thankless: within each new attempt lies a fresh work of creation.

Indeed, experience has taught us that there is no all-purpose formula for making radio-reportage; that in order to deal appropriately with a topic it is not enough to be able to speak with ease at a microphone; and that the art of radio-reportage consists in finding for each theme the formula that is best able to enhance the interest which it is likely to ignite.

If sports reportage has led to many genuine successes of late on the radio, that is because it has been practised since the first hour and, little by little, experience has borne fruit.

This cannot be said of other topics, which are approached with a great deal of audacity no doubt, but for which, most of the time, one cannot resort to experience. Nevertheless, no one can say that the radio-reporter works blindfolded, for no matter how much the topics of the radio-reportage differ from one another, they all share a common logic in terms of how they are presented. We are now beginning to understand the essential rules.

The Académie des Arts Phoniques – which by the way has displayed a somewhat paradoxical inertia – should produce a primer for radio-reportage.[2] There has to be within this Academy a competent figure capable of writing a booklet that all people who have ambitions to play the role of radio-reporter would be able to consult and would benefit from.

While the official rules are not yet issued, permit me to anticipate some of them and share some remarks.

PREAMBLE

Since the radio-reporter is the worst placed to assess the fruit of his efforts, the critics need to play their role (which in this case is a most laborious role) in a frank and direct way. It is up to the radio-reporter to avoid becoming resentful in response to negative comments made by those who are trying to analyse his work, when their judgements are supported by coherent arguments. Only on that condition will he improve.

PRECEPTS

- Radio-reportage is nothing but a new form of journalism.
- It is instantaneous journalism.
- It is not possible to become a journalist overnight.

---

[2] The French Academy of Phonic Arts, founded in May 1931 and gathering artists, technicians, writers and lawyers. It dealt with all forms of sonic art including radio, recorded discs and film; its annual prize rewarded French-language sound works including radio plays, reportage and recorded discs.

- In matters of journalism it is necessary to specialise in order to produce good-quality work.
- While relating a fact implicitly requires the ability to observe, commenting and judging, on the other hand, require in-depth knowledge of the subject addressed.
- One can only speak well about what one knows.
- This knowledge becomes all the more necessary with radio-reportage, since it is also instantaneous journalism.
- In an article, between one sentence and the next, there is always space to reflect and even collect information over an undetermined period of time. In radio-reportage there is scarcely enough time to swallow one's saliva between two improvised instalments.
- Just as there is such a thing as poor writing, there is such a thing as poor speaking, that is to say that badly-spoken radio-reportage is as off-putting as a poorly-written article.
- In speaking matters just as in writing matters, one should not confuse verve and prolixity.
- A journalist who knows how to see and how to write will take great care in coordinating the different elements of his work with enough coherence to enable his evocation to be not only truthful but above all capable of enhancing the emotion emanating from his subject. There is no better example for the radio-reporter to follow.

ON RADIO-REPORTAGE STRICTLY SPEAKING

- The greatest difficulty lies in translating a visual impression verbally and instantaneously; it is essential to train oneself in this kind of exercise as often as possible.
- It is an excellent thing to ensure that one does not fall silent, no matter what happens, but this does not mean that one must speak without saying anything: that would be falling from Charybdis to Scylla.
- Underneath the improvisation, the solid frame of a preestablished plan must show through.

  It is just as dangerous for the radio-reporter to feel that he has become familiar with the microphone as it is to feel daunted by it; indeed, excessive confidence is often accompanied by a degree of negligence, which encourages improvisation in content as well as form.

- Improvising content is like asking chance to do the work of the artist; the radio-reporter is far more competent than chance, too competent to do that.
- If one has gaps in one's knowledge, one should not feel compelled to profess ignorance when imparting information to listeners. There are other ways of dealing with the microphone.

- Be coherent: the atmosphere is everything that surrounds, everything that encircles, everything that envelops.
- News reportage depends on the duration of the event that it relates. Anecdotal reportage must take the listeners' attention span into account. We know that it is limited.
- If two speakers are better than one, this is also because they allow reflection and documentation to come to the rescue of the radio-reportage during its realisation.
- The team of two speakers is to the lone radio-reporter what the stereoscope viewer is to the photographic camera.

This is enough for today. The need for a school of radio-reportage has often been discussed and, as a matter of fact, it genuinely seems as though experience has begun to yield, little by little, a beneficial education.[3] We hope that radio-reporters will draw inspiration from it all.

4.9 HERMANN KASACK: MICRO-REPORTAGE

Translated by Marielle Sutherland. First published as 'Mikroreportage,' *Die Sendung*, 6 September 1929, 587–8.

Hermann Kasack (1896–1966), a German novelist, poet and playwright, was deeply dedicated to radio. Between 1925 and 1933, he was a prominent presence at the Berlin Funkstunde: he delivered talks about literature and poetry, read from his work and presented programmes for adults and children. He wrote over a hundred radio programmes, including talks about theatre, portraits of German writers, radio plays (sometimes under a pseudonym) and radio poems. He was also a prolific radio critic. A member of Gruppe 1925 alongside leading anti-Nazi and Jewish writers, he saw his

[3] Calls for the creation of such a school were issued throughout the 1930s by French radio journalists including Carlos Larronde, Alex Surchamp, Georges Delamare and Jean-Gabriel Poincignon, but no such school was created then in France. By May 1933, Germany had schools of radio reportage in Berlin and Munich, founded by Richard Kolb, a fervent Nazi who directed the Berlin Funkstunde after Hans Flesch's removal.

radio commissions dry up in 1931 and 1932, and was banned from public speaking and broadcasting in March 1933 (he eventually returned to broadcasting in 1946). He continued to write after Hitler's accession to power, producing prose works as well as coded resistance poems. From 1941 onwards, he worked for the publisher Suhrkamp; in 1953, he became president of the Akademie für Sprache und Dichtung, the German Academy for Language and Literature.[1]

● ● ●

'Micro-reportage': this is the dynamic reporting of events and activities that are transmitted in situ through the microphone.[2] The very first time a journalist abandoned the custom of talking through the microphone in the broadcasting studio and took the microphone outside into the open air was the moment that marked the birth of radio reportage. The first time such an event took place was in Berlin in the spring of 1925, when a horse race was broadcast from Karlshorst.[3] Initially, this type of reportage was limited almost exclusively to short reports of sporting events. Gradually, the sphere of micro-reportage expanded to include current daily events too.

[1] Charles W. Hoffmann, *Opposition Poetry in Nazi Germany* (Berkeley: University of California Press, 1962), 154–5; Martina Fromhold, *Hermann Kasack und der Rundfunk in der Weimarer Republik* (Aachen: Alano, Rader, 1990).

[2] *Mikroreportage* in the original, translated as micro-reportage to retain the inventiveness of Kasack's term, which also conveys the focus of the reportage on chunks of life and its presentation of a contained world. English sources from the late 1930s refer to 'radio-reportage,' with 'microphone reportage' only appearing much later.

[3] From the Berlin-Karlshorst racetrack. The first German sports broadcast was, however, transmitted earlier than that: it was a rowing regatta broadcast by Norag, the Hamburg station, in July 1924. By 1925, the mobile microphone was an accepted notion in Germany, widely relayed in radio-related headlines, slogans and press articles. In 1928, in *Der Deutsche Rundfunk*, von Heister expressed his wish for a 'travelling microphone,' 'at one moment [. . .] at a football match, and at the next moment [. . .] already transmitting the finish of a horse race derby.' Calling for more live reportage and for more broadcasting outside the studio, he hoped for a radio that would offer an 'acoustically tactile' contact with 'everyday life in all its manifold color' (trans. Brían Hanrahan). The wandering microphone also provided a frame for outdoor broadcasts focused on city sounds, examples of which included Paul Laven and Paul Hindemith's experimental series on the concept of the 'disoriented microphone,' relaying sounds from across streets, railway stations and the Frankfurt docks, or one of its sequels featuring radio reporters speaking from multiple popular locations in Paris. See Hans Siebert von Heister, 'Unser Osterwunsch – Aktualität, Aktualität, Aktualität!,' *Der Deutsche Rundfunk*, 3 April 1928, 957–8; Brían Hanrahan, 'The Mobilization of Weimar Radio: Actuality, Microphone, Radio-film,' *Transfers* 3, no. 2 (2013): 8, 12–13; Kate Lacey, *Listening Publics: The Politics and Experience of Listening in the Media Age* (Cambridge: Polity, 2013), 103–5; Paul Laven, 'Aus dem Erinnerungsbrevier eines Rundfunkpioniers,' *Literatur und Rundfunk 1923–1933*, 16–25.

Today, reportage is the principal component in modern radio programming, along with presentations related to the arts and entertainment.

What is the nature of reportage? First of all, the number of participants in a particular event is not restricted to the number of people present; rather, the general public becomes a witness to the event. A major difference between micro-reportage and mere news broadcasting is that in the former we experience the tension of the moment, and in the latter we are given the ultimate, conclusive result from the outset. This is the case with, for example, all sporting events, races and contests. Skilful micro-reportage turns every radio listener into a viewer. Consider, for example, the broadcasting of the two rounds of the Davis Cup tennis tournament, the Six-Day Race and football matches.[4] Even though the boxing match between Schmeling and Paolino, broadcast from America, did not depict the action directly from the ringside but sent progress reports on the individual rounds from an editorial office to Germany a few minutes later in each case, this meant much more to the listeners than a retrospective news report on Schmeling's success, albeit the atmosphere (the crowd's expressions of acclamation, etc.) was entirely lost in the process.[5] Another example: How different the experience of all those people who heard the bells of liberation ringing out from Cologne Cathedral at midnight from the experience of those who merely read about it the next morning in the newspapers . . .[6] The sound of the bells still resonates unforgettably in the ear of the radio listener, as if he himself had actually been there. Micro-reportage also includes broadcasts from Zeppelins and excerpts from broadcasts of public gatherings: this is broadcasting in the service of the speaking object.[7]

---

[4] Six-day races, appreciated across the world and particularly popular in Weimar Germany, were cycling events that provided prime broadcasting material.

[5] The German boxing champion Paul Schmeling, who defeated the Basque boxer Paulino Uzcudun in a well-publicised match in 1929.

[6] A broadcast from 3 January 1926 celebrating the withdrawal of foreign troops from areas of the Rhineland and other parts of Germany that had been under British, Belgian and French military control since 1918; British troops had left the area around Cologne the previous day. The German writer Otto Alfred Palitzsch summarised the event as follows: 'Hundreds of thousands in the most distant provinces took part in this festival, with its speeches, the rumbling confusion of voices, the echo of the city astir, and the chimes of the German bells upon the Rhine. A singular event, a piece of history, was captured by the radio and transmitted just as it proceeded in reality.' Otto Alfred Palitzsch, 'Broadcast Literature,' trans. Don Reneau, in *The Weimar Republic Sourcebook*, eds. Anton Kaes, Martin Jay and Edward Dimendberg (Berkeley: University of California Press, 1994), 601.

[7] Types of reportage involving physical and technological feats were practised from the mid-1920s onwards, including broadcasts from mountain tops, the ocean bed, the bottom of mineshafts, and exercises in actuality broadcasting such as the live transmission of Clarence Chamberlin's transatlantic flight in 1927. 'Extreme' broadcasting enabled radio stations and reporters to push the boundaries of what was technically achievable. French radio

The bells ringing from Cologne Cathedral, the whirring of the Zeppelin's propellers, the thunderous applause of a large crowd of people, etc. – radio reportage can portray many things without needing the personal involvement of an announcer or speaker. Yet there are also many cases where a supporting commentary, namely 'oral reportage' – as Alfred Braun once termed it – is required.[8] Alfred Braun has a pronounced gift for radio reportage, which must be handled very differently to newspaper reportage.

There have been many cases where excellent newspaper reporters have completely failed in front of the microphone because rather than producing spoken words, they have, as it were, merely reproduced written words. Micro-reportage is the art of 'ad libbing.' Not only the events, but above all their intensity, their atmosphere, their reflection of reality must be transmitted through words, sounds, pauses and announcements. In this respect, Braun is unsurpassed in the whole of Germany. He has the ability to adapt to an unknown situation in such a way that he not only makes audible what he sees and observes, but above all what is *worth* seeing and observing from the point of view of the person listening on his device. His best reports are those in which he is wholly reliant on his presence of mind. An excellent combination of factual information, momentary ideas and expert intimacy with the microphone! A good radio reporter must always put himself (like a radio producer) in the position of the radio listener; he must answer the listeners' questions, despite them in fact never reaching his ear, as effortlessly as he would if they had been asked of him in reality.

The role of good radio reportage is to do justice to the vitality of the moment. This is why it also adheres to a principle peculiar to radio. The principle of uniqueness. The appeal of self-contained fleetingness. Recently, Berlin has made some outstanding progress in the development of micro-reportage. There are three different kinds of micro-reportage: reportage on sports and current affairs, as well as reportage on everyday life. Current affairs often require reportage that interrupts the normal programming, as happened recently in the case of the

stations, for example, practised the airship reportage from 1929 onwards, and attempted broadcasts from the top of Mont Blanc and from a high-speed train in 1932. See Hanrahan, 'The Mobilization of Weimar Radio,' 12; Roger Frison-Roche, 'Un radioreportage au Mont-Blanc,' *Annuaire de la Radiodiffusion Nationale, année 1933* (Paris: Ministère des PTT; Service de la Radiodiffusion, 1933), 267–76; Léon Plouviet, 'La radio en aérostat,' ibid., 277–84; Méadel, 'Genèse du radio-reportage,' 87–101.

8 *Mundreportage* in the original. The reporter and producer Alfred Braun (1888–1978) was a pioneer of radio reportage and live commentary. Braun's documentaries for the Berlin Funkstunde included the programme series *Mit dem Mikro durch Berlin* ('Around Berlin with the Microphone'), which began in October 1928. See Carolyn Birdsall, 'Sonic Artefacts. Reality Codes of Urbanity in Early German Radio Documentary,' in *Soundscapes of the Urban Past: Staged Sound as Mediated Cultural Heritage*, ed. Karin Bijsterveld (Bielefeld: Transcript, 2013), 140–1.

interview with Sven Hedin, for example.[9] The extemporaneous interview is, in general, a form of reportage that has scope for further development, especially considering the possibilities offered by the capital city of the German Reich: 'The Voice of the Day' two or three times a week for ten minutes (it does not need to be any longer); this is how to offer topicality.[10] Other types of reportage on current affairs could be built into the normal programming. We may recall here the launch of the SS Bremen and Hans Bodenstedt's experimental attempt to broadcast regular reports from on board the ship during its maiden voyage.[11]

What I call everyday reportage may also be valuable: wandering around a zoo with the microphone, walking through a warehouse or a large train station, visiting places of entertainment or going behind the scenes at a hotel.[12] We have heard much of this type of reportage before – and it has had varying degrees of success –, but we would not wish to risk too much repetition. This is why we should welcome the idea of sending radio reporters into foreign cities and thereby attempting to create a new kind of urban and rural reportage. Here, as well as conveying over the radio what is happening on the spot, the radio reporter has another task: to vividly illustrate what is characteristic about the different cityscapes.[13] Everyday reportage: this allows the cities to speak, the workplaces, the mines, the phenomena of social life – without, however,

[9] The Swedish explorer Sven Hedin (1865–1952), a Nazi sympathiser and later friend of Hitler's, was a popular public figure.

[10] The evening programme 'Stimme des Tages' broadcast throughout November and December 1938 by the Prague station Praha II-Mělník, which transmitted German-language programmes.

[11] Hans Bodenstedt (1887–1958), director of the Norag, was renowned for adventurous reportage; his early experiments included an interview with a zookeeper and a telephone conversation with a deep-sea diver at the bottom of the sea. See Palitzsch, 'Broadcast Literature,' 601.

[12] Broadcasts from zoos were popular elsewhere too; examples beyond Germany include a reportage conducted by Alex Surchamp from the lions' enclosure at the Paris Foire du Trône in 1934 (a lion urinated on him halfway through), and a radio visit of Manchester's Belle Vue Zoological Gardens hosted by 'Mrs Rooney of Belfast,' one of the BBC's many radio characters, for her many followers in 1935. See Surchamp, 'Tribulations et tartarinades d'un radioreporter,' *Annuaire de la Radiodiffusion Nationale, année 1934*, 307–10; 'On the Wireless,' *The Irish Times*, 16 May 1935, 4.

[13] Such sound portraits were first made by Hans Bodenstedt and Hans Flesch in 1924, when they conceived *Hörbilder* or cityscapes for Norag; these were a streetscape and a portrait of the port of Hamburg, which Bodenstedt described as an attempt to draw on the 'sounds of reality.' Through such sound portraits, he argued, 'the whole world offers itself as studio.' See Hans Bodenstedt, 'Spiel im Studio,' in *Aus meinem Archiv: Probleme des Rundfunks*, ed. Hans Bredow (Heidelberg: Kurt Vowinckel, 1950), 145; Reinhard Döhl, *Das neue Hörspiel: Geschichte und Typologie des Hörspiels* (Darmstadt: Wissenschaftliche Buchgesellschaft, 1988), 127; Mark E. Crory, 'Soundplay: The Polyphonous Tradition of German Radio Art,' in *Wireless Imagination: Sound, Radio, and the Avant-Garde*, eds. Douglas Kahn and Gregory Whitehead (Cambridge: MIT Press, 1992), 339; Birdsall, 'Sonic Artefacts. Reality Codes of Urbanity in Early German Radio Documentary,' 137.

embellishing the abhorrent side of reality! And what about court reportage? Every week, from Moabit, we hear an hour-long transmission of some sort of 'public' trial![14] And this does not mean the big exemplary cases but the minor trial proceedings that unfold every day. It is incomprehensible that the Reichstag has thus far resisted broadcasting. Hence, we have all the more need for the 'contrived' reportage currently produced in Frankfurt and Berlin in the form of newspaper reports and chronicles (on original disc records) – albeit such a thing should, under normal circumstances, be rejected.[15] It will only become possible to implement dynamic micro-reportage systematically once the question of the indispensable short-wave transmitter has been resolved. This is because the speaker must have some freedom from the microphone's technical demands and functions. After all, the role of reportage on current affairs becomes this: not to beat around the bush when confronting reality – rather to search out reality in every place where it speaks to us through rhythm, life and intellect – and not to shy away from the darker side of life. For micro-reportage really does have the potential to let life speak without falsification or distortion, and to turn radio into an authority on objective observation.

4.10 OLIVE SHAPLEY: NIGHT ROMANCE OF THE ROADS

First published as 'Night Romance of the Roads,' *Radio Times*, 28 October 1938, 8.

Olive Shapley (1910–1999) was a British radio producer celebrated for her imaginative approach to the radio documentary and dedication to social issues. She started

---

[14] From the Kriminalgericht, the Central Criminal Court in Moabit, in Berlin's Mitte district.

[15] Gramophone and wax disc recording, used in Germany for news gathering from mid-1929 onwards, played an important role in the rise of outdoor broadcasts and offered new editing possibilities. To mark the end of 1929, for example, Hans Flesch made the first attempt at a gramophone news compilation, which he called *Rückblick im Schallplatte*. This became a monthly occurrence the following year, and included additional short clips from Reichstag speeches. See Birdsall, 'Sonic Artefacts,' 141, 146.

working for the BBC in 1934, as Children's Hour organiser for the North region; in 1937, she became assistant producer for the North region, a post she held until 1939. She created new types of documentaries for the BBC Features Department, travelling across the North of England with a van fitted with a mobile recording unit, and using inventive sound montage to capture voices and atmospheres. She celebrated the lives of ordinary people, notably in documentaries such as 'Night Journey,' about night lorry drivers (1938), 'Homeless People,' about the homeless (1938), and 'Miners' Wives' (1939), which compared the lives of mining communities in County Durham and the North of France. Shapley also produced radio plays, arranged radio programmes, and adapted and translated plays for the BBC's Children's Hour. Joan Littlewood and Ewan MacColl (as Jimmie Miller) were among the presenters she often used for her documentaries; she worked with Littlewood on 'The Classic Soil,' a documentary contrasting Manchester in 1939 with Engels's portrait in *The Condition of the Working Class in England*. When Shapley married another BBC staff member, the BBC's rules for couples forced her to resign; during the Second World War, she nonetheless continued to work freelance for the BBC; she produced documentaries giving voice to women and, after moving to the United States, she continued to contribute to the BBC's Children's Hour and created a new programme, 'Letter from America.' Thereafter, from 1949 to 1953, Shapley was presenter and producer of the BBC's Woman's Hour. She was rarely invited to comment on her work in writing; her print journalism for the *Radio Times* and the *Listener* amounts to a handful of short articles.[1]

●　　●　　●

Each night the roads of this country change their character completely. The process begins almost imperceptibly in the early evening, and by midnight the transformation is complete: the roads are alive with heavy, steadily-moving traffic. Near London especially they are much livelier than they have ever been by day. These journeys go on every night of the week; snow and ice and fog may slow them up, but will never stop them altogether. Locomotives and cabbages, heavy machinery and sewing-needles are all carried along the roads in this way, from seaport to seaport, from one great industrial centre to another.

The individual units in this nightly trek are of every variety, from the smartly-painted light van to the lumbering eight-wheeler with its misshapen load tied down with tarpaulin. There are hundreds of cafés which exist only for this night traffic. Any night you will find ranks of lorries drawn up outside them, the drivers slewed across the wheel asleep. When they wake they will have a cup of tea, perhaps a meal, and set out on another four or five-hour stretch.

Again, you may travel for miles and not catch a glimpse of another human being in the dark cabins of the lorries, but the roads will be alive with conversation, the sign language of the headlights, dipping and flashing.

---

[1] See Olive Shapley and Christina Hart, *Broadcasting: A Life, The Autobiography of Olive Shapley* (London: Scarlet Press, 1996).

This is one of the aspects, the romantic aspect if you like, of road transport that we want to bring out in this programme.[2] You may say that all this is a visual thing, but we think it can be brought to your ears too. We shall spend a good deal of time making sound recordings – of lorries thundering along the new, straight roads, of lorries grinding up the steep side of Shap, of lorries leaving a depot under the echoing railway arches and setting off over Manchester cobbles on an eleven-hour run.

The other thing we want to do in this programme is to give some idea of the lives of the men who operate this intricate road service. We shall spend two nights in a transport café, recording conversations all the time. Not more than ten minutes of this will be used in the completed programme, but it is obvious that none of this can be rehearsed, and we may have to 'shoot' for an hour or so before we get anything useful.

Unofficial Interviewer

It may be rather disturbing to go in to your usual café for a cup of tea and half-an-hour's sleep, and find that you are expected to talk into a microphone, so we are taking with us someone who has had experience of road-transport work and, at the same time, has a clear idea of what we want for this broadcast. He will act as an unofficial interviewer, and will ask the kind of questions that everybody is interested in: Do you ever want to sleep on the road? What does it feel like to set out in a thick fog? Do you mind giving up an ordinary home life? And so on. We hope, however, that we shall not have to use an interviewer at all, and that the drivers who drop into the café will talk without any prompting.

How Others Work

One night I rode on a lorry for ten hours. This particular lorry was twenty-six feet long; it had eight wheels, seven gears, and weighed eight tons. The load, consisting of valuable chemicals and textiles, weighed another fourteen tons. There was a fine rain falling and I should have found it a strain driving an ordinary car on that road. The noise was shattering most of the time, and it was very hot and stuffy in the cabin. I learnt from first-hand experience that the lorry-driver must be very strong physically, have no nerves at all, and be a first-class driver. In addition to this he must make up his mind to a very lonely life, a life almost cut off from the rest of the world. 'Night Journey' will give him a chance to speak for himself, and will give those who work in the daytime and opportunity of hearing something about those who work at night.

---

[2] 'Night Journey,' arranged and produced by Shapley, broadcast on the BBC Regional Programme in October 1938.

4.11 B.E.N.: FEATURE PROGRAMMES

First published as B.E.N., 'Feature Programmes,' *Radio Times*, 31 August 1928, 367, 376.

The identity of the author, clearly a member of staff at the BBC, is not indicated in the original. The initials point to B. E. Nicolls (Basil Edward Nicolls, 1893–1965), the BBC's General Editor of Publications from 1928 and, prior to that, Station Director of 2LO London (1926–1928) and 2ZY Manchester (1924–1925), and Assistant Director of Education (1925).[1] 'Feature programme' was the term employed at the BBC for broadcasts that combined speech, music and factual information. Two decades later, Val Gielgud defined the feature programme as 'the most essentially "radio" of all programmes broadcast,' but also as a difficult notion, which covered an 'exceedingly wide' range of possibilities. Originally, Gielgud observed, the term would 'cover programmes without obvious labels – programmes that for some quality of the unusual stood out from the generally flattish plain of normal programme output'; the feature programme, he pointed out, was soon used to designate 'any programme item – other than a radio play – whose author makes use of the specialized technique of radio-dramatic production.'[2]

• • •

From the earliest days of broadcasting special programmes have been devised which could not be claimed either as musical programmes, plays, or talks, but were in fact a combination of all three. These were special programmes in the sense that they were out of the ordinary, involved research and thought, and had some claim to being considered an original form of expression, peculiar to broadcasting and not suited to the public stage or concert platform. For convenience in administration some generic title was required to denote the programmes which could not be classified as one of the ordinary forms of programme activity, and 'feature programme' insensibly established itself as convenient and descriptive. The phrase may not occur often in the BBC's

[1] My thanks to Kate Murphy for identifying Nicolls as the most likely author and sharing biographical information.

[2] Val Gielgud, *Years of the Locust* (London: Nicholson & Watson, 1947), 74. See also footnote 2, p. 116.

published programmes, but the listening public is quite familiar with the type of programme which it indicates.[3]

Feature programmes are almost as old as broadcasting. The *Radio Times* goes back as far as the autumn of 1923, and they figure occasionally in its columns even then. Major Corbett-Smith, when Director of Cardiff Station, was the pioneer; under his pilotage the Magic Carpet visited China on the first of its twenty flights,[4] and other real feature programmes such as 'The Mariners of England' and 'Nature Pictures' were supplemented by 'Literary Nights' and 'Mr Everyman's' informal commentaries on symphony concerts.[5] Bournemouth produced one of the earliest feature programmes under the heading 'Eighty Years Ago,' the forerunner of other period programmes such as '1770' and 'In a Victorian Drawing-room.'[6] Early in 1924 Major Corbett-Smith came to London, and was responsible for several elaborate productions, of which 'Under the White Ensign,' 'Moods in a Garden,' and 'Sportsmen All' were typical.[7] Some of these experiments were less successful than others, but all were interesting and the historical programmes often definitely stimulating. [. . .]

The real feature programme combines speech and music to produce an artistic result which could not have been produced by either separately. A talk on London is a talk; poems about London may form part of a poetry reading; the *'London' Symphony* and *Cockaigne Overture* are music:[8] combine the three and you have the makings of a feature programme. It is essential that the thread running through a feature programme should be a strong one and that none of the musical or spoken constituents should be irrelevant. It may sometimes take a week to find an appropriate piece of music, but the programme fails if it is not found, and there is no real substitute. Some seeming feature programmes are merely titles and nothing else, or titles and a quotation, followed by one or two more or less appropriate items. At one time every evening concert, almost, had

---

[3] [Author's note] A series of programmes of chamber music and songs broadcast from Cardiff, early in 1924, was presented under the heading of 'Feature Programmes,' but the use of the words for that type of programme did not find general acceptance.

[4] 'The Magic Carpet 1: China,' broadcast on 5WA Cardiff in 1924, featured Corbett-Smith as a pilot flying a magic carpet over China.

[5] Programmes broadcast in December 1923, on 2LO London and 5WA Cardiff respectively. A series of 'Literary Nights' were broadcast in 1923 and 1924 on various BBC stations. Mr Everyman was a popular speaker in 1923 and 1924, and presented programmes on 5WA Cardiff.

[6] Programmes broadcast on 6BM Bournemouth in 1923 and 1924; '1770,' on Samuel Johnson, Boswell and Oliver Goldsmith, was broadcast in 1927 on 2LO London and 5XX Daventry; 'An Hour in a Victorian Drawing-room' was broadcast on 5NO Newcastle in 1925.

[7] These programmes from 1924 were broadcast on all BBC stations.

[8] Edward Elgar's *Cockaigne (In London Town)*, Op. 40.

a special title, and the pages of the *Radio Times* bristled with 'Fun and Frolic,' 'Powder and Patches,' 'A Summer Soufflé,' 'A Mixed Grill,' and even doubtful improvisations such as 'High-Low,' 'Lightsome,' etc. A heading does not make a feature programme, unless the actual programme is worked out very closely.[9] A composer programme is not a real feature programme, nor is an illustrated musical lecture.

A word as to the devising of feature programmes. This makes an amusing hobby, and any listener who cares to try it will find it both interesting and instructive. The difficulty depends on the subject. Anyone can knock together musical and literary items to form a programme under the heading of 'The Open Road'; but try, say, 'Joan of Arc' or 'Give a Man a Horse he can Ride' and you will find it rather more difficult. If your programme is to be designed for broadcasting, the greatest danger that you will have to surmount is that of having too much spoken matter. Really suitable musical items are often difficult to find for some particular programmes, *e.g.*, a Dr. Johnson programme, where conversely there is plenty of literary material; and there is always the danger of allowing the announcements and linking material to destroy the balance between speech and music.

In the studio there is one fundamental difficulty which faces the producer of anything more elaborate than the miniature programmes in which not more than two or three persons are involved – that is the difficulty of creating 'atmosphere.' Every listener knows that atmosphere in the studio is passed on out of it to the listener, just as much as the individual broadcaster's personality. With three or four persons in one studio, atmosphere is easy to obtain. When, however, owing to the size and variety of the constituent orchestras and players, the programme is performed in several studios simultaneously, or when it is performed in one large studio with some forty of fifty persons in it, the atmosphere that is created by the collective interaction (both in sight and sound) of all the artists is very difficult to obtain. The problem is best illustrated by the latter case. In, for instance, a historical programme the linking notes and announcements are of the greatest importance in carrying on the action and creating a mood for the music or play that follows; and it is really almost as essential that the musicians and players should hear the announcement and catch the mood as that the listeners should. In the early days of broadcasting, this was possible, owing to the fact that the studios were very small and the announcer had to speak loudly enough, into the comparatively insensitive microphones then used for the whole of the orchestra and other artists in the studio to hear every word. In the modern large studio with sensitive microphones, the orchestra cannot hear the announcement, and finds it difficult in consequence to follow the programme with close interest or share any of the dramatic excitement

[9] Titles used for BBC programmes from 1923 to 1927.

that may be affecting the announcer or producer. The announcer, on the other hand, cannot speak loud enough for the orchestra to hear or his voice would sound unnatural to listeners and the effect of the announcement be lost. He, in his turn, and the other readers and soloists, will be affected by the unavoidable lack of interest of those members of the orchestra, etc., who cannot hear what is going on. The atmosphere of the programme suffers, and the listener finds himself merely interested where, in other circumstances, he might have been enthralled or deeply moved.

4.12 LAURENCE GILLIAM: 'ACTUALITIES' AND 'FEATURES'

First published in 'Sidelights on Radio Drama,' *Radio Times*, 30 August 1935, 7.

Laurence Gilliam (1907–1964) was a British radio producer who led the development of feature programmes at the BBC. Before his BBC career he worked for the British Gramophone Company and as journalist, actor and producer. He joined the staff of the *Radio Times* as writer in 1932, then the BBC Drama Department in 1933, where he experimented with sound pictures and mobile recording vans and arranged, adapted and produced a vast range of programmes, including radio plays, Christmas programmes, actuality features, and sound montages merging the factual and the fictional. The BBC's Drama and Features departments were twinned until 1936; when they were split, Gilliam was appointed Assistant Director in charge of Features, becoming Head of Features in 1945. The present piece appeared in the *Radio Times* alongside commentaries by ten authors involved in broadcasting (Barbara Burnham, L. du Garde Peach, Peter Creswell, Robert Chignell, Howard Rose, Lance Sieveking, Harcourt Williams, Barbara Couper, Gordon Gildard, Wilfrid Rooke Ley), who had been asked to discuss how radio plays are made.

• • •

The appeal of 'the real thing' is the essence of actuality broadcasting. These programmes deal in 'the real stuff,' but the fact that the stuff is real is not enough. Life in the raw is indigestible; it must be presented, and that is where the job of the radio producer comes in.

If this job is well done, the 'real thing' is presented without strain and given emphasis, comment, colour, and contrast. Any methods are justified – mobile recording van, direct relays, short-wave relays from the other side of the earth, direct or recorded, studio scenes here and there if necessary – the end justifies the means. There are only two final tests of good 'actuality.' Does it sound real, and is it interesting? It may be as real as yesterday's weather, but no one may care.

Think of some treatments of reality that you have seen or heard; of films like *Berlin, Drifters, Man of Aran*, the recent BBC film *The Voice of Britain*, or the authentic African dances in a fictional film like *Sanders of the River*;[1] or of such recent 'actuality' programmes as the Christmas Day programmes, 'In Town Tonight,' 'Owt about Owt,' sudden flashes in the News Bulletins, microphone tours of Midland and Northern villages, the Dales programme, '*Opping 'Oliday, Gale Warning, Cable Ship*, or even a complicated mixture of the real and the reconstructed like the Silver Jubilee programme, *Twenty-Five Years*.[2]

Features like these, from far or near, recorded or direct, are remembered, if at all, because they bore the stamp of truth and reality, because their subjects were interesting, because they touched some deep quality of sentiment, reminiscence, technical interest or human curiosity. They were reassuringly real and alive.

Half-way between the radio-play and the actuality programme stands the 'feature' programme, applying the technique of the radio play to a real, that is, actual or historical, subject. Its main field has been the reconstruction of the past, gaining authority by the use of contemporary sources and interest from the radio dramatic method. There are subtle differences between such strictly documented dramatic narratives as *The King's Tryall, Air Race*, and *Twenty Years Ago* and the elegiac quality of *Gallipoli*, or, again, programmes like *Sedgmoor* and *Gordon of Khartoum*, which were to all intents historical plays, but they all bear an unmistakable family likeness.[3]

Two other types of feature programmes have firmly established themselves. One is the anthology type, which illustrates a central theme with music, poetry, dramatic scenes or descriptive prose; such as *Miscellany, Mosaic*, and *Pilgrim's Way*.[4]

---

[1] Documentary films by Walter Ruttmann (1927), John Grierson (1929), Robert J. Flaherty (1934); *BBC: The Voice of Britain* (1935), a film scripted by Stuart Legg; a film by Zoltán Korda (1935), decried for its racism and xenophobia.

[2] BBC programmes and plays broadcast in 1934 and 1935.

[3] These were historical reconstructions and historical plays broadcast in 1934 and 1935, but there are no definite records associated with some of these titles.

[4] Regular BBC programmes shaped as thematic anthologies, in which poetry often dominated.

The other is the biographical programme – *Coleridge*, *Peter Porcupine*, or *Sir Thomas More*. These programmes have sought a swift evocation of the central figure, and have succeeded in avoiding the limping pedestrianism of the usual biographical play.[5]

Most feature programmes have made use of music as an integral part of the general design. Sometimes it is present purely as a link, sometimes it rises to the dignity and significance of a protagonist. Sometimes original music is specially commissioned, but more often the rich store of recorded music is drawn upon.

But the essentials of the good feature programme are: A firmly-defined theme, accurate but imaginatively handled research, and, above all, good writing. The niceties of radio production can then be applied to enhance the final effect; but without these firm foundations they are but sound and fury.

4.13 CHARLES SIEPMANN: TALKS

First published as 'Talks,' *Radio Times*, 8 September 1933, 527.

Charles Siepmann (1899–1985) joined the BBC in 1927 as an Education Assistant, then became Head of Adult Education from 1928, working closely with Hilda Matheson. He replaced Matheson as the BBC's Director of Talks in 1932, a role he held until 1935, in which he furthered her innovations, and the Talks Department's progressive agenda and readiness to deal with contentious social issues. In 1935, he became the BBC's Director of Regional Relations; in 1936, Director of Programme Planning. Over the course of his career at the BBC, he occasionally stepped on the other side of the microphone, giving readings from Vita Sackville-West's and W. B. Yeats's poems in 1929 and 1936. Relations with John Reith became increasingly fraught (like Matheson, Siepmann was felt to be too radical); he resigned from his post, left Britain for the United States and began an academic career at Harvard in 1939, where his research focused on the social and educational significance of radio. From 1942 to 1945, he served as assistant director at the US Office of War Information; from 1946

---

[5] Three biographical programmes by D. G. Bridson, broadcast in 1934 and 1935. The radio biography of Coleridge was baptised 'Radio-Dramatic Survey.'

to 1967, he was Professor of Education at NYU, where he continued to write about radio broadcasting.[1]

• • •

Many thinking people have hailed broadcasting as potentially the widest civilising influence since the invention of printing. This judgment seems to be confirmed by the rapid and steady rise in the licence figures during the last ten years. By and large, no one can now seriously question its importance nor even its popularity; and yet in detail how little one knows, despite the passage of years and the accumulation of experience, of the influence of broadcasting and of the changes it has wrought in the habits and the pleasures and the outlook of listeners.

That for many thousands of people it has banished, or at least mitigated, loneliness, that it has provided new means of enjoyment and maybe influenced or even radically changed men's outlook and values on issues large or trivial, one can fairly confidently claim. But are we as a nation, after ten years of broadcasting, greater and more discriminating lovers of music, wiser, and more temperate judges of political and social events, as readers more fastidious in our tastes, and in our laughter and enjoyment more civilised or more intelligent? These are the questions to which the answer still remains intangible. And yet, in taking stock, we should surely be capable of some measurement of progress and be able to say whether or no as the servant of democracy 'the labourer has been worthy of his hire.' Even after ten years it is almost certain that the popular vote on the apportionment of time to this or that item in broadcast programmes would sweep away much, if not most, of what is most significant in the achievement of the BBC

This does not argue that wireless has functioned as a tyrannical pretender to a place in the loyalties or even the affections of listeners to which it has no right, nor that democracy, in the sense of the will of the majority of listeners, is an impossible criterion by which our programme policy should be guided. The BBC has consistently believed that its listeners are capable of response not only to the lowest but to the highest. There is no other working faith for this or any other great public service catering for the needs of the majority. But the problem of realising aims that may seem to some so fantastically high is not only a matter of reasonable faith but of a day-to-day practical appreciation of the means that it will get us to the end.

The technique of broadcast talks is worth considering from this point of view, both in respect of the selection of subjects and of their means of presentation.

[1] See Richard J. Meyer, 'Charles A. Siepmann and Educational Broadcasting,' *AV Communication Review* 12, no. 4 (1964): 413–30; Scannell and Cardiff, *A Social History of British Broadcasting vol. 1*, 68–9; Murphy, *Behind the Wireless*, 174–5.

That something has been achieved is proved by the fact that in the first six months of this year the correspondence that comes to the BBC shows a significant and even startling alteration in the balance of interest and appreciation of different sections of the programmes. For many years past, the broadcasting of Dance Music has provoked consistently the largest number of appreciative letters. For the first six months of 1933, and for the first time in the history of broadcasting, the appreciation of talks has climbed to first place in the statistics of correspondence. Moreover, not only is appreciation greater, but complaints are less. For the same period in 1932 the percentage of criticism of broadcast talks was 30 per cent odd. For the first six months of 1933 the figure had dropped to 10 per cent. Correspondence is a fickle and an inadequate guide, but the figures must mean something. If they do not reflect, at least they coincide with a definite advance in the technique of broadcast talks. The belief that there is practically no subject incapable of stimulating interest and enjoyment, if it is well and simply presented, is being steadily confirmed by experience.

What is it that listeners look for in talks?

First and foremost, personal contact with men of outstanding ability and character. Personality (there is overwhelming proof of this) is the first requisite of a good broadcaster. And so in the programme for the coming season there will be found names familiar to millions of listeners, men and women whose personality has survived the curious and exacting tests of the microphone. And next to personality comes the whole complicated field of presentation. The need for a simple, direct, and personal style of speaking, sincerity and candour, and that intangible factor of integrity which is more easily recognised than defined. Controversy, too, the opportunity to hear men speak out their convictions on issues great or small and to catch the excitement and the stimulus of a clash of views. The political talks on Thursday nights will be all controversy.

And another series that, on the face of it, seems to smack more of history or of exposition will, in fact, provoke, if it does not present, controversial opinion. But nothing is, perhaps, so new or has been welcomed so readily as recent experiments in the presentation of the life and circumstances of our time through the eyes of a practised observer. Housing and Unemployment are in themselves abstract themes, but many listeners will remember how these subjects came alive when presented in terms of the fresh and immediate experience of things seen and heard, of persons and scenes visited and recorded post-haste at the microphone, by such speakers as Mr S. P. B. Mais and Mr Howard Marshall.[2] It remains perhaps wearisomely true that we are chiefly interested in ourselves and in our neighbours. The further we explore and venture beyond the

---

[2] The British novelist and journalist S. P. B. Mais (1885–1975), who appeared in BBC programmes during the 1920s; Howard Marshall (1900–1973), who then specialised in sports commentaries.

immediate environment of our daily life the more we stand in need of the gift of imagination and the discipline of thought. It is, therefore, for the broadcaster, whether on things near to or far from our common experience, to quicken them to a new life by the gift of vivid, true, and imaginative description. It is, after all, no more than the old art of the story-teller. And so in this programme, again and again it will be found that this method has been tried, that men are to be sent far and near to bring back breathless to the microphone the freshness of personal and recent experience. [. . .]

Wherever possible there will be coupled with this personal description of immediate experience an exploitation of the magic power of wireless to conquer space and make a fool of time. Following hard upon the heels of technical development, talks are to come to you not only from the studios of Broadcasting House, but from all over Europe wherever hot news is to be found, and from three thousand miles across the Atlantic in a series that may make history in broadcasting. [. . .]

All this represents new method in presentation. [. . .]

Though the brush may falter here and there, the unified conception of the whole, and the richness and grandeur of the theme will surely make the attempt worth while.

4.14 DESMOND MACCARTHY: THE ART OF BROADCASTING TALKS

First published as 'The Art of Broadcasting Talks,' *BBC Handbook 1929* (London: British Broadcasting Corporation, 1929), 223–5.

Desmond MacCarthy (1877–1952) was a British writer associated with the Bloomsbury group, and an eminent journalist who wrote a great deal of literary and drama criticism, notably for the *New Statesman*, for which he acted as literary editor from 1919 to 1927. During this time, he became a resident literary critic at the BBC, giving fortnightly talks on literary criticism from 1925 to 1929, then contributing radio reviews of recent books from 1930 to 1935. From 1928, he gave regular lectures on topics related to the novel and to theatre, and contributed to educational literature programmes for schools. He was also a frequent contributor to the BBC magazine the *Listener*, writing book reviews and articles on drama, biography and poetry until 1950.[1]

• • •

It is a new art different from that of the orator, the author, or the lecturer. Although the broadcaster may be addressing an audience a hundred times larger than any which has ever assembled to hear the most famous orator, he is not addressing them in a mass, but privately, one by one. Dramatic emphasis and images, which would be appropriate in a speech, or phrases and transitions which are characteristic of good prose, do not necessarily sound right when they reach the ears of a solitary person by the fire or a small group of people in a room. Some master this new art at once, but the vast majority require to learn it.

It used to be the privilege of exceptionally favoured hosts to be able to invite specialists, travellers, or literary men and get them to talk about their own subjects. Now, thanks to wireless, all can enjoy that privilege. The broadcaster is in the position of 'a lion' who has been persuaded one evening to expound what he knows, or to describe what he has seen, to a few acquaintances – thoroughly, because his little audience want to learn; clearly, because they may be puzzled or ignorant; and informally, because they have not assembled to hear a lecture. The occasion is 'social' rather than public. If the broadcaster imagines that he is addressing a few people who happen to be ignorant about what he knows best himself but are interested in it, he will hit upon the right kind of words and sentences. He should also himself be a listener, for he can learn as much from hearing others broadcast as from practice. Yet it is a mistake to imitate any particular model. Just as stolen jokes are seldom successful, so a manner extremely agreeable in one person may not fit another. The public ear is sensitive to artificiality. Be yourself, whatever limitations that implies. It is safer. When you are sitting in front of the little cube in that empty, muffled room you have dwindled to a voice; you have been deprived of all means of expressing yourself except one. Ordinarily we get our impressions of each other through our eyes; we read from looks and gestures. When we are listening we discover – what every blind man knows – that tones of voice also convey character.

In daily life we smile when we wish others to know that we are pleased, or that we want to please; and since we are at once understood, few of us learn to make our voices subtly expressive. It is enough to grin agreeably, but it is no use grinning into the microphone. One vocal habit, however, everybody learns

---

[1] See Todd Avery, 'Desmond MacCarthy, Bloomsbury, and the Aestheticist Ethics of Broadcasting,' in *Broadcasting Modernism*, eds. Debra Rae Cohen, Michael Coyle and Jane Lewty (Gainesville: University Press of Florida, 2009), 158–75.

more or less – namely, to use a polite or conciliatory tone on special occasions. Unfortunately, this accomplishment does not carry the broadcaster far. The tone in which one apologises for not passing the potatoes is not suitable for explaining the habits of the shark, or describing an ascent of Mount Everest. The broadcaster should therefore avoid the ingratiating tone if his subject is explanatory or descriptive. It may, however, be necessary in the course of a talk to apologise for dwelling on some point, and this is better done by a slight change of voice than by a verbal apology; for the broadcaster who confesses that he feels he is boring his listeners communicates that feeling.

There are many different kinds of discourses which come under the head of 'BBC Talks.' Some are not exactly talks, but brief expositions of technical subjects. It is not so necessary to disguise the fact that these are being read from a manuscript. They should convey information as concisely and clearly as possible. In preparing them the important thing to remember is that short sentences are easiest to understand, and that qualifications of any statement should be added after it, not inserted as a clause in the statement itself – unless the broadcaster is a very skilful reader.

At the other end of the scale are talks which depend more upon personality and the illusion that the broadcaster is in the room with the listener. These must, of course, be written in a conversational style; and although this style has an easy air and reads as if it had been written straight off, it cannot be achieved by scribbling down sentences no editor would pass without correction. It is not a bad plan for a beginner to write out first, as elaborately and carefully as he can, what he wants to say (the effort will fix in his memory his happiest phrases and sentences), and then, putting the manuscript aside, to spout it all again to a stenographer. The result ought to prove a good discourse in the conversational style. Something approximating to the same result may be reached by reading aloud what he has written before delivering it. While he reads he will discover which phrases and sentences sound pretentious or unnatural. He will say to himself, 'I can't imagine *talking* like that!' He will also discover that correct punctuation is often too logical for a would-be spontaneous discourse. He will find he pauses longer at a comma, sometimes, than at a semi-colon, or that he even hurries over a grammatical full-stop. He should mark these natural pauses with pencil lines and observe them while broadcasting. He should also vary the pace of his reading: this is most important.

Clear enunciation is essential, but it is fatal to allow listeners to perceive that you are taking desperate pains to articulate correctly. Such pains must be taken in rehearsal; in front of the microphone it is best to forget yourself. I have sometimes listened with more pleasure to a delivery in which both accent and enunciation left much to be desired, than to one marked by a too silvery, too self-conscious distinctness. In short, when preparing material think of your audience; when rehearsing, of yourself; and when actually broadcasting – only of your subject.

4.15 ANDRÉ SAUDEMONT: THE RADIO INTERVIEW

Translated by Emilie Morin. First published as 'L'interview par radio,' *Annuaire de la Radiodiffusion Nationale, année 1933* (Paris: Ministère des PTT; Service de la Radiodiffusion, 1933), 249–54.

André Saudemont (1900–1970) was a French radio journalist, lawyer, drama critic and occasional songwriter. He worked for the radio station Paris-PTT, where he contributed to the Radio-Journal de France, the evening programme of national news launched in 1927, and he was among the first to explore the possibilities of the radio interview. He specialised in radio chronicles about theatre and about the law; he published an early book on radio and the law, *La radiophonie devant le droit*, in 1927. He was associated with the anti-Semitic right before and during the Second World War, and acted as Louis-Ferdinand Céline's lawyer in 1938 and 1939, when Céline was sued for libel and defamation for his anti-Semitic pamphlet *L'Ecole des cadavres*. After 1940, Saudemont continued to work for Radio-Paris, then under Nazi control. Owing to his propagandist work as radio journalist, he was debarred from practising as a lawyer in 1944 and was sentenced to partial national indignity (one of the sanctions taken against collaborationists). He continued to work in radio broadcasting thereafter, for the news bulletin of the ORTF (the French national broadcasting service) in the Ile-de-France region, and occasionally presented theatre broadcasts and interviews.

•　•　•

The radio interview is a formula that is admirably well suited to the wireless. It is partly thanks to the radio interview that the news bulletin has an originality and a life of its own: the newspaper cannot compete with the interview conducted before the microphone!

With radio there is no cheating, no denying. The interviewee is there, in the studio, answering the questions that are put to him. We get his exact turn of phrase, his style, his intonations, and even his hesitations. And through him we disseminate across the world a slice of real life and current affairs.

When I say 'no cheating' . . . some cheating would nonetheless be possible. I am thinking of Max Dearly,[1] who, when someone asked him for an interview,

---

[1]　French actor and director (1874–1943).

said in the hoarse voice we all know well: 'Why not? And if I can't make it I will send in Henry Laverne.[2] He imitates me so well.'

For a long time now, the interview has been given its rightful place in the *Radio-Journal de France*,[3] and this requires the broadest eclecticism: we remain at the command of current affairs, of changing circumstances.

Which one of us was the first to practise this formula? Idle question. There is always someone ahead of us, even when we think of ourselves as precursors.

Indeed, when I started conversing with Jules Berry[4] on the occasion of what I thought was his microphone baptism, he said with a smile: 'I did the same thing a few years ago, in Lyon.'

And others in Germany thought of interviewing a great juggler such as Rastelli[5] long before I did.

So . . . we should stop searching for the first 'radio interviewer.'

Is it easy for us to bring the personalities of our choice into the studio, and do they graciously accept our invitation? Fairly easy, as a general rule. This new way of working is favourable to them; everyone likes publicity; well-known people need it and will always need it, and they want to be in a studio at least once in their lives. It is not unusual for them to say, when they leave the station, that they remain at our disposal.

Are our interviews improvised or scripted? There are three ways to proceed: complete improvisation; a prepared plan, with questions organised so as to leave room for the inspiration of the moment; a text rigorously scripted like a dramatic dialogue, in which each person has their own lines.

Which procedure is best? It depends on the circumstances; it depends on the interviewee as well as the interviewer.

The goal, it seems to me, independently of the means deployed, is to give the listener the impression that a free and spontaneous conversation is taking place. Even if one is reading a script, one must pretend otherwise.

Complete improvisation is extremely rare. I once sat behind the microphone with Jules Berry and Suzy Prim[6] without knowing what we would talk about, and we just talked . . .

Like Peeters,[7] I prefer the second method: a preliminary conversation, a basic plan, an approximation of order for the questions. After that, you can go where the fancy takes you. [. . .]

---

[2] French actor and comedian (1888–1953).

[3] The daily evening news programme broadcast by Paris-PTT and relayed by the state-owned regional network. The Radio-Journal de France became the sole official channel for radio news in 1939 and was integrated into the Vichy regime's official structures from 1940.

[4] French actor (1883–1951).

[5] Enrico Rastelli (1896–1931).

[6] Jules Berry (1883–1951), French actor, and Suzy Prim (1896–1991), French actress.

[7] Georges Peeters, a fellow journalist at Paris-PTT.

As for the interviewees, some (very few) improvise with such facility that it is difficult to stop them (I remember Dussane and Simone).[8] Others are happy to start from a simple plan. Many prefer to have a printed script, because they suffer from nerves and this gives them peace of mind.

As for nerves . . . Experienced orators are obviously more at ease. When Lutigneaux interviews the masters of contemporary thought, like Léon Brunschwig, Julien Benda or Fortunat Strowski,[9] why should they suffer from nerves, beyond having that strange feeling the microphone gives to those who are new to this kind of sport?

But when Peters interviews a boxer, even a world champion like Young Perez,[10] who seems so slender in the studio, the words only come out of the mouth of his victim (I mean interviewee) with difficulty. The art of using one's fists has nothing to do with the art of Cicero and Demosthenes . . .

Artists are not conference speakers either, generally speaking, and standing in front of a microphone instead of standing in front of a public is disconcerting for many of them.

If Grock, André Baugé, Germaine Dermoz, Georgius, Pomiès, Musidora remained absolutely cool-headed, others seemed troubled, more or less intensely so.[11]

I remember the poor great Marie Delna,[12] whose mouth became dry and who struggled to speak. Lucienne Boyer was so disconcerted that she proved unable to remember the lyrics of *Parlez-moi d'amour* when she sang at the microphone after our conversation . . .[13] And yet . . .

Paul Colin repeated 'erm . . .' throughout and admitted feeling as though he had stepped into a void; Serge Lifar kept on shaking my arm as though I were a rag doll; Max Trébor felt paralysed by the emotion and always resented me for it, especially as I had forced him to improvise; Marie Dubas was nervous; Raquel Meller only answered with yes or no; Mistinguett was rather intimidated, and Catherine Fontenay got lost in her notes.[14]

---

[8] Béatrix Dussane (1888–1969) and Madame Simone (Simone Le Bargy, 1877–1985), French actresses.

[9] Léon Brunschvicg (1869–1944), French philosopher; Julien Benda (1867–1956), French novelist and philosopher; Fortunat Strowski (1866–1952), French literary historian and critic.

[10] The Tunisian boxer Messaoud Hai Victor Perez (1911–1945), known as Young Perez.

[11] Grock (1880–1959), Swiss clown; André Baugé (1893–1966), French opera singer and actor; Germaine Dermoz (1888–1966), French actress; Georgius (1891–1970), music-hall singer; Georges Pomiès (1902–1933), French actor; Musidora (1889–1957), French actress and director.

[12] French opera singer (1875–1932).

[13] French singer (1901–1983).

[14] Paul Colin (1892–1985), French painter and poster artist; Serge Lifar (1905–1986), French ballet dancer and choreographer; Max Trébor (1897–1944), French singer; Marie Dubas

As for nerves . . . Sometimes it is the interviewer who suffers from nerves. Jacques Bernier, when he is facing an artist whose talent he greatly admires – Gaby Morlay or Florelle, say – becomes worried, agitated; his face becomes redder than usual.[15]

Are the listeners more likely to join us in the studio when interviews are broadcast? This is rare. Only two interviews have really drawn in a large crowd: the interview of Costes and Bellonte by Georges Lion, and the interview with Jeanette MacDonald.[16] Journalists, photographers, admirers and hunters of autographs flooded into the station. Jeanette listened to me with indifference as I was introducing her . . . for the simple reason that she could not understand a word of it. The heroine of *Parade d'amour* then simply read a few sentences that had been written for her.

Some interviewees are troubled when they see the public. When she arrived in our large studio and saw people, Damia stepped back, terrified, and refused to speak in these conditions, and I took her to our small studio; there, we were alone, and no one could see whether or not she was reading, gesticulating, whether or not she was a little scared . . .[17]

I don't know how our listeners remember our interviews, but I do know that they are for us a source of great pleasure. [. . .]

Our studio on rue de Grenelle has received many illustrious visitors who have confided their secrets to the microphone.[18] Soon, without a doubt, we will be able to go outside looking for them and we will collect our sound news from elsewhere, by using recorded discs that will then be broadcast. Mr Edouard Belin, the famous inventor, President of the Association Générale des Auditeurs de TSF,[19] announced the news recently: our domain of operation will grow wider, to the great satisfaction of our public.

(1894–1972), French singer and comedian; Raquel Meller (1888–1962), Spanish singer and actress; Mistinguett (1875–1956), French singer and actress; Catherine Fontenay (1879–1966), French actress.

[15] Jacques Bernier, journalist at Paris-PTT; Gaby Morlay (1893–1964), French actress; Florelle (1898–1974), French singer and actress.

[16] Dieudonné Costes (1892–1973) and Maurice Bellonte (1896–1983), French aviators; Jeanette MacDonald (1903–1965), American singer.

[17] French singer (1889–1978).

[18] The Paris-PTT studio at 103 rue de Grenelle, Paris.

[19] General Association of Wireless Listeners, an organisation created in 1924, which had oversight of programming at state-funded radio stations.

4.16 HENRY LYTTON: THE MYSTERY OF RADIO HUMOUR

First published as 'The Mystery of Radio Humour,' *Radio Pictorial*, 18 January 1935, 5–6.

Henry Lytton (1865–1936) was a British actor and singer best known for his long career as Gilbert and Sullivan performer with the D'Oyly Carte Opera Company. In this capacity, he contributed to BBC broadcasts of Gilbert and Sullivan compositions between 1930 and 1935. He occasionally wrote articles for the BBC magazines the *Listener* and the *Radio Times*.

• • •

[. . .] Up to now, comedy has been judged by 'audience response.' With radio humour this is impossible.

It seems to me that this factor has been neglected or ignored, yet surely it is the key to the whole situation? Both BBC and performers have argued that as comedy has always been tested by 'audience response,' an actual living audience is necessary for wireless humour in addition to the great unseen audience of listeners. Artistes have said it was impossible to put any life into their work unless they had an audience to play to.

The BBC has claimed that the studio audience can be regarded as a representative section of listeners, and if the studio audience is amused, the other listeners will be too.

This is only begging the question.

The studio audience may be amused for the very reasons that the listener is bored. The studio audience hears and sees the complete show. The listener only hears the spoken word. If a man with a funny face says something foolish, people will laugh because he *looks* so funny. If a voice issuing from a loud speaker says the same thing with the same intonation, the listener at home irritably thinks to himself 'How fatuous!' and switches off.

So long as he has an audience in front of him, a comedian will, consciously or unconsciously, appeal to the eye as well as to the ear. Yet the perfect radio comedian must appeal *only* to the ear.

There is only one solution.

A new race of radio comedians must be created who do not depend on 'audience response.' For the present the BBC must persevere with the established comedians. There is none better. But they should be straining every nerve to discover and develop young men who will think and act only in terms of the microphone when creating their comic effects.

So far as I know, this is not being done. New artistes are discovered, but they appear on the same programmes as the older ones, they watch them at work, they have the studio audience to address themselves to, and they are in fact learning to perpetuate the old and worn-out technique instead of trying to discover a new one of their own.

The next problem is to discover how to do without 'audience response.' Goodness only knows what ingenious methods will be discovered in the future, but for the present why not test comedy by the simple expedient of reproducing it under the actual conditions in which it is designed to be heard? Radio comedy is not intended to be heard by an assembled audience, but by two or three or four people sitting in a drawing-room. Fit up half a dozen small rooms in Broadcasting House as ordinary middle and working class sitting-rooms, let the present studio audiences be split up into twos and threes and each little party be given a room to itself, and give each listener a *brief* printed questionnaire to fill in to record his or her impressions, and then we get as fair a test as it is possible to make.

In addition, let there be concealed peepholes through which the reactions of these audiences can be observed, and the BBC would soon learn which types of humour most consistently failed to register. This obviously involves a great deal of work, but surely when one is blazing a new trail a certain amount of detailed and properly controlled experiment is infinitely preferable to years of haphazard efforts?

Now we come to a consideration of the most difficult problem of all – the kind of humour that is wanted and how it is to be put on the air. Obviously anything I can say on these points will only be theoretical, but all the same, there are one or two details that appear to me to be important.

Let us try to learn a lesson from another quite new art – the films. There is a great deal of money to be made out of a successful film, so there was every inducement to discover as quickly as possible how a successful film is made. Unlimited money has been spent on this and now, as far as anything in the world of entertainment is capable of being foretold, it is possible to produce a successful film to order. Here in England we haven't quite reached that pitch of perfection, but in Hollywood a first-class organisation can say with such accuracy that the expenditure of a certain sum on a film of a certain type will result in a certain minimum of profit that hard-headed bankers will advance money on the proposition!

How has this been done? Naturally, many details have a bearing on it, but the one I am concerned with at the moment is this – every story, every scene, every action in a film has been translated into film terms by experts who have made an exhaustive study of the art. If a stage play is bought for production as a film, everything right down to the tiniest detail is converted into film technique.

This procedure has, to some extent, been followed on the radio. Full-length plays – notably musical comedies – are drastically revised for radio purposes. This largely means they are condensed, that spectacular scenes are deleted, that the whole show is closer knit. What is done is good – but in my opinion not nearly enough is done. The result is a musical comedy that sounds something like a gramophone record of a stage production – not a radio musical comedy that has its own individuality and its own characteristics and which is expressed in a technique that is entirely different from stage technique. Just as the film which is only a photographed stage play has almost invariably been a failure, so the radio musical comedy which is only a mechanical reproduction of the theatrical version cannot be anything but a modified success.

I have admitted that a good deal of expert radio technique is put into full-length musical comedies, but how much is allotted to variety programmes or to individual comic turns? Very little, I fear. The artiste may be given a few hints which result in correct intonation and delivery, but that is not enough. No matter how good his songs and patter may be, they should be taken by experts and re-written in terms of radio technique.

If a stage comedian was engaged to do his own special act in a film, he would have to submit to this revision of his material. He would be carefully rehearsed in the precise way he would have to perform his act for film purposes. He would submit to it without a second thought – and he should do the same when he goes on the air.

Some comedians have been clever enough to make a special study of radio comedy. They write all their own broadcasting material, it is entirely different from the stuff they use on the stage, and they have naturally become very popular. But a man might be an inspired radio comedian and yet be utterly unable to write a line of his own stuff. As things are, he would almost certainly be wasted. He would never get the chance of making a hit – would never even dream of his own potentialities.

How is this special radio technique to be discovered? Some of it is known already. That is to say, a great many individual broadcasters have their own ideas and theories which they keep safely locked in their own bosoms for fear rivals should 'steal' them. Also, they feel that if they have found these things out by experiment and hard thinking, why should others get the benefit free of charge? The BBC should pay handsomely for constructive additions to the science of radio technique. These payments would bring them handsome dividends in years to come.

When all the available knowledge had been collected, sifted and analysed, there would be enough to form a working basis. The whole problem should then be put in the hands of a small staff of enthusiastic experts who would devote all their time to the technical side of radio comedy. Their job would be to see that every comic performance in front of a BBC microphone was first translated into a form that would display it to the best advantage.

In building up their technical skill, the experts would have to proceed always with the idea of that suburban drawing-room in their minds. So frequently the BBC appears to think of its audience as grouped in a super Albert Hall, instead of as scattered in hundreds of thousands of little rooms.

But even more important than that is the acquisition of exact knowledge concerning the power of the ear to form mental pictures. I believe that a properly educated ear can, when aided by speech, enable the brain to visualise with remarkable clarity what is supposed to be going on. But instead of encouraging the ear's latent ability, most of our wireless comedians ignore it. They just stand in front of the microphone and talk. It may be very witty, clever and amusing talk, but I feel I want a loud speaker to do something more than talk to me, to recite anecdotes to me. I want it to build up in my mind an irresistibly comic picture of something that is actually happening.

That is what wireless lacks – humour with some action in it. Let me give an example. I have heard dozens of jokes about Belisha Beacons.[1] I have not yet heard a comedian take the infinite comic possibilities of, let us say, a nervous little man piloting a large and obstinate wife over a herringbone crossing, with a full accompaniment of traffic noises, hoots, uncomplimentary remarks from motor drivers, and so on. Properly handled, with suitable sound effects, such a scene could produce hysterical laughter, yet if it did occur to the average wireless comedian to use this idea, he would simply stand in front of the microphone and tell us what happened when he was out with his wife the other afternoon.

It is from such errors that the technical experts would save him. They would take his anecdote, convert it into radio technique, arrange the sound effects for him, write in any additional material that was necessitated by the new form, rehearse him in delivery till the timing between the effects and his remarks was accurate to a split second, and finally send him into the studio with a show that created gales of laughter instead of bored smiles.

I sometimes think that loud speakers ought to be made transparent – or at any rate, translucent. They should look like windows instead of boxes. That is what they are – windows that enable us to look out of our little drawing-rooms into the great world and see the laughter and tears, the comedies and dramas that the world is playing for us right on our own doorsteps.

---

[1] The Belisha Beacon, a flashing light used to mark zebra crossings in Britain, is made of a pole with black and white stripes and an orange globe.

Most people think of a loud speaker as a voice which comes into their rooms. It is not. It is a magic door through which we can pass and discover the great wonderland of life that lies all around us. At present the technique of the wireless comedian is that of the man who calls on us, stands in front of the fire and tells us the funny story he has just heard. What is wanted is the comedian who metaphorically exclaims 'Here! Look what's happening just down the road. Come along and let's see it all. You will laugh!'

4.17 GRACE WYNDHAM GOLDIE: LISTENING TO COMEDY

First published as 'Listening to Comedy,' *Listener*, 15 April 1936, 744.

Grace Wyndham Goldie (née Nisbet, 1900–1986) is best known as a pioneering television producer. Before her career in television, she was a radio drama critic for the BBC's weekly magazine the *Listener*, and specialised in witty and erudite reviews of BBC radio plays. When she was hired by the *Listener* in 1935, the radio drama column was thought of as a temporary experiment, but it became a long-standing feature, and Wyndham Goldie became the most prolific British radio drama critic thereafter. Initially, she was unfamiliar with radio broadcasting, but fought to become an insider and immersed herself in the theatre and radio worlds, attending numerous rehearsals, talks and productions. Her radio journalism led her to write about experimental television, too, during the 1930s, and she became the *Listener*'s first television critic.[1]

• • •

I wonder what proportion of listeners switch off during the performance of a wireless play. It would be interesting to know. At a guess I should say a large one. Yet the proportion of audiences who walk out of a theatre while

[1] See Grace Wyndham Goldie, 'Double Vision,' *Listener*, 18 January 1979, 59–60.

a play is going on must be a very small one indeed. Is this because broadcast drama is so much less interesting than the drama of the stage? Not a bit of it. If by pressing a button on our seats in the theatre as soon as we were bored we could instantaneously and without expense be transferred to a music-hall, a concert or our own firesides the auditorium of many a theatre would look strange. But would we really gain by possessing so magical a device? On the whole, surely, no. For there are very few even of the best plays which do not contain moments of dullness and it is usually worth while putting up with them for the sake of what follows. Yet if we listeners meet such moments in a wireless play our first instinct is to switch it off and switch on to something else.

Now the moral of all this, no doubt, is that if listeners were more patient they would be rewarded in the end. But in practice it is no use telling listeners or audiences what they *ought* to do. So the writers and producers of wireless plays have to reckon with the fact that we are an impatient lot and endeavour to make their entertainments much more continuously interesting and exciting than a production in the theatre needs to be. And here they immediately come up against another idiosyncrasy of listeners. Which is that it is much more difficult for us to enjoy a play when we listen to it in our own homes than when we listen to it in a theatre. Most of us go to the theatre to indulge our emotions. The theatre is designed for such indulgence. During the performance we sit in a comfortable darkness; we can gulp in comparative privacy when we are moved, and yet when we laugh it is with the added enjoyment of laughter shared. But in our well lighted sitting rooms, with the eyes of our families upon us, it is not easy to indulge either in surreptitious gulps or in really hearty laughter.

Now here are two of the main reasons why it is so difficult to produce comedy successfully over the wireless. Good comedies are scarce, even in the theatre, and good comedies which have the strong thread of interest or suspense that is essential for a wireless play are as scarce as strawberries in December. Add to this the fact that laughter is essentially a social act, and that the more is certainly the merrier when it comes to the enjoyment of farce and comedy, that comedy acting depends even more on facial expression and the contrast between words and behaviour than the acting in serious plays, and it begins to seem impossible that comedies should ever be given successfully over the microphone at all.

[. . .] Comedy which is essentially radio, as some fantasies and some plays of adventure have been essentially radio and as the Walt Disney cartoons and the René Clair comedies are essentially film, has yet to be discovered.

4.18 ROBERT DESNOS: 'THE KEY TO DREAMS' ON THE POSTE PARISIEN

Translated by Emilie Morin. First published as 'La clé des songes au Poste-Parisien,' *Radio-Magazine*, February 1938.[1]

Robert Desnos (1900–1945) was a French writer renowned for his capacity to fall into 'sleeping fits' when he was a member of the Paris Surrealist group in the 1920s and early 1930s. He wrote poetry as well as travel reportage, songs and films, and a great deal of journalism, sometimes under a pseudonym. After his break from the Surrealist group, radio broadcasting became his primary activity. His first radio appearance was in June 1931, for a talk on Surrealism on Radio-Paris, and his radio creations thereafter were imaginative and memorable. Much of Desnos's radio work was conducted in the context of Paul Deharme's advertising company Informations et Publicité, which Desnos joined in 1932 as advertising broker for the cinema section, subsequently taking charge of all pharmaceutical advertising. After Deharme's death, and until 1939, Desnos worked at Foniric Studios, which produced radio advertising as well as original radio works, and he became Foniric's main advertising copywriter. He used his talent for word play and thought association to craft new kinds of advertising for radio stations in France and the French colonies; his quirky, charming rhymes and songs advertised anything from vermifuge to nit-killing products, and were so successful that he liked to describe himself as the most widely heard poet in Europe. Desnos's other notable radio creations included, from 1933 onwards, a weekly programme on Radio-Paris called 'La demi-heure de la vie pratique' ('The half-hour for practical life'), to which he contributed a dialogue or sketch about a literary, historical or scientific event or figure whose anniversary it was that day; 'La grande complainte de Fantômas,' a song detailing the exploits and misdemeanours of the hero Fantômas, broadcast in 1933 to music by Kurt Weill; a celebrated radio rendering of excerpts from Walt Whitman's *Leaves of Grass*, broadcast by the Poste Parisien in 1936; and 'La clé des songes' ('The key to dreams'), a weekly programme that ran from February 1938 to June 1939 on the Poste Parisien. The latter arose from a blanket invitation to listeners to send letters about their dreams. For each instalment, Desnos and his collaborators Colette Paule and Jérôme Arnaud would devise radio sketches around a few letters selected from the mass of correspondence. The selected dreams would be re-told by Desnos on air and embedded into ambitious sound montages, and Desnos would

[1] The only copy that has survived in French archives is part of the Desnos collection at the Bibliothèque Jacques Doucet (folder DSN 450, La clef des songes, pièces annexes), and precise publication details are missing from the presscutting, which is misdated from 1937.

interpret each story using Artemidorus's *Interpretation of Dreams*. The programme was so popular that it continued in 1940 and 1941 in writing, in the women's magazine *Pour Elle*, for which Desnos wrote under a pseudonym, Hamidas Beloeil. During the Second World War, Desnos's broadcasting work largely came to a halt, and he published odds and ends of literary journalism and contributed poetry to clandestine publications. He joined the French Resistance in 1942, collecting information, making false identity papers, and writing against collaboration under various pseudonyms. He was arrested in 1944, imprisoned, and deported to the Buchenwald, Flossenbürg, Flöha and Theresienstadt camps. He died of typhus in Theresienstadt shortly after the camp's liberation. His co-detainees remembered his extraordinary courage and the ways in which he had used oneiromancy to give others courage and hope.[2]

•   •   •

Who among us has never received a visit from strange characters or famous people in their dreams?

Who among us has never travelled through strange countries and lived through burlesque or tragic adventures in their sleep?

The world of dreams has preoccupied humankind from the beginning of time. The Greeks and the Romans practised oneiromancy and searched for good and bad omens in their dreams. The belief in dreams endured throughout the Middle Ages and the Renaissance. Athalie still tells schoolchildren and the spectators of the Comédie-Française about her dream. And many among us own a copy of *La clé des songes*, that dreadful brochure anyone can get hold of for a few coppers, which is generally just as stupid as it is coarse.[3]

When Jérôme Arnaud and I made 'La clé des songes,' the programme you can hear every week on the Poste Parisien, we tried to invent a new poetic game. We wanted to bring back to life a domain that fundamentally belongs to the radio. We do not, of course, practise psychoanalysis or psychiatry, and we have not attempted anything scientific in the real sense of the word.

We simply draw on the abundant correspondence that we receive week after week. First, we select the two dreams that are the most radiophonic; two dreams in which the acoustic dimension takes over the visual dimension. In this respect our game has taken a singular form and exceeds the scope that we had first intended for it. We are offering a ready-made dream to our listeners, a dream that many of them would not otherwise have encountered since the dream, in its general form, is above all individual.

---

[2] See Chevrier, *La 'clef des songes' de Robert Desnos*, 83–101, 91, 127–303; Dumas, *Robert Desnos ou l'exploration des limites*, 191–219.

[3] *La clé des songes* was a popular volume listing symbols, proverbs and popular sayings first published in 1901 by the Parisian publisher Vermot.

Yet it soon became clear to us that, beyond the individual dream, whose clothing or disguise, as we might call it, differs from person to person, there is such a thing as a genuinely collective dream. Indeed, there are many points of concordance between all the accounts of dreams that listeners send us every week.

We also read accounts of other dreams that do not lend themselves to radiophonic reconstitution, and we make a second selection: we choose between the dreams that do not carry an omen and those that, on the contrary, signify something about the future.

It will be easy, we hope, for our listeners to understand that there is nothing absurd about using dreams to try and predict the future.

Indeed, what is a dream but a symbolic reconstitution of events that have been genuinely lived, a momentous allegory conveying a mindset and a corporeal state at a given time?

Since in most cases we can think of the future as a quasi-logical consequence of the past, it follows that if we exercise great precaution and approach the dream with a little bit of subtlety it becomes possible to deduct from it an omen about the days to come.

Who did we consult to discover the essential principles of divinatory science? After searching for a long time we turned to the classics. We would like, notably, to pay tribute to Mr Henri Vidal, who published in 1921 an excellent translation of *Oneirocritica* by Artemidorus of Ephesus, who lived in Greece at an obscure time.[4] There is no doubt that his interpretation of dreams is subtle, artful, intelligent, and philosophers and scholars as difficult to read as Professor Freud himself have said so. However, in order to be used, such a book must be interpreted first. For if we dream of automobiles, for example, Artemidorus naturally writes about *horse carts*.

We find our listeners' dreams immensely amusing. We are delighted to read them and hope that our listeners, too, are delighted to hear these stories! There is such great variety in the adventures we hear about and the stories that we relate! Think, for example, of the man who once dreamt that he was walking all over Max Régnier,[5] who was 30 metres long and as flat as a sole; think of the woman who nearly wed the Prince of Wales,[6] and think of the listener who

---

[4] Vidal's translation is entitled *La clef des songes d'Artémidore d'Ephèse, ou les cinq livres de l'interprétation des songes, rêves et visions* (1921). The original, the only surviving dream-book from Graeco-Roman antiquity, insisted on the allegorical dimensions of dreams and their deep social significance, and provided a nomenclature of common dream motifs based on a vast enterprise of dream collection. For a recent appraisal, see Peter Thonemann, *An Ancient Dream Manual: Artemidorus' The Interpretation of Dreams* (Oxford: Oxford University Press, 2020).

[5] Max Régnier (1907–1993), French dramatist, actor and theatre director, who featured in the programmes of Radio-Cité as singer, comedian and humourist during the 1930s.

[6] A reference to Edward VIII's abdication and marriage to Wallis Simpson in 1937.

went through the same adventure, but with Lindbergh. Véra Korène, Yvonne Printemps, Stalin, Sacha Guitry, Pierre Dac, Professor Picard, Paul-Boncour, Shirley Temple, and so many others: such are the distinguished guests who pay a visit to our dreamers.[7]

As for the events that our listeners dream about, they range from tragedy, sometimes of a grandiose kind, to irresistible comedy; take, for example, the listener who undertook a long journey on a camel with a moustache, then found herself sitting inside a pumpkin; or the listener who invented an extraordinary automobile-piano which made it possible to play music and drive along the roads at the same time.

I can already guess the objections to be levelled at us. What about the hoaxers, you will say. What about those who send you stories of dreams they have not dreamt, dreams they have invented? So what? This is of no importance whatsoever, since the imagination works in the same way whether we are awake or asleep. We never make up complete nonsense, and the made-up dream gives away the same secrets, carries the same omens as the authentic dream.

Dream away, dear readers. Your time will never be wasted when you are asleep. You will rest and accumulate poetic treasures at the same time. Who knows? If you decide to write to us perhaps you will learn precious things about your future. Some say that a dream is worth more than a piece of advice. That much is true.

If wisdom comes from sleeping on an idea, is that not because we can dream? When you listen to 'La clé des songes,' don't believe what it says entirely, but do believe in it a little bit all the same; and then dive without fear into the vast oceans of your own dreams, into the depths of the night.

---

[7] Véra Korène (1901–1996) and Yvonne Printemps (1894–1977), French singers and actresses; Sacha Guitry (1885–1957), French actor, director and playwright; Pierre Dac (1893–1975), French humourist; Auguste Piccard (1884–1962), Swiss physicist and inventor; Joseph Paul-Boncour (1873–1972), French politician; Shirley Temple (1928–2014), American child actor and singer.

PART 5
A THEATRE FOR THE EAR

5.1 GEORGE BERNARD SHAW: THE DRAMA AND THE MICROPHONE

First published as 'The Drama and the Microphone,' *The Playgoer, Organ of the Liverpool Playhouse Circle*, 25 March 1925, 3.

The Irish playwright George Bernard Shaw (1856–1950) is better known for his theatre plays, political activities and literary criticism than for his radio work; however, he was among the first writers to become involved with the BBC. He first went on air in November 1924, for a reading of his play *O'Flaherty VC* in which he performed all the roles himself. He subsequently gave many radio talks and contributed to radio debates with other authors. None of Shaw's plays were written specifically for radio, but over twenty of his stage plays were broadcast in full by the BBC between 1923 and his death in 1950. He was particularly sensitive to questions of copyright and remuneration, and played a key role in the establishment of copyright law in broadcasting: he asked for payment and recognition of his copyright on all materials as early as 1923, when arrangements tended to be informal, few authors looked after their rights, and the British Society of Authors had not yet taken a clear stance in relation to broadcasting. Shaw's relationship with the BBC was deeply fraught yet hugely significant for both parties. He was one of those dissenting figures that large organisations need to function well; he remained a fierce critic of the BBC and expected it to live by high moral and political standards. He became a member of the BBC's small Advisory Committee on Pronunciation in 1926 (the committee soon exceeded its advisory remit and issued rules for pronunciation and language at large) and a member of the BBC's General Advisory Council in 1934. This text was a contribution to a symposium to which Edward Gordon Craig and Hilaire Belloc also contributed, which was organised around the following question: 'Will broadcasting be detrimental to the art of the theatre?'[1]

• • •

I really do not know whether it will or will not because I have never heard a play broadcast and, therefore, cannot judge what chances broadcasting has

---

[1] See Allan Monkhouse, 'The Words and the Play,' in *Essays and Studies by Members of the English Association vol. 11*, ed. Oliver Elton (Oxford: Clarendon, 1925), 33–34; L.W. Connolly, *Bernard Shaw and the BBC* (Toronto: University of Toronto Press, 2009); Jürg R. Schwyter, *Dictating to the Mob: The History of the BBC Advisory Committee on Spoken English* (Oxford: Oxford University Press, 2016).

as against sitting in a theatre and watching a performance; nor can I foresee what developments are possible in the way of television and of making a group of speakers all equally audible, which I understand they are not at present any more than all the instruments are satisfactorily audible when an orchestral performance is broadcasted. All I can say is that if I could see and hear a play from my fireside I would never enter a theatre again. The theatres would then be all stalls and dress circle, filled with people who wish to show off their clothes, their jewels, and themselves. There would be no stage, because the real show would be the front of the house; but there would be a band and bars. The drama would not suffer: it would only have discarded a worse system for a better.

Quite a separate question is whether broadcasting will oust theatregoing as a way of passing the evening no matter what the thing broadcast may be. It is cheaper; it is more comfortable for those whose homes are at all fit to live in; it is available in town and country and can, in fact, be carried about; to many people it has made the theatre and the trouble of getting there as intolerable as the motor car has made the railway train. In the end it may force even conjurors to invent some means of broadcasting their illusions. I shall not prophesy, but I again remind our managers that theatregoing is very dear, very inconvenient, and horribly stuffy and promiscuous; unless they overcome those disadvantages by the overpowering fascination of good plays, good acting, and theatres that are like enchanted palaces instead of hotel smoking rooms, broadcasting will knock them out.

5.2 AUGUSTIN HABARU: WE MUST DISCOVER THE RADIO

Translated by Emilie Morin. First published as 'Il faut découvrir la radio,' *Le Populaire*, 13 December 1936, 4.

Augustin Habaru (1898–1944) was a Belgian journalist and poet who wrote for French communist and socialist publications, and had particularly close associations with *Le Peuple*, *L'Humanité* and the magazine *Monde*. He was the first editor of *Monde*. He also wrote for newspapers in Belgium, Switzerland, Germany and Austria, occasionally published poetry and translations, and championed working-class writers and Belgian writers. His journalism focused on social and economic questions and industrial techniques, and encompassed literary criticism and journalism on radio in Europe. He published a pamphlet on radio and internationalism, *L'Organisation internationale de la radiodiffusion* (1929), wrote radio columns for *Le Haut-Parleur* and *Mon Programme*, often under the pseudonym Georges Fleurigny, and documented broadcasting developments in the Soviet Union, Spain, Germany and Czechoslovakia. The present essay complements an earlier article advocating the need to write specifically for radio in the manner of Hermann Kesser and other German authors.[1] Habaru also gave talks on Parisian and French regional radio stations (Radio Tour Eiffel, Radio-Paris and Rennes-Bretagne) in 1937 and 1938, talks on French theatre, culture and history on German radio (Frankfurt and Stuttgart) in 1930, 1931 and 1932, and on Dutch radio (Hilversum) in 1932 and 1933. The French Communist press was dissolved by the French government in August 1939, but Habaru was able to continue his activities as a journalist. During the Second World War, he contributed information he had collected on German industrial activities to the Belgian and French Resistance, and led various types of resistance actions in the south of France. He was summarily shot by the Gestapo in June 1944.[2]

•   •   •

Aeschylus has been resuscitated. We owe this miracle to the radio.

You are alone in a room and, all of a sudden, voices come to you from a faraway past. Voices, only voices: around them, you imagine an unknown territory, disappeared peoples. There are no cardboard sets, no costumes borrowed from the cloakroom of the Quat'z'Arts.[3] The Persians mourn the annihilation of their armies, Xerxes bewails, Darius steps out of his tomb. In a theatre, the helmets, the weapons, the shields, the clothes, the language, the gestures make you smile: everything seems artificial. But now that visual conventions have been abolished, naked voices just come to you. And perhaps you have turned off the light in order to be alone with these voices, with these souls. Between you and Xerxes the abyss of the centuries has disappeared . . .

---

[1] A. Habaru, 'Un art nouveau: Le théâtre radiophonique,' *La Voix*, 27 April 1930, 12.

[2] See Michel Aguettaz, 'Habaru Augustin (Pseudonyme: Monsieur Paul),' *Le Maitron: Dictionnaire biographique, mouvement ouvrier, mouvement social*, https://maitron.fr/spip.php?article144823, last accessed 24 August 2021; Paul Aron, *La littérature prolétarienne en Belgique francophone depuis 1900* (Loverval: Labor, 2006), 62–70.

[3] The Cabaret des Quat'z'Arts, a Parisian venue favoured by artists and writers, and renowned for its annual ball.

It is only when we hear a radio broadcast of Greek theatre that we can understand the immense possibilities of radio drama. Théo Fleischman, with his adaptation of *Les Perses*,[4] has reminded us of this important fact on the air waves of Paris-PTT.

Radio drama, born about ten years ago, has not yet found its path. All too often, it seems sufficient to adapt the classical repertoire or the boulevard repertoire for the microphone. No one has yet understood that if radio can resuscitate the masterpieces of antiquity and even Racine's masterpieces – which are rarely accepted on stage nowadays – it must also create its own original art without borrowing anything from the stage.

The cinema was born on the day it moved away from theatre. Radio drama will be born the day it does precisely this.

A little book by Carlos Larronde, *Théâtre invisible*, features two plays by this author who, in France, is among the very first to have dedicated himself to radio drama. These texts are difficult to read, and this is the best compliment one can pay them: they are not written to be read but to be heard.

Along with the much-missed Paul Deharme, Théo Fleischman and very few pioneers, Carlos Larronde has tried to create a new art form that obeys the laws of radio. He defines his conception as such: 'a drama played by naked souls or, if you prefer, faceless actors. A drama that forces us to close our eyes, not because the décor is invisible, but because another scenery, purely ideal and abstract, is being built in our imagination. A drama that unfolds within the human mind . . . Radio has given the marvellous its true home.'

Carlos Larronde relates his microphone art to the symbolism of Maeterlinck or Charles Van Lerberghe (who in *Les Flaireurs* seems to be have predicted the invention of radio twenty years in advance), but the 'naked souls' into which he breathes life for our benefit remain close enough to individual and social realities to stir our emotions.

Another conception of radio drama is possible: as a theatre that is less intimate, more social, more 'unanimist,'[5] closer to the tradition of Walt Whitman than to Maeterlinck. This orientation, which has produced abroad, in Germany especially, some remarkable works and, in France, a beautiful performance by Charles Wolff at the Poste Parisien,[6] is far removed from the concepts advanced

---

[4] Adapted from Aeschylus and first broadcast in 1926; it was broadcast again in 1936.

[5] Illustrating the ideas of Unanimism, a French movement founded in the 1900s with which Fernand Divoire was briefly associated.

[6] Charles Wolff was a collector of phonograph records and author of early books on discography, and gave talks on music on French radio. He contributed to the acoustic backdrop made by Foniric studios for 'Salut au Monde!,' the tribute to Walt Whitman conceived by Desnos for the Poste Parisien in 1936.

by Carlos Larronde. Between these two extremes, the field of possibilities remains sufficiently broad to allow rich, varied, original creations. The possibilities of the radiophonic art are infinite.

Yet, apart from Larronde, Divoire and a few others, French writers continue to ignore the radio. The repertoire of our national and private radio stations is often so poor that it would be cruel to linger on it. The theatre companies that work for our radio stations usually perform in plays that are so mediocre that adapting the dramatic repertoire seems to be the best solution for the time being.

Some writers have launched manifestoes but have done nothing. F. T. Marinetti, three or four years ago, solemnly announced a new art and defined characteristics that he presented as a tremendous revolution.[7] Marinetti and the Futurists have done nothing. In the Soviet Union, in 1928, Mayakovsky proclaimed the reign of the 'radio-agitator.'[8] Soviet radio, although it has produced some great social documentaries, has not created a truly new radio-dramatic art. In Germany, Goebbels has killed the efforts of radio writers; the very best, such as Hermynia Zur Mühlen, are in exile.[9] In the United States, the best creators are slaves to advertising.

Today, French writers are the best placed to create the radiophonic art of tomorrow. Larronde, Fleischman, and a few others are showing the way. Three million listeners are waiting. There is no totalitarian orthodoxy that can pretend to enlist their thoughts. The publicity advertisers cannot ask them to flatter their own public. They are free – almost free.

What are they waiting for to discover the radio?

[7] This is a reference to Marinetti and Masnata's 1933 manifesto 'La Radia.' In parallel, Marinetti wrote various radio works or radio syntheses, which were published later.

[8] Mayakovsky's poem 'Radio-agitator' (1925) celebrated radio's capacity to overcome distances and move across cultures, and reflected on its ability to bring about a Communist future for all: 'And maybe / we / will soon hear / through the air / something like this: / A worker / of America and a worker of Chukhloma / will join their voices / in a single chorus. / So that the ages without chains / pass / more quickly, / So that this date / becomes nearer – / Drum out / with your million / tongues, / Radio-agitator!' Trans. Robert Bird, in Bird, 'Envoicing History: On the Narrative Poem in Russian Modernism,' *Slavic and East European Journal* 51, no. 1 (2007): 65.

[9] Austrian anti-Nazi writer; see her 'Radio Programmes for Women' (4.2).

5.3 RENÉ CHRISTAUFLOUR: WILL RADIO CREATE 'SUPERHEARING,' AS CINEMA CREATED 'SUPERIMPOSITION'?

Translated by Emilie Morin. First published as 'La radiophonie va-t-elle réaliser la "suraudition" comme le cinéma la "surimpression"?,' *Comœdia*, 13 January 1929, 1.

René Christauflour (d. 1944) was an amateur playwright considered by other radio authors as a pioneer owing to his risky and imaginative radio play about a train accident, *L'Express 175*, which was frequently revived after its first broadcast in 1929. His concept of *suraudition* (superhearing) resonated with many of his contemporaries and was often evoked thereafter. Christauflour was severely disabled, having caught polio as a child, and he died at a young age. He wrote *L'Express 175* in response to a writing competition organised by Radio Tour Eiffel in 1928. Two speakers, Georges Delamare and Paul Castan, had asked listeners to send them information about the kind of drama that they wanted to hear, and how it should be structured and composed; using their responses, they compiled a list of what listeners deemed to be the most desirable features in a radio play, and invited their listeners to write plays in that model. Christauflour won the competition. In a letter to the newspaper *L'Intransigeant* a few months later, he pointed to four possible directions for the radio play: taking plays from the common theatre repertoire and adding explanations to clarify the scenery and actions at the start of each act; asking the actors to present the character they are impersonating before each act (an approach commonly taken for adaptations of classical plays); adding an entirely new character whose sole mission is explaining the action (an approach advocated by the writer and radio critic René Sudre); inventing an entirely new dramatic form, free from the rule of the three unities, and predicated on a free exploration of movement and sound. The latter option, he explained, was the one he had pursued with *L'Express 175* and new plays he was writing.[1] He did not bring these other plays to completion, possibly because he lacked support and professional contacts; nothing by him was ever broadcast beyond *L'Express 175*.[2]

• • •

[1] 'Le théâtre radiophonique: Le point de vue de l'auteur. Une lettre de M. Christuaflour' [*sic*], *L'Intransigeant*, 24 June 1929, 6.

[2] On Christauflour's life, the only information available consists of brief recollections in a tribute programme on early radio: 'Dramaturgie des voix: *L'Express 175*,' Radiodiffusion Française, 2 July 1945, INA archives.

238

Radio drama must uphold a new conception of the spectacle that is exclusively applicable to the microphone.

To this end, some very interesting creations have already been broadcast, among which we include *L'Incident du Pont du Hibou* [*sic*], the very peculiar play by Mr P. Deharme;[3] the author wanted to put the listener in a dream state so that he could experience the action heard (the play did not have all the success it deserved).

And the even more interesting play by Mr Bernard Dupeyrat, *Le dernier des Valois* [*sic*], in which the music commented on the words; this play was very new and very adventurous, especially in its first version.[4]

L'Express 175, which will be broadcast today, 13 January, by the national radio-telephone station Tour Eiffel, represents an entirely different point of view.[5]

Owing to its presentation, radio drama is liberated from the constraints imposed by the theatre set, and it has an immense advantage over the cinema, in that it has ownership over the marvellously imaginative power of words.

The listener is blind, if I may use that word, and has to translate the sounds that he perceives into three dimensions; this restriction – what a paradox! – should also yield an immense freedom; the old rule of the three unities can be exploded: why confine oneself to an action taking place at one time and in one place when, by opening and closing the microphone, the place, time and action can change instantaneously within the same scene?

To break free of the shackles that are already unsuitable on the theatre stage is also to develop one of the most wonderful means of expression given to us by radio and enable this art to take on a life of its own, for only radio has been granted such an immense creative power.

I wrote *L'Express 175* by using such complete freedom as my formula.

I had to find new modes of presentation, including what I called 'superhearing,' in an analogy to superimposition in the cinema.

Superhearing enables the action to travel into the past or into the future instantaneously.

The play is taking place aboard a locomotive while the machine is moving at full speed; on three occasions the mechanic remembers his past and on three occasions the microphone, having slowly closed, reopens, on the scene of the

---

[3] *Un incident au pont du Hibou*, one of Deharme's celebrated radio plays, which was based on Ambrose Bierce's short story 'An Occurrence at Owl Creek Bridge,' about a plantation and slave owner who is about to be executed.

[4] *Le dernier Valois* was first broadcast by Radio Tour Eiffel in April 1928. It was repeated to great acclaim in June 1928, in a second version with music by Gaston Selz and accompaniment from a jazz band; on that occasion it was announced as an 'acoustic film.'

[5] Christauflour's first play about a locomotive accident, first broadcast in January 1929.

automobile accident, then his arrival home, then finally a visit to the Punch and Judy show.

Another very delicate scene could never have been realised without radio's admirable imaginative power: in the final scene, the soul of the dying mechanic's wife and the soul of his daughter come to fetch him.

The great advantage of the new art of radio is that it shall give free rein to the dramatist to construct his play just as he feels it living within his mind.

To create an atmosphere, we need the moving matter of noise. I have presented noises in a new way by letting them move through the action: we hear the noises of the locomotive at full speed and they accompany the voices of the characters, becoming either weaker or stronger depending on whether the action becomes tender or dramatic, and reach their full height when the tragedy occurs.

Producing these noises will be very difficult, because they should not cover the voices of the characters: the words must come out of the loud-speaker clearly, to avoid causing fatigue for the listener.

I am persuaded that radio will bring about a new mode of expression in the theatre and that the theatre will be transformed by it.

5.4 R. E. JEFFREY: WIRELESS DRAMA

First published as 'Wireless Drama,' *Radio Times*, 6 June 1924, 438–9.

R. E. Jeffrey (Ronald Ernest Jeffrey, 1886–1957) was the BBC's first Productions Director, credited with many innovations in radio drama. He worked on both sides of the microphone, as announcer, speaker and reader of poetry, and adapted and produced many plays for radio including Richard Hughes's *A Comedy of Danger* (1924), widely seen as the first British radio play. Before joining the BBC, he was a theatre actor, a playwright, and lectured in public speaking at the University of Glasgow. His path at the BBC took him to 5SC Glasgow, where he worked as drama producer, then to 2BD Aberdeen, where he became station director. His early experiments included an ambitious production of *Rob Roy* (the BBC's first attempt at literary adaptation) featuring a choir and an orchestra, broadcast in October 1923 on 5SC Glasgow, which Jeffrey adapted and produced, and in which he also performed. In 1924, he was appointed director of the BBC's Productions Department in London, a post in which he worked intensively on the aesthetic of the radio play. He resigned from the BBC in 1929 to pursue a career in the film industry and was replaced by Val Gielgud. Jeffrey was among the first to conceptualise radio drama as a form in its own right in the *Radio Times* and elsewhere; he believed that radio plays should appeal to the imagination without adhering to the conventions of the theatre and initially defined three categories of radio plays: radio plays 'with action set in one scene,' which create mental images and include enough pointers in terms of sound effects or within the dialogue to enable listeners to follow the movements of the action through time and space; radio plays 'with action set in one scene [that] introduce imaginative pictures' and borrow from cinematic techniques; radio plays 'where the action moves swiftly from place to place and so follows the characters' adventures,' requiring 'a different kind of dialogue.'[1]

● ● ●

My experiences in producing wireless drama prove to me beyond doubt that it has several advantages over stage productions.

Almost all of us have, consciously or sub-consciously, a strong sense of the dramatic. The hidden books of our lives are, for the best part, made up of pages full of dramatic incident. We have all been thrilled by joy, or fear, agony, love, hate, inspiration, anger, and other emotions. Strict training and temperamental reluctance to allow these feelings to take possession of us, have, perhaps, caused us to exercise restraint, and these soul-moving moments have been rigorously repressed. But here we must remember that the sub-conscious mind stores up every experience, and these experiences may provide the mental understanding to appreciate incidents outside ourselves, if they are motivated by similar feelings.

POWER OF THE SUB-CONSCIOUS MIND.

With broadcasting there is no need to perpetrate the crudity of a papier-maché ship on rolling billows of canvas, unwarranted absurdities presumed to produce an illusion on an intelligent mind. Thus, although we have never actually been in a disaster at sea, our sub-consciousness will supply a personal analogy, if we have ever passed through a moment's experience which prompted the feeling of fear of death, or steadfast courage, or resignation. Which of these feelings is recalled is dependent upon the point from which we view the disaster.

Not only is this feeling supplied by sub-conscious analogy, but an imaginative scene is also provided – it being mentally impossible to experience an emotion without also conceiving a personally acceptable appreciation in which to set it. All the accumulated knowledge of sea, ships, storms, etc., which we have

---

[1] 'British Producer Explains How to Write Radio Plays,' *New York Times*, 12 July 1925, 13; Christina S. L. Pepler, *Discovering the Art of Wireless: A Critical History of Radio Drama at the BBC, 1922–1928* (PhD diss.: University of Bristol, 1988).

read, heard, or seen, will supply a picture with a wealth of infinite detail and truth. This is a most vital point, so far as broadcasting is concerned.

Now, when we are stirred by an emotion aroused by the efforts of actors on the stage, the reality is seriously counteracted by the fact that an obviously artificial setting – probably the direct opposite of the sub-conscious picture – is facing us.

A Personal Picture.

The amazing advantage of listening without sight to words which are arranged to build emotion-compelling situations is that every person places the emotion in a setting fitted to or known by him. Thus, the emotion becomes a power inter-acting with a personal experience. Here the artificiality is entirely done away with, and if the ability of the speakers is of a high order, the emotion of the situation is universally accepted – it becomes a personal picture adapted to the mentality of the individual and assumes a reality which can be far greater than any effect at present provided on an ordinary stage. This is but a development of Shakespeare's idea that curtains of unostentatious appearance should be used for backgrounds. His intuitive knowledge of psychology was particularly true.

In the theatre, everyone, of whatever class, type, or education, is compelled to look at the same setting. With the applying of these psychological facts to broadcasting, a suitable setting for every sentiment is instantly provided by the listener.

At the theatre, a king may see a bad, or, at least, indifferent representation of a palace reception chamber; a scientist may be confronted with a laboratory, quite unacceptable when compared with the one in which he habitually works; an East-End Chinaman may see a travesty of an 'opium dive'; or an architect may see a structurally ridiculous portion of a house. These things observed, the full effect of the play and the efforts of the actors are militated against. But with broadcasting, the listening audience is given the opportunity of supplying individual pictures suited to its mentality, experience or habits; this reality must strengthen the uttered lines.

The same with persons of the stage. The voice may be a stimulant of a thousand reminiscences, conscious or sub-conscious, but let the owner of the voice be seen and the illusion generally crashes to the ground.

There is yet another aspect. Plays of mystery – I mean, embodying mystic or divine characters as players – will always be more powerful and real by wireless than by stage. The above reasons operate here, but they are reinforced by the element of religious mysticism inherent in us all. When producing plays of this type, I have always wished (and, indeed, endeavoured to contrive) that divine characters should not be seen, although it is necessary, of course, that their voices should be heard. Their presence should be *felt*. Immediately they are seen in the flesh, material takes the place of the mystic.

242

5.5 ROLF GUNOLD: ROUTES TO ACOUSTIC DRAMA

Translated by Marielle Sutherland. First published as 'Wege zum akustischen Drama,' *Der Deutsche Rundfunk*, 2 August 1925, 1948.

This essay is the published version of a talk Gunold gave to introduce his play *Spuk* ('Ghost apparition'), on the occasion of its first broadcast by the Schlesische Funkstunde, Breslau, in July 1925. A biographical sketch is included with 'The Seventh Sense' (3.7).

• • •

The acoustic drama, or the radio play, is on the rise, and nothing can put a stop to its development, even though, at present, it is coming up against so much resistance. Christian Aloys Wilsmann discusses the theoretical prerequisites in his essay.[1]

We must now also consider what it is that connects our new art form with the past, the present and the future, and what seems to be required in terms of implementing the radio play in practice.

We all no doubt recognise that, in principle, humanity has from the very beginning harboured the essence of radio, i.e. the contact between transmitter and receiver. It is the mysterious event between question and answer, between sympathy and antipathy, which encompasses all living creatures and constitutes the only bridge to communication. In the first instance, this event is consciously reflected as an artistic means of expression in the theatre. The stage represents the transmitter or loudspeaker, the audience the receivers. Over time, this device has perfected itself, becoming the cultural pinnacle of our modern theatre.

[1] Gunold is referring to an essay entitled 'Probleme des Hörspiels' by the German journalist Aloys Christian Wilsmann (1899–1966), which appeared in *Der Deutsche Rundfunk* in July 1925 alongside his own. Like Wilsmann, Gunold wanted to establish radio drama as a genre in its own right, and was keen to differentiate between the theatre play that might lend itself to broadcasting but was not written for radio, and the radio play conceived especially for broadcasting. These essays are part of a longer conversation in *Der Deutsche Rundfunk*; see also Aloys Christian Wilsmann, 'Zur Dramaturgie des Hörspiels: Eine Studie über Klangprobleme im Rundfunk,' *Der Deutsche Rundfunk*, 19 April 1925, 994–6.

When civilisation – and with it, the natural sciences – arrived, this was the beginning of the battle between theatre and machine technology. Steam power and global communication threatened to displace drama, the most vivid of all the arts, along with its satellite: acting. Richard Wagner recognised this danger and appropriated technology by virtue of the idiosyncrasy of his music dramas and his eminent theatrical instinct. This was the turning point. In order not to perish miserably, theatre had to keep up with machine technology. As a result, hydraulics, electricity and chemistry found their way onto the stage. Nevertheless, the dramatic muse was still restless. A new machinery appeared: film, which, from a historical perspective, harboured within it the first comprehensive breakthrough of technology into dramatic territory. The silent optical device began speaking, by means of silent signals, to the silent person. In-depth psychology was denied; the superficial observation of images was decried as unknown dramatic territory. In place of the stage was a section of screen and a machine. It seemed likely that acoustics would soon follow optics. It started with the phonograph, and the wireless perfected the breakthrough. For the first time, the waves on the sea of metaphysics were audibly breaking on the shore of human existence. However, the electrical wave has treated dramatic literature no differently to the way the optical wave has treated it, leaving the performing arts to wander blind and deaf through the world, robbed of their most precious components. The only way out of this, the only salvation, is either to exit the arena of art or create a new work of art which, having developed together with the machine, has an artistic justification for its existence. This is the threshold into acoustic drama. It is essential to unite aesthetic literature and machine technology. If we attune ourselves in such a way, we do not need to be afraid, for the old Pan is in the act of playing his flute in an entirely new way, and the best way of listening to it is to engage closely with the melody right from the beginning.

As we all know, the first step is always the most difficult, both for the author and for the audience. Initially, it is the listener who is the most important; he has to be taught how to use an organ that has thus far proceeded through life very much weakened by the supremacy of the optic nerve: the ear. The success of the acoustic radio play is predicated on a disciplined audience. This discipline consists precisely in the keenest form of listening, and it must not be disturbed by anything. Sounds and acoustic moods, to which the human being has thus far paid no attention, become the main focus and the point of departure for dramatic concentration. Perhaps radiophonic theatre[2] is also performing a cultural function here, in that it simultaneously educates people in proper listening.

---

[2] *Funkbühne* in the original.

It was the Schlesische Funk-Stunde, under its artistic director Ernst Fritz Bettauer [*sic*], which took the first step towards implementing the radio play in practice.[3] After the premiere of the first German radio drama, 'Bellinzona' – written on an intuitive basis by myself –, had to be postponed until the production of the necessary acoustic apparatus, Bettauer nonetheless experimented with establishing, in the first instance, the potential audible shape of the new art form, and this is what ultimately led to the premiere of my ghost sonata 'Spuk'.[4] This route proved to be the right one, and the artistic director embarked upon it courageously. It became clear that the acoustic scenery[5] – a theoretical requirement – really must form the basis of a radio play, and that this is what immediately shifts the radio drama into the artistic domain. Music, direction and technology have come together organically as servants of the new acoustic muse.

5.6 GABRIEL GERMINET: FROM *RADIO DRAMA: A NEW MODE OF ARTISTIC EXPRESSION*

Translated by Emilie Morin. First published as Pierre Cusy and Gabriel Germinet, *Théâtre radiophonique: Mode nouveau d'expression artistique* (Paris: Chiron, 1926) 13–16, 17–22, 23–5, 35–8.

[3] Silesian Radio Hour, Breslau (now Wroclaw, Poland), which began broadcasting in May 1924; Friedrich (Fritz) Ernst Bettauer (1887–1952), a German writer, theatre director and early artistic director of the Schlesische Funkstunde.

[4] *Bellinzona* was not broadcast until 1978. Gunold's *Spuk* ('Ghost apparition'), subtitled *Eine Gespenstersonate in fünf Sätzen nach Motiven von E.T.A. Hoffmann* ('A ghost sonata in five motifs after E.T.A. Hoffmann') revolved around the disembodied voices of ghosts naturally attracted to radio.

[5] *Akustische Kulisse* in the original, a term first used by von Heister in *Der Deutsche Rundfunk* earlier in 1925. The discussions around the concept of acoustic scenery or sound set (*Geräuschkulisse*) started in 1925 in German radio publications, and were emulated elsewhere, for example in France, from the mid-1920s to the early 1930s. See Hans Siebert von Heister, 'Das Hörspiel: Klangraum – Akustische Kulisse,' *Der Deutsche Rundfunk*, 19 April 1925, 993–4.

Gabriel Germinet (pseudonym of Maurice Vinot, 1882–1969) was an indefatigable advocate of radio and wrote numerous radio plays. Trained as an engineer in fluid mechanics, he worked in different strands of the French industry alongside his radio work. He was also an inventor, and his inventions included a telephone news service planned in 1922 and named Paris Informations Sans Fil, which he called 'Radiogazette'; the invention was a failure but anticipated later news bulletins on the radio. He was director of programmes at Radiola (Radio-Paris's predecessor) from 1923 to 1927, then advisor at Radio-Paris until 1931, and played a leading role in organisations of radio professionals such as the Union d'Art Radiophonique (the French Union for Radiophonic Art). *Théâtre radiophonique: Mode nouveau d'expression artistique* – the first book-length discussion of radio drama as a coherent genre, with its own principles – was widely discussed and had a global reach; a Japanese translation, for example, appeared in 1929. A collaborator, Pierre Cusy, contributed the first chapter on theatre history; Germinet wrote the chapters on radio and coined many important notions and terms, including *décor de bruits* (noise décor). Together, before publishing this book, Germinet and Cusy wrote *Marémoto* ('Seaquake', a play situated onboard a sinking ship), in response to a competition advertised by the newspaper *L'Impartial Français*; *Marémoto* won the first prize jointly with *Agonie* by Paul Camille (a monologue by a dying character that was never broadcast). *Marémoto* has a peculiar history, to which this text alludes. A few days before its intended official broadcast in October 1924, the play was rehearsed live on wavelengths not used by French radio stations. But some wireless listeners accidentally tuned in and thought that they were witnessing the sinking of a real ship; they alerted the authorities so that the crew could be rescued. The French Ministry of the Navy withdrew permission to broadcast the play. To circumvent the ban, *Marémoto* was performed a second time in a Radio-Paris auditorium, off-air, for French journalists and *théâtrophone* subscribers; thanks to the publicity the event received, the play was translated into English by C. A. Lewis and broadcast by the BBC in February 1925. Subsequently, it was translated into other languages, and broadcast in other countries including Italy, Austria, the United States and Argentina. Radio-Paris was only allowed to broadcast *Marémoto* for the first time in 1937.[2]

• • •

[1] Cusy's own radio work was confined to his collaboration with Germinet; there is no information about him anywhere, but handwriting samples in the Germinet-Vinot archive (Bibliothèque Nationale de France, Paris) suggest that Cusy was the pen name of Pierre Giroud, a Parisian printer who later printed brochures for Germinet.

[2] See Cécile Méadel, ed., 'Mare-Moto. Une pièce radiophonique de Pierre Cusy et Gabriel Germinet (1924),' *Réseaux. Communication-Technologie-Société* 10, no. 52 (1992): 75–94; Cécile Méadel, ed., 'Maremoto: A radio play (1924),' by Pierre Cusy and Gabriel Germinet, trans. Pauline Ridel, *Réseaux. The French Journal of Communication* 2, no. 2 (1994): 251–65; Christopher Todd, 'Gabriel Germinet and the "Livre d'or du théâtre radiophonique français" (1923–1935),' *Modern & Contemporary France* 10, no. 2 (2002): 225–41; 'Gabriel Germinet: Les carnets radio,' France Culture, 26 January 2006, INA archives.

Radio forces the listeners to make the effort to imagine, an effort they are not normally accustomed to making.[3] As part of the radiophonic presentation of a scene taken from the common theatre repertoire, the listener will hear one voice, then a second answering the first and, soon thereafter, a third voice. What is the relation between this third character and the first two?

Was this character standing on stage alongside the other two, or has he joined them without having heard the first dialogue?

It is not possible for the listener to understand.

A preliminary explanation of the play can, at best, lift some uncertainty around the intrigue and alleviate incomprehension; nevertheless, in many cases, the intrigue will remain just as obscure from the perspective of the listener. [. . .]

Let us not forget that although the radio provokes intense emotions, it also lacks an essential dimension for which authors will need to compensate by trying to create extreme emotions.

The wireless listener is confronted by a lack of atmosphere: indeed, in a theatre, the audience is, in theory, isolated from any influence external to the spectacle; in practice, it is submitted to the influence of the room just as much as to that of the stage.[4]

This phenomenon, tied to the psychology of the crowd,[5] can also be observed in other domains; as we have previously noted, it has been one of the theatre's essential conditions.

With the radio, on the contrary, the listeners do not leave their home, where everything is familiar, and nothing prepares them for the strong emotions of the stage; the public cannot be considered as one block, and the action must speak to each listener in isolation.

---

[3] Germinet's study features occasional footnotes cross-referencing other parts of the book; such footnotes have not been included in this translation. Only his discursive footnotes have been translated, and they are marked as [Author's note] here, to differentiate them from the rest of the anthology's editorial apparatus.

[4] [Author's note] Mr H. Delobière published an interesting article entitled 'La musique et la radiophonie' in the issue of *Radio-Concert* of 20 December 1924, from which we extract the following observations: 'When we are at a concert, we can see the conductor, the beautiful singer, the great virtuoso. Clearly, contact is established and a tangible link, which proves irreplaceable, is created between the main actors in the musical drama and the public. As a matter of fact, as soon as the musicians have taken their seats, as soon as the conductor has appeared on the podium, and even before the first sound has been heard, an atmosphere is created, through which all individual sensibilities fuse into one, forming a collective and happy soul (which naturally becomes even happier when applause erupts later). The atmosphere is irreplaceable too. The concerts broadcast on the radio will for a long time, if not always, lack such an atmosphere.'

[5] [Author's note] See the works of Mr Gustave Le Bon.

On another level, when, in a concert, we hear a piece that captures our attention, so much so that we become eager to have the score, are we not often surprised when we later try to play it, or when we read it, to find it a lot less attractive than when we heard it?

The public of the theatre hall is a group of individuals who find themselves in emotional conditions that are optimal for witnessing the performance of dramatic works.

This is what makes a theatrical performance successful, and since it is incompatible with the principle of radio broadcasting, it is easy to understand how obvious its absence can become.

But how will we be able to conceive radiophonic versions of, on the one hand, the setting for the action, which we do not know, and, on the other, the facial expressions and the technique of an artist whom we can hear but cannot see?

The future of radio drama depends on the solution to this question [. . .].

THE ATMOSPHERE

Radio drama must be to theatre as we already know it what a sketch or a poster are to a finished painting: composed to reflect the fact that the observer will scrutinise it in detail.

A sketch, a poster, as we have noted, are made to be looked at by an observer who is in a hurry, to produce impressions that are short-lived, yet sufficient to strike the mind and capture the attention.

From a radiophonic perspective, because radio requires the mind to adapt, which cannot happen instantly, and because listeners are separate individuals with different temperaments, the wireless public is only open to simple yet strong sensations – those strong sensations that men were looking for a very long time ago when they gathered around makeshift boards and travelling actors.

If strength cannot be broadcast on the radio, strong emotions can be, and admirably well.

The topic that creates extreme or highly dramatic sensations, or very joyous sensations, will be more comprehensible than other topics, given the current state of radio and – permit us to insist on this point – given how perceptive listeners currently are.

On the other hand, because it addresses a large public, radio drama should be neither subtle nor refined; this does not mean that sophisticated ideas will not be pursued or implemented, but that it is premature to think of it as an exceptional art for an elite public, given that listeners are still imperfectly trained to listen to radio transmissions.

To this we shall add that it is always advantageous to collaborate with artists whose voice, timbre and pitch differ sharply from one another, so that the listeners can understand the action as clearly as possible. Furthermore, we cannot insist enough on the necessity of a careful execution, which can only be created through rehearsals. It is indeed regrettable that radio-scenarios and radio-texts are often insufficiently prepared, on the pretext that it is possible to perform at the microphone without calling upon one's memory, that it is possible to read without being seen and without affecting the listeners' experience.

THE DÉCOR

[. . .] [W]e noticed that creating, and sometimes sustaining, different sources of sounds or noises whose point of emission is suitably situated in relation to the microphone, over the whole course of the action, enabled the listeners to imagine the atmosphere through which the characters evolved.[6]

This condition can be met, and has already been met,[7] through the use of noises whose position in relation to their point of emission and the actor's mouth creates what we might call 'phonetic volume.'

This is how it becomes possible to create an arrangement that feels very alive, as we have shown in the experiments we undertook for the broadcasting of the radio-drama *Marémoto*, which called for noise décors [*décors de bruits*][8] that created a perfect illusion.

Music emanating from far away can, in some cases, be used in order to form a *musical backdrop* that will be to radiophonic production what the stage backdrop is to the theatre, in a way.

The sound décors that are created on the radio will enable its theatre to become humanised.

Just like symbols in dramatic art, music remains the primary vehicle for the sensations in this invisible art. [. . .]

FACIAL EXPRESSION

[. . .] [N]oises can lay claim to being much more than noise.

A listener who heard *Marémoto* wrote to us saying that he had 'heard the wind in the boat's ropes.' Others said that they felt as though they were cold, although none of the characters had alluded to the temperature at any point.

The wind, perfectly imitated[9] and blowing like a storm in the background, was enough to create that impression. [. . .]

---

[6] [Author's note] In the very near future, listeners will subscribe to publications conceived for this purpose, which will enable them to better situate the scenes they are listening to and better understand the works transmitted on the radio.

[7] [Author's note] See the third part of *Marémoto*.

[8] [Author's note] An expression we coined in April 1924.

[9] [Author's note] Thanks to impeccable technical work and to noise equivalences directed by Mr Robert Bugnon, Engineer for the Compagnie Française de Radiophonie [French Radio Broadcasting Company].

During the broadcast of *Marémoto*, wireless listeners who were not conversant with the maritime wireless service became anxious and regretted being unable to call for help, and a few listeners even sent telegrams and telephoned the maritime authorities in their region.

Given that noises have the power to create fully-fledged sensations by themselves, it is logical to assert that noises must succeed at putting the listener in a mindset that makes him better able to appreciate the value of the words.

Noise is what creates the imaginative counterpart to facial expression.

GESTURE

Finally, authors should not forget the particularities of radio drama as they are developing their topic.

The characters must do or say everything that will enable the action as such to be imagined, as well as everything they would need to do or say to enable a blind public to comprehend and perceive the action.[10]

Just as the first scenes in a stage play tell us how the characters are situated in relation to one another, on the radio the first dialogues will need to give these indications as well as brief, yet highly evocative, information about the setting.

As they are playing their roles, the actors must constantly remember that their movements are invisible. No character, for example, shall say, 'I will leave it there' when speaking of something they are holding, because the listener would not be able to understand what they have just done.[11]

All words, just like all noises, must concur to create and sustain the illusion through hearing; this will mean using brief sentences, condensed arguments, faster dialogues and onomatopoeia, while making space for judiciously placed silences.

The performance should be entrusted to artists who express themselves without emphasis and whose diction remains sober and without accentuation.[12] On this matter, it will be necessary to take into account the progress accomplished every day through research on how to modify some parts of language in order to compensate for the distortions created during transmission and reception by machines that are not as perfect as the human ear.

---

[10] [Author's note] This proposition, made by Mr Maurice Vinot in 1922, was reiterated in 1924 by Miss Miller, winner of the first Wireless Competition in the United States.

[11] [Author's note] We saw, in the issue of the magazine *Le Studio* from 1 March 1925, the text of a broadcast play in which the following indications appear: '. . . The stage is empty; a servant enters, followed by X. Second tableau: same backdrop, etc.' These indications, which the author had obviously planned for the text destined for the stage, become genuine barbarisms in radio broadcasting.

[12] [Author's note] The Radio Actors' Competition organised by *L'Impartial Français* (1924) has demonstrated that the study of diction, as it is currently taught, is very far removed from what the study of radio-diction should be.

Various Studies and Realisations

'I can hear the light,' said Tristan.[13]

The ear of the wireless listener, presented with a work whose topic has been chosen well and executed well, will not only hear but also transpose into three dimensions the forms that have been 'perceived' through hearing, be they inert or animated.

In order to create a complete illusion, radio drama will need to draw upon its own means to create impressions similar to those generated by the dream, which is frequently so strikingly close to the truth. Indeed, what is a dream if not a spontaneous manifestation of the unconscious which has been translated into images? As a matter of fact, we can find in music an example of the power of suggestion that takes place through hearing. Indeed, does music not 'create, for many people, visual images that surface in the mind more or less quickly, more or less clearly, and constantly move'?[14]

Before *Marémoto* was broadcast, a few attempts at a radio drama were made.

The prose pieces that were transmitted using wired or wireless transmission borrowed from staged theatre and were never fully understood by those who did not know them beforehand.[15]

A first attempt was made at Radio-Paris, with a play by Paul Ginisty, *Les Deux Pigeons*.

For this, noise décors were used.

The action was fairly comprehensible for the listeners because the play has a very simple structure and there are few characters.

Rosalie, by Mr Max Maurey, a very amusing play, also very timely, came across as dull when it was broadcast, although it has long been part of the repertoire, and in spite of an excellent interpretation. [. . .]

Mr Bertram Fryer, Director of the Bournemouth station in England, has had the very ingenious idea of offering a radiophonic transposition of a painting by Mr Alfred Von Wierusz-Kowalski, 'Through the Steppe in Winter.'

The idea was to animate a pictorial artwork through radio.[16]

Over the course of this radio-scenario, which lasted a few minutes, we heard the wolves howling, the bells of the horses pulling the troika, and the conversation between a young lady and her driver.

---

[13] A reference to Wagner's opera *Tristan and Isolde*.

[14] [Author's note] Paul Ramain in *Le Courrier Musical*.

[15] [Author's note] For example, the radio-telephonic transmission of *Knock*, by Mr Jules Romains, was only entertaining for the wireless listeners who had previously seen this brilliant satire performed at the Comédie des Champs-Elysées.

[16] [Author's note] 'Which radio-advertiser will succeed in creating, in the spirit of the radio listener, a vivid sense of the real form and colours of the object, of the work subject to radio-discussion?' (Conference presentation by Mr Maurice Vinot, November 1922, Hôtel des Centraux).

Her cries of anguish merged with the words of reassurance uttered by the man and his gunshots.[17]

We wish to applaud this successful adaptation, which possesses, in our view, the qualities essential to a radio-scenario: a very brief plot, suggestive noise décors, and the construction of a very vivid impression in the mind of the listener.[18] [. . .]

Conclusion

If we compare ancient theatre to radio drama, we realise that the latter is nothing but the brilliant generalisation of a formula that is as old as the world itself.

Just as a photographic chamber is the projection of our sense of sight, just as the telephone is the projection of our sense of hearing, radio is, most certainly, the projection, in the three-dimensional world in which we live, of the phenomenon of telepathy, hence of the nervous system, onto the social realm. [. . .]

In ancient times, it was necessary to gather people in immense theatres; in the Middle Ages, almanacs were often used in order to spread ideas and ensure some unity of vision, and, consequently, some collective will among men from the same country; in modern times, newspapers can very quickly reach the citizens of a nation. Likewise, in the future, radio will become the preferred instrument for disseminating ideas.

We can understand why it is the focus of such great preoccupation from the perspective of governments, who consider it dangerous if it remains within hands that cannot be controlled; let us remark, nonetheless, how simple it would be to consider radio as a spoken press, enjoying, as a consequence, a status similar to that of the printed press.[19]

[17] [Author's note] This radio-scenario was heard by Mr Rambaud (7 Passage des Lions, Geneva) among others; he writes to us: 'It truly seems as though these noise décors, as you put it so well, are by nature destined to do a great service to Radio Drama through their impact on our reflexes and our nervous system.'

[18] [Author's note] The first radio-play broadcast in Germany by the Schlesische Funkstunde, on 21 July 1925, is entitled *Spuk* (ghost apparitions). The author, Mr Rolf Gunold from Charlottenburg, delivered a lecture entitled 'Towards an Acoustic Drama' before the broadcast of his work. The *mise-en-scène* was by Mr Fritz Ernst Bettauer. The lack of details about this radio-scenario does not enable us to discuss it at length, to our regret. [. . .]

[19] [Author's note] '. . . We ask that news on the wireless be incorporated into the private telegraphic or telephone lines used by the press: indeed, unless more generous guarantees are offered, the Radio-Press cannot logically come into being, its non-existence maintaining the unacceptable level of privilege that the printed press enjoys.' Excerpt from the report presented on 6 September 1922 by Mr Maurice Vinot to Mr Paul Laffont, Deputy State Secretary of the PTT [the French postal, telegraph and telephone service], at his invitation, following the plans drawn for the first decree aiming to regulate radio broadcasting in France.

As the resources of radio stations are expanding, it will become possible to dedicate large amounts of money to radio drama and to envisage the broadcasting of scenarios that will frequently be costly, owing to the need to be attractive.

We will then enter an era comparable to the current era of the cinema, in which scriptwriters and film directors often enjoy considerable financial resources.

Radio-scenarios of this nature will be amply justified because, as we are writing,[20] we can already count in France, Belgium and Switzerland more than 600,000 wireless sets owned by radio enthusiasts, representing over two million French-speaking listeners.

Nonetheless, as in England, all those who own a wireless set will need to contribute regularly, through annuities, to the costs of exploitation as well as the technical and artistic costs incurred by the radio stations that prove the most popular.

Indeed, it will be necessary to ensure that radio stations are able to pay adequately for radio-scenarios; such scenarios will only be broadcast once or at intervals far removed from one another, for it is impossible to expect the same radio-scenario to be broadcast several days in a row.

Authors of theatre plays can, according to the current arrangements of the societies of authors, receive royalties from all the channels through which their works are presented.

With radio, the author will only be paid once, more or less.

Special plays demanding that their authors have a deep knowledge of the conditions of transmission and reception for radio should not be put in the same realm as works that are played under the pretext of providing publicity to their authors; with radio, authors' rights must be the same as the rights they enjoy in the theatre. This is in the interest of radio drama, for the latter will be systematically ignored if authors are not assured that they can derive advantages from the broadcasting of their works that are comparable with those from which they benefit in relation to the theatre. If in the very near future a special treatment is not reserved for authors and composers working especially for radio, then radio is irremediably condemned to mediocrity. What will happen to radio is what we can currently see happening to films in France; authors prefer to restrict their activity to traditional theatre, which proves more advantageous for them [. . .].

We hope that those who preside over the administrative routes shaping the destiny of radio in France will be mindful of these facts.

It is not sufficient to organise groups proposing to guide the choice of works to be broadcast, although these groups are obviously well-intentioned; it is necessary, rather, to examine the means through which dramatic authors can

[20] [Author's note] In December 1924.

become interested in the new mode of expression, which, even for those who have an experience of the stage, requires a fairly long period of initiation.

By way of illustration, we would like to draw attention to one of the prerogatives that authors of radio drama enjoy: an abundant correspondence from listeners, who cannot applaud the author and the actors as they would in a theatre, and send their impressions in writing instead.

After the second broadcast of *Marémoto*, several thousand letters were written by listeners living in France, England, Belgium, Switzerland, Holland, Italy, Spain, Austria and Yugoslavia; an unsuspected public, consisting at least of two million listeners spread across the whole of Western Europe, was listening.

5.7 LANCE SIEVEKING: FROM *THE STUFF OF RADIO*

First published as *The Stuff of Radio* (London: Cassell, 1934), 15, 38–9, 74–5, 77–81.

Lance Sieveking (Lancelot de Giberne Sieveking, 1896–1972) was a British radio producer and author who used modernist techniques to craft new types of storytelling and sound montages. He joined the BBC in 1926 as Assistant Director in the Education Department; he tried his hand at different kinds of programmes, from talks to news bulletins, presided over the creation of running commentaries, and devised feature programmes merging music, spoken word and sound effects. His radio pieces became increasingly ambitious over time, as studio equipment became more sophisticated and as he developed his mastery of the BBC instrument called the 'Dramatic Control Panel,' a forerunner of modern mixing desks. His most celebrated work – *Kaleidoscope*, subtitled *A Rhythm, Representing the Life of a Man from Cradle to Grave* (first broadcast in September 1928 on 2LO London and 5XX Daventry) – was a sound montage bringing together sound effects, poetry and fragments of dialogue, designed to be performed live. Using the Dramatic Control Panel, Sieveking conducted the first broadcast; the adventure involved three orchestras, a wide range of sound effects and performers in seven radio studios simultaneously. As part of his work in the Variety Department, he produced a large number of radio plays (about 200, in David Hendy's estimation). Later, he acted as script editor and made forays into television; in 1930, he directed the BBC's first television play, his own adaptation of Pirandello's *The Man with the Flower in his Mouth*. He was interested in the techniques honed by filmmakers such as Vsevolod Pudovkin and G. W. Pabst, and emulated their strategies in his radio work.[1]

●　●　●

In spite of the fact that radio-plays are apparently performed in public, they are not. They are performed in private.

Everyone who has anything to do with a radio-play subconsciously makes a great act of faith before it begins. He privately asserts his belief that the sounds he is about to make will be carried to other places, and there heard, in private, by a number of other people for ever invisible and unknown to him. He then privately gets on with it.

Radio-drama is in fact such an extraordinarily personal and private matter that it may be difficult to avoid appearing egotistical in writing about it. It is a 'mystery' in the old sense; a thing beyond human reason; a kind of secret rite.

[. . .] In 1930 Mr Pudowkin shot a man's smile in slow-motion, and in 1929 I shot his voice in the same way.[2] The smile will always remain in the province of the visual camera, and never come within the province of broadcasting except in the form of a televised film containing a slow-motioned smile. At least it is difficult for me to believe that we shall have a television apparatus capable of slow-motioning at given moments during a transmission of a live actuality. That would open up a new set of possibilities which I do not permit myself to contemplate just now for fear of confusion.

But at any rate, Mr Pudowkin's remarks have served to show that a man absorbed in thinking about the cinema will come upon identical problems and similar solutions to those encountered by a man absorbed in thinking about radio-plays. On the film he finds that a significant movement emphasised in a special way in its presentation to the audience, can be a useful short cut to quick and complete understanding. In the radio-play he finds that a significant and imaginatively evocative sound presented in a special way can give a listener in one second a visual image which it might otherwise take two hundred and

---

[1]　See David Hendy, 'Biography and the Emotions as a Missing "Narrative" in Media History,' *Media History* 18, no. 3&4 (2012): 361–78; David Hendy, 'Painting with Sound: The Kaleidoscopic World of Lance Sieveking, a British Radio Modernist,' *Twentieth-Century British History* 24, no. 2 (2013): 169–200; Lance Sieveking, *Airborne: Scenes from the Life of Lance Sieveking, Pilot, Writer and Broadcasting Pioneer*, ed. Paul Sieveking (London: Strange Attractor Press, 2013).

[2]　The Russian filmmaker Vsevolod Pudovkin (1893–1953) had a particular interest in the expressivity of the smile and commented on it on several occasions in his writings on cinema.

fifty words to create. He might make a narrator describe in a series of vivid word pictures, a desolate stretch of sandy shore. Not a soul in sight. The tide is out. Dreary little waves lap on damp rocks. The sun is sinking. And a lot more. Without a narrator the radio-producer simply evokes all this in his imaginative listeners' minds by (1) a small wind; (2) a faint plashing of water on sand; (3) a distant dismal sea-gull calling in the grey sky; and (4) an even more distant church clock striking five. All this will take about six or seven seconds, and the exactness of its timing will be the criterion by which to judge the capacity of the producer, for exact *rightness* of timing is everything or nearly everything. And this is not achieved with clocks, but with an instinct similar to the musician's.

Of course the sea-gull and our old friend the Broadcasting House train, have done a good deal of work in past years. But it is still possible to use them with *great* care.[3]

But the visual slow-motion and close-up of the cinema screen have been just as much overworked and mishandled by scores of film directors.

[. . .] The art of writing plays for the wireless medium is an art, the practice of which may be treated of in the same general terms as any other art, since it is subject to the same aesthetic and emotional laws as any other art. The same qualities that make for good (or great) art in any medium, make for good (or great) radio-drama. And those qualities which make for bad art in any medium will infallibly make for bad radio-drama, for the same reasons, and in the same way. And since it is quite unnecessary for me to embark upon a disquisition about art in general, I will confine myself to a few observations about the technical problems that face a radio dramatist. For it is in their technical problems that arts differ from each other.

To begin at the beginning: the radio dramatist must ask himself, what are all the things that people see subconsciously? In his play, what are the things which, not seeing, they will desire to see? What are the things which, desiring to see, they *will*, in some form, see? Helped and prompted by him, to what degree? And the degree of his mastery of the technique by means of which those problems can be solved, may be estimated by the degree in which not only he but his audience is unaware of its presence. If anyone except a fellow-practitioner involuntarily perceives the presences of a *device*, or piece of *machinery*, then the dramatist has failed, and/or the producer has failed; while the unfortunate actor and actress are handed over to the audience bound and helpless. There is an analogy applicable to every art.

The radio dramatist, once the early stages of technique learning are over, and the basic part of his work occurs without obtruding itself, now becomes like the composer of music, in that he *hears* what he writes, conceives and works out his play before his mind's ear. He is more like the composer than

---

[3] The most commonly used sound effects, which listeners could recognise instantly.

the theatre playwright in this respect, for whereas the theatre playwright has to *see* his play as it goes along and hear it also, the radio dramatist and the musician are dealing only with things to be heard: the radio dramatist having by far the greater orchestra to write for (since he is not limited to what are generally accepted as 'musical instruments') and an infinitely larger field of tone, pitch, volume, timbre, and general character of sound, for he deals not only in words, not only in music, but in every sound in the world which may be taken in its original form, or imitated; which may be used realistically or in some abstract way. The radio dramatist writes his play, as it were, with his ear alone. The world his audience and his orchestra . . .

[. . .] An author, writing for the stage, or the screen, knows that he can rely for a great measure of his effectiveness upon the collective response of the assembled mass of people. He knows that a crowd probably will respond in such and such a way. The radio audience, however, is composed of a vast number of people who are separately listening in different places, and therefore not subject to mass psychology. The dramatist constantly remembers that there are quite a large number of legitimate devices with which on the radio he cannot 'get by'. Never was this so glaringly illustrated to me as when I listened in London to Hitler speaking in Berlin. He was addressing a crowd of many thousands, who kept perfectly silent for the most part, but who suddenly roared applause. The applause was staggering. One felt at those moments with what certainty the speaker was holding the huge crowd, and doing with them as he pleased. But when they kept silence, they passed out of the picture entirely and utterly, leaving the orator with his rhetoric pouring forth in an unstemmable stream, *alone* – alone in an empty room; and one listened to his unflagging voice with nothing but quiet attention. Then the crowd roared again suddenly, and one had a brief but quite startlingly strong emotional experience, a sort of *reflected* mass influence at a distance.[4]

The dramatist remembers that most of his audience, which may number over a million people – out of the fifty million who listen to one or other part of the programmes – are sitting in rooms alone or at most with one or two others. He remembers that a man's reactions are very different when he is not surrounded by crowds of other people. And the playwright weighs the 'truth' of a line, the inevitability of a piece of dialogue, or movement in the plot, or the goodness of a joke, with an extra, a special care. He knows how magically acute the ear becomes when the eye is not functioning to cloud or dress up its

---

[4] Sieveking referred to the Nazi takeover of the German press and radio in similar terms, as a spectacle to be watched and heard, in his novel *The Woman She Was* (also from 1934). His non-judgemental tone reflects the most prevalent stance in 1934: those who were lucid about the tenor and content of Hitler's ideas were a minority; they belonged to persecuted Jewish communities and anti-Nazi groups in Germany, and to communist and socialist circles elsewhere.

impressions. Pretty or interesting faces, dresses, lighting, scenery, nice legs and clever gestures conspire together to deceive the ears of the audience. They don't always succeed. But they frequently have a partial success. But poor words, second-rate writing, are exposed naked and dreadful by the relentless microphone.

In England, radio is, so to speak, owned by the nation. It has not been commercialised. It has therefore been able, and one trusts, will continue to be able, to concern itself primarily with ideals and only secondarily with what are called 'box-office considerations'. But while supplying entertainment year in year out, its equally important duty has always been, particularly in the department of drama, to discover the new possibilities latent within itself, and the best means of using them in terms of contemporary life. This latter has been inevitably limited to a certain extent by the narrowing down of the field of subject. The very universality of audience precludes for radio an absolute universality of subject, at present.

So two great basic ingredients of life are, to some extent, missing. They are: sex and humour. These two are inextricably mixed up together. All the best and most robust humour has in it an element of sex; and sex itself is not always unrelated to humour. (By 'sex' I do *not* mean wanton bawdiness.)

The reason why radio lacks these is two-fold. First because it is so difficult to make humour 'get across' through the microphone; and second, because it is so difficult to prevent sex from 'getting across.' One day this may no longer be true. But remember, there have always been limitations of one kind or another. And in a period of great limitations, *i.e.* between 1850 and 1906, many great writers flourished. The rising generation of writers – dramatists and poets – have before them a tremendous opportunity. It remains to be seen whether lack of big money attractions, or lack of realisation of the opportunity – or something else – will lead to their failing to take it. I hope they will take it. For in this new form, at its present stage of development, and in the stages of development into which it will soon enter, lies the possibility of restoring the drama to the place which it once occupied in the life of the community. The poetic drama, a form used by Goethe, Shelley, Swinburne, Hardy and Browning, among others, is a form comparatively unsuited to the modern theatre, but one which may now come into its own. There have been several examples broadcast in the last few years with some success. And it seems to me that among the thirty or so different genres of radio-play and 'programme' the poetic drama is as likely as any to be found to contain most of the qualities peculiarly suitable to the broadcast medium. I am not suggesting that writers of the new generation will, or even should, attempt to produce works closely following the design of, say, *The Dynasts* or *Prometheus Unbound,*[5] but I

---

[5] Scenes from *The Dynasts* were played in BBC broadcasts in 1926, 1927, 1929 and 1933, and readings from *Prometheus Unbound* were broadcast in 1926 and 1933.

am suggesting that a form not entirely dissimilar from those may eventually turn out to be a good form for what Mr Guthrie has so light-heartedly called 'the canned medium'.[6] My cousin the late Gerard Manley Hopkins would have found radio a very congenial medium as any who study his highly individual manner of poetry will perceive. In architecture, new materials such as steel and reinforced concrete have given with their elasticity and strength the possibility of entirely new forms in building, embodying the cantilever and multi-unit construction. But practically no one among the architects in this country is using the new materials for any purpose except to make the shapes always possible with the old materials. This in spite of the fact that the innumerable modifications of our contemporary life have long since created a strong demand for the new forms in construction that are possible with the contemporary materials. The cinema too has always been to a large degree in the hands of people who could only see one way to do with it: to take theatre plays exactly as they stood and photograph them – photograph the three or the four acts, with the scene set firmly round them, because, in the theatre, the audience couldn't be expected to wait several hours while they built new scenes. Radio has its theatre votaries no less renowned than the cinema, and no less dull. Given elastic steel their grandfathers made a marble bath, indistinguishable from the marble baths of the past three thousand years, except that the 'marble' was put on with a paint-brush, and exhibited it with pride in the great Exhibition of 1862. But Leonardo da Vinci made an aeroplane in 1482 that looked extremely like the aeroplane of Mr Grahame White.[7] Only Grahame White lived at a time when the right materials had been discovered, and da Vinci was some centuries out in his form. Some of the writers of poetic drama were writing, perhaps too soon. Perhaps also, there are writings existing to-day that are suitable only to a medium not yet discovered! But it is too easy to be carried away into windy speculations.

It may well be, as we have already said, that the radio-play is a sport of nature – a phenomenon peculiar to this decade only – a thing in which, while we speak of it, the worms of decadence and dissolution crawl in and out. It may be. Maybe. But one thing is certain. When vision is added to sound and yet another new form becomes possible, while new work will be done in terms of it, there will remain all the work done for the old medium. Can it be adapted? Can the radio-plays of sound only be adapted to the look-listen conditions of the future? Of course they can. But it will take considerable art and ingenuity. The scenarios of silent films have been adapted for talking pictures. Even silent films themselves have had sound ruthlessly attached to them with all sorts of

---

[6] Guthrie refers to 'canned drama' in his introduction to *Squirrel's Cage and Two Other Microphone Plays* (5.11).

[7] The British aviator Claude Grahame-White (1879–1959).

quaint and grotesque results. Now, slowly and late, after their nature, men of the film are awaking to the fact that the radio-play is in many cases ready, almost as it stands, to be made into a film. But what has to be done to the script of a radio-play before you start to make the film, is not quite what will have to be done to a radio-play script by the adapter for look-listening, at least not in more than a few cases.

5.8 TRISTAN BERNARD: FOR THE INVISIBLE BLIND PUBLIC

Translated by Emilie Morin. First published as 'Pour des aveugles invisibles,' *Sketches radiophoniques de Tristan Bernard*, *La Petite Illustration*, 11 October 1930, 3–4.

Tristan Bernard (pseudonym of Paul Bernard, 1866–1947) was a popular French writer and journalist renowned for his wit. He made his debut before the microphone in November 1923, on the French radio station Radiola. He started to write for radio after hearing one of his theatre plays – a comedy in verse entitled *L'Ecole des quinquagénaires* – broadcast on Paris-PTT in February 1930 and failing to understand it. The broadcast was an example of what was called *théâtre radiophoné*: it was a retransmission of a performance by the Louis Cognet theatre company to which no modifications had been made (Cognet's approach simply entailed giving brief explanations of the setting and the action at the beginning of each act). In a strongly-worded letter that appeared in *Le Journal*, Bernard complained that he had been unable to distinguish between the characters and understand the action in his own play, and he presented the broadcast as an example of the ignorance, incompetence and negligence that technology could unleash.[1] In the wake of this letter, the Compagnie Française de Radiophonie, the French national broadcasting service, invited Bernard to write a play especially for radio; his radio play *Le narcotique*, broadcast in March 1930 by Radio-Paris, was followed by other radio plays. With radio drama, Bernard favoured adaptation: he believed that radio did not require new writing techniques, only some simple tweaks, and that most theatre plays could be fruitfully adapted for radio simply by

---

[1] Tristan Bernard, 'Plaintes d'un diffusé,' *Le Journal*, 12 February 1930, 1–2.

creating a sense of continuous action. His radio work was never as successful as his theatre plays, but his commitment to radio was genuine; he also contributed to other radio genres, creating crosswords for a radio series launched by Radio-Paris in 1928. Bernard was Jewish, and his work was banned by the Vichy regime during the Second World War; he was arrested in October 1943 and sent to the Drancy concentration camp, an experience that left him greatly weakened. His co-detainees remembered how he would recite poems and classical plays to help them keep hope. He stopped writing after his release.[2]

• • •

I must confess that I was seized by a passion for radio broadcasting quite suddenly, and entirely by chance.

A wireless salesman lent me a set so that I could try it out. The music lovers around me became intoxicated with music whenever we spent evenings at home.

Sometimes they listened to plays spoken in ordinary language, transmitted from different parts of Paris, Lille or Toulouse.

One day I heard that one of our national radio stations had included one of my plays in its programme. I was somewhat suspicious and made arrangements to listen to it. I tried to understand it but found it terribly difficult. And yet I have a good memory. I can only guess what the other listeners thought. They probably turned the dial towards another station.

The people who had organised this radio audition had chosen the actors for my little play somewhat haphazardly. They were talented comedians, but their voices were poorly 'matched' and sometimes resembled one another too closely. And, because the characters could not be seen, and because there was nothing to indicate that someone had entered the stage and someone else had left, the whole experience was somewhat confusing.

After this I decided to adapt plays or write plays especially for the wireless, taking as my starting point a very simple idea: that the public of listeners can see neither the actors nor the place from whence they speak and are supposed to gesticulate.

I wanted to write theatre for the blind, in which the dialogue creates the décor within the listener's imagination.

My first writing attempts were greeted with warm appreciation, I must say, if the many letters that listeners sent me are anything to go by. But I was

[2] See Cornelia Otis-Skinner, *Elegant Wits and Grand Horizontals: Paris – La Belle Epoque* (London: Michael Joseph, 1963), 135–48; René Duval, *Histoire de la radio en France* (Paris: Alain Moreau, 1979), 53, 67; Robert Prot, *Précis d'histoire de la radio et de la télévision* (Paris: L'Harmattan, 2007), 42.

subjected to violent attacks from the 'technicians' of the wireless. With every new invention comes the rise of new technicians. Inevitably, they lack experience, but their views become all the more authoritative, at least as far as they are concerned.

If anyone paid a visit to a craftsman from the Gobelins[3] in order to reprimand him, he would laugh and would be right to do so. Indeed his craft is five centuries old. Through practice, a long line of generations has been able to gain the necessary experience. They have had many successes but have learned just as much from the many errors made along the way.

In response to my first radio attempts, the technicians reprimanded me for reinventing myself as a radio dramatist. To this I responded with humility: I explained that I was new to radio broadcasting, and that my work over the past forty years had been about trying to reach the public and kindle people's interest. The soul of the public does not change, no matter whether we speak of 'spectators' or 'listeners.' When the means of expression change, only the faculties of attention change, and this is what we should take into account. This is a matter for authors, not for engineers. To each their own business.

Let me sketch the situation briefly:

Three arts that mirror one another and yet are different.

Silent film, which only calls upon the eye.

Radio broadcasting, which only calls for headphones. In between, another art, that makes itself seen as well as heard: theatre – and, if you like, the talking films, which is a kind of theatre printed onto a roll of film.

Writing for radio means speaking to the imagination of the listener without forgetting that the characters cannot be seen. The task of the author is to create dialogue that is sufficiently evocative to dispense with real décors. The author must compensate for the paucity of resources by becoming more ingenious and remedy the insufficiency, the void inherent in the material realisation of the radio play by painting the scene as richly as possible. Richly: let me linger on that word, for one realises quickly that radio's precarious resources are also unlimited and that imaginary décors can be created using words that would cost millions if they were made of wood or canvas. Those who build castles in the air are admirable architects when their talents are used well.

We have a whole host of great dramatic authors at present. I encourage these authors to write for radio with as much energy as I can muster every time I meet them. I am persuaded that they will find radio to be an occasion for excellent training. Radio makes authors more accustomed to giving words the highest level of evocative meaning. And this is always a useful skill, even when one is not writing for the wireless.

[3] The Gobelins Manufactory, a French tapestry factory founded in the 15th century.

The Société de Radiophonie Française, or Radio-Paris if you prefer, generously put its auditorium at my disposal for all nine of my broadcasting attempts. I was well seconded by my colleague Jean Bouchor and, for the *mise-en-scène*, by Georges Colin, who has not only a great talent for acting but also a great curiosity for these new questions.[4] The actors who were put at my disposal were highly gifted artists. This is how I was able to broadcast a good number of sketches, the majority of which are being published today in *L'Illustration*.

We will continue with these experiments during the next season, I think. Many of those who spoke to me during my travels this summer expressed their approval, without being prompted. The authors who will follow in my footsteps will see for themselves how pleasurable it is to see one's public expand in this way.

I will only start working on a new series of broadcasts once we have pulled together a good collection of 'noises,' however. At present, in that regard, even in the foreign studios that are said to be perfect and are lauded far and wide, the creation of noises leaves much to be desired. Indeed it poses difficulties that are not obvious at first sight.

When you listen to a fine orchestra playing on the wireless, you can hear the audience applaud after each piece. You know that it is applause. But it is necessary to know it, for applause has been translated into a ferocious sort of spittle, into some hoarse, bizarre snoring, which bear no resemblance to a demonstration of enthusiasm.

In the same way, shooting a gun next to the set does not mean that the listeners will hear a real gunshot. Phonographs have been used to make disc records of authentic train station noises, but once they were played they stopped being train station noises. Some wireless sets, as we know, are more precise when they transmit interferences than when they render such noises.

Without a doubt, these issues are the work of the wireless receiver, not the work of the wireless transmitter; yet even when wireless sets are improved and no longer distort the noises that they carry, the problem will not be resolved entirely.

There are some noises that we cannot recognise even when they are faithfully rendered. Think, for example, of street noise. In our everyday lives, we hear it constantly, but we do not listen to it. You may remember that game we played as children, which entailed blocking and unblocking our ears with our fingers several times in a row. The successive oppositions of silence and noise would enable us to hear something resembling chimney bellows. That is when we as children first became aware of the hubbub on the street.

---

4 Jean Bouchor (1882–1953), French author and journalist; Georges Colin (1880–1945), French actor, radio producer and director of radio plays.

Little by little, the ears of the public will become better educated. The public must learn to hear, then to listen. I have received letters about some of the sketches you are about to read from experienced wireless enthusiasts who observed that the plays I write for radio present somewhat violent plot twists and adventures from time to time, and they objected to the fact that I do not always write comedies when I write for radio.[5] I answered that listeners have not yet been equally trained in listening, and that it is sometimes necessary to capture and hold their attention in a manner that is a little brutal. Indeed the wireless public would find it difficult to endure tirades that already come across as lengthy in a theatre, where other spectators are present and can make such tirades bearable.

If the crux of the matter is making people laugh, then we must acknowledge that the laws of humour are not the same on the radio and in the theatre, for laughter is contagious. Indeed, it is easier to amuse and entertain spectators who are assembled together than listeners who are dispersed. I experienced this first-hand when I wrote for spectators who were full of intelligence and good will but had received different levels of education. Some of them had not frequented the theatres assiduously. They had not all had the same occasions to refine their minds . . . A good story taken from folklore, tried and tested, would immediately make at least fifty spectators laugh. Then in a split second another two hundred would join in . . . After that, the rest of the theatre would follow. The public cannot come together in this way with the wireless, which only enables contact between listeners who are sitting in the same room. And even then, the contact that they establish is neither as powerful nor as stirring as it would be in a full theatre.

The comedy writer must take this into account.

I pondered asking Radio-Paris to tell listeners that we were recording a conference in front of an audience, instead of announcing talks as usual. My plan was to invite a good team of cheerful spectators into the auditorium, and make them rehearse ten times or so, in order to obtain from them peals of laughter that could have seemed entirely spontaneous. But I don't even know whether we would have been able to pull all our isolated listeners along with us, even if we had used this kind of artificial help, which reminds me of a stage claque. We must search for another kind of comedy. And it may be that this constraint, this search, just like many other constraints and searches, will produce good results.

---

[5] Indeed, several of Bernard's radio sketches involved robberies and criminal investigations.

5.9 HANS KYSER: HOW DO WE CREATE RADIO PLAYS AND A DRAMATIC LITERATURE FOR RADIO?

Translated by Marielle Sutherland. First published as 'Wie schafft man Hörspiele und Hörspielliteratur?,' *Die Sendung*, 14 February 1930, 107–8.

Hans Kyser (1882–1940) was a German novelist, playwright, screenwriter and film director who specialised in historical dramas. He had a background in journalism, and acted as the *Vossische Zeitung*'s Russia correspondent during the First World War. His cinema work included collaborating with F. W. Murnau on the scenario of *Faust* (1926). Readings from his works were broadcast on German radio from 1927 onwards, and he wrote radio portraits and radio plays – including, between 1929 and 1933, plays about Socrates, a trilogy about Napoleon, and a play about Rembrandt. His experiments with sound and silence struck Rudolf Arnheim, who thought highly of his radio work.[1] Kyser was a Nazi Party member and he continued to make films until 1936; he produced work notable for its anti-Polish stance and rabid nationalism. How to make a living from writing remained a chief concern. In 1938, invited by Goebbels to an event celebrating improved economic conditions for writers under the Nazi regime, he protested, objecting that they were all struggling to make ends meet; he was briefly imprisoned.[2]

• • •

At the Kassel conference, which was conceived as an internal debate about radio and poetry between the Reichsrundfunkgesellschaft and representatives of German literature, I felt compelled to become very prosaic in the discussion about a particular radio play.[3] I used numerical examples to point out

---

[1] Rudolf Arnheim, *Radio*, trans. Margaret Ludwig and Herbert Read (London: Faber and Faber, 1936), 183, 199.

[2] See Stefan Priacel, 'Soirées de Berlin,' *Les Nouvelles Littéraires*, 19 December 1931, 10; 'Grève sur le tas chez Goebbels,' *Messidor*, 29 July 1938, 10; Wayne Kvam, 'The Nazification of Max Reinhardt's Deutsches Theater Berlin,' *Theatre Journal* 40, no. 3 (1988): 369.

[3] Kyser is referring to the conference on poetry and radio held in Kassel in the autumn of 1929, organised by the Prussian Academy of Arts and the Reichsrundfunkgesellschaft (the Radio Broadcasting Corporation of Germany, which oversaw all regional German broadcasters). He contributed to the closing discussion.

the unprofitability thus far of this new artistic genre for writers, expressing my fear that it will not be possible to create an independent and valuable art of the radio play that goes beyond casual labour as long as there is no basic regulation on royalties across all broadcasting corporations and as long as there are no compulsory provisions on implementation that can be applied in order to regulate in matters of repetition, exchange and acquisition by radio stations.

What are the conditions like today? The Reichsrundfunkgesellschaft has developed and concluded a tariff contract with the Vereinigung der Bühnenverleger,[4] which regulates the radio stations' own performances and their broadcasting of stage productions of opera, operetta and drama. The provisions of this contract are reasonable; I would like to take this opportunity to emphasise here that, in my experience and according to polls, the radio fees for talks, etc. can be described as adequate, even though the principle that operates here, too, involves placing a lower value on talks developed specifically for the wireless than on readings of literary works, by dispensing with the line fee.

In terms of the tariff agreement on the broadcasting of theatrical works, the Reichsrundfunkgesellschaft found itself dealing with a powerful partner in the Vereinigung der Bühnenverleger. This contract set out minimum and maximum fees, stipulated the provisions to be implemented for both of these, allowed plenty of scope for the valuation of any intermediary works when it came to transmissions from one main radio station to another, and, in the case of musical works, made it obligatory to obtain the material from the publisher.

Since, when it concluded the contract, the Vereinigung der Bühnenverleger had not yet given any consideration to the distribution of radio plays, and the radio play itself was still only in its infancy, neither side had any reason to include it in the tariff contract. The writers, translators and editors of all kinds of dramatic works are nowadays able to base their negotiations on clear contractual provisions. It is only the radio play that is still unregulated; the radio playwright is reliant on individual negotiations with the individual broadcasting corporations, and the fees the corporations are willing to pay are dependent upon the esteem in which they hold the individual author, or upon other imponderables.

Every theatre play earns its royalties, in the first instance, from stage productions, and successful plays might be performed as repertory plays on over a thousand stages. For the author, radio transmission merely means one more performance, so the radio fee is included in this, and there is no further payment. It is very different in the case of the radio play if it represents a

---

[4] German Association of Theatre Publishers, founded in 1919.

genuine attempt to fulfil its own artistic form and has not already distanced itself from its own form by having been constructed with a view to a later stage production.

A radio play, too, is required to be a full-length work. This work may, however, at best, be acquired by ten broadcasting corporations. There are almost never any repetitions, and there can be no question of a repertory play. The radio playwright, however, has produced the play specifically for this broadcast, and this broadcast is the only remuneration for his achievement.

It therefore seems self-evident that the tariffs for broadcasting radio plays should be significantly higher than those for broadcasting stage plays. (Usually, the opposite is true.) It seems just as necessary for the Reichsrundfunkgesellschaft to create, in the interests of the radio play (which of course the Reichsrundfunkgesellschaft wishes to promote), a special fund to support the corporations who work without any surplus money available, or whose limited listener numbers do not allow for higher fees. Successful works must be repeated, and there must be more precise provisions in order to ensure these are acquired by all broadcasting companies. Even if the value of radio plays is not immediately recognised – whether this is due to the novelty of their form or their new content – such repetitions are important for cultivating a taste for the radio play. Merely being advised by the programming council is not enough here. Ultimately, if we wish to boost the incentive to create radio plays by increasing potential revenue, the Reichsrundfunkgesellschaft needs to support the cheap printing of these works, and their announcers must draw attention to them before they are broadcast. It used to be possible, for example, to buy the text of operas or operettas on the street. It is to be hoped that the content of radio plays – which are, after all, often distorted by poor reception – will make this printing even more worthwhile.

I will refrain from describing the current conditions, which we have to accept are due to the novelty of this artistic genre. Competitions and honoraria, which are no more than a rare and wonderful gesture, do nothing to promote radio plays in a serious way. We must initiate business-oriented and economic discussions. Authors' associations like the Bühnenverleger, who are already distributing radio plays, will gladly enter into negotiations with the Reichsrundfunkgesellschaft, who, for their part, have a strong interest in these, too.

Even if the radio play is only a small, and perhaps not the most important, element in the totality of radio presentations, it is nonetheless the only creative phenomenon to come out of this new technological art. It must be nurtured all the more carefully to ensure it does not sink to the level of cheap economic labour before it has even got off the ground, and the person who has channelled his artistic will and productive labour into this new form must receive better pay – and please, let us make sure this is not only in Berlin.

5.10 ALIDA AND PIERRE CALEL: A CONCEPTION OF RADIO DRAMA

Translated by Emilie Morin. First published as 'Une conception du théâtre radiophonique,' *Radio-Magazine*, 23 August 1931, 2; *Radio-Magazine*, 30 August 1931, 2.

Alida Calel and Pierre Calel were the pseudonyms of writers Alida Lafforgue (d. 1946) and her brother Jules Lafforgue (1873–1947). They wrote about Quercy, their native region in the south of France, and often wrote together. Pierre Calel, also a journalist, had an interest in radio reportage and created broadcasts about the South-West of France during the early 1930s. Prior to the publication of the essay that follows, several of their joint works were broadcast on French radio, including poems, in 1926 and 1927. Thereafter, plays they had initially written for the stage were broadcast in 1933 and 1934, and a special programme celebrating their poetic and dramatic achievements was broadcast by Strasbourg PTT in 1933. Neither their radio play *Les moins de cent ans* nor their conception of radio drama attracted the attention they had hoped for, although much of what they argue here resonates with ideas advanced by prominent contemporaries, notably the writer and critic René Sudre, who believed that, to create a satisfactory radio play, it was necessary to add a character solely in charge of introducing and commenting on the action.[1]

• • •

We are grateful to *Radio-Magazine*[2] for giving us such a valuable occasion to tell readers about our recent experiment in the domain of radio drama, which we shall continue to develop, since our playlet *Les moins de cent ans*, broadcast by the Toulouse-Pyrénées station,[3] was greeted by initial responses that are very encouraging.

Above all, we would like to hear what listeners think of our work; what they believe we should and could do, how they believe we should develop or

---

[1] Sudre summarised his ideas in *Le huitième art: Mission de la radio* (1945).

[2] A weekly French radio magazine that published literary articles, scientific information about broadcasting technologies and international radio programmes like several other radio magazines.

[3] In June 1931.

modify our idea. Any criticism, any suggestion from them will be gratefully received.

We believe that everyone – editors of newspaper, directors of wireless stations, authors of radio plays, faithful and competent radio listeners – should bring their collaboration to what we are doing.

We have neither desire nor wish to keep our idea for ourselves. We want to do the opposite of that. And this letter proves it. If what we believe is right, every author will find in our method something suited to his personality, and will be able to transform and adapt it to his character and talent, without impinging upon the discoveries made by other authors. This is a vast field, open to everyone. Everyone will reap something different, depending on their activity, their know-how, their artistic talent, their sensibility and their temperament.

Now that we have clarified these issues, let us explain what this is all about.

Everyone has had occasions to see that, compared to ordinary theatre, radio drama has a serious handicap.

Indeed the only kind of perception that the wireless allows is through sound. We hear words and various noises. That is all.

Ordinary theatre involves sight as well as hearing; not images, but the direct, real sight of artists on the stage.

This is a considerable difference, and it works to the advantage of ordinary theatre.

Many among our artists who are fans of the wireless noticed radio's serious inferiority very quickly.

Some attempts were made to rectify this state of affairs. Some big radio stations, such as Radio-Paris,[4] have prefaced the transmission of theatre plays with commentaries explaining to the listeners the main aspects of the *mise-en-scène*, the setting and the meaning of the work performed.

Introducing performances in this way made them easier to understand. Nonetheless, they were still relatively difficult to follow.

The listeners knew little or nothing of the characters' costumes, facial expressions, development and attitudes. It was impossible to interpret their silences. The listeners were also likely to misinterpret the noises they could hear coming from the stage.

These are the difficulties we tried to overcome.

How can this be achieved with sound (voice or noise) as the sole means of expression? How can the action be dramatised over the radio as well and as fully as in an ordinary theatre?

---

[4] A French radio station founded in 1922 as a private station, under the name Radiola, and renamed Radio-Paris in 1924. It became state-owned in 1933; it is widely remembered for its role during the Second World War, when it became the prime vehicle for pro-Nazi and Vichy propaganda.

It occurred to us that we ought to compare theatre when it is performed and watched with theatre as it is written and read. We noticed that the written play is more or less in the same situation as radio drama, since it has only one means of expression: sound. We can read it, but we cannot see it. We can see the words clearly, but the words can only be translated into sound perceptions.

And yet the text of a play, when we read it, produces a more complete perception than a play transmitted over the radio.

This, it seems, comes from the fact that when we read a play we are given explanations about all the things that we cannot hear: the setting, the costumes, the development of the characters, their facial expressions, the quality of their silences, their mindset and even, sometimes, some of the intentions that animate the characters on the stage.

One may object that this is what the big radio stations already do when they broadcast plays. Yet there are differences; the two things are not at all identical. The big radio stations initiate the public into the play before its commencement, whereas the written play transmits information *just as the changes, evolutions and shifts in performance are taking place*. The text acts as a step-by-step commentary on the action.

Our concept arises from an acknowledgement of this fact and this difference.

We spent time thinking about our idea and we developed it and, after many attempts, we produced our broadcast of *Les moins de cent ans*.

We imagined a character who is always present on the stage, so to speak, whom we called the *playmaker*, if we may use that word.[5]

Perhaps our master of ceremonies has ancestors in the theatre of yore, in which one of the actors would address the public to explain the dramatic situation and the rudimentary setting, and enable a sumptuous backdrop to emerge in the spectators' docile imagination. Our playmaker also owes something to the ancient chorus who comments, warns, responds, rejoices, cries and remains part of everything that has taken place, takes place, is about to take place.

However – and this is the essence of our conception of radio drama – the playmaker is not there to explain the action, and his role is not make the action clear in all of its details and as it is developing; his work is of utmost significance and should not be conducted dispassionately, in an impersonal and lifeless fashion, without momentum. Rather, the playmaker must be the living soul

---

[5] *Meneur de jeu* in the original. A similar idea was advanced by the French writer René Sudre: *le spectateur de la coulisse*, the spectator in the wings, an additional character who would describe the set, introduce the action and describe the characters' movements. Sudre's model was discussed by René Christauflour in *L'Intransigeant*; Christauflour advocated for a more radical transformation, including the disappearance of any reference to anything visual, and called for a better recognition of radio's singularity and novelty. See René Christauflour, 'Lettre de l'auteur,' *L'Intransigeant*, 24 June 1929, 6; René Sudre, *Le huitième art: Mission de la radio* (Paris: Julliard, 1945), 130.

of the drama, the most important and the most vibrant character, who comes the closest to us, reaching into our minds and our hearts. He must be like a mirror who reflects the play and the listeners at the same time.

His comments, his warnings must be performed in a dramatic fashion, tailored to his personality: with irony, with subtlety, with severity, with affability, with passion, as the nature of the situation requires. The dramatic author must principally focus his efforts on the playmaker. He is not a parasite but the voice leading the play.

This method will yield the same results as the written play, the same results as the play we see performed on a stage.

Moreover, if the playmaker is judiciously used, we believe that the listeners will perceive everything *even more clearly than if they were watching a play on a stage*. This is a device that can enable radio drama to achieve everything that a play does on a stage; moreover, it can explain or suggest intimate secrets and divulge hidden intentions to the listener. This would be impossible with a play staged in a theatre, no matter how skillful the author is.

Herein lies an inexhaustible source of artistic and dramatic possibilities that have the power to transform the art of tomorrow, and turn radio drama into the most captivating and the most complete of theatres. [. . .]

5.11 TYRONE GUTHRIE: INTRODUCTION TO *SQUIRREL'S CAGE AND TWO OTHER MICROPHONE PLAYS*

First published as 'Introduction,' in *Squirrel's Cage and Two Other Microphone Plays* (London: Cobden-Sanderson, 1931), 7–11.

Tyrone Guthrie (1900–1971) was a British author, actor and theatre director renowned for his innovations with the staging of plays and operas. He was also a familiar voice and presence in BBC programmes. In 1924, he was hired by the Belfast station 2BE, and was the first voice that 2BE listeners heard when the station was launched in September that year. He proved a most versatile employee, writing radio plays, working as announcer, and arranging, producing and performing in various spoken word and musical programmes, as Tyrone Power and as Tyrone Guthrie. The independence that he and others at 2BE enjoyed in those early years enabled him to develop a distinctive approach to radio drama, and to merge music, sound effects and imaginative dramatisation in his radio productions. In 1926, Guthrie left the BBC to work with the Scottish National Players in Glasgow; he dedicated himself to his theatre career from then on, but kept on creating innovative 'microphone plays,' as he called them. He also produced fourteen plays for the radio documentary serial *The Romance of Canada* for the Canada National Railroad network in 1931.

●　●　●

It is my regretful belief that the Drama of the Stage is going to be forced, by economic pressure, to abandon the unequal struggle with the 'canned' products of the Film industry and Broadcasting corporations. Already, by slow degrees but sure, 'the legitimate' is being forced off the road and confined to select nooks and corners of the largest metropolitan cities. Soon theatre-going will have become, like polo, attainable only by the rich.

Believing this, I wanted to try some experiments in 'canned' drama. Radio offered a more promising field than the cinema, because, in Great Britain at all events, it is free from the anxieties of commercial competition. As a result of this the BBC has subordinated the question of Popular Appeal to Principles of Moral Philosophy; but has, none the less, been moderately adventurous and quite encouraging to technical experiment.

Hitherto, and possibly for some years to come, the progress of the films and radio have been hampered by the rapidity of mechanical development. The concentration upon things mechanical has set a standard of reception and transmission far superior to the quality of the programmes. From the beginning the programme designers have been panting after the engineers and they will not overtake them until the focus of public interest shifts from the practical and mechanical to the artistic and philosophical applications of this new medium.

Meantime I offer these three microphone plays to the public as straws in the wind – indications that, in some not too distant future, the human spirit may find sincere and effective expression in terms of mechanised drama. By then the technique of these three plays will be as dead as Queen Anne, as dated as the dodo. But meantime, I hope they may perhaps seem technically amusing because experimental; and, in addition to their technique, I sometimes hope that they may have something to say.

It has possibilities – the microphone play – that are inherent in neither the film nor the stage. Since the audience is dependent upon one sense only, it follows that the impression they receive, though limited, is highly concentrated in quality. Perhaps this would be more comprehensible by analogy with another form of theatrical art – grand opera for instance. In opera the impression, instead of being concentrated, is diffuse and multiplex. Appeal is made both to hearing and to sight; the mind endeavours to grapple with simultaneous impressions of acting, singing, orchestral playing, costumes, lighting, *mise en scène*; to say nothing of ermine in the 'horseshoe,' tiaras on the grand tier. *C'est magnifique* – a welter of opulence; the voice of reason is drowned in the blare of trombones, smothered in ruby velvet.

The broadcast play on the other hand, is deprived of all these sensual sops to Cerberus; but for that very reason the mind of the listener is the more free to create its own illusion. Playwright, producer and actors combine to throw out a sequence of hints, of tiny clues, suggestions; and the mind of the listener collects, shapes and expands these into pictures. Admitted that this is difficult; it demands a great deal of creative energy and technical ingenuity of the artists, a great deal of imaginative concentration of the listener. But it can be and has been achieved; *Brigade Exchange* achieved it;[1] *Carnival*, though far too long and uneven to retain one's concentration throughout, at times captured the imagination with amazing power and subtlety.[2]

The microphone play lacks the glamour and physical magnetism of the stage, but lacks also the too too solid flesh. Because its pictures are solely of the mind, they are less substantial but more real than the cardboard grottoes, the calico rosebuds, the dusty grandeur of the stage; less substantial and vivid, because not apprehended visually, more real because the impression is partly created by the listener himself. From the author's clues the listener collects his materials, and embodies them in a picture of his own creation. It is therefore an expression of his own experience – whether physical or psychological – and therefore more real to him than the ready-made picture of the stage designer. For example, the author suggests 'moonlight night.' The stage picture would express the designer's idea of the author's idea of moonlight night; but the listener's picture, created from his own associations, derived from his own experience, expresses his own particular brand of moonshine. I do not deny that the stage picture will probably be more academically correct, but it remains, none the less, no more than a translation, an interpretation of someone else's experience.

Again, the impressions of the microphone play are more intimate than those of the stage, because neither the writing nor the playing needs to be pitched high enough to carry to the back of pit and gallery.

Finally, they are more subtle because received by each listener privately at home, not coarsened by being flung into an auditorium, where individuals are

---

[1] An English translation by I. D. Benzie of Ernst Johannsen's popular radio play *Brigadevermittlung* (1929), performed on BBC television in August 1938; it was broadcast as a radio play on the National Programme the following month.

[2] A radio adaptation of Compton Mackenzie's *Carnival* by Mackenzie and Holt Marvell (Eric Maschwitz), broadcast on 5GB Daventry in November 1929.

fused together into one mass, which becomes a single crowd personality, easily swayed to laughter or tears, but incapable of the minute pulsations of feeling, the delicate gradations of thought, which each member of the crowd experiences when alone.

Technically these plays approach their aim by two different routes. In *The Flowers Are Not For You to Pick*,[3] I have tried to exploit the peculiar intimacy that the microphone makes possible, and to treat both the dialogue and the characterisation rather more obliquely and economically than is usual on the stage. I have taken pains, too, in the more important scenes to provide the listener with the material to create his own *décor*. For the 'Robbers' Island' scene, for instance, I have indicated that it is evening, that there are trees on the little island; a glassy lake, shadows, reflections of trees, birds, and sunset, two people in a little rowboat, the first star. The detail of this picture, its composition, colouring, the stress laid on this feature and on that, becomes a matter of individual selection.

In *Matrimonial News* the effect aimed at is primarily musical.[4] Picture is all the time subordinated to rhythm; the characterisation is not subtle, but broad and flamboyant, because the contrast in pitch and colour between one voice and another is more important as a musical contribution to the *ensemble* than as an expression of individual character.

Squirrel's Cage attempts to combine both methods; pictorial in the scenes, musical in the interludes.[5]

Perhaps the stage directions 'Fade-in,' 'Fade-out,' 'Cross-fade' require a little explanation. A Microphone Play is not performed, as a rule, in one 'Studio,' but in several. *Squirrel's Cage* for example uses four – one for the actors, one for the chorus, one for the 'noises,' and one for the orchestra. A device known as a 'Mixing-panel' enables the director of the play, by twirling knobs, to increase or reduce the volume of transmission from each Studio. To fade-in is so to twirl that transmission from a given Studio increases steadily from an inaudible pianissimo to maximum volume. Cross-fading implies fading-in of one Studio simultaneous with the fading-out of another. The effect rather resembles that of superimposed photography in the films.

The punctuation of these plays may seem irregular. It is intended rather to express the rhythm of the lines than their grammatical construction.

I want to express sincere thanks to the actors and actresses who have interpreted these plays. They contributed qualities of humour, delicate feeling and subtle intelligence, that will be sadly missed by those who merely read the printed word.

---

[3] First broadcast on the BBC Regional Programme in April 1930, in a production by Tyrone Guthrie, and on the National Programme the following day.

[4] First broadcast on the BBC National Programme in June 1938, in a production by Guthrie.

[5] First broadcast on 5GB Daventry in March 1929.

5.12 MARC DENIS: AN ESSAY ON RADIO DRAMA

Translated by Emilie Morin. First published as 'Essai sur le théâtre radiophonique,' *Le Petit Radio*, 7 July 1934, 1–2.

Marc Denis, pseudonym of Maurice Zeller (1895–1946), had two personalities and two lives, which have been discussed in histories of the Second World War but not in scholarship on radio. Maurice Zeller was an officer in the French Navy from the Alsace region; after his dismissal for opium consumption, he became a radio salesman, then turned to radio broadcasting. After 1929, he became a prominent radio journalist, working under the name Marc Denis; he covered major sporting events for French radio stations, worked for the Poste Colonial (the broadcasting service for the French colonies) from 1931 to 1937, and wrote successful radio plays, co-authoring some of them with his wife, Denyse Denis (also a pseudonym). During the Second World War, as Maurice Zeller, he joined a pro-Nazi organisation, the LVF (Légion des Volontaires Français contre le Bolchévisme), and was assimilated into the German Wehrmacht. In 1943, he joined the Abwehr, the German military intelligence service, and became one of the most feared and ruthless French agents in the service of the SD, the intelligence service of the SS, hunting down, torturing and killing members of the Resistance and the Maquis in large numbers across Brittany. He fled to Berlin and Sigmaringen in 1945, was sentenced to death in absentia, and was arrested and executed in Rennes in 1946. To the close reader of his radio plays, kept at the Bibliothèque Nationale de France, his sinister life trajectory does not come as a surprise: notably, his radio play *Et in terra pax* (first broadcast in 1935 on Radio Tour Eiffel) presents war as a necessary purgative and a solution to social ills.[1]

•　•　•

[. . .] Is there a linguist who will be capable of creating the new, appropriate vocabulary that we are waiting for and find a name, once and for all, for what we call radio drama, for lack of a better term? Indeed this radio drama of ours (let us continue to call it thus since we have to) is taking a long time to forge a

---

[1] See Eric Rondel, *Zeller, un des espions du IIIème Reich: Un Français de la LVF au service de l'Abwehr* (Erquy: Editions Astoure, 2017).

personality of its own, in my opinion, and that is because it has kept the awkward and unsuitable label of 'drama.'

Drama strictly speaking is one thing and radio drama should be another entirely; yet the taxonomy imposes to the latter the routines and the customs of the former. Professional habits die hard, and it is easy to annex the brand new art of the air waves to the art of the stage.

Of course, I am not talking about what has already been baptised *théâtre radiophoné*,[2] a neologism that I did not invent; that is, the transmission of plays performed in theatres, or the broadcasting of a theatre repertoire more or less suited (all too often unsuited, alas) to the necessities of the microphone. Here, I shall restrict my commentary to the pure radio drama, this new thing that a few of us are working on, that we are starting to apprehend, to accept, to understand.

It is important to grasp the fundamental difference that separates these two modes of theatrical expression: *théâtre radiophoné*, the theatre performance transmitted over the radio, is the means; radio drama is the ends. The means, firstly: we are now confronted with a new technique that has been put at the disposal of authors in order to enable a larger public to come into contact with works that were conceived and written long ago. The ends: with radio, we are at the threshold of a new world; we are entering into a sacred wood that has barely been explored and whose detours are still unknown to us, and we must annex it to augment what we already own.

I hope those who disagree will forgive me: what else can I say? I have been asked for my opinion, and I am giving it to you unequivocally. The day will come, this much I know, when the theatre, the cinema and the radio (the latter will soon become the most perfect mode of expression at our disposal) will enable us to express everything that remains beyond our reach at present and will expand infinitely what the human brain can produce.

The most perfect dramatic creation always seems very limited when it is confined within three walls, in spite of all the improvements of modern *mise-en-scène*. It seems to me that the cinema, with its gift of ubiquity, is capable of doing more with time and space, owing to the camera's mobility and the tricks made possible by editing. The cinema enables movement within a widened conception of space that uses time as its fourth dimension, whereas the theatre must abide by the laws of three-dimensional space. But only the radio can explore all the incommensurable worlds within which our imagination travels. Through the wonders of the air waves, we can now venture into all the marvellous worlds of subjectivity, into these dream worlds that populate our thoughts. And do not tell me that the instrument is too limited or that our ears are not up to the task. Hearing is, most certainly, the most subtle and self-sufficient of our

---

[2] A radio broadcast of a stage play performed in a theatre.

senses. Anyone who listened to moving radio-reportage created by my Belgian colleague Théo Fleischman for the funeral of His Majesty Albert can testify to this.[3] I am convinced that no collection of photographs, no film of the ceremony (a silent film, of course) would have been able to stir emotion in the same way as this voice coming to us from Belgium, accompanied, like a hallucination, by the sound of veterans marching, the noise of horses stamping the ground and, paradoxically, the audible silence of a people in pain.

Radio drama – our elusive goal – is also, just like ordinary theatre, its elder, a way of representing action without compare, and it is marvellously well suited to the Cartesian rectitude characteristic of the French spirit. And this is not another one of those paradoxes I am fond of: with radio, things can only be suggested, sketched out, with each listener completing the edifice within his mind, constructing, from the foundations that are offered to him, the desired building with the lines and forms begotten by his dreams. A shared conception, a unique theme; multiple realisations, each one of them perfect since they are all different, and they suit everyone. This is the miracle of radio in general, and of radio drama in particular.

The wonderful possibilities that I began to foresee a long time ago were revealed to me by 'Le Pont du Hibou' [*sic*], by the much-missed Paul Deharme.[4] It took me a long time to become personally involved with radio, but one day (one evening, rather), the spark came. In collaboration with my wife, I wrote 'Le maître des âmes,' which was performed by Louis Cognet's company on the Paris-PTT station on 13 December 1930. 13: a fateful number that has always been my lucky number. After this, and up to now, a dozen plays have followed, including 'Dernières manoeuvres,' 'Sous le masque,' 'Le bracelet,' 'Etrange escale,' which was broadcast recently, and 'Et in terra pax . . .,' still under consideration.

I am far from thinking that we have reached our goal; radio drama in France and abroad is only an adolescent, still caught in a difficult phase. That is why I consider all the plays I have written to be nothing but mere exercises, experiments conceived in order to discover a technique, to hone the methods we need to allow us to use the whole of the treasure that has been put at our disposal. Will we succeed and will this goal be reached one day? Nothing is less certain, for radio drama will, above all, always be ripe for improvement; the goal will always elude us, and will appear more beautiful, yet less accessible, perhaps, after each new step forward. Let us not lose heart, however, for what we manage to do will be a fine achievement, marking the necessary step at

---

[3] Using new technological possibilities, Fleischman transformed Albert I's funeral march into an acclaimed broadcast in February 1934.

[4] *Un incident au pont du Hibou*, the radio play through which Deharme pioneered a new adaptation method.

which we can pause for a while, to enable our radio drama to rival and match the achievements of its elders and earn credentials so often denied today.

Radio and cinema have often been compared to each other. I have already discussed the areas in which I believe the latter to be superior to the former, owing to the fact that cinema addresses the mind by calling on our senses first and foremost. By this I am not suggesting that the work of the cinema is only material; rather, I am suggesting that, while the screen can only act on our intelligence and our sensibility, the wireless set can cooperate with these faculties, transforming us into docile artisans crafting the action.

It cannot be denied, however, that radio and cinema share some common ground, since they only speak to one of our senses (I am here talking about pure cinema, about silent cinema, whose masterpieces still remain unrivalled by the talking films, whose sonorous voice is all too often discordant and mostly indiscreet). I have discussed these ideas previously, a few years ago; moreover, they are not specific to me, and I hope the reader will forgive me for repeating my arguments: I need to present these ideas again, as I would like this commentary to be as full as possible. It was logical to use, for the purposes of radiophonic creation, some processes taken from the cinema which, once transposed from a visual plane to sound, could serve us well. Each one of my plays was nothing but an attempt at a play, and over the course of these successive attempts, as I used some new methods specific to radio, I also used many tricks borrowed from cinema directors: the dissolve, superimposition, the close-up, etc. Superimposition enables the juxtaposition of two distinct sound planes, two distinct actions; the dissolve enables movement without transition from one action to another simultaneous action; the close-up divides and sequences the sound planes, and immediately gives volume to the actors' performances.

Then I ventured into the realm of dreams and unreality, which has never been, in my view, satisfactorily explored on a theatre stage. Let us take the example of 'L'Oiseau bleu.'[5] Each spectator builds an idea of the realm of the future, for example, that differs from what their neighbour imagines. How can everyone be satisfied by what is shown on a stage? In a radiophonic creation, the situation is different: the listener is only given an indication and then creates and imagines the setting he is yearning for. Did you not think that the unreal Chantecler of radio had, of late, become more real than the real Chantecler of the stage?[6] This is why I am against exact representation and painstaking description on the radio. If it is possible to let the imagination of your listeners run free, if it is possible to perform for each listener as though they were alone, within the setting that suits them, how can one wish to impose the same backdrop upon everyone? This would be a mistake. Radio drama is essentially

[5] A 1908 play by Maurice Maeterlinck.
[6] Edmond Rostand's play *Chantecler* (1910), broadcast many times after 1927.

278

subjective and must remain so. This is, and I am not afraid of repeating it, what extends its possibilities infinitely and transforms it into a mode of expression capable of expressing everything.

The progress made in that direction has become very clear, particularly for sound scenery. A few years ago, radio authors would try to objectively reconstruct, as precisely as possible, the atmosphere in which the action was taking place, through the use of ingenious sound effects, which were sometimes created through unexpected means. Today, such sound effects have not been abandoned, but music is used more frequently; such music is of an evocative rather than imitative nature, and sketches out the scenery subjectively, through impressions and sound memories that all listeners are free to fill as they wish, in accordance with their own beliefs.

I realise that I am now talking about the material realisation of radio drama . . . and that is another story. It would take too long to get to the bottom of this question; as I cannot address it fully here, I will leave it aside today in spite of the interest that it may ignite. But perhaps you are beginning to find this discussion somewhat lengthy? Without expressing opinions, theories or conceptions, I shall discuss the technique of radio drama some other time, if I am given this chance, along with its evolution, its current state, the results that it has generated and the wonderful hopes that it enables us to entertain.

5.13 LUGNÉ-POË: RADIO DRAMA'S MARVELLOUS RESOURCES

Translated by Emilie Morin. First published as 'Les ressources merveilleuses du radio-théâtre,' *Comœdia*, 12 January 1934, 4.

Lugné-Poë (Aurélien-Marie Lugné-Poë, 1869–1940) was a French actor and an influential theatre director and stage designer, remembered for his championing of Symbolism and foundational productions of plays by Maeterlinck, Ibsen, Strindberg and Jarry at his Théâtre de l'Œuvre in Paris in the 1890s. He does not seem to have written about radio beyond the present piece, but radio programmes from the period reveal his sustained engagement with broadcasting. His contributions to the offerings of Radio-Paris during the 1930s included talks on elocution and diction and on the theatre, a reading from Alphonse Allais's stories and a performance of scenes from Jules Renard's novel *Poil de Carotte*. He also introduced radio adaptations of stage plays for Radio-Paris and Paris-PTT from 1929 onwards and throughout the 1930s, including works by Ibsen and contemporary French dramatists. In May 1939, he acted in a 'radio-scénie' (the term coined by Radio-Cité for a series of plays performed in front of an audience that year); this was an adaptation of *The Odyssey* by Jean Grimod, with Radio-Cité's acting company.

● ● ●

[. . .] The radio style is becoming an absolute necessity at the microphone. As a matter of fact, in as little as a few months, the miracle of radio-vision could come into our world by surprise, change all the domains from which we obtain artistic fulfilment, and open up new resources concealed within us, whose presence we do not suspect. Who knows?

Today, the radio-performance has an existence of its own alongside the theatre performance, and radio deserves its place alongside the theatre, alongside the 'spectacle of the stage' that in my opinion continues to be neglected. The illusion gifted to us by radio brings new advantages, new possibilities. Should we feed it with tinned theatrical goods?

Who among the dramatic authors of yore, in France or abroad, had predicted that the microphone would unveil a new theatre? . . . The answer is: no one. Today, we certainly have some competent authors, but they must study the technique of the microphone and they must sacrifice their interests in the short term. The microphone has become a strange genie that makes demands, that must be cherished, nurtured, in a corner of one's mind.

Only rarely can we confront yesterday's or today's dramatic masterpieces with the microphone. Try to imagine a powerful automobile with a 20 CV engine, to which is harnessed an old nag, as elegant as you can possibly make it: the position of the horse represents fairly well that of our ancient theatre. The automobile starts just as the coachman shouts: 'Giddy-up!' What will become of the horse? (The horse, here, is the theatre.) Shudder and tremble! And take pity upon the horse who collapses immediately, before anything has even started . . .

It is evident that I only have dramatic theatre and comedy in mind here, not musical theatre; let us not mix up the marvellous goods that science has gifted upon us. Although the secrets of comedy or pathos have not yet been fine-tuned on the radio, we can hear a revolution rumbling! We – authors, men of letters, artists – must take part in this revolution alongside the scientists and, for as long as radio remains separated from our experience of watching and listening to the talking films and theatre, we must learn how to love radio, and how to make others love it.

There is a time of day when the listener regards a theatrical work transmitted through the microphone as tedious and it is best avoided. The work that the microphone author needs to do can be thankless and involves much trial and error, flotsam and jetsam. The ear is much more sensitive than the eye and sound itself: silence and speech encompass a thousand emotions and thousands and thousands of notes, still unknown for the most part; what a vast world opens up to the thinker or the philosopher when they know how to make themselves heard!

Microphone work is not tedious, not tedious at all, and it shall never be so; let us agree that radio drama is unique; let us respect the science that gave birth to it; let us give everything we can give to it in exchange for all that it gives; indeed its mystery is a source of infinite artistic effects; let us express our gratitude to the pioneers who have put all their energies into presenting us with all things possible and impossible at the microphone, all the dramatic works of yesterday and today. And now, let us find our direction!

It seems that, to attract the gregarious mass of the public who is becoming interested in radio plays, we must search for simple texts that use a concise and very literary language and, within a few minutes of listening, will bring us back to the most extraordinary debates and conflicts that humanity has known. Form, style, words will have a considerable value. Some words will need to be used, but not others, and they cannot be replaced. Who knows? Before long, we may have to accept, to create an international language for radio able to speak to two, three or four nations of listeners. I am already aware of all the ironies that can arise from such a proposition, yet the science says so; science is indomitable, and art can no longer keep its power and its cruelty contained! We must become canny enough, or wise enough, to work with that.

It is possible to foresee a radio drama that will create powerful masterpieces, full of pathos, confronting the great problems, passions, debates of humanity in a shortened form close to the great Greek tragedies. Comedy writers can contribute to this effort too.

It seems necessary to acknowledge radio technique as a dramatic science of the first order, which will help us invent a multi-faceted, complex art, served by the many domains of the spirit, and create a new artisanship around the theatre of the stage, to which we shall all be proud to contribute, and will eagerly contribute, as good French artists. Our task is to help authors, train them, give them an idea of our hopes and fears, and let our artists-assistants work on diction to bring it to the right 'scale,' to make it clear, simple, suited to the texts we are looking for. Excessive flourish, false eloquence, grandiloquence have become unacceptable. Radio drama is not on the side of work that is too academic, too pompous; keeping to this path would place us in severe jeopardy since all the other nations are thinking about the future. Let us not kill the goose that lays the golden egg! Let us, as precise and careful artisans, come closer to the technicians, and the dramatic art for the radio of the future will discover itself, will discover its own formula.

5.14 GEORGES COLIN: IN THE SERVICE OF RADIO DRAMA

Translated by Emilie Morin. First published as 'Au service du radio-théâtre,' *Comœdia*, 12 May 1933, 4.

Georges Colin (1880–1945) was a popular and prolific French radio actor and radio producer. He was initially a theatre and cinema actor, and his radio career began in 1924, when he joined Radio-Paris as speaker. He directed Radio-Paris's acting company, produced radio plays and reportage, occasionally wrote radio plays, and acted in a very large number of radio plays during the 1920s and 1930s on French radio stations, public and private. He specialised in dramatic reconstructions of historical events and was celebrated for the care with which he mined historical documents to create soundscapes for radio.

•　•　•

At the start of the season this year the future looked bright for radio drama. Works written specially for the microphone by Fernand Divoire, Carlos Larronde, Mrs Douglas d'Estrac, Suzanne Malard, etc., attracted the attention of listeners and critics.[1] We felt as though we could have high hopes. Unfortunately, for mysterious reasons, all of this has stopped yet again . . . and we are waiting yet again . . .

It is impossible to ever do enough for radio drama. The microphone devours everything . . . The repertoire wears out . . . It is always necessary to create new works. But the adversaries of radio are numerous and powerful, and radio dramatists, poorly rewarded for their efforts on all levels, tend to lose heart. If nothing is done to encourage them, this could be the end of radiophonic creation for some time.

I know that the style and rhythm of pure radio drama have not yet been discovered, and that we will need to find ways to enable listeners to grow accustomed to this new language . . . In his great book, *Etudes de psychologie*

---

[1] Colin may have in mind Fernand Divoire's play *Marathon* and his 'symphonic poem' 'Naissance du poème,' broadcast on Radio-Paris in 1932, Carlos Larronde's *L'Autre soleil*, Douglas d'Estrac's *Leur silence*, Suzanne and Cita Malard's *Central-Éternité*.

linguistique, Father Marcel Jousse writes: '*The arrangement of language into words is an operation that did not take place spontaneously.*'[2] Likewise, the work leading us to the creation of a true radiophonic language, with its own rhythm, could remain at a standstill for a long time and yet, inevitably, eventually, a new theatre will emerge, a theatre that will be at home in the auditorium, and the air waves will disseminate plays written specially for radio.

In the meantime . . .

In the meantime, the microphone makes new conquests, slowly but surely, particularly with plays from the common theatre repertoire. The authors of these plays are more willing to allow radio stations to broadcast their works and sometimes they even agree to facilitate a play's transformation and adaptation for the microphone. Some very modern plays have been broadcast recently. These broadcasts were meticulously arranged and sometimes, when the means allowed it, the actors were cast well. As a matter of fact, all artists, and above all the greatest, should venture into the auditorium: this would be in the interest of radio and radio listeners. A good theatre actor, if he accepts to submit to the discipline of the microphone, is almost always a good radio actor (in any case, the role of the radio producer is precisely to assist him).

In the current circumstance, all sound effects have not yet been discovered, but those that are being used are known to the listener and no longer add novelty. The work selected and the quality of the performance thus remain of primary importance. We must make sure that mediocrity does not take over; performing frequently at the microphone can encourage the formation of certain habits, and does not necessarily create the flow, sensitivity and talent that have become indispensable to radio broadcasting.

The listener is delighted when he can feel, within the auditorium, the living presence of personalities whose knowledge, experience and legendary career grant a mysterious sex-appeal to radio, the art of concealment. The men and the women who create plays in the theatre should come to the microphone more often to give the performances they have created. After rehearsing their part for weeks on end they know the faintest movements within the thought of the author, and the company of radio actors is always galvanised when great fellow actors come into the auditorium to perform their creation.

For the performance of Charles-Henry Hirsch's *Les Emigrants*, Léon Bernard agreed to come to the microphone to play the magnificent role that he

---

[2] Marcel Jousse (1886–1961) specialised in the anthropology and psychology of gesture, and saw gesture as the origin of all human communication, including speech. The quotation is based on an unreferenced quotation that appears in Jousse's *Études de psychologie linguistique. Le style oral rythmique et mnémotechnique chez les verbo-moteurs* (1925), itself loosely based on a teacher training manual by Alphonse Piffault (*Psychologie appliquée à l'Éducation*, 1922). Piffault's philosophy of language, a catalogue of deep prejudices, doesn't align with Jousse's humanism.

had created.[3] The first rehearsals had felt somewhat precarious . . . As soon as Léon Bernard arrived – he understood the whole discipline of radio in a split second – the other actors were invigorated and followed in the footsteps of their great comrade. The performance was magnificent . . .

On other occasions, when Suzanne Desprès, Mary Marquet, Véra Sergine, Marcelle Géniat, etc. were in the auditorium, the quality of the performance always improved.[4]

We shall serve the dramatic repertoire with all our good will, and create the most appealing cast we can, every time we have such an opportunity. Let us, also, continue to hope for the *purely radiophonic* masterpieces that will undoubtedly be created.

5.15 MADELEINE MONTVOISIN: ON THE POSSIBILITIES AND EXIGENCIES OF RADIO DRAMA

Translated by Emilie Morin. First published as 'Des possibilités et exigences du Théâtre Radiophonique,' *Comœdia*, 2 October 1936, 4.

Madeleine Montvoisin (fl. 1935–1940) was a French author who decided to write for radio because she felt that the theatre world was beyond her reach.[1] She lived in Rouen during the 1930s. She wrote various radio plays, now long-forgotten (*Mamiche, Grisou, Cendas, Coups de griffe, Les rescapés, Le bercail*), which were all broadcast by the Poste Parisien between 1935 and 1939, and she adapted for radio Honoré de Balzac's novel *Le père Goriot* in 1938 and Charles Dickens's novel *Oliver Twist* in 1940. Thereafter, there is no trace of her in radio programmes beyond a play titled *Les*

---

[3] This was Charles-Henry Hirsch's play *Les Emigrants* (1909), which may have been broadcast under a different title; Léon Bernard (1877–1935), prominent French actor who taught at the Paris Conservatory.

[4] The French film and theatre actresses Suzanne Desprès (1875–1951), Mary Marquet (1895–1979), Véra Sergine (1884–1946) and Marcelle Géniat (1881–1959).

[1] 'Une rouennaise: *Mamiche* et Madeleine Montvoisin,' *Rouen-Gazette*, 30 July 1937, 2.

Sébastien, broadcast in 1953 by the RTF's Programme Parisien. It is possible, though not certain by any means, that she joined the French Resistance during the Second World War and worked for the intelligence service of the Free French after 1942.

• • •

[. . .] Radio drama is destined for an audience who must understand it, grasp its every nuance, eyes closed. To reach this audience, the writer has words and nothing but words at his disposal. If he does not know how to capture the right expression, he will unavoidably fall into insipid and uninteresting chatter. Yet, more than any other branch of the dramatic art, radio drama requires a kind of attention that is sustained and constant.

Words and nothing but words; but also a concert, a verbal music that enchants the ear, attracts attention, sparks feelings within the mind; every word, when it is employed to such ends, has a profound and just emotional reach.

Because the actors only have words to utter, we must create for them a colourful and vivid form of expression, full of images, to give their role all the emotional power it needs.

The characters in a radiophonic work are born in the Word; they must be impregnated with it, adorned with it.

The absence of backdrop forces the author to master the art of the sketch-maker. With three words, as the sketch-maker does with three lines in pencil, the setting for the action must appear, clear and firmly delineated, in the mind of the listener. The atmosphere must be created by a few sentences, which means that every word must have a clearly defined and precise reach.

After that, what is at stake is no longer to charm the spectator through the grace or the skills of such and such star actor. A glance, a facial expression will not make the listener smile or cry. He sees nothing; he can only hear in the way that the blind do, withdrawing into himself, shut within the depths of his soul, surrounded by darkness, but with a receptivity to sound that is naturally increased.

No word will be masked by a trick of gesture, a grimace or a wink. Radio actors are well aware of this and watch their diction closely.

As for the author, he knows that each word will fall into a deep silence and a deep darkness. To each word he must give its exact meaning, its beauty, its own colour, if he wants to create something worthwhile . . .

Radio drama rarely allows for vulgar expressions: vulgarity stands out too much; it becomes shocking.

Owing to the purity of language, the refined choices of expression that radio requires, we are witnessing the rebirth of the Word along with the advent of radio drama. The Word, the almighty master of radio, must remain distinguished, just like any aristocrat. Will these developments extend to the stage? We should hope as much.

Radio drama enables a return to theatre's classical form, and herein lies its greatest advantage. It is no longer possible to speak and say nothing: radio demands a precise construction and a dialogue purged from vulgar expressions; above all, this dialogue must remain alive, without chatter, without tasteless or meaningless flourish.

Finally, radio drama enables an externalisation of psychological disturbances, no matter how slight. What cannot be rendered through facial expression must be explained to the public. The public consents to this because one does not listen to a radio play at home, with one's family, in slippers, in the same way that one would listen to a play staged in a theatre. The audience dressed in formal attire and the audience sitting by the chimney are not the same. As soon as the collar comes off, one becomes oneself again; and it is without a cravat, without gloves and without snobbishness that one becomes a listener – as a good man, as the head of a family or as a bachelor, always more inclined to be moved by the drama and more prone to introspection. Between the family table and the sideboard it all becomes so easy.

In a theatre, one is more inclined to think that the words of the actor playing the young hero, who does not yet have the corpulence of middle age, does not look anything like oneself, are twaddle.

But at home, with one's eyes closed, the illusion can so easily be created. The most hardened minds will shed tears over an adolescent's heartache because, even if they refuse to admit it and are not aware of it, this adolescent they cannot see is a reminder of their own youth, resonates with a memory held within. Can the spinster see herself in the young actress performing on the stage? Of course not: she was young once but she knows that she was not young in that way. Before her wireless set, she will find herself again and will only need to imagine that the young heroine is wearing the hat she wore for her sixteenth birthday . . .

All this complacency, all this juvenile credulity can offer tremendous resources to the radio author if he knows how to draw upon them. He can use them; he has at hand everything he needs. The obligation to use nothing but words allows well-crafted returns to the past, a dissection of the human heart, a psychological analysis reaching into the very confines of the soul.

The more the author is sincere, and the more he does away with all sentimental modesty, the closer he will be to his audience. One will never think that the author has gone too far if one has been taken to unexplored regions of the soul. Everything that one still ignores about oneself, even after half a century on earth perhaps, one will learn through the revelations of an anonymous voice, through words – simple words, yet so heavy with eloquence and expression.

While the laws of snobbishness have constrained the stage and turned it into an increasingly superficial representation of real life, the capacity to listen to radio as one is – at home, in a dressing gown – has turned radio drama into a true and humane theatre. The microphone can stake a claim over all the things that are still forbidden on the stage: it lets the listener enter the scene, delve into his own mind, and explore the furthest recesses of his emotions and sentiments.

In this way, radio offers authors a treasure trove of resources and possibilities that have otherwise long been forbidden. Authors no longer need to sacrifice the study of psychology to the demands of stage action, which have been all too often deployed to dissuade the spectator from making an effort of comprehension and analysis.

Radio drama contributes to the education of the masses, enabling them to free themselves from an existence entirely dictated by materialism. It can transform them into thinking beings who take an interest in themselves and are aware of how their actions are determined by their own reactions.

From this we can conclude that radio drama can become one of the most precious instruments of social evolution if we let it fulfil this purpose, and if we make plans for a type of progress that is not simply about celebrating the machine.

5.16 CARLOS LARRONDE: THE POETRY OF SPACE

Translated by Emilie Morin. First published as 'Poésie de l'espace,' in *Théâtre invisible: Le douzième coup de minuit, Le chant des sphères* (Paris: Denoël & Steele, 1936), v–vi.

A biographical sketch is included with 'Radio Drama' (3.12).

• • •

Let us distinguish, once and for all, between the means and the goals, between radio as a vehicle dedicated to the transmission of music and words, and radio as an original form of expression, as an autonomous art.

Radio must be the latter as well as the former.

But radio will only really exist once it brings to humanity an order of sensations that is different, sufficiently distinctive to become a source of attraction in its own right.

The common formula whereby radio drama is defined as a SPECTACLE FOR THE BLIND is nothing but mere convenience, more or less. Those who are still wondering, with astonishing ingenuousness or disarming bad faith, whether it is truly necessary to write plays specially for the microphone would not entertain, even for a moment, an idea as baroque as going into a theatre and witnessing the performance of a comedy or a tragedy with their eyes closed.

The listeners should not be considered as blind. They are something else. They have the gift of 'super-hearing.'[1] Let us give them everything that hearing, that most subtle sense, the sense of interiority par excellence, can yield in terms of lyricism, dreaming or suggestion. Let us turn them into SEERS.

I am not saying that the practice of broadcasting plays written for the theatre should be condemned as a whole. There are two definitions of a radio play. The first definition is absolute: 'A work that could not be performed on a stage.' The second is more supple: 'A work that is more striking when it is heard, by virtue of its conception and its form, than it would be if it were staged in a theatre.' A drama played by naked souls or, if you prefer, faceless actors. A drama that forces us to close our eyes, not because the décor is invisible, but because another scenery, purely ideal and abstract, is being built in our imagination. A drama that unfolds within the human mind. Once again, this is not about compensating for an absence, but about creating a presence.

Radio has given the marvellous its true home.

Radio has created a new poetry: the poetry of space.

5.17 CARLOS LARRONDE: A LESSON IN ATTEMPTING A RADIO PLAY

Translated by Emilie Morin. First published as 'L'enseignement d'une tentative,' *L'Intransigeant*, 16 October 1932, 11.

The following text provided the basis for Larronde's 1936 foreword to his radio plays, 'The Poetry of Space' (5.16). Here, he reflects on his experience with *L'Autre soleil*

---

[1] In reference to René Christauflour's ideas (5.3).

('The other sun'), a radio play first broadcast in October 1932 on Radio-Paris. A biographical sketch is included with 'Radio Drama' (3.12).

• • •

Keeping to oneself a lesson learned from experience, when that experience holds general significance, is nothing but an expression of false modesty. I would like to present, succinctly, some observations that arose from the broadcasting of a play I wrote for the wireless.

There are two definitions of the radio play. The first definition is absolute: *a work that could not be performed on a stage.* The second is supple: *a work that is more striking when it is heard, by virtue of its conception and form, than it would be if it were staged in a theatre.*

A drama played by naked souls, or, if you prefer, faceless actors. A drama that unfolds within the human mind. A drama we can listen to with our eyes closed. In either case, this is what a radio play should be.

As a matter of fact, it is difficult to implement a strict separation between these two definitions. That is why the visual element, which is inseparable from the theatre, sometimes benefits from being merely suggested.

Let me reaffirm a previous statement. The art of the microphone involves finesse, not complications.

The value of the slightest detail is amplified for the person who is listening. This is another reason to avoid dispersing the attention of the listener.

Creating subtlety from simplicity: perhaps this is what we need to learn . . .

The same thought, the same feeling, no matter how nuanced, require far fewer words to be voiced at the microphone than literary expression demands.

As a consequence, when one rewrites for the wireless a play previously performed in a theatre – if the play lends itself to rewriting – the text will lose two thirds of its length.

Radiophonic dialogue allows neither detours nor long transitions, but it magnifies audacity, accentuates brutality.

The value of noise is essentially emotional. There is lyricism within sound, which works in parallel to the lyricism of language, but only does so intermittently.

What is at stake is to establish the points of coincidence between sound and speech.

Unlike the eye, the ear does not accept continuity easily. That is why permanent noise can weaken a play instead of intensifying it. However, letting noise intervene can also be a way of extending the dialogue.

On stage, most of the time, a detail that has been missed has no repercussions. To the ear, however, even the beginnings of an error can compromise the whole listening experience.

There is such a thing as theatrical diction, and it is based on the distance separating the actor from the spectators who are the furthest away from the stage. First and foremost, one must use one's voice to aim beyond the footlights. The actor's profession (and the orator's, too) involves adjusting the flow of words to the room.

Instead of creating a distance between the person speaking and the person listening, the microphone brings them closer together. Hence the necessity of letting speech begin at a low volume.

Any word uttered before the microphone is a secret.

In the auditorium, what matters first and foremost is the entire compass of tones, which grows from pianissimo. Precisely for this reason, a rehearsal is only useful if it can be held live.

When a noise is accompanied by its spoken designation, the listener can understand the action better. But we should merely see this as a stopgap. A perfectly realised noise is sufficient in and of itself.

The actors do not have to know their parts by heart, but only if they own the text as completely as they would if they knew it by heart.

It is impossible to judge how good a radio play is before listening to it.

There is a difference between the play on the page and the play on the stage, and it can be considerable. Radio broadcasting transforms the text on the page into another work entirely.

There is such a thing as a 'language of listening' that is absolutely autonomous.

'Writing for the microphone': this is an unsuitable expression. One must write for the loud-speaker.

Radio has created a new poetry: the poetry of space.

5.18 GRACE WYNDHAM GOLDIE: LET US BE THRILLED

First published as 'Let Us Be Thrilled,' *Listener*, 25 March 1936, 571.

A biographical sketch is included with 'Listening to Comedy' (4.17).

• • •

Do thrillers thrill on the radio? This is not, though I offer it freely to Mr Henry Hall,[1] the title of a new song hit. It is a solemn enquiry into the ability of the microphone to make our flesh creep. Do we want our flesh to creep? Speaking for myself, 'Yes, certainly. From time to time.' Taking our fiercer emotions out for a little run on a lead is always pleasurable, and fear, which is too overwhelming to be pleasant in real life, becomes fun when given gentle exercise in the safety of the theatre or our homes.

There were two thrillers last week. One, 'Death in the Dressing Room,' was a mystery play with musical accompaniments.[2] It contained two murders, daggers dripped with blood, screams were heard in the dark, blunt instruments were put to their habitual use, detectives snapped handcuffs on deep-dyed villains. And did my flesh creep? Not for one moment. Yet on the following Thursday, as I listened to 'The Green Goddess' I was genuinely thrilled, and my flesh crept to quite a pleasurable extent.[3] Why?

You may say that the music mixed with the story in 'Death in the Dressing Room' lessened rather than heightened the tension, that the dialogue was banal and the acting poor, whereas 'The Green Goddess' had a first-rate story, a heaven-sent main part and Mr Cyril Maude to act it.[4] I agree. But I do not think that all this accounts completely for the failure of the one play and the success of the other. The real trouble, I am sure, was that although 'Death in the Dressing Room' was specially written for the microphone it was attempting something that the microphone must do less well than the stage, whereas 'The Green Goddess,' in spite of being a thirteen-year-old stage play, was highly radiogenic.

I do not believe that the ordinary murder play, of which 'Death in the Dressing Room' was a variation, can ever be satisfactory over the air. After all, bodies are static things and if we are to play the parlour game of 'Who Killed Cock Robin?' we must stay more or less put and look round the faces of the potential murderers to see who is showing signs of guilt. This used to be all very well in the theatre where everything has to take place in one or two scenes and where we can see the faces of the actors. And even there it has palled of recent years. And the newer thrill of watching the murderer at work and guessing at what he feels, as in 'Payment Deferred' and 'Night Must Fall,' seems to me to be equally stuff for the stage rather than for the radio.[5]

---

[1] Conductor of the BBC Dance Orchestra.

[2] An adaptation by Max Kester of a thriller about a murder in a theatre dressing-room by Betty Laidlaw and Bob Lively, broadcast on the BBC National Programme.

[3] Howard Rose's adaptation of William Archer's *The Green Goddess*, broadcast on the BBC Regional Programme. This was the BBC's second radio adaptation of Archer's play.

[4] A British actor who appeared frequently in radio programmes after 1933.

[5] Thriller play by Jeffrey Dell from 1934, based on a novel by C. S. Forester; thriller play by Emlyn Williams from 1935.

If we cut out murder plays, what about thrillers which depend on horror? There seems to be no reason why these should not be highly effective over the microphone. A world of horror should be as easy to create in the imaginations of listeners as a world of fantasy. And as for plays which depend on physical violence, these are far more possible over the air than on the stage, since we can bear to hear what we could not bear to see. But it seems at least doubtful whether plays of either imaginative and physical horror are desirable. What, then, is left if we are to have thrillers at all? Quantities of stuff; quite sufficient to keep the Drama Department busy and ourselves amused almost indefinitely.[6] There is every kind of play which depends on adventurous action and strangeness of atmosphere: 'Lost Horizon' showed how well atmosphere can be created by the microphone.[7] The schoolboy serial in 'The Saturday Magazine' proved that if we have movement and continuity we can be excited and amused even by the silliest story.[8] The microphone can let us move with the characters through a series of events. It has only to let us be off into curious worlds, let us meet one excitement after another, pursue villains and be chased by criminals and we shall be happy. This is the sort of thing the radio can do better than the stage. This, surely, is the line upon which radio thrillers should develop.

5.19 LEOPOLD JESSNER: RADIO AND THEATRE

Translated by Marielle Sutherland. First published as 'Rundfunk und Theater,' in *Film und Funk. Sozialistischer Kulturtag in Frankfurt am Main, 28–29 September 1929* (Berlin: Sozialistischer Kulturbund, 1929), 55–60.

---

[6] The BBC Drama Department. On the broader context, see Richard J. Hand, *Listen in Terror: British Horror Radio from the Advent of Broadcasting to the Digital Age* (Manchester: Manchester University Press, 2014).

[7] A radio play by James Hilton and Barbara Burnham.

[8] 'The Saturday Magazine,' broadcast weekly on the BBC National Programme from October 1935 to June 1936.

Leopold Jessner (1878–1945) was an actor, a theatre director associated with German Expressionism and renowned for his innovations in stage design and acting, and a filmmaker, remembered for his silent film *Hintertreppe* (Backstairs, 1921). He directed the Berlin Staatstheater from 1919 to 1930, and from 1925 to 1931 he led the teaching of drama and acting at Berlin's Staatliche Schauspielschule, which was part of Berlin's Hochschule für Musik, the Berlin Conservatory. There, he became involved in the work and experiments conducted at the Rundfunkversuchsstelle, a radio research laboratory; the facility, created in 1929, equipped musicians and composers with the skills needed to work in radio broadcasting, and conducted its own broadcasting and sound film experiments, using professional equipment. Jessner's other radio activities included broadcasts about the theatre and a 1928 adaptation of *Othello* for Norag (Nordischer Rundfunk AG, North German Radio Company, Hamburg). In 1933, the Rundfunkversuchsstelle was closed by the Nazis for 'cultural bolshevism,' and Jessner came under threat as a socialist and a Jew; dismissed from his post, he left Germany for England, then worked with touring theatre ensembles in Rotterdam and Tel Aviv. In 1939, he moved to Hollywood, where he worked anonymously as a script reader for the film industry until his death. The present piece was originally a talk delivered at the 1929 Frankfurt convention of the Sozialistischer Kulturbund, the Socialist Cultural Association founded in 1925 to serve as cultural arm of the SPD, the Social Democratic Party of Germany. The convention focused on the social function of film and radio and their potential for socialism; it featured talks defining the SPD's future film and radio policy, and discussed how the SPD could further its cultural work.[1]

●　●　●

My subject requires me to touch once again on questions that have no doubt already been covered in detail here. However, it is difficult to enter into the middle of a debate without having at least summarised the main points of context beforehand.

Ever since rulers, citizens or nations have engaged in cultural politics, they have employed various means of transmission. To this day, the primary means has been *school*. As the centuries have passed, *theatre* has advanced into an important position within cultural politics. The further theatre has moved away from improvisation and mere comedic acting, the more it has appropriated both historical material from the past and topical present-day problems, the more it has become a lectern from which to transmit cultural events to the

---

[1] See Christine Fischer-Defoy, *Kunst, Macht, Politik: Die Nazifizierung der Kunst- und Musikhochschulen in Berlin* (Berlin: Elefanten Press, 1988), 33–58; Bruce Murray, *Film and the German Left in the Weimar Republic: From* Caligari *to* Kuhle Wampe (Austin: University of Texas Press, 1990), 173–6; Dietmar Schenk, 'Die Berliner Rundfunkversuchsstelle (1928–1935): Zur Geschichte und Rezeption einer Institution aus der Frühzeit von Rundfunk und Tonfilm,' *Rundfunk und Geschichte* 23, no. 2&3 (1997): 124–7; Palmier, *Weimar in Exile*, 147, 511, 796 n28;

public from a height and in a, shall we say, entertaining and uplifting way. Up to the present day – and in fact today more than ever – theatre has been one of the most important instruments in a nation's cultural politics.

For a quarter of a century now, these two phenomena have been joined by a third, namely film, which was at first regarded as a purely industrial product but is now, like theatre, developing into a cultural element beyond the technical-industrial sphere. – Although film was initially regarded as pure entertainment, now it is impossible not to acknowledge it as a cultural and political force. In this respect, the possibility of both national and international dissemination has created an instrument of cultural politics which, if used correctly, could very much become a lynchpin of propaganda. And so it falls to us, the socialist cultural politicians, to undertake the immense task of organising the film audience in the same way theatre has already organised its audience. What I am referring to here is that kind of consumer organisation which, like the Freie Volksbühne, an example of classic consumer organisation, has introduced new audiences to the theatre.[2] Just as the very powerful Freie Volksbühne community is a lynchpin of theatre today, this kind of organisation could also prove considerably helpful in German film production, even extending into international export regulation. The initiative to incorporate this important area of cultural politics into our sphere of activity must come from our own circle.

Now, over the past few years, we have been seeing the emergence of a new phenomenon in the field of cultural politics – *radio*. And with radio, the possibility of cultural dissemination has exceeded that of film. For what are the spatial reaches of film in comparison with the physical possibilities of radio? And if, once we have got over our initial astonishment, we realise that what we have here is actually a real opportunity to socialise cultural politics, then we must understand the responsibility that comes with this recognition. And this is when we begin to hear the voices of those demanding greater courage from the management boards of the individual broadcasting companies. Being courageous does not always mean being extremely radical. Just as we in social politics long ago moved beyond the so-called immiseration thesis, neither do we need black and white representations in the politics of art anymore. On the other hand, there is a misplaced fear of clearly articulating the facts. In radio, too, it seems *censorship* issues not so much from the higher-ranking authorities but is dictated by this fear, a fear felt by everyone involved, and yet one that they have invoked themselves. And it must be pointed out here that, instead of demanding courage from its exponents,

---

[2] The Free People's Theatre, a theatre organisation founded in Berlin in 1890, aimed at the working class and dedicated to offering performances at affordable prices. Its network of branches grew steadily; by 1930 there were 305 Volksbühne societies across Germany, with a membership of half a million. Dissolved by the Nazis in 1933, the Volksbühne was revived in 1948. See Cecil Davies, *The Volksbühne Movement: A History*, 2nd ed. (Amsterdam: Harwood, 2000), esp. 158.

the Republic's[3] approach has been not to demand a state of compromise, yet at the same time often not to look upon this negatively either. And this danger has already proved to be present in radio, even though it is still only in its infancy. As damaging as this careful manoeuvring within theatre has been, as guilty as theatre has proved to be in this respect – and that is not to say your speaker has played no part in this himself –, radio has already become just as guilty.

Only radical updating, only proactive vigour can protect it from premature senescence.

I felt it was my duty to emphasise this before introducing the separate issue of *broadcast theatre*[4] and thereby moving on to the actual question of radio and theatre.

In order to give proper consideration to this question, we must examine the points of contact between these two forces and, furthermore, differentiate clearly between them.

Apart from the mere fact that radio and theatre serve as evening entertainment, there is a closer point of contact between them in the sense that radio has commandeered the stage play and presented radio plays taken from the spheres of operatic and dramatic literature. In other words, this means we no longer need to go to the theatre to hear *Egmont*, *Don Carlos* and contemporary literature today.[5] We no longer need to go to the theatre to hear the *Meistersinger*, *Martha* and the *Rosenkavalier* tomorrow.[6] So, what is this all about?

If, for the time being, we disregard whether, in principle, this undertaking is correct or incorrect, the first question that arises is: what kind of dramatic works might be particularly suitable for radio broadcasting? In the field of drama, it will be those dramatic texts within world literature that are wholly reliant on the spoken word, works in which the movement of the plot is secondary to that which is their primary feature: their inherent intellectual and phonetic capital. On the other hand, it might be theatre pieces in which all mimic and plot-related elements are already contained within the language, creating a particular linguistic rhythm that reflects the shape of the events.

In terms of operatic literature, it seems to me that the most suitable operas are those that border on the oratorio.

So much for the question of the repertoire when it comes to the broadcast play.

The more important question, however, is this: can opera really be reduced to purely acoustic possibilities? The response here must be that the effect of the *Schauspiel*, the dramatic spectacle, is created wholly by the unification of word

---

[3] The Weimar Republic, the German state from 1918 to 1933.

[4] *Sendespiel* in the original: a play broadcast on the radio, but originally written for the theatre, not for radio.

[5] Plays by Goethe and Schiller.

[6] Richard Wagner's opera *The Master-Singers of Nuremberg*; Friedrich von Flotow's opera *Martha*; Richard Strauss's opera *The Rose-Bearer*.

and movement, that it is not called *Schauspiel* without reason, for its power issues not least from the three-dimensional spectacle of action. Even if we are very familiar with the content of a play, even if we have already read it and seen it on stage, a reproduction on the wireless can do nothing more than evoke a weak recollection of something previously experienced.

And as regards opera, its direct reproduction in front of the microphone is no less problematic. – An artistic genre that is already seen as a problem from a critical perspective dispenses with personal actors at its peril. What differentiates opera from absolute music is of course the fact that it is both heard *and* seen. And seeing is certainly not secondary here – not only because of the set but primarily because it conveys the three-dimensional aspect of the personality; it seems to me that this personality will be a form of protection and a refuge for opera if one day, due to the costliness of running an operatic institution, small and medium-sized opera stages were to be replaced by the *sound film*. For no matter how close the sound film comes to the reality of opera, this lack of proximity to a three-dimensional personality means it will never be a fully valid replacement.

It is even less likely, however, that radio will threaten the existence of opera with its purely acoustic effect.

My view is that radio directors will, sooner or later, abandon the attempt to appropriate dramatic and operatic, and even operetta and revue, literature for radio, and that it is – so to speak – only a matter of time before we see the emergence of the purely acoustic radio play. This is because even if a drama and opera programme that is adapted for radio does emerge, this situation in itself is, in general, no different to a film company coming up with the idea of sending their film operator to a theatre to film the events on stage, i.e. record the A to Z of the performance and then screen it for the public in their picture palace. Even in its timid beginnings, when it was lacking in subject matter, film never hit on this idea. The men responsible for film knew right from the start that this genre is predicated on a wholly different kind of dramaturgy, one that differs significantly from the dramaturgy of theatre.

We should not overlook the fact that the beginnings of such a separate dramaturgy are also noticeable in radio; this dramaturgy is in fact based wholly on acoustic possibilities. Of course, we have already discovered so many technical tools for the radio play and acquired so many experiences, and all these ideas have developed into such distinct expertise that the recipes for radio dramaturgy have, to a large extent, thrived.

This dramaturgical insight has already produced evening entertainment that has brought us considerably closer to a solution to the question of the radio play. The fact that music is now playing a predominant role here is related to the regularity of radio. For example, a 'Songabend' [Evening of Songs] was recently broadcast in Berlin to great acclaim from the press – it was a kind of revue for the ear, with loosely sequenced scenes that were both educational and entertaining, and it managed to create an exceptional kind of tension without, as is common, needing to invent a supplementary tale, i.e. without what we refer to as plot.

The value and lack of value of an evening of 'songs' may well be disputed. But at all events, it represents the exploitation of purely radio-based possibilities. We urgently need to conquer these possibilities in their hundredfold variations and derive the best possible performance from them.

Radio directors should be conscious of what it means not to have to carry the burden of tradition. Whereas theatre has to reckon with, and often do battle with, fixed conventions and sacred traditions, the phenomenon of radio, still in its infancy, inherently has scope for experiment and therefore for the most productive means of any affirmation.

Generating new, fertile subject areas that are commensurate with the purely acoustic form – this may lead to an entirely new artistic genre, to a new kind of art of the people, i.e. an art that is comprehensible to everyone without lowering the standard, an art that plays to the masses but nevertheless stops being art, an art that is primitive without becoming banal, an art that is aggressive in an agreeable form, tearing up the backdrop.

And this is exactly the point where the task of radio and the task of theatre converge. Only the poet who writes for everyone is the poet of today's theatre. Only the actor who can make the most sceptical of all sceptics laugh or cry is the actor of today's theatre.

The artistic performances on both the radio and the stage must, at present, stay as far away as possible from the idyll of the garden arbour and the *l'art-pour-l'art* point of view! This is because the human being of today, i.e. the non-psychological, unsentimental, non-melodramatic human, disaffirms these. This human being wishes to encounter his own likeness in whatever clothing art offers him, whether this be a knight's costume or a jacket or a smock. The clothing is of no consequence – what matters is the attitude and the language.

This trend towards the present in art, which is always a sign of revolutionary times, has already led to theatre being identified with the form of a documentary newspaper report. A newspaper report may certainly take on a theatrical form, but the question of the effect will always be a question of coercive shaping. No matter how aggressive the reportage on the stage, it does not carry as much weight if it lacks those formal principles that elevate the actualities beyond the contingency of the singular event.

Now, if we regard the entire programming over one day as one single, extensive radio play, then we must make clear that, in contrast to theatre, radio reports on the individual case without shaping it. Only the facts as such are of interest here. Nonetheless, radio reportage as a whole differs significantly from newspaper reportage.

A good radio director must become, so to speak, a dramaturg of daily events. His job is to create, out of each day and each event, a radio revue on the grandest scale – compiled like an acoustic film: with moments of tension, intersections, intensifications, dramatic climaxes. It is conceivable, for example, that an important news report and some other report on some kind of exciting occurrence – perhaps an expedition to the South Pole, a flight across the ocean or a sensational political event – might be inserted into the middle of an important lecture on beekeeping.

The more we see the disappearance of the nice, neat categorisation of daily reports, the more radio will become a reproduction of the simultaneous phenomena of life.

Nowadays, theatre has to take into account the particular audience 'face,' i.e. the audience's particular traits. Depending on the geographical location and the tastes and tendencies of the individual theatre, this might be a high-society audience, a middle-class audience or a working-class audience.

Radio, however, is not confronted with such a precise audience. Its audience is the totality. It is a newspaper for everyone; its audience, in reality, is the people in their entirety. This is why its programmes must increasingly be attuned to the masses. This is why the individual radio directors must listen to the wishes of the masses.

Theatre today has forms of consumer organisation such as those I mentioned earlier. The film industry will soon resort to forms of consumer organisation. These have already begun to develop within the field of radio, and we must do everything to ensure that their exponents have some influence over the radio directors' programme design. For it must be repeatedly emphasised that, particularly in relation to the working class, radio has a politico-cultural mission to fulfil, a mission no less productive than the setting up of schools or the performances offered by film and theatre.

However, I must conclude by saying here – since nowadays we all too often hear to the contrary – that theatre will survive despite film and radio. If theatre really is going through a crisis, then the main reason for this, I believe, lies in that sense of an all too willing resignation in the face of the ascent of film and radio, a resignation that has given rise to an oppressive atmosphere of pessimism around theatre.

Individual poets and individual men of the theatre have tended to come to the false conclusion that what they need to do in response is to increasingly adapt theatrical performances to film and radio performances.

The regeneration of theatre is only possible if it comes from within theatre itself. I would be the last person to argue that theatre should hermetically seal itself off from the technical achievements of our times. However, directors make the mistake of transferring these technical achievements, all too often crudely and shapelessly, onto the stage from the outside, without allowing them to fuse organically with the idiosyncrasy of theatre.

This is the only way of avoiding a watering down of theatre, which would of course lead to the catastrophic decline of theatre once and for all.

Theatre will, however, go on and on if it draws on the vitality of existence for the sake of the vitality of existence, and if it meets the demands of education just as much as the demands of combat.

Radio, however, will produce its best performances if it becomes increasingly aware of its duty to present its listeners with an image of life as it is happening in the present: topical and uncompromising, educational without being pretentious, aggressive, but at the same time with attention to detail. It has the broadest, most ambitious boundaries. Its empire is expansive; it does not wander off into provinces that do not intrinsically belong to it!

This is the task of theatre. – And this is the task of radio.

These tasks are sometimes aligned, yet they do not intersect. And they are united in striving for a particular effect, one that is moving further and further in the direction of the popular.

5.20 ERNST HARDT: DRAMA

Translated by Marielle Sutherland. First published as 'Drama,' in *Dichtung und Rundfunk. Reden und Gegenreden, als Verhandlungsniederschrift gedruckt* (Berlin: n.p., 1930), 59–66.

A biographical sketch of Ernst Hardt is included with 'The Echo of the Listeners' Needs' (3.10). This is the script of a talk delivered on the second day of the 1929 *Dichtung und Rundfunk* (Poetry and Radio) conference in Kassel, Germany (30 September 1929 and 1 October 1929), as part of a discussion on radio drama to which Hermann Kasack also contributed.

• • •

We already mentioned yesterday, for example, radio's curious capacity for not merely broadcasting pure physical sound dispassionately, but, on the contrary, for conveying to us as receptive listeners, almost miraculously, the subtlest emotional modulations and tensions in the sound – in the case of poetry, in the spoken word – more unequivocally and insistently than is the case within the visible world. It is this ability that has made radio suitable, right from the beginning, for disseminating works of poetry and, in particular, dramatic poetry. The principles of dramatic effect pertaining to the new theatre, the radiophonic theatre[1] or the 'theatre without eyes,' as Schmidtbonn has called it,[2] were such that their directors very soon began to speak of a new dramatic art form, which they referred to as the radio play;[3] you will find countless theoretical discussions on this in the radio literature. I do not intend to talk to you about this art form – which is, at present, more a fancy of the imagination than something that has taken on a discernible, recognisable shape in reality –; rather, I will talk to you about the principles and rules of this new theatre and the way in which the radio director is able to adapt a work created for the stage for radiophonic theatre. This kind of artistic work on his part is also best placed to reveal, I believe, the rules and principles of this new and still anticipated dramatic form. Above all, it seems important to recognise the following: the development of our stagecraft has meant that the director – whose job it is to transform the dramatic script given to him into sensory perception on the stage – now strives for such a high degree of physical realisation that preferably nothing at all is left to the audience's imagination. Whatever the intended style of the drama, the director endeavours to create its corporality with such plastic tangibility that the audience members' own sensory perceptions validate the perfection of his directorial decisions precisely when the theatrical reality impacts upon them with such force that any other productive or even creative imaginative activity on their part becomes impossible. Herein lies what all those who create the visual elements of the drama script – the actor wearing costume and mask, the stage designer using light, colour and all concrete forms of representation, and furthermore the director as their leader – see as the highest objective of the dramatic script. Let us recall that many years ago, in addition to the eye and ear, Reinhardt even tried to prevail over the audience's sense of smell with a 'suggestion of reality,' filling the air of the entire auditorium with incense on one occasion and the aroma of oranges on another. In short, the role of the theatre director, in a sense, is to make it absolutely impossible for the audience to exercise its imagination in any way that might be productive by presenting a directorial work of such harmony and plastic tangibility that it holds all the senses captive to an almost violent degree.

---

[1] Hardt uses the term *Hörbühne*, to differentiate radio drama from staged drama, *Schaubühne*.

[2] *Theater ohne Augen* in the original. Wilhelm Schmidtbonn (1876–1952), German writer and dramaturg.

[3] *Hörspiel* in the original: a play written specifically for radio.

The role of the radio drama director, gentlemen, is the absolute opposite of this. He can only have an effect on a single human sense: the sense of hearing. He has to employ every conceivable force and, at the same time, every conceivable subtlety and sensitivity in his use of this sense of hearing if he is to force the miraculous power of the listener's imagination to engage in the richest possible but also the most carefully managed dream activity. He must play the human imagination, if I may use this expression, with perfect virtuosity and unfailing artistic accomplishment, like a pianist at the piano, with all its chords subjugated to his fingers. Within this sphere, the human imagination cannot bear nothingness, unlimited space, corporality or events; the radio drama director must therefore know how to affect the ear, as a sensory organ, in such a way that the listener's imagination performs automatically, so to speak, all that activity pre-empted by the stage designer, the lighting technician and the corporality of the actor under the auspices of the director on the visual stage. Gentlemen, the people on the radio stage are as characteristically beautiful or as characteristically ugly, as unequivocally particular and as physically present as is ever possible for human souls to dream; all reality is but vapid and pale in comparison. These people make their way through the inexhaustible magic of dream landscapes, the gruesomeness of nightmares or the shimmering colourfulness of glass castles in the air – unreal – hyperreal. And the fact that they have emerged and unfurled out of the darkness with increasing luminance on thousands and hundreds of thousands of stages, each of which with only a single, deeply engrossed listener – this entire sorcery, gentlemen, is dependent on the extent to which the director is capable of employing everything that makes a sound in contributing to the birth of the most formidable human power: the imagination and reverie of the human soul. This not only moves mountains but piles them one on top of the other! Employ sounds of the wrong kind, however, and nothing will be created – one false sound, and the entire glorious edifice will collapse in the darkness.

In school we learned that on the primitive stages of Shakespeare and antiquity a large proportion of the visual elements was likewise left to the audience's imagination, that this imagination built an even more Roman Rome and allowed stiff masks to cry and laugh more inwardly than a screen or the naked countenance of an actor would be capable of doing today; and if I am not very much mistaken, the contemporary art of directing is, once again, seeking a way back from a theatrical form that is overly predicated on the viewer not as a co-creative creature with a heart and soul but as a creature who, although certainly sentient, is still merely a photographic plate registering external impulses.

When the curtain rises before the viewer at a theatre play, he sees a scene, created by light, form and colour, in which the action will play out. Either the director has tried to create the playwright's inner image of the scene as set out in the script, or he has followed the playwright's direct instructions.

The beginning of a performance of the same drama on the radio stage is nothing more than the sound of a gong, and if the director were to now simply utter a stage direction into the ear of the listener, who is listening deep into the darkness, he would certainly be able to create in the mind of the listener an impression of how he should be conceiving the scene's setting, but he would not be able to compel the listener's imagination to automatically construct the setting itself. To do this, he would have to invent words or sounds, or sounds *and* words, which force the imagination, via the ear, to produce a clear idea of the scene. The audible voices must be selected on the basis that their sound – which is not, as may be the case on stage, corrected by visual elements – is capable of evoking the clearest possible idea of the personality of the speaking character. This is why, for instance, we rarely hear a boy's or youth's role spoken by a girl in radiophonic theatre; the correction offered by visible trousers is missing, and the microphone is as merciless as the graphologist, who would rarely ever mistake female handwriting for male handwriting. The radio director must make sure no words are spoken by any person who is not immediately and clearly characterised in the mind of the listener, either through address or through some other means; otherwise, instead of triggering the creative power of the imagination, the director will engage the listener's intellect in uninspiring speculation around who might currently be speaking. Word by word and sentence by sentence, the director must acquire a feeling for whether what is emerging in an audible sense is developing in proportion to the imaginative work already undertaken by the listener; for that which the theatre director has already constructed out of light, colour, cardboard and screen in advance, as a given, must, in the imagination of the listener, be gradually blended in with increasing clarity as the scene develops, whether this be through words, noises or sounds.

In theatre plays we occasionally find that it is precisely the climax of a scene that is shaped purely by gesture, purely by something visible. The radio director must translate this purely visual climax into an audible one. In stage plays there are figures whose ambivalent existence or insubstantiality is characterised for the audience precisely by something visual about them; for example, the Departmental Director in *Armut* by Wildgans, who is also death,[4] and, in my opinion, the ghost in *Hamlet*. This ambivalent or spectral reality on the stage must be created in auditory terms in such a way that not only does the listener's intellect comprehend immediately, but his imagination is stimulated by the ear so effectively that it is capable of first constructing and then experiencing such fluctuating ambivalence or uncanny insubstantiality as is found in something that has a mere semblance of existence. The radio director has a wealth of auditory effects at his disposal here, by far surpassing the range of effects on

---

4 *Armut* (Poverty, 1915), a tragedy by Anton Wildgans.

the eye. Because the presentation of a drama purely for the ear lacks that to-ing and fro-ing between eye and ear that allows first one then the other of the two senses to rest a little and, to a certain extent, catch their breath while taking in the visual play, the script must be revised remorselessly down to the essential. Theatre directors do indeed strive for this, yet it is only radio play directors who are truly capable of learning how to do it, and in fact, in my experience, of bringing out the best in the poetry. In addition to this necessary compression into what is intrinsic and essential, what we hear in radiophonic theatre is the inexorable development of a poetic work, not disrupted by any modifications. This poetry subjugates the entire intellectual and emotional essence of the listener to the poet's will, keeping it in breathless tension and inescapably under the spell of the inexorably resonating auditory world.

A philologist and expert in German culture and literature has indeed contradicted me in this, however I wish to repeat again: I believe the primary element of the dramatic script is the word, i.e. language, and radio represents the re-inauguration of the original power of language, a power we had almost forgotten. The radio play actor, released from the inhibitive obsession with not forgetting the text, freed from make-up, costume and all bodily distraction, is reliant solely on his inner intellectual and emotional richness, which can only manifest itself in the thousands and thousands of tonalities he accomplishes in the interplay between sound and words. Absorption in poetry and through poetry is therefore life and death to him, and woe betide him if he does not bring his humanity to bear; the microphone is capable of shattering even the greatest, the most famous actor to the point of abject pitifulness.

Gentlemen, some of you, in astonishment, will take from my attempt to discuss the radio stage and the drama unfolding upon it, a certain partisan preference for precisely this kind of theatre. In conclusion, therefore, I do not wish to shy away from a full confession. I have watched an entire series of theatrical performances of one of my own works – partly in a collaborative capacity, and partly because I was obliged to watch them –, two of which were, in and of themselves, among the most famous performances of their time: the second performance of Tantris under the direction of Brahm, and the Burgtheater's performance with Kainz in the lead role;[5] yet, two years ago, I was almost alarmed to find that what I felt was the first perfect rendition of the poetry was in a radio performance. I was even more confused and alarmed when two critics, referring to different performances they had attended that also included the two I mention above, both individually came to the same conclusion. Meanwhile, there have been many assertions about this or that drama by this or

---

[5] *Tantris der Narr* (*Tantris the Fool*, 1907), Hardt's celebrated play on the Tristan and Isolde myth, which won the Schiller-Preis, was directed by Otto Brahm at Berlin's Lessingtheater in 1909, and at the Burgtheater in 1908, with Josef Kainz in the role of Tristan.

that listener; but I would not wish to conclude my advocacy of radiophonic theatre, which is ultimately focused on the radio play, without incorporating a testimony that seems to me to be of extreme importance in terms of both the person and the work.

In July I attempted, with some trepidation, to adapt Hamlet for radiophonic theatre.[6] Schmidtbonn, with whom I am not personally acquainted, wrote to me to tell me that the performance had brought him closer to the work than any other Hamlet performance he had seen in his life. I asked him to do the German radio director and radiophonic theatre itself the infinitely valuable service of describing in detail the impressions of the performance that caused him to experience it in this way. I shall now quote a few sentences from his reply, which is currently being printed. It is an essay entitled 'Theater ohne Augen':[7]

'There are many doubts about the ability of the classics, even of Shakespeare's works, to stay fresh and relevant to our own times. It is certainly the case that the more theatre employs external means in order to keep the classics alive, the more quickly the classics die away. They die away because the theatres are murdering the word within them . . . Radio returns to these works their innate and specific power, the power of the word, and indeed it returns it to them in an unforeseen, compelling, victorious form. Who among us, upon feeling particularly moved in the theatre, has not closed his eyes in order to experience the play more intensely, more inwardly? Indeed, we may even say, paradoxically, in order to see better? . . . Radio offers us the deliciously rich feeling of a mysteriously creative power starting up within us precisely because our eyes must remain inactive, because only the sound of the word touches the membrane of our ear, of our soul. Soul speaks directly to soul. Are we lacking the image of the setting? Are we missing trees, rocks, sea, a palace hall, the factory floor? Not at all! The infinitely wakeful procreative force of the human brain bestows upon us – including the most ordinary among us – a wealth of breathing, constantly self-transforming visual power, next to which the stiff, alien structure of scenery made of cardboard and wood virtually descends into the ridiculous . . . How in Hamlet we inhale the ghastly air on the terrace over the sea; we freeze, we are tempted to bury ourselves deeper into our clothes against the damp chill which then, by force of nature, engenders the ghost. Up until now, we have sat before this ghost in the theatre, defying Shakespeare, at best content to be sceptical, but superior, provoked into derision. Here, though, derision never crosses our minds! Arising out of barely determinable noises, out of the clanging of a door, followed by silence, out of the pressing sound of a shuffling step now and then, as if made by a creature at pains to move its

---

[6] This production has not left clear traces.

[7] Theatre without eyes. The bibliographical information could not be recovered; other sources that cite this piece do so via the present essay.

lifeless legs, out of a voice that seems to come directly from outer space, from where the ghosts reside: how we see the figure of doom emerge, and how we are paralysed like Hamlet himself! I can offer no better example of the superiority of radio precisely in terms of its visual dimension, precisely where everything depends upon the listener's own creativity. In all frankness, where else would I have felt the power of poetry so uninhibitedly, with such unearthly apprehension, touching my innermost being so deeply, indeed, so perfectly? . . . Is it not also strange how not only the general setting takes on a shape but also the individual speaker? Who would feel the urge to see one of these actors? How? That would be a terrible awakening, a moment of total return to sobriety! It is within us that the actor takes on face and body. The image of this Ophelia, whom I never saw, will never leave me. This Ophelia, whom I crept up upon almost as an eavesdropper hiding behind a wall, who made my soul tremble with the heartfelt sincerity of her voice, and whose sweet image arose within me, unattainable, the image of the unearthly. The music of all those voices, out of which Hamlet's voice sounded forth as solitary as a violin note. What a happy evening that was; something new, something that could not have been anticipated a few years ago. Not once did this secret music of the word stifle thought. This music was there, constantly. But it arose, as did the image, out of the words by its own force . . . Things such as Hamlet's monologue, which, in truth, can barely be heard on the stage: here they were new, as if spoken for the first time. They affected us as if heard for the first time, and continued to beget new emotions. We, the few listeners gathered around the device, saw for the first time into the innermost heart of all these figures from this great poetry; for the first time into the innermost heart of Shakespeare himself.' – . . .

May this echo of a radio performance, resonant with profound experience, help to bring the work of German poets to the kind of theatre that can offer such effects, just as soon as they have mastered its principles.

PART 6
RADIO POLITICS AND
RADIO FRONTIERS

6.1 SUZANNE CILLY: WOMEN AND RADIO

Translated by Emilie Morin. First published as 'Les femmes et la radio,' *Radio-Liberté* 4 (June–July 1936), 1–2.

Suzanne Cilly (1905–1972) was a French journalist, writer and illustrator. The newspapers for which she worked included *Radio-Liberté*, where she published a radio column entitled 'Voix sans visages' (voices without faces) from 1936 to 1939, consisting of witty and impressionistic vignettes, reviews and reflections. *Radio-Liberté* was the magazine of Radio-Liberté, an association of radio listeners created in 1935, associated with the French Left and subsequently close to the Popular Front. Initially, Radio-Liberté campaigned for greater state scrutiny over the broadcasting power and financial affairs of private radio stations; for state control over the manufacturing of wireless and electrical equipment; for women's programmes that would be more effective and less clichéd, and would include information about their legal rights; for better educational provision for children; and for an improved coverage of social and political topics, free from lobbying pressures and propaganda. Cilly was married to the writer Pierre Autry, a key figure in the French proletarian literature movement, who worked as a radio and music critic for *Le Peuple* and was co-editor of *Radio-Liberté*. During the Second World War, the anti-Hitlerian views they had both expressed in their pre-war journalism were investigated, and Cilly was prosecuted for anti-German propaganda.[1] She is remembered for her feminist convictions.

• • •

Among the large volumes of letters that readers send to radio magazines, complaints and suggestions about women's issues are fairly rare, if not inexistent. This is remarkable. If, sometimes, we find in this mass a letter written by a woman, then it complains about the irregularity of certain programmes and asserts that radio ought to include more 'entertainment' and no 'serious' music.

---

[1] See Jean Prugnot, 'Cilly Suzanne, Marie-Louise,' *Le Maitron: Dictionnaire biographique, mouvement ouvrier, mouvement social*, https://maitron.fr/spip.php?article105858; Jean Prugnot, 'Autry, Pierre,' ibid., https://maitron.fr/spip.php?article10540, last accessed 30 November 2021.

About the so-called women's programmes, nothing is ever said. This may be because women are wise enough to listen to programmes that have not been made especially for them, and because they have resigned themselves to the low quality of women's programmes like fashion talks, 'La demi-heure de la jeune fille de France' or 'Le quart d'heure de la femme,'[2] to which they simply stop listening after trying once or twice.

I defy any woman with a critical disposition and common sense to not shrug her shoulders and not feel humiliated at the thought that someone believes she could be vain enough, stupid enough, immature enough to enjoy listening to such mediocre creations.

Let us be fair. Sometimes, among the mountains of gossip, advice and recommendations from well-intentioned radio hosts, we get some displays of good sense and intelligence, although they never amount to more than five minutes in any given week. I would put in that category the words of wisdom that Madame Colette uttered recently in such a measured way, with the melodious Burgundy accent that enhances her peasant persona.[3] With charming humour, and with great ease, she was able to denounce the outrageous behaviour of all the women who felt compelled into orgies of food buying by the strikes.

But for each intervention of high quality, we have to put up with myriad recipes detailing ingredients that no one can afford or cook, which are nearly impossible to transcribe for anyone who is not an experienced stenographer! . . . Why such quantity of beauty tips? The vast majority of listeners will never be able to try them (anything involving plastic surgery, for example, costs thousands of francs)! . . . Why so many self-righteous, unthinkingly orthodox talks about Catholic saints like Jane Frances de Chantal or historical figures like Madame de Maintenon? . . . Why so many interviews of film stars, sports athletes or theatre celebrities? All they reveal is a striking degree of intellectual indigence and a self-contented, unquestioning outlook . . . Why should there be so much empty chatter about pleasantries, so much vanity and pretension? I am thinking of Madame Fernandez's talk on Paris-PTT about how important optimism and serenity are to keeping one's looks.[4] Do we care to hear about Maurice de Waleffe, born Kartoffel [sic], who, as his name suggests, is an exporter of the French taste as well as beauty queens, and about his every memory of Buenos Aires?[5]

---

[2] Programmes broadcast by the private station Poste Parisien and the state-owned regional PTT network respectively; literally, 'the half-hour for the young woman of France' and 'woman's quarter-hour.'

[3] The French writer Colette (1873–1954) contributed regularly to 'La demi-heure de la femme' (woman's half-hour) on the Poste Parisien in 1936.

[4] One of the speakers presenting fashion programmes on Paris-PTT.

[5] A Belgian-French journalist who invented the Miss France contest; his surname was Cartuyvels.

And what about all the Pierrettes, Bluettes, Wafflettes and Machinettes – all those silly wireless creatures? . . . Words fail me.

Is there anyone out there who truly believes that women who enjoy listening to radio, and young women generally, have no other preoccupations? That serious topics are of no interest to them?

For my part, I place my trust in the women of Radio-Liberté. They have demonstrated, in the midst of current events, that they are aware of many pressing issues, and know when they ought to take their responsibilities and stand by men's side, without being under their tutelage, without being subject to tyranny, but as comrades, equal to them.

To these women, who are courageous, hard-working, positive, I ask: what do you think of this Radio we have been given?

Our comrades, by joining Radio-Liberté, have joined the vanguard of the wireless world. It is up to them to fight for a better radio, to campaign so that women's programmes lose their superficial, silly and pointless character, and are replaced by programmes that are more enjoyable, more interesting, more rewarding.

I call upon all the women who are sickened, revolted or simply bored by the tepid programmes currently on offer, like 'La demi-heure de la femme' (which are broadcast so parsimoniously anyway), all the women who want to see change, all the women who have ideas, to write to us. Radio-Liberté, through its action and through its magazine, will dedicate itself and campaign, in whatever ways it can, to disseminate, define and implement their suggestions.

6.2 YVANE ARTHAUD: WOMEN'S VOICE IN THE WORLD

Translated by Emilie Morin. First published as Yvanne [*sic*] Arthaud, 'La voix des femmes dans le monde,' *Lumière et Radio*, 10 February 1930, 5.

Yvane Arthaud (1895–1944) was a French journalist and feminist militant associated with the Union Nationale des Femmes de France (the National Union of the

Women of France) and the Union Nationale pour le Vote des Femmes (French Union for Women's Suffrage) during the late 1920s and 1930s. She believed that radio could act as a powerful social force,[1] and the title of this essay is a reference to *La Voix des Femmes*, a feminist newspaper created in Paris in 1848, revived in 1917. During the interwar period, most radio stations had a female announcer, but female journalists were a small minority. Arthaud was one of two female journalists delivering Paris-PTT's Radio-Journal de France, a national evening news bulletin launched in June 1927, to which she contributed a daily item for women (the other female journalist, Andrée Guérard, talked about fashion). She occasionally contributed talks to other Paris stations, generally about matters seen as women's issues. Her journalism for the printed press focused on social questions and social progress, and she frequently wrote about feminism and about the need for women to have the right to vote. Her views were tinged by her Catholic faith. During the Second World War, she worked for the French railways; she died of meningitis in 1944. French women were eventually granted the right to vote in 1945.

●　　●　　●

The history of civilisation shows how, during different eras, groups of individuals were able to make their voices heard with more or less authority.

The intellectuals opened up the study of the world to the troubled masses of the Middle Ages; thereafter, the artisans transformed the economic lives of nations; the voice of scientists changed our ways of living; the voice of workers modified our conception of authority and discipline. Now the voice of women can be heard; all women are eager to ensure that they are not forgotten in the current effort, be they intellectual or manual workers who have availed themselves of their rights as citizens, or workers who are still demanding those rights, be they mothers within families or isolated mothers.

As a matter of fact, we may see women initiate change in the world, like the groups of individuals we have mentioned above as exemplars.

If we tried to offer a prognosis on their influence, this would perhaps be a prognosis on the ailment from which modern civilisation suffers. But we shall not go as far as that: it is not in the midst of the anxious storm raging within humanity that we can discover the leader of the day, and it would be arrogant to believe, because millions of women have voiced their new aspirations, that our direction for the future will come from women; but it would also be imprudent to fail to listen to the women of the twentieth century. When we read the

---

[1] See Yvane Arthaud, 'Influence sociale de la radiophonie,' *Annuaire de la Radiodiffusion Nationale, année 1933*, 179–83.

conclusions published by the many women's congresses and gatherings that were held this year [. . .], we can see that they are animated by the same energy: hunger for individual dignity, thirst for activity.

Indeed, for as long as women have found enough within the home to satisfy their aspirations, they have failed to make demands, for doing so would have been fruitless. However, now that the home is no longer a refuge or a domain of activity, the voice of women has made itself heard; at first, anxious and timid like the voice of an aggrieved person, then gradually more precise, able to move from personal grievances to collective demands, and from the latter to asserting the need for general reorganisation.

Everywhere, this movement upwards has taken place in two stages.

First stage: women liberate themselves from the civic tutelage that stifles their family activity and is no longer adapted to social customs.

Second stage: women join a national delegation and succeed in imposing reforms.

In this way, women speak and act as part of a regular pattern, and it is becoming evident that something new is happening in the world. It is almost as though forgotten forces were starting to emerge again.

In this process, radio becomes a friend for women of action. They can issue their call to the world without being told that their voice is inferior to the task. They can speak the good words without disrupting their labour for their family. And within their own homes other women, to whom the Hertzian waves are bringing distraction and education, are listening too; to those who are idle and alone, radio is a long-awaited pastime and a long-awaited voice; to those who are absorbed in domestic chores, radio brings peace and a remedy for boredom. The wireless brings an echo of the world outside. The news enters the drawing room, the children's bedroom, the space by the stove.

Women now have access to a new source of education that can enable them to develop: they must ensure that they learn from it.

Their voices have been granted a new power to be heard, and this should not be underestimated.[2]

The new mode of thought disseminated through the radio nonetheless needs to survey its own field of action with vigilance, to take stock, before venturing into the wider space; perhaps our task is to support this process.

---

[2] Similarly, the British Labour politician Margaret Bondfield observed: 'Radio has brought revolutionary changes in the lives of millions of women. To my mind the greatest change of all is the fact that the slender wire brings the world and its affairs into the tiny kitchens and living-rooms which hitherto had isolated so many housekeepers in the performance of their duties.' Bondfield, 'What Radio Can Do for Women,' *Radio Times*, 12 November 1937, 7.

6.3 EGON ERWIN KISCH: RADIO REPORTER FROM RED SQUARE: 'THE MOSCOW MICROPHONE NEVER LIES!'

Translated by Marielle Sutherland. First published as 'Der Funkreporter vom Roten Platz. „Am Moskauer Mikrophon kann man nicht lügen!,"' *Arbeiter-Sender*, 18 November 1932, 3–4.

A biographical sketch of Egon Erwin Kisch discussing his work for Radio Moscow is included with 'Woe Betide the One Who Sees' (2.9). *Arbeiter-Sender* was a German Communist radio magazine published in Berlin, which emerged from the Communist opposition to Weimar radio and from the German Communist Party's growing interest in establishing an influence over radio broadcasting. It often reported on Radio Moscow in 1931 and 1932. The magazine began to appear in February 1930 and was banned by the Nazi chief of the Berlin police in February 1933. Its leading journalists were imprisoned or died in the resistance movement.[1]

• • •

'*The poisoned wave*,' they write. A shudder goes down the reader's spine as evening falls and the hour draws closer. The teeth-baring Bolsheviks appear before his wireless eye, getting down to their work, full of scorn. They smear the Soviet trade unions' short-wave transmitter with potassium cyanide, the Welle 50 transmitter with arsenic, the Welle 1000 transmitter with strychnine;[2] then they give the frequencies a dose of mustard gas as they travel through the ether.

And so the Bolsheviks disrupt the harmony of the spheres, singing the praises of capitalist society, and other popular songs, throughout the universe.

---

[1] See Thomas Bauer, *Deutsche Programmpresse 1923 bis 1941: Entstehung, Entwicklung und Kontinuität der Rundfunkzeitschriften* (Munich: Saur, 1993), 146–47, 188–89.

[2] This is a reference to the national broadcaster Deutsche Welle, formed in 1926, which supplemented regional stations and broadcast across Germany. From 1927, it relied on the high-power Deutschlandsender transmitter (initially 40 kW) near Zeesen. While countries across central and northern Europe soon had equivalent high-power transmitters to broadcast nationally, the range never reached anything resembling 1,000 kW, and here Kisch mocks German technological ambitions and the role of propaganda.

Moscow's voice echoes throughout; the cosmos becomes nervous, the Milky Way rancid, the politicians deeply worried.

What is to be done?

You dig into the earth where the antenna is grounded, and you seize it. You go up into the sky and interfere with the air waves through disruptive transmitters (!). You climb up the pulpit and excommunicate those Christian souls who have leverage over Moscow. You enter parliament and threaten war against the Soviet Union if it does not stop broadcasting cultural Bolshevism. You go to the newspapers with cautionary images of 'marriages destroyed by listening to Radio Moscow, the degeneration of children and insurgency among the housemaids' . . .

Horrified, the newspapers report that yesterday evening, Moscow calmly broadcast a business report in the *Daily News* slot and a concert of new work music, even though a few hours beforehand, 'Voroshilov had occupied the Kremlin and murdered Stalin,' and even though the streets of Moscow were running with the blood of millions of murdered bodies and cold corpses, from Kusnetzki Most into the Moskva River.[3] '*Have we ever*,' says the press, 'have we ever seen such *raw* cynicism? We hope these programmes, calmly broadcast from Moscow yesterday right in the middle of a bloodbath, will open the eyes of those listeners who believe that what they are hearing from Moscow in the evenings is a new gospel . . .'

It is true. It is a *poisoned* wave. But what it is poisoned with is not potassium cyanide, it is not arsenic, and neither is it strychnine or mustard gas. It is something quite *different*, a very different, very *devilish* poison . . .

And this very different, very devilish poison is infused into the listeners while a noise machine deafens them. And what a noise machine! *No* radio station in the West has such a machine, no matter how many millions they have spent on their equipment, no matter how many elaborate, new-fangled and deceptively well-functioning noise machines they may possess.

But what – please tell us; we are all ears! – but what – just whisper it to us; we will turn the loudspeaker on! – but what *is* this poison? Where can we *buy* it? What is its chemical formula? What is it *called*?

Here is the answer: the poison is called *truth*; you cannot buy it, because it is a dangerous poison; you cannot produce it, because its chemical formula has, well advisedly, not been disclosed by the owners of the capital.

And the *noise machine*? Is it *expensive*? Is it complicated? Could we capitalists not manufacture it *too*?

No, the noise machine is not expensive, it is not complicated, it is not patented, but you capitalists *cannot* manufacture it! It consists of the sound of

---

[3] Kliment Yefremovich Voroshilov (1881–1969), prominent Soviet military and political leader close to Stalin.

millions of new machines, new industries, millions of hammers at work on new buildings, turbines rotating at the Dnieper hydroelectric power station; it is the clatter of new furrowing machines in the Don territory, the hissing of blast furnaces in Kusnetzk, the rattling of tractors on collectively owned land, the sigh heaved by the chest when difficulties arise, and the bright jubilation resounding through the air when these have been overcome.

No, you do *not* wish to produce, and nor are you capable of producing, this noise machine; it must be produced despite you and *against* you. And *neither* would you wish to plan, nor would you be able to plan, Moscow's programming. If *you* were to tell the truth about *your* system, that would be the *end* of your system.

In Moscow they do not *need* to lie; they are not *permitted* to lie, and they *cannot* lie.

They *cannot*? No, they cannot. When the radio reporters stand on *Red Square* and two million people march by, workers in civilian clothing, in blue shirts, their rifles on their shoulders, their shell pouches in their belts, when children rescued from child neglect – pupils of the technical school – march by with drums and music, when the Red Army and the Red Navy wave the flags of international solidarity in the air and kneel at the grave of Lenin, our leader and theirs, when the factory workforces appear on Red Square with the best examples of their manufactured commodities, when STALIN and the Party's *Central Committee* are greeted by millions of cries of jubilation and solidarity,[4] when four-engined aeroplanes whizz through the air, aeroplanes produced by what was yesterday the least advanced country in the world, when factory workers with red headscarves flood the square, clasping one another, playing the accordion or singing, when the little children are so enthusiastic that they let go of their balloons on the trucks, and a whole city is singing the 'Internationale' . . .

No, no such genius of a reporter has yet been born who could lie or exaggerate in this situation; no, no such censor has yet been born who could prescribe what one should or should not say in this situation. – Incidentally, as regards censorship: the radio reporter in Moscow knows only one kind of censorship, and this consists in the Director of the *Gewerkschaftssender* sometimes saying to him,[5] before a report on Labour Day or at the Revolution celebration:

'Please, Kisch, just tone down the enthusiasm! Stay objective; agreed?'

Yes, yes, I intend to stay objective. I won't let myself get too enthusiastic. If only it weren't so damned hard sometimes!

---

[4] The Central Committee of the Soviet Communist Party.
[5] *Gewerkschaftssender*: Radio Moscow, known as 'der Große Gewerkschaftssender Moskau.'

6.4 ALFONS PAQUET: RADIO AND THE STATE

Translated by Marielle Sutherland. Lecture from 1933, first published as 'Rundfunk und Staat,' in Gerhard Hay, ed., *Literatur und Rundfunk 1923–1933* (Hildesheim: Gerstenberg, 1975), 241–7.

The German writer Alfons Paquet (1881–1944) wrote poetry, plays, novels, essays and travel writing. He was also a publicist and a journalist; he worked as the *Frankfurter Zeitung*'s political correspondent during the First World War, then in Sweden, Finland and Moscow during the Russian Revolution. He was a militant pacifist and a Quaker. With Bertolt Brecht, Alfred Döblin, Hermann Kasack, Ernst Toller, Kurt Tucholsky and others, he joined Gruppe 1925, a group of leftist writers, theatre directors and critics formed to provide mutual support and protest against the Weimar Republic's increasingly repressive approach to culture and the arts. He was involved in radio broadcasting from 1926 onwards, and his name remained a staple in German radio programmes until the start of 1933. He wrote many plays and talks for radio, gave readings and published radio journalism. He was one of the speakers invited at the 1929 *Dichtung und Rundfunk* (Poetry and Radio) conference in Kassel, where he discussed how he, as an autodidact, had learned how to speak and improvise at the microphone. A member of the Prussian Academy of Arts, he was expelled after refusing to declare loyalty to the Nazi government, along with Alfred Döblin and René Schickele. His radio activities slowed down dramatically after March 1933, but he continued to give occasional talks, and his last radio talk dates from the end of 1943. This essay is the script of a lecture delivered in Berlin on 12 January 1933.[1] He died of a heart attack during an air strike in Frankfurt in 1944.

•　•　•

In its thus far tempestuous development, radio has affected everything: the newspaper, the book, the theatre, the concert hall. Domestic entertainment,

---

[1] It is unclear whether this lecture was a radio broadcast or not; Marie-Henriette Paquet's bibliography, based on the Paquet archive, identifies it as a public, non-radio talk, while Franz Steinfort lists it as a radio broadcast. Paquet gave another radio talk in early January 1933, but there is no record of him speaking on the radio on 12 January 1933 or of a talk titled 'Rundfunk und Staat.' See Marie-Henriette Paquet, ed., *Bibliographie Alfons Paquet* (Frankfurt: Lothar Woeller, 1958), 103–8, 109–11; Elmar Lindemann, 'Senderaum als

school and church – everything is beginning to accommodate radio. At first, it seemed the purpose of radio was merely to further reinforce the effect of every form of publication it incorporated. However, radio practice is increasingly and ever more clearly setting itself apart from the practice of writing books, newspaper reports and plays. In radio, the written word, the printed word, disappears. Its experiments are focused on the spoken word and on complementing this with an art of sounds and noises that primarily serves to invigorate the reproduction of the word, to create a new and vivid imagination.

The spoken word is beginning its reign over the world. The oration, the catchword, voices speaking in unison: these things stir the masses. The newspaper reader is turning away from the folded sheet to hear the conversation. Today, men of state exert greater influence through their gift of oratory and the tone of their voice than through written instruction and decrees.[2] The ear of the listener has become an eye, and the inner vision gained thereby is generating 'feeling for the world.' A new sense of vision through the ear is forming. The domain of the word has not expanded in such a volatile way since the invention of the printing press.

Radio's spiritual home is among the masses. And how dearly I would like to add: in the hand of genius. Radio reaches everyone, even the loneliest, even the most isolated individuals. Radio ensures the whole world holds its breath when someone flies across the ocean. It sends laughter from a concert hall billowing across the whole of the continent. The communication transmitted to everyone at lightning speed through radio requires only that the words mean something to everyone, otherwise it limits its own radius. Immediacy is the primary stylistic principle here. Radio is also free to take the most local circumstances as its point of departure and, in turn, to influence these, but it must then imbue these

Podium. Zu Alfons Paquets Rundfunkschaffen,' *Literatur und Rundfunk 1923–1933*, 237–41; Franz Steinfort, *Hörspiele der Anfangszeit* (Essen: Klartext, 2007), 61–157, 307–21; Jan-Pieter Barbian, *The Politics of Literature in Nazi Germany: Books in the Media Dictatorship*, trans. Kate Sturge (New York: Bloomsbury, 2010), 14–15; Harry T. Craver, 'The Abominable Art of Running Away: Alfons Paquet and Concepts of Travel Writing in Germany, 1900–1933,' *Colloquia Germanica* 46, no. 3 (2013): 284–302.

[2] This certainly proved true of Hitler, Goering and Goebbels, who understood radio's power early on. In August 1933, notably, Goebbels delivered a speech presenting radio as 'the eighth great power' and the ideal vehicle for Nazi ideals. His Ministry of Propaganda was planned around five departments: Radio, Press, Active Propaganda, Film, and Theatre and Popular Education. See Anson Rabinbach and Sander L. Gilman, eds., *The Third Reich Sourcebook* (Berkeley: University of California Press, 2013), 612–13; Carolyn Birdsall, *Nazi Soundscapes: Sound, Technology and Urban Space in Germany, 1933–1945* (Amsterdam: Amsterdam University Press, 2012); Horst J. P. Bergmeier and Rainer E. Lotz, *Hitler's Airwaves: The Inside Story of Nazi Radio Broadcasting and Propaganda Swing* (New Haven: Yale University Press, 1997).

circumstances with new value. The difference between radio and the newspaper or the book is similar to the difference between taking a photograph from the ground and taking a photograph from an aeroplane. Modern photography has discovered the oblique image. The view is directed at the objects from above, but it stays close enough to them to record their outlines. Good radio programmes can be compared to oblique photographs. The vertical view from above can only take in roof surfaces, or at best the ground plot. The oblique-angle view from above is what reveals the most.

Radio is always about integrating things that are happening into thought and imagination, even if these are phenomena we cannot possibly see, such as the state. Each person has a different concept of the state. Some say it is an idea, perhaps even a moral idea, but only a few are capable of imagining anything in this regard without the aid of an image. Some people think of the state in terms of a pyramid, a geometric figure, perhaps a scattering of government buildings interconnected by invisible lines, perhaps also an enormous spider's web from which no one can escape. Otherwise they understand it in terms of symbols such as figures, uniforms, historical dates. These are all concepts, but we cannot photograph them. In this regard too, radio remains as distant as the aeroplane. It is certainly the case that the state becomes conscious of itself through radio when the heads of government are speaking; this is because it is impossible to show or broadcast governance. And just like the state, the nation too perceives itself through the transmission of the word; as does, at times, the linguistic community, which extends beyond the boundaries of the state, even the nation, and encompasses communities of like-minded people that deviate from the government's understanding and representation of them. However, there is always a feeling in the air that the state of things needs to be changed. The role of radio is precisely to get a sense of what things are *in the air*. Radio thrives on paradoxes, in fact, and is capable of any comparison, any juxtaposition. It demonstrates the connection or disconnection between ideologies and situations through the manner in which it compares and contrasts these. It does not evade reality. The question is merely whether it approaches ideologies and situations creatively or with a declaration of war. It is of course entirely natural to make the mistake of believing that having radio in the palm of one's hand is all that is needed in order to have at one's disposal the power of unlimited influence over the masses and, furthermore, over the creative individuals within a nation. Even if an individual buys up all the musical instruments in the world, this does not mean he owns the hands that play them. An artless (in all probability, unartistic) owner is of course incapable of recognising the artistic potential harboured by these instruments. Radio may indeed have the best artists at its disposal, but it will reduce them to mere clerks implementing processes, to disgruntled workers, if it takes the initiative away from them, the joy in coming up with ideas, the means available to them. We need only consider the current state of radio to see how the prevailing, traditional concept of education – not to mention politics – is an obstacle to the possibilities for educating the people of today in tasks that are, in and of themselves, vitally important to them. German radio's preference is for the literary and musical treasures of previous centuries. The programming is saturated with Bach and Schubert, with military marches and sentimental ballads. It is certainly very meritorious to be able to make the treasures of the archive of bygone times accessible to millions of listeners, however the mass erosion of things that were never conceived or written for radio is a ruthless exploitation that destroys treasures and valuable rarities, and even hinders the development of radio itself. The old, manually operated music, as it were, developed out of the march, the dance step, the walk. Its forms stay close to the ground. Real radio music belongs to a very different sphere. It always seems impersonal, but its impact can also be powerful, refreshing and captivating. Once again, its origins are elemental. We might be more inclined to trace it back to the humming top or the Aeolian harp than to sheet music. It is the humming top as the archetypal mechanical instrument that outrageously disrupts the music played by fingers or breathed tirelessly through wind instruments, and it is the Aeolian harp that is the archetype of cosmic demonic possession. One might of course argue that the mechanical instrument is the destroyer of all historical feeling for music. I believe, however, that the historical feeling for music is destroyed more by misuse than by objects which are only superficially connected with the feeling for music and which go back to the elemental. This is because even mechanical music, the broadcasting of which is suited to radio above all else, expands the creative possibilities of music in general. Nowadays, however, we content ourselves with playing disc records. I have nothing against disc records. I merely object to them becoming processing mills, mechanically reeling off music that has not been created for the purpose of mechanical reproduction. It is also highly likely that the disc record is used – either out of idleness or out of hostility – as a means of obstructing radio music, which requires no engraved musical score as its template, and stands in the same relation to the music of yore as the spoken word to the printed and the written word.

The same principle, the same distinctions, apply to radio as a political instrument.

The intellectual potential of radio can only develop if it is passionately sympathetic to collective concerns, perceiving the collective as much in terms of its differences as in terms of its commonalities. The mere question of whether the intellectual possibilities of radio are keeping up with technological inventions is enough to bring forth political considerations. Whenever an idea is entirely lacking in the prerequisites for its implementation, it risks degenerating into a utopian idea. Nothing in the political sphere has taken the high value we place on the imagination out of circulation as much as utopia. Radio is able to juxtapose utopia and reality in such a way as to give rise to a third dimension: an ideal that can take concrete shape within the human and the social realm.

Much of what can be said in books and satirical magazines, on the stage and at school cannot be appropriated by radio. Radio must, for example, refrain from publicly performing a radio play about a heart operation, even if it is a masterpiece of precise, artistic compilation, for such a broadcast might also be heard by patients who are about to undergo such an operation and who may become alarmed to the point of mortal danger. Yet beyond the elementary limits presented here, what breakthroughs have been made through radio, and what possibilities it offers us for communication! To dwell for a moment on the medical sphere: tremendous transformations are currently underway in medical science! Public opinion is in a state of great agitation about it. New questions are arising, and there are hints of radical upheaval, yet these are met with a narrow-minded and anxious hostility. The same is true of the judicial sphere, which almost seems to have come to a dead end in Germany. Law and regulation are everything here. But where is the jurisprudence? Where is the judge as the bearer of living law?

And above all, the religious sphere, so anxiously guarded! Thus far, radio has carefully refrained from addressing questions pertaining to decisions made in the spiritual realm and their bearing on deeds in the social realm. The sluice gates of the communicable have remained locked. There is a general lack of broad-ranging debate to stir and invigorate the public interest. Never again, however, will a nation as riven with questions and as affected by new forces as Germany have the opportunity to earn the kind of intellectual greatness that must be striven for and preserved, or to avail itself of the services of those who are engaged not only in disseminating more profound, reformed ideas, but also in securing their acceptance.

The German people are now at a crossroads. Either we choose armament – i.e. the translation of all organic national substance[3] into tanks, heroism and ammunition – or we strive for an intellectual accomplishment that will allow us to negotiate the great questions, questions that other nations are of course fretting over too. The highest level of such an attitude cannot be the martial form. Threatened and beleaguered, we still dare to hope for a life liberated from despair, one way or another. If fate grants nothing better to the German people than a re-immersion in the obsolete eighteenth- and nineteenth-century feeling for the world, then radio will be limited to providing non-committal entertainment to millions of listeners. In this case, it would have to satisfy itself with mediating intellectual matters to these listeners in such a way that

---

[3] The German term in Paquet's text, *Volkssubstanz*, was used in racialised Nazi discourses presenting the nation as a 'pure' ethnic group, denouncing hypothetical threats to its integrity, and describing its expansion as a struggle for survival.

they would not feel the need to make new decisions, in fact in such a way as to merely generate boredom. Then, the purpose of radio would merely be to pump the people, like an accumulator, full of tension and feelings of unease, to intensify their animosity towards certain neighbours in such a way that all it would take would be for someone to sound the alarm bell and issue the war cry at the specified moment. Then, radio would be nothing more than a cog in the wheel of weapon technology, and it would be *deployed* as such.

Another development could proceed from the tactfulness that is one of radio's inherent characteristics. Perhaps, through its intrinsic nature, radio might be able to accomplish substantial feats, make unexpected discoveries, and become more important to Germany than an army. At all events, radio also brings people from all countries together – even if only loosely – into a community. It is able to cement this union. For the first time we have an instrument that is capable of making such progress possible! Groups of people, tribes, nations, countries: all these appear in radio from a bird's eye perspective, yet all countries are simultaneously recognisable in their natural conditionalities. One of the most wonderful possibilities offered by radio is precisely that of clarifying these conditionalities and contextualities, yet radio is no less capable of making visible those matters that lie beyond the boundary posts. Radio can follow the events journalistically, but it may also race ahead of them. Nowadays, there are many challenges in dealing with the outside world that can only be resolved through nations working together. No printed document, no written propaganda will suffice to show the myriad ways in which millions of people can be guided towards cooperation. The foreign policymakers of all countries have been very active in recent years; there has certainly been no lack of will to find new ways of cooperating. Nothing has been lacking as much, however, as the will to gain an overview of the tasks that lie ahead of us, and a creative imagination with room for manoeuvre in engaging and testing the masses. Instead, what comes to the fore in radio are those forces of bureaucratisation, regulation and barracking that have always spelt disaster in our nation's fate.

The now pressing question of the development of German radio is therefore indeed connected with greater decisions. If radio lags intellectually far behind the technological developments that created it, it will at best remain as it is: a mosaic of mediocre individual performances with occasional flukes, vegetating like a mollusc, with neither beginning nor end in sight, an endeavour with little enthusiasm for experimentation, and one with low remuneration and high budgets. The alternative to this is that radio conceives itself as an orchestra, as a building cooperative for symphonic architecture composed of a broad range of instruments, as the executor of an important duty in the intellectual and spiritual life of the nation. Here, the primary requirement is that artistic and intellectual energies should take precedence. This does not mean that radio should disregard its day-to-day work. However, in terms of the overall shape of the programme plan, it would make sense to slightly restrict broadcasting times. In addition, the creation of a repertoire within radio would entail a periodic series of selected broadcasts extending over the months, building up, as it were, with the special programmes organised for the feast days, into seasons. This would make it possible to insert into the infinitely flowing stream of transmissions something approximating to a cantus firmus, thereby keeping the listeners waiting for more. On special occasions, the different radio stations may complement one another in many respects. Once the key idea and the common format have been established, they can come together to offer common broadcasts relayed by all stations. Last New Year's Eve's coordinated all-stations programme *Hier sind alle deutschen Sender!* was an example of this; an example, however, in the sense that as well as excellent individual pieces of work, such as that by the Königsberg station,[4] it featured a series of disappointing broadcasts. There was no sense at all of a unifying idea. However, the very fact that an all-station relay such as this is technologically possible represents an intellectual challenge. And this challenge does not stop at our national borders, nor even at the borders of the continent.

It may be that Germany, as a great political power among other great powers, was founded too late. We can expect no more conquests by land or sea. Our only consolation is that we have Schiller's famous words, imputing to the Germans the 'land of dreams.'[5] Perhaps German aviation and radio will populate this land of dreams and its castles in the air with a little reality. Yet here, too, there can be no country unless it is underpinned by a moral idea that is based neither on war nor on the oppression of others. Thus far in its development, German radio has acquired a modest capital in terms of renown and prestige even beyond its borders. Foreign countries such as Denmark have seen the emergence of communities of listeners who have even learned German in order to understand the programmes better. These communities of listeners have dissipated, however, on account of the regressive route radio is currently following. Hard-won capital is in danger of disappearing rapidly, and an auspicious trajectory, barely begun, risks being aborted.

---

[4] 'All German Radio Stations are Here!', broadcast on 31 December 1932 by Orag (Ostmarken Rundfunk AG), Königsberg (now Kaliningrad, Russia) – the main radio station in the Free State of Prussia, Germany's easternmost region, cut off from the rest of the country.

[5] *Reich der Träume* in the original. From Schiller's poem 'Der Antritt des neuen Jahrhunderts' ('The Start of the New Century'): 'Freedom is only in the Land of Dreams; / And only blooms the Beautiful in Song!' Bulwer Lytton, trans., *Schiller and Horace* (London: Bradbury, Agnew, 1875), 194.

6.5 KURT TUCHOLSKY:
FREE RADIO! FREE FILM!

Translated by Marielle Sutherland. First published as Ignaz Wrobel, 'Freier Funk! Freier Film!,' *Die Weltbühne* 18 (May 1932): 660–3.

Kurt Tucholsky (1890–1935) was a German writer and journalist. He was closely associated with *Die Weltbühne*, the influential literary magazine based in Berlin, which he edited before his friend Carl von Ossietzky took over, and *Die Neue Weltbühne*, its counterpart in exile. Alongside his journalism, Tucholsky wrote satires, songs and political revues. He became a pacifist after serving in the First World War, and was known for his anti-Nazi and moderate leftist views. He often used pseudonyms. He moved to Paris in 1924 out of disappointment with the Weimar Republic, then back to Berlin in 1926, and to Sweden in 1929. His journalism dealt with many topics including music, politics and radio. He denounced as a fallacy the idea that radio could be apolitical: this claim, he argued, was the hallmark of a politically conservative worldview, and radio was inherently a deeply politicised medium. His name and works occasionally appear in German radio programmes from the period; he gave talks and readings on two occasions in March 1929, on the Frankfurt and Cologne radio stations, and may have given other readings thereafter. In 1933, his books were burned and he was stripped of his German citizenship by the Nazi regime owing to his Jewish roots. He sank into deep despair and took his own life. He died in Sweden.[1]

• • •

We must not give up our fight against censorship.

Rudolf Arnheim recently asked in this regard: 'Should the democratic principle of freedom of speech in publishing have unlimited application, or must the state have the right to suppress hostile and damaging opinions?'[2]

A state can only be granted the right to exercise censorship if it knows what it wants in the first place. This means that one of the prerequisites for censorship

---

[1] See Jelavich, *Berlin Alexanderplatz*, 54; Palmier, *Weimar in Exile*, 69–70; 258–59; Sabrina Ebitsch, *Kurt Tucholskys Journalismuskritik: Kritik als Berufsstörung* (Munich: GRIN, 2008), 96–100.

[2] Rudolf Arnheim (1904–2007), prominent film and radio theorist; the piece cited is Arnheim, 'Petzet, Kuhle Wampe, Albers,' *Die Weltbühne* 13 (March 1932): 486–8.

we would endorse would be a categorical worldview on the part of the censor. There is no such thing in Germany at the present time.

The Catholic state in the Middle Ages was able to demand the right to exercise censorship in religious matters because its worldview was clearly delineated. It was the worldview of the Catholic Church. It of course has given its blessing in some cases, for it generally prefers to exercise a presence rather than issue condemnations – but back then, the Catholic worldview had a clear shape: there was a degree of certainty around obligations and freedoms, what was permitted and what was sinful, and the censor possessed something to which no German censor may have recourse today: an original moral yardstick by which to measure things.

The Russians have stipulated a categorical worldview; their censorship is based on what they call the proletarian interest, and this is defined, with a fair amount of precision, in the teachings of Marxism-Leninism; at least, it should be.

In the case of the Italians, it is more difficult; Fascism is an end in itself.

What we are seeing in Germany is the brazen hubris of musty circles in our society who like equating the interests of the civil service with those of Germany. This is simply not the case.

Germany is not shaken if someone attacks the Reichswehr.[3] Hitler, that 'abject Mongolian vagabond,'[4] is not Germany; nor are his hordes alone Germany; nor the great landowners; nor Groener's military officials[5] – none of these groups, alone, are Germany. They all make up Germany together – and then, of course, there are other groups too.

We see how false and deeply dishonest this censorship is in the fact that it never dares to encroach upon printed matter to the extent that it does upon film and radio, which today are as good as worthless because they are not free.

We all know that in legal terms, dissemination by radio and film is no different to dissemination by the printing press. It is, for example, an offence to disseminate an as yet unprinted manuscript against the will of the author – it would likewise be an offence for the propagator to type up the manuscript and sell it as a book, read it on the wireless or turn it into a film. There is no doubt about that.

Things look very different, however, when it comes to censorship.

Radio has never been free. Film became subject to censorship when it wanted to expand beyond the fairground domain – censorship suppressed it

---

[3] Armed Forces of the Weimar Republic.

[4] *Hergelaufene Mongolenwenzel* in the original, between inverted commas. This is one of the insults that Tucholsky crafted for Hitler, and it refers to an article by the anti-Nazi journalist Friz Gerlich that dismissed Hitler's theories about race and applied them to Hitler's own appearance. See Philipp W. Fabry, *Mutmaßungen über Hitler: Urteile von Zeitgenossen* (Düsseldorf: Athenäum-Droste, 1979), 63; Tobias Ronge, *Das Bild des Herrschers in Malerei und Grafik des Nationalsozialismus: Eine Untersuchung zur Ikonografie von Führer- und Funktionärsbildern im Dritten Reich* (Münster: Lit Verlag, 2010), 243–4.

[5] Karl Eduard Wilhelm Groener (1867–1939), Minister of Defence of the Weimar Republic.

again. The old ideas of the authoritarian state went something like this: religion must be preserved among the people. And not only religion but also all other forms of illusion. Initially, everything is forbidden. Thereafter, we will allow some things. And yet, it should be precisely the other way round:

Anything that does not directly violate legitimate public interests should be free. Only the rest should be forbidden. [. . .]

The existing penal laws of all civilised countries fully suffice to prevent what any decent intellectual would himself wish to prevent:

Causing a public nuisance; revilement; insult; defamation . . . in short, anything perpetrated via these methods. What we cannot tolerate, however, is the barefaced hubris of smaller circles in our society who like to make the intellectual views they happen to hold the measure of all things. Every minister has the right to form and express an opinion on abortion, homosexuality, pacifism, Russia, the distribution of goods. We prefer, however, to compile our library differently; we select from the infinite diversity of existing ideas those that befit ourselves.

And this is where we see the absolute weakness of any attempt – even the Russian attempt – to stipulate a narrowly delineated worldview: any proponent of such coercion prevents his subordinate from forming a free opinion. He does not allow him access to any counter-arguments.

I do not intend here to discuss the extent to which this is necessary in Russia. The Russians may in any case point out that their worldview is a general one and that the great edifice of their philosophy always provides them with an answer to any question.

The German concept of the state, however, cannot provide this. It is a patchwork, an eternal compromise, a vague fabric composed of tentative regressive movements and that concept that is actually not a concept at all: we must exist so that we exist.

What kind of moral views are permitted in our films? What kind are permitted in radio? If we look more closely, we find only those that no longer have any substance. The slightest objection to anything leads to censorship. Of all the conceivable objections, only one is exempt: that of the working class. This is of no interest.

We must be permitted to declare artistic works of this kind null and void; it is a miracle if anything useful can ever be derived from them.

They are an exercise in futility. Imagine if there were only one newspaper in Germany, and imagine if this newspaper were published by the government – would you wish to read it? I, for one, would not. With the best will in the world, it is impossible to see why no one is permitted to express his political or ethical opinion on the wireless – radio broadcasting aims to be neutral, but of course, it is not, and neither can it be, for there is no such thing as neutrality.

Radio could, however, be non-partisan.

Why should a film be banned for glorifying the war? Banning it does not achieve anything. All you need to do is screen an equally resolute pacifist film that shows the wretched deaths in the trenches and for whose sake these people are dying; a film that shows the well-known generals and the unknown soldier! You screen anti-capitalist films and films financed by IG Farben.[6] You show black and white, blue and red.

Why should Hitler not speak on the wireless? Only, of course, if you also let Thälmann speak – it works if there is parity.[7] That said, as in any democracy, this also raises the question of whether democracy must put up with somebody using its freedom of speech to suppress democracy itself. In my opinion, it does not have to do so – but our democracy is by no means capable of this yet. In actual fact, we have already gone much further the other way – democracy has blissfully acquiesced in this and is now, quite rightly, paying the price with its demise.

The main reason why film and radio are subject to censorship – and, moreover, this dangerous, silent censorship – is because they are new inventions. It is of course more difficult with books; we can still hear echoes of the old battle cries: Freedom of the press! Down with book censorship . . .!, which means there is at least a prospect of one truth or another being published. These cannot be filmed or broadcast, though – the channels to this are obstructed.

I know very well that the call for press freedom is no longer meaningful; the 'exertion of influence' over the press is so great . . .

In film and radio the power is concentrated within a relatively small stratum; the very stratum that feels threatened if censorship is attacked. And just as the world's distribution of goods benefits a few hundred thousand people, censorship is exercised for the sake of the malign spirit and narrow-mindedness of a few million people who each time have the audacity to claim they are 'the country.' They are not.

We are not at all interested in the moral views of the censors; no one has enquired as to these. And I think it would be a wasted effort to try and influence these men or even to find more judicious replacements for them. They simply have to go.

It is fear that has put them in post.

Every country is a large-scale nursery. If I wish to know what military plans Germany is making, I have to read the French press; although incidentally, what is grotesque about this is that French newspapers are allowed to be imported into Germany – it is only when they are translated that interventions follow. As long as the masses don't read them! As long as the masses don't watch any films that are 'derogatory about Germans'! As long as the masses don't hear anything on the radio . . .!

---

[6] IG Farben, the largest chemical and pharmaceutical corporation in the world.

[7] Ernst Thälmann (1886–1944), leader of the KPD, the Communist Party of Germany, from 1925 to 1933.

The self-same masses who are called up when there is a war on. Then they are good enough to be taken into battle. For a cause they know nothing about.

But to let them know what is actually going on; to inform them in advance of what is really happening in the world – that just won't do. Instead, censorship keeps watch.

Absolutely every kind of censorship is an evil. It is no way to educate a nation. How the education bigwigs in the SPD subjected us to their collective snivelling when the law on Tawdry and Filthy Writings, which they had helped to pass, went through![8] It was insincere, petit-bourgeois and stupid.

Free the cinema screen! Free the ether!

These are becoming so important to the people. Because where would it leave religions, and above all, where would it leave patriotism if people knew what was going on?

Censorship is employed in the protection of the few against the many.

6.6 KURT TUCHOLSKY: RADIO CENSORSHIP

Translated by Marielle Sutherland. First published as Ignaz Wrobel, 'Rundfunkzensur,' *Die Weltbühne* 24 (April 1928): 590–3.

A biographical sketch is included with 'Free Radio! Free Film!' (6.5).

•   •   •

---

[8] Sozialdemokratische Partei Deutschlands, the Social Democratic Party of Germany. The law's full name was 'Gesetz zur Bewahrung der Jugend vor Schund- und Schmutzschriften' (Law for the Protection of Youth from Tawdry and Filthy Writings). Passed in 1926, it existed until 1935. An inspection authority was set up to provide a list of texts which were banned from being sold or advertised to anyone under eighteen years of age. The law did not set out the criteria for what was classified as 'tawdry and filthy,' but in practice the texts on the list were generally either pornographic, or popular, cheap, commercial writings featuring sex, alcohol, romance and adventure.

The censorship of radio is one of the unacknowledged products of bourgeois dictatorship. Kurt Hiller once explained in this regard that the main objection to Mussolini's dictatorship is its underlying objective – and although dictatorship always has the same flavour, it may have any of a thousand different objectives.[1] Of all the different forms of such dictatorships, however, there is one that is hateful wherever it appears: clandestine dictatorship.

What is happening in radio – and, to a somewhat lesser extent, in cinema – would, if it were happening in the press, be a call to all custodians of unfilled advertising space to man the barricades and fight for radical change; if newspapers were subject to the same gagging order to which radio listeners and cinema-goers acquiesce, unperturbed, their turnover would suffer – as would, consequently, their sales of advertising space, and as would, consequently, the publisher. It is usually at this point that somebody cares to do something about it. And yet, in the case of radio – an instrument of sound –, all we are hearing is silence. What is going on here?

Radio today still finds itself in the position of the press before the year 1848: however, because it is new, either the German public does not have enough of a feel for the immense political danger inherent in this ridiculous paternalism, or it supports this censorship. Any typically German misgivings that caricature freedom in such a way as to make it impossible ('But what if that leads to . . .?') are false: the present, amply reactionary penal law is quite enough to make insults, treason and high treason – and whatever else we say when we are referring to police rule – impossible. Today, the democrats point out with a smirk that smoking was forbidden on the streets of Berlin during the Vormärz,[2] yet, apart from a few exceptions, they keep shamefully quiet about the fact that smoking is not permitted on the radio, even though radio itself is clouded in smoke.

In radio, not a single word may be spoken that has not been recognised and approved by an irrepressible, irresponsible and almost secretive horde of tenured and unaffiliated reactionaries, average citizens and obedient busy-bodies. Consequently, radio can never progress beyond a certain mediocrity, which would not be all that bad – were it not for the fact that large swathes of the population are being deprived of the opportunity to express their ways of life, their political requirements, their ideals, desires and opinions in a manner befitting a republic that proclaims itself a democracy. The censors hide their true objectives behind two excuses: firstly, that radio should be apolitical; and secondly, that listeners would complain if the lectures were too flagrant, too radical.

---

[1] The German author, Communist and early gay rights campaigner Kurt Hiller (1885–1972). Hiller was imprisoned in Nazi concentration camps in 1933 and 1934.

[2] The period in the run-up to the 1848 March Revolution.

It is not possible for radio to be 'apolitical,' for there is nothing anywhere that is apolitical. It is just as impossible, for example, for a human being to be 'unmedical' – everyone is subject to the laws of nature, anatomy, biochemistry; even Goethe, even Stefan George,[3] even Edison. A rational view of the world requires that its viewer refrain from considering all aspects of life at once; so, if someone is studying Schopenhauer's life's work, he may well, in so doing, mention the philosopher's economic circumstances as one of the bases for his work, yet he cannot let this detain him; at particular junctures in this investigation, he will have to leave this finding aside. This does not mean, however, that he is dispensing with it altogether. Neither does radio eliminate its political basis by apparently ignoring it. It continues to exist.

In fact, it exists so clearly that radio, far from being politically neutral – as it envisages itself to be –, is without doubt politically biased. The muted tones of vengeance, the fusty undertones of the German Reich, the philosophy of landowners, former army officers, current judges, big industrialists, their morality and their moral convictions – these attitudes find a favourable reception in radio, indeed as such a matter of course that the class to which the censors belong is easily identifiable. Should a free-thinker, a radical worker [. . .] attempt to articulate such views as are as self-evident to us as the others' own views are to themselves, he can be sure of being censored. This is an ugly injustice.

The second excuse for censorship is that the listeners do not want these kinds of lectures. This is where we need to begin to educate the German people in something that they have thus far been lacking: tolerance. There are only two ways to do this. Either a ruling caste exercises a clear and explicit dictatorship, discernible to everyone – and that is that. Or, we live in a democracy.

In such a democracy, every individual has a duty to allow his opponent to operate and deliver the full force of his argument; both sides must be granted the same opportunity and conditions to advance skilful argumentation and unleash the power of propaganda. I believe it is a crime to make films that glorify war; if the wholly inadequate and criminal penal code that will be bestowed upon us does not provide for such a delict, I have no right to forcibly prevent the showing of such films. I can cause a disturbance at the screening – and I will certainly do so; I can lambaste the film, take it to task, work against it in some way – yet I am not allowed to prevent it being shown. If a pacifist does not wish to see a war film, then he simply need not go to see it.

It is exactly the same, however, the other way round. If somebody does not wish to listen to his Holy Father being ridiculed on the radio, then he should switch it off; he has no right to force his opinion on others. A radio management

---

[3] The German Symbolist poet Stefan George (1868–1933), who enjoyed widespread popularity during the Weimar period and whose visions of an almighty Germany appealed to the Nazis.

board that acquiesces – and indeed takes great pleasure in acquiescing – in rampant bourgeois narrow-mindedness is not apolitical, not even politically neutral, rather it represents, purely and simply, the interests of the ruling class and the latter's conceptions of morality. This censorship must be abolished entirely. It is not enough, for instance, that the League for the Protection of German Writers is allowed to delegate its people into committees;[4] that the Poetry Academy – which remains curiously uninfluential – has put a stop to this or that outrage; that an individual such as Wolfgang Goetz, a bad writer, but without doubt an upright and honest man in an intellectual sense, has been given, quite by chance, the opportunity to prevent particularly dirty tricks from behind a desk in a censorship department: no, radio and film censorship must be abolished.[5]

The artistic consequences of such censorship are as peculiar in the case of cinema as they are in that of radio.

Since it is impossible to get anything onto the radio that the average listener regards as 'eccentric' in his letters of complaint; because it seems it is possible to print a book for eight hundred readers but not screen a film for eight hundred viewers – other than in the case of a rare act of patronage –, cinema and radio are destined to remain on the middle rung of the ladder. Although the genius of such a rare and exceptional person as Chaplin has managed to flourish on the basis of general comprehensibility, this is merely an isolated case. Years ago, when Hans Siemsen was the first to demand educated film criticism, he was certainly justified in doing so; in the meantime, he will have himself realised where the limits of cinema as an art form lie.[6] They lie precisely on the threshold where there is a failure of imagination – not that of the viewer but that of the producer: nothing makes it to the screen that General Director Klitzsch does not understand, and the results are indeed telling.[7] Although the artists involved in a film may raise the standard in terms of its quality, they cannot raise the level of the foundation on which it stands. ('Potemkin' is the exception to the rule).[8]

Hence, film is lacking in the many thousands of subtleties found in literature. And hence, radio is lacking in almost any new, colourful, subtle, sophisticated experimentation; barely any sound arising from this makes it onto the air waves. Disregarding the fact that the ear – except where it is engaging with

---

[4] Schutzverband deutscher Schriftsteller, founded in 1909 and disbanded in 1933.

[5] The German writer Wolfgang Goetz (1885–1955) worked as a civil servant for the German film censorship office until 1929.

[6] Hans Siemsen (1891–1969), German writer and journalist, who wrote essays and cinema reviews for *Die Weltbühne* during the 1920s.

[7] Ludwig Klitzsch (1881–1954), director of the leading German film company UFA (Universum Film-Aktien Gesellschaft).

[8] Eisenstein's silent film *Battleship Potemkin* (1925).

331

music – absorbs more slowly and in a more rudimentary manner than the eye, the radio censor (so he can sleep at night) needs to demonstrate his recognition of the unconventional: he presumably allows readings of Stefan George's poetry because 'we' have heard of him. He would never, however, allow radio to become a mouthpiece for the young Stefan George – which, on the other hand, is at least logically consistent, and perhaps even welcome. Radio, in its current state, finds itself in an intellectual limbo.

Radio censorship is, in the lowest and the worst sense, a half-flaunted reactionary weapon. These committees, boards, authorities and bureaus are superfluous, because they – like a large proportion of the German civil service – do not perform any productive work; instead, they hinder the work of others. Radio censorship depresses the intellectual level of the nation in the same manner as a particular section of the press: both distract the audience from matters of essential importance. Radio censorship must be abolished.

6.7 RENÉ SCHICKELE: A PAN-EUROPE OF RADIO STATIONS

Translated by Marielle Sutherland. First published as 'Paneuropa der Sender,' *Die Sendung*, 27 February 1931, 135–6.

René Schickele (1883–1940) was a German writer and journalist from Alsace, then a contested territory between Germany and France. He was born in a town annexed by Germany in 1871 and returned to France in 1918; like Annette Kolb and others, his dual sense of belonging shaped much of his life. He took French citizenship after the First World War but lived in Germany until 1932; he wrote novels, short stories, poems and plays in German but rarely wrote in French. His work focuses mostly on Alsace and promotes harmony between France and Germany. He was one of the founders of the Alsatian literary magazine *Der Stürmer* and edited *Die Weissen Blätter*, a magazine dedicated to Expressionism, which Thomas Mann saw as 'anti-militarist, anti-imperialist, anti-bourgeois and pro-pacifist.'[1] His involvement with radio began in 1926, when he contributed a first talk on autobiography to the Elsässische Stunde (Alsatian Hour)

---

[1] Thomas Mann, 'René Schickele of Alsace,' *New York Times*, 26 May 1940, 8.

created by the Stuttgart station, which also broadcast his stage play *Hans im Schnaken-loch* ('Hans in the gnat-hole,' 1916) that year. Readings from his poetry and novellas and talks about his work followed until early 1933, on the Langenberg, Leipzig, Berlin and Strasbourg stations. He read from his work on the Frankfurt and Langenberg stations in 1927, 1928 and 1929, and gave talks on the Frankfurt station in 1932. That year, he settled in the south of France, and lived alongside German émigrés in Sanary-sur-Mer until 1934. In 1933, he was expelled from the Prussian Academy of Arts. He was aware that dark times were ahead, confiding in his diary: 'If Goebbels manages to wipe our names from the German picture, we are dead. Phantoms of a diaspora in an arid land. Even the next generation will know nothing more of us.'[2] He died of a heart attack in Italy.[3]

●   ●   ●

A person lives in total isolation on the edge of a forest. The most southern mountain of the Black Forest rises up just behind the house, and if this hermit sets off in this direction, he might wander for days through the woods, only ever through woods, the valleys lying between them like the offspring of giants, exposed, naked and shivering in the sun. If, however, he looks over to the other side, then he sees the Rhine Rift Valley spreading out before him up to the Vosges Mountains. On bright days he can make out the cross on top of the Hartmannsweiler Kopf mountain, the enormous grave of sixty thousand soldiers, French and German, who for years and years competed for ownership of the peak – the space they were fighting for is no larger than the Belle-Alliance-Platz in Berlin. It might also be that the man in question can see from his desk, at the same time, the French and the German Riviera Express chugging south, and, up in the sky, the Basel airmail flying north.

The wireless stands in the entrance hall of the house; you only need to turn the dials a little in order to hear Stuttgart, then a moment later Strasbourg, Paris, then a moment later Berlin, and Radio Milano announces itself just as clearly as 'This is the Süddeutsche Rundfunk'[4] – and these are only the stations that are in the immediate vicinity. This means that in reality the hermit is never really completely alone, that (and though he may sometimes curse this) when he casts his gaze upon the present – a gaze that in effect remains destined to the present only – his attention is never lost in the hum of the forest or the immeasurable sky across the plain.

---

2 Cited in Palmier, *Weimar in Exile*, 7.

3 See Rainer Schickele, 'René Schickele,' *Books Abroad* 15, no. 3 (1941): 273–5; Eric Robertson, *Writing Between the Lines: René Schickele, 'Citoyen francais, deutscher Dichter' (1883–1940)* (Amsterdam: Rodopi, 1995); Palmier, *Weimar in Exile*, 108, 279, 286, 390, 478; Áine McGillicuddy, 'René Schickele: A Misunderstood European Regionalist,' *Europäisches Journal für Minderheitenfragen* 5, no. 1 (2012): 41–52.

4 Süddeutsche Rundfunk AG (Sürag), the South German Radio Company, created in Stuttgart in May 1924.

On the contrary, it is precisely this silence and privacy that allow him to listen in to the present moment with the same attentiveness a doctor would employ when listening to a person's heartbeat. Nowadays, it is possible to be lonely without losing the world.

As unimpeded as our eyes sweep across the German-French border, so do the sonorous waves roam freely across from Stuttgart-Freiburg to France and from Strasbourg to Germany. However, for a long time, this 'minor frontier traffic' in the air encountered far greater difficulties than the other 'minor frontier traffic' on land. On land, every bridge had a toll-keeper, and every toll-keeper on the bridges from Baden to the Alsace behaved like a gendarme. And although the toll-keepers took a martial approach, there were always, in addition, real gendarmes in their vicinity. And, in conjunction with one another, they made sure that those crossing the border were not smuggling insurgent leaflets in the lining of their garments, or the equivalent ideas in their heads, into the French Alsace. They frisked people, searching for leaflets and letters; they read the dangerous ideas from their passports or from their faces. This was a kind of secret science that yielded very few returns for its practitioners but caused its victims much displeasure.

So, how was it in any way possible to stop the messages the Stuttgart Radio was sending to its Alsatian listeners? They tried to do this by 'interfering until the cows came home' in the transmission of the Stuttgart station's 'Alsatian Hour.' It is certainly true that that terrific crackling of Morse code reminded listeners of the machine gun fire accompanying a military assault. The disturbance was indeed unpleasant for the listeners, but it soon became clear that speech over the air waves could not be obliterated as completely as silent written characters on paper or soldiers in war. It was hard to know what to do. The then president, Mr Poincaré, took advice. During his military campaign against the Alsatian autonomists, he announced he was setting up a major broadcasting facility in Strasbourg that 'will reply to the German propaganda against the French Alsace – politely, but firmly – by spreading the truth.' Hence the creation of the Brumath transmitter. It had a wavelength of 345.2 m, whereas Stuttgart transmitted to a wavelength of 360.1 m. In such proximity, and with its 869 Hz and 12.2 kW, it would have been easy for the Brumath transmitter to knock Stuttgart out of the ring. Ten days later, the new Mühlacker transmitter was put into operation on the western border.

And it is more powerful than Strasbourg-Brumath.

Nonetheless, there is – thank goodness – no prospect of France building an even more powerful transmitter on the border; in fact, all the signs point not only to a ceasefire between the German and French radio stations but even to a lasting peace.

Strasbourg began broadcasting on 11 November, the day on which the war ended twelve years ago, with Mozart's 'Requiem' – without an inaugural address, without a national anthem. Announcements are made in French and German; there are talks in French and German; the programming takes all social strata into account. It is not far off the highest standard it can possibly be, taking into account the limited resources of the broadcasting company. In France, for example, listeners do not pay any fee, which is disadvantageous to both French and foreign listeners. The French listener has no idea how advanced foreign radio is, whilst his own is barely getting off the ground, and the foreign listener is missing out on the best that France has to offer.

On the eastern border too, the arms race between the big-hitting broadcasters will soon come to a standstill. What the radio stations have in common with Gandhi's teaching on non-violence is that they may well harass their opponents, but they may not kill them. They cannot do this. It is precisely this welcome impotence that points them towards seeking a common understanding. This path has been trodden several times already. In the foreseeable future, not only friendly appreciation will be a matter of course, but also mutual facilitation through programme exchange and other forms of cooperation. It would already be possible today for a central station for all European radio stations to carry out, relatively undisturbed, European projects that would benefit each of the countries working together and put none of them at a disadvantage, not even the most minor among them.

6.8 LOUIS LE CRESTOIS: RADIO AND PEACE

Translated by Emilie Morin. First published as 'La radio et la paix,' *La Parole Libre TSF*, 12 July 1931, 1.

Louis Le Crestois (fl. 1930–1932) was a French journalist who contributed occasional articles on the politics and technology of radio broadcasting to *La Parole Libre TSF*, a French weekly radio magazine, from 1930 to 1932.

• • •

Today Europe is at a crossroads. No serious mind can ignore this fact. If the next disarmament conference, due to convene in 1932,[1] fails; if European states cannot agree on a precise and extensive programme for simultaneous and controlled general disarmament, then the armament race will start once again, igniting among all nations a psychosis aggravated by fear and insecurity. Once again, the slightest incident can bring about war. War, that abominable and unforgettable nightmare: we must avoid it at all costs. We must make sure that the general disarmament conference succeeds.

If general disarmament, the only true guarantor of peace and security, appears difficult, if not dangerous, in the eyes of some, that is because the mistrust, the hatred and the fears caused by the war have not yet abated. To create a spirit of harmony, trust and international solidarity, radio possesses particularly effective virtues. Broadcasting does not recognise borders; within the peaceful atmosphere of our homes, away from the screaming crowds and the passions of the forum, it brings us in direct contact, instantaneously, with a manner of thinking that expresses itself in a familiar and friendly way. Radio is trusted; radio is respected and, whenever it manifests its sincerity clearly, we are moved by it. The great spiritual powers of the world have already understood the value inherent in its force of persuasion, in radio as a peaceful weapon of propaganda and conversion. All religions use radio in order to make contact with their congregations; why should the pacifists neglect it?

Some efforts have already been made. During its session of July 1930, after examining the report presented by a subcommittee of experts, the League of Nations' International Commission on Intellectual Cooperation adopted a resolution recommending that educators should inform the youth as much as possible about the life and work of the different nations and the League's aims, and should use radio broadcasting widely.

They write: 'It would be possible, for example, to broadcast eminent personalities speaking about questions related to the League of Nations or the rapprochement between nations, or a series of short and well-documented programmes on these topics, or else commentaries on world politics made in a spirit of peace.'

The Commission is convening again this month in Geneva and will examine responses to a questionnaire sent to the major radio stations of Europe through the intermediary of the International Broadcasting Union.[2] It would be interesting to know the content of these responses. Will they be published?

---

[1] The Disarmament Conference opened in Geneva in February 1932, gathering delegates from sixty-two countries.

[2] Union Internationale de Radiophonie, created in Brussels in 1925 to represent European broadcasters and resolve international broadcasting problems.

This would be desirable. The radio public has the right to know what instructions are given to radio stations on such important subjects. Let us also hope that the League of Nations will concern itself with the establishment of a shared programme for all countries. The work begun last year by the International Commission on Intellectual Cooperation must be vigorously pursued;[3] armed with tenacity and pacifist good will, the International Broadcasting Union must stand up to all the chauvinistic excitement sadly brought about by the economic crisis, the wounds inflicted by the treaties and the incomprehension manifested by large parts of the public. The voice of the air waves must be the voice of peace.

A practical programme must be put in place.

Let us sketch out a few points that are essential from our perspective.

The educational effort must be principally aimed at the youth, with the help of talks that can invigorate interest and deal with life in different countries, the specific features of the different nations, and the goals and work of the League of Nations.

Highly-regarded international figures should be asked to undertake a 'mass tour' before the microphones of Europe, in order to campaign for the pacifist organisation of Europe.

International relays and special international days should feature more often in radio programmes; German radio stations should arrange French hours, and French radio stations should create German hours. Thus radio broadcasting, as it brings together thousands of listeners, would teach humanity trust, solidarity, international brotherhood. It would not merely teach such values; it would give practical examples and create new habits, which is even more important. It would enable these new feelings to filter through every mode of thought and would progressively neutralise the old hereditary venom.

There is little time left, but Europe can still be saved from an irremediable decadence. If the continent shows enough courage and manages to overcome the divergences and aversions that are currently so divisive, peace and prosperity are guaranteed; if the forces of hatred and distrust triumph, chaos and the ruin of occidental civilisation will ensue.

Radio broadcasting is one of the most beautiful discoveries invented by humanity's fecund genius; will it know how to play, and will it be willing to play, the salutary role to which it is inherently destined?

---

[3] An organisation attached to the League of Nations, which promoted the exchange of intellectual, artistic and scientific ideas.

6.9 GABRIEL GERMINET: RADIOPHONIC ART IN THE SERVICE OF MORAL DISARMAMENT

Translated by Emilie Morin. First published as 'L'Art radiophonique au service du désarmement moral,' *Le Front*, 30 October 1937, 3–4.

For a biographical sketch of Gabriel Germinet see 5.6. The present text is the conclusion of a report read at the first French International Congress of Radiophonic Art and at the 1937 Paris conference of the Rassemblement Universel pour la Paix (International Peace Campaign), an organisation founded in 1935 to support the League of Nations and coordinate pacifist movements across the world. Germinet was one of the main organisers of the Congress (held in Paris from 8 to 10 July 1937), as Treasurer of the Union d'Art Radiophonique (the French Union for Radiophonic Art) and Treasurer of the Association Syndicale des Auteurs et Compositeurs de la Radiophonie et de la Télévision (Union of Authors and Composers for Radio and Television).

• • •

[. . .] We propose that a pacifist programme be created by the main radio station of every country and broadcast at pre-arranged times so that the counterparts created in neighbouring countries can follow one another, forming a chain that will encircle the globe when all the men of goodwill are listening in and pondering the daily appeal for peace.

These programmes shall be composed by drawing on the radiophonic arts represented at this Congress.

These broadcasts shall be animated by a constant and benevolent desire to proselytise, together with a commitment to high-quality ideas, to which thinkers as well as the best interpreters shall contribute.

To obtain the maximum level of effectiveness, the word 'peace' shall only be uttered in exceptional circumstances. It will be sufficient for the broadcasts to generate pacific reflexes. In this domain we are likely to see the emergence of a specific technique that is firmly embedded in an understanding of psychology.

We are persuaded that all those who bring their heart, their sensitivity and their imagination to bear upon their collaboration with radio broadcasting can only be pacifists. If they wish to do so, they have the capacity to elevate the radiophonic art and enable it to become a noble art by excellence, by drawing upon poetry, the art of oratory, music, singing and theatre, and by allowing their creations or their interpretations, which enrich the leisure time of hundreds of thousands of human beings, to be augmented by their contributions to the pacification of the human spirit.

We conclude this call by affirming forcefully that, thanks to the art of radio, thanks to other means also arising from the will to see the power of peace extended, the whole of Humanity can hope for a better future. I hope, gentlemen, that you will become associated with this work of salvation. [. . .]

6.10 PAUL VAILLANT-COUTURIER: RADIO AND PEACE

Translated by Emilie Morin. First published as 'La radio et la paix,' *Radio-Liberté: Bulletin de l'Association d'Auditeurs de TSF*, 13 November 1936, 2.

Paul Vaillant-Couturier (1892–1937) was a French writer, journalist, laywer and politician, and a prominent figure in the French pacifist movement and the French Communist Party. His activities centred on his commitments to pacifism and Communism. Notably, he was editor-in-chief of *L'Humanité*, the French Communist Party's daily, from 1926 to 1929 and from 1935 to 1937, and Deputy of the Seine department from 1919 to 1928 and from 1936 to 1937. He also wrote novels, poems, plays, literature for children and reportage. In 1936, he became patron of Radio-Liberté – a prominent French association of radio listeners which drew some of its membership from the trade unions and from anti-fascist, communist and socialist organisations – and was subsequently made its vice-president. The association had its own radio magazine, *Radio-Liberté*, and published a counterpart dedicated to film, *Ciné-Liberté*.

● ● ●

The civil war in Spain fills the radio and echoes through it . . . The listeners are assailed by lies, amplified by relays of General Queipo de Llano's harangues and statements from Lisbon.[1] Hitler is having his appeals for a crusade against democracy broadcast on the radio, Mussolini his apology of violence and his contempt for the League of Nations.

Radio is turning into a closed world.

The powers of chaos and hatred are bringing violence into the listeners' homes. And public opinion is becoming accustomed to these displays of belligerence.

Let us say it loud and clear: Radio-Liberté will fight, with all its might, against the utilisation of radio by the peace-killers.

To unite humanity: such is radio's vocation.

With radio, human beings have gained the marvellous power to converse beyond the mountains, the plains and the sea, and through borders and walls. Humanity now possesses an extraordinary lever of peace.

It must be utilised to create a world insurrection against war.

It would be in the honour of this government, born out of the Popular Front, if it drew on German, Italian and Spanish philosophy and literature to search for everything that can bring human beings closer together and counter the propaganda of hatred that disfigures national cultures and serves the cause of war.

New kinds of radio programmes, broadcast in foreign languages and in French, could be created so that every nation can understand other nations better and so that human beings can ponder the tradition of generosity within their own country.

Bringing texts closer together would be edifying. Listeners would be able to measure the distance separating Heinrich Heine from *Mein Kampf*.

As President Herriot stated at the Biarritz Congress, Voltaire's France will always be the friend of Goethe's Germany.[2] Already, the broadcasting of music on the radio has enabled every nation to look into the soul of other nations . . .

In order to serve the cause of peace, radio should enable human beings to encounter one another without being hindered by the partitions imposed by political partisanship – in the intimacy of their homes, in the comfort of their culture.

Then, and only then, will radio honour its destiny.

---

[1] Queipo de Llano (1875–1951), a highly controversial figure in Franco's Nationalist Army and in the Spanish anti-republican movement, renowned for his radio harangues and, later, for orchestrating mass killings.

[2] The French statesman Edouard Herriot (1872–1957), who gave a widely debated speech on foreign policy at the 1936 congress of the French Radical-Socialist Party.

6.11 ERNST TOLLER: INTERNATIONAL RADIO

Translated by Marielle Sutherland. First published as 'Internationaler Rundfunk,' *Die Sendung*, 30 May 1930, 347–8.

Ernst Toller (1893–1939) was a German writer affiliated with Expressionism, and a prominent advocate of pacifism and Marxism. Discharged from the German army in 1917, he participated in various pacifist organisations, and his political activities led to his arrest and imprisonment in 1918. Thereafter, he joined the Independent Social Democratic Party of Germany and became a leader of Bavaria's revolutionary movement, briefly acting as army commander of the short-lived Bavarian Soviet Republic and as President of its Central Committee. Sentenced to five years of imprisonment for high treason, he continued to write while in prison and built a considerable reputation as one of Germany's foremost playwrights. He was opposed to Hitler long before his accession to power and was seen as a particular threat by the Nazis. In 1933, he narrowly escaped arrest, was stripped of his German citizenship owing to his Jewish roots, and moved to London and Paris. In 1936, he emigrated to New York, where he worked as screenwriter for Metro-Goldwyn-Mayer. The last cause he fought for was Spanish republicanism. He had a keen interest in radio; several of his theatre plays were broadcast on German radio, and he wrote two radio plays: *Berlin, letzte Ausgabe!* (broadcast by the Berlin Funkstunde in 1930) and *Indizien* (broadcast by Radio Wien, Vienna, in 1932). His first radio appearance was a poetry reading on the Berlin Funkstunde in February 1927; thereafter, he gave various readings on German radio stations. He began to think about radio while in prison: the present essay replicates phrasings from a letter sent to B . . . from Niederschönfeld prison in 1924 and expands on these early ideas.[1] He relished radio's ability to overcome borders: his correspondence from the late 1930s mentions talks delivered in the United States and Spain, and being heard in Germany and China.[2] He took his own life in May 1939, soon after the Nazi invasion of Czechoslovakia.

● ● ●

---

[1] Ernst Toller, *Letters from Prison*, trans. Ellis Roberts (London: John Lane, 1936), 356–7.

[2] See Ernst Toller, *I Was a German*, trans. Edward Crankshaw (London: John Lane, Bodley Head, 1934); Michael Pilz, 'Masse – Medium – Mensch: Medienreflexion und Medienkritik in Ernst Tollers Radioarbeiten am Beispiel des Hörspiels *Indizien. Drama für Rundfunk*,' *Text+Kritik* 223 (2019): 67–75; *Ernst Toller: Digitale Briefedition*, http://www.tolleredition.de/, last accessed 1 December 2021.

All instruments of technology harbour two forces: constructive and destructive forces. Up until now, humans have used the boldest calculations and the most superb inventions to strike each other dead, gas cities and lay waste to countries. This dangerous twin force is also inherent in radio. – I can imagine how, in future wars, the rulers will broadcast lies upon lies, confusing the world, delaying peace even longer. We can only deal with this danger by, in times of peace, working extremely hard to turn radio into a means by which people from different countries may get to know one another. By increasing people's knowledge and insight, we ensure the apostles of agitation meet with no response.

Do you remember what we thought of the French, the Russians and the English during the war? All Russians were barbaric illiterates, all the English were disingenuous and small-minded, and all the French were degenerate weaklings.

And how were we Germans portrayed by the other side?

Most people lack imagination.

If they could imagine the sufferings of others, they would inflict less suffering. What was it that distinguished a German mother from a French mother? Clichés, which deafened people to the truth.

This is where the great pioneering and preparatory work of radio begins. The people of Germany must acknowledge that the people of France experience the same daily pleasures and hardships, that people feel the pinch of taxes both here and there, that burdens are unevenly distributed both here and there, that the causes of poverty and misery are not to be found beyond the borders.

We in fact know so little about each other. Our school education is patchy and permeated with prejudices.

For us, the Black man is an exotic creature who plays jazz music now and then, and the Jew is an extortioner intent on taking us for a ride on a daily and hourly basis.

What do we know of the life of the Black man in Africa? Of the major social and political conflicts of the Black man in America? Who would think it possible that in the southern states of North America, despite a free constitution, the majority of coloured people do not have the right to vote, and that in Poland the Jews are not all merchants and intellectuals but also craftsmen and labourers?

Other countries are as ignorant as we are. In America, I was asked whether it was true that in our country school children are given beer for breakfast, and whether the Bavarians speak German.

Just think what radio could do here!

In the newspapers we are always reading about other countries' appetite for war. What would be the upshot if we could hear the major peace demonstrations in England, France, etc. in Germany, and the German peace demonstrations could be heard in the other countries?

The prerequisite for this would be courage on the part of radio. It should not be put off by chauvinist attacks. What is ostracised today will be praised by everyone tomorrow; what is regarded as utopia today will be 'plain' reality tomorrow.

And what new perspectives does this open up for the realm of art?

We will acquire a feel for the untranslatable by listening to dramas we are familiar with from German translations, performed in their mother tongue; music and songs, cultivated in the atmosphere of a particular landscape, broadcast by a radio station, will bring that landscape closer to us; experiences of everyday life shared through broadcasting will sharpen our perspective and enrich our knowledge. But the most distinguished task of radio in the political field remains the fight against clichés that engender hatred.

The role of radio cannot be overestimated. In order to ensure it fulfils this role, we have to turn it into a tool for those who are toiling, with their hands and their minds, trying to build a humane society.

SELECT BIBLIOGRAPHY

This is a selection of recent English-language books on European radio before 1939. Scholarship published before 2000, scholarship in languages other than English, primary sources, and shorter book chapters and journal articles are cited in footnotes throughout.

Andrews, Maggie. *Domesticating the Airwaves: Broadcasting, Domesticity and Femininity*. London: Continuum, 2012.

Avery, Todd. *Radio Modernism: Literature, Ethics, and the BBC, 1922–1938*. Abingdon: Routledge, 2016.

Birdsall, Carolyn. *Nazi Soundscapes: Sound, Technology and Urban Space in Germany, 1933–1945*. Amsterdam: Amsterdam University Press, 2012.

Bloom, Emily C. *The Wireless Past: Anglo-Irish Writers and the BBC, 1931–1968*. Oxford: Oxford University Press, 2016.

Campbell, Bruce B. *The Radio Hobby, Private Associations, and the Challenge of Modernity in Germany*. Cham: Palgrave Macmillan, 2019.

Campbell, Timothy C. *Wireless Writing in the Age of Marconi*. Minneapolis: University of Minnesota Press, 2006.

Cohen, Debra Rae, Michael Coyle and Jane Lewty, eds. *Broadcasting Modernism*. Gainesville: University Press of Florida, 2009.

Connolly, L.W. *Bernard Shaw and the BBC*. Toronto: University of Toronto Press, 2009.

Crook, Tim. *Audio Drama Modernism: The Missing Link Between Descriptive Phonograph Sketches and Microphone Plays on the Radio.* Singapore: Palgrave Macmillan, 2020.

Currid, Brian. *A National Acoustics: Music and Mass Publicity in Weimar and Nazi Germany.* Minneapolis: University of Minnesota Press, 2006.

Fisher, Margaret. *Ezra Pound's Radio Operas: The BBC Experiments, 1931–1933.* Cambridge, MA: MIT Press, 2003.

Gilfillan, Daniel. *Pieces of Sound: German Experimental Radio.* Minneapolis: University of Minnesota Press, 2009.

Hennessy, Brian. *The Emergence of Broadcasting in Britain.* Lympstone: Southerleigh, 2005.

Jelavich, Peter. *Berlin Alexanderplatz: Radio, Film, and the Death of Weimar Culture.* Berkeley: University of California Press, 2006.

Lacey, Kate. *Listening Publics: The Politics and Experience of Listening in the Media Age.* Cambridge: Polity, 2013.

Lommers, Suzanne. *Europe – on Air: Interwar Projects for Radio Broadcasting.* Amsterdam: Amsterdam University Press, 2012.

Lovell, Stephen. *Russia in the Microphone Age: A History of Soviet Radio, 1919–1970.* Oxford: Oxford University Press, 2015.

Murphy, Kate. *Behind the Wireless: A History of Early Women at the BBC.* London: Palgrave Macmillan, 2016.

Neulander, Joelle. *Programming National Identity: The Culture of Radio in 1930s France.* Baton Rouge: Louisiana State University Press, 2009.

Potter, Simon J. *Broadcasting Empire: The BBC and the British World, 1922–1970.* Oxford: Oxford University Press, 2012.

Potter, Simon J. *Wireless Internationalism and Distant Listening: Britain, Propaganda, and the Invention of Global Radio, 1920–1939.* Oxford: Oxford University Press, 2020.

Purcell, Jennifer J. *Mother of the BBC: Mabel Constanduros and the Development of Popular Entertainment on the BBC, 1925–1957.* New York: Bloomsbury, 2020.

Scales, Rebecca P. *Radio and the Politics of Sound in Interwar France, 1921–1939.* Cambridge: Cambridge University Press, 2016.

Street, Seán. *British Public Service Radio and Commercial Competition, 1922–1945.* Eastleigh: John Libbey, 2006.

Wrigley, Amanda. *Greece on Air: Engagements with Ancient Greece on BBC Radio, 1920s–1960s.* Oxford: Oxford University Press, 2015.

INDEX

EU Authorised Representative:

Easy Access System Europe Mustamäe tee 50, 10621 Tallinn, Estonia

gpsr.requests@easproject.com

Printed and bound by CPI Group (UK) Ltd, Croydon, CR0 4YY

16/04/2026

02091744-0001